Women in the Gospel of Mark

Women in the Gospel of Mark

Characterization through Literary and Gender Analysis

David E. Malick

Foreword by Johannes N. Vorster

☙PICKWICK *Publications* · Eugene, Oregon

WOMEN IN THE GOSPEL OF MARK
Characterization through Literary and Gender Analysis

Copyright © 2025 David E. Malick. All rights reserved. Except for brief quotations in critical publications or reviews, no part of this book may be reproduced in any manner without prior written permission from the publisher. Write: Permissions, Wipf and Stock Publishers, 199 W. 8th Ave., Suite 3, Eugene, OR 97401.

Pickwick Publications
An Imprint of Wipf and Stock Publishers
199 W. 8th Ave., Suite 3
Eugene, OR 97401

www.wipfandstock.com

PAPERBACK ISBN: 979-8-3852-2588-0
HARDCOVER ISBN: 979-8-3852-2589-7
EBOOK ISBN: 979-8-3852-2590-3

Cataloguing-in-Publication data:

Names: Malick, David E. [author]. | Vorster, Johannes N. [foreword writer].

Title: Women in the Gospel of Mark : characterization through literary and gender analysis / by David Malick.

Description: Eugene, OR: Pickwick Publications, 2025 | **Includes bibliographical references.**

Identifiers: ISBN 979-8-3852-2588-0 (paperback) | ISBN 979-8-3852-2589-7 (hardcover) | ISBN 979-8-3852-2590-3 (ebook)

Subjects: LCSH: Women—Biblical teaching. | Bible.—Mark—Criticism, interpretation, etc. | Women in the Bible. | Women in Christianity—History—Early church, ca. 30–600.

Classification: BS2585.52 M35 2025 (paperback) | BS2585.52 (ebook)

VERSION NUMBER 01/02/25

Diagram of Narrative Text from *Story and Discourse: Narrative Structure in Fiction and Film*, by Seymour Chatman, Copyright (c) 1978 by Cornell University. Used by permission of the publisher, Cornell University Press.

Synoptic diagram of pertinent oppositions, taken from *The Logic of Practice* by Pierre Bourdieu, Copyright (c) 1980 by Stanford University Press, 1990. Used by permission of the publisher, Stanford University Press.

Diagram of The Sower, taken from *Interpreting the Parables* by Craig L. Blomberg. Copyright (c) 1990 by Craig L. Blomberg. Used by permission of InterVarsity Press, P.O. Box 1400, Downers Grove, IL 60515, USA. www.ivpress.com.

Table of Sower/Interpretation/Gospel Group taken from *Sowing the Gospel: Mark's World in Literary—Historical Perspective* by Mary Ann Talbert. Copyright (c) 1996 Augsburg Fortress. Used by permission of the publisher, Augsburg Fortress.

Diagram First/Second/Third Degree Narrative, taken from *Sowing the Gospel: Mark's World in Literary—Historical Perspective* by Mary Ann Talbert. Copyright (c) 1996 Augsburg Fortress. Used by permission of the publisher, Augsburg Fortress.

Diagram of the chiastic structure of Mark 3:20–35, taken from *Mark: A Theological Commentary for Preachers* by Abraham Kuruvilla. Used by permission of Wipf and Stock publishers, www.wipfandstock.com.

To my wife,
Mary Lynn Gannett-Malick,
without whose self-denying love and commitment
this work would not have been written.

Contents

List of Illustrations and Tables | xi
Foreword by Johannes N. Vorster | xiii
Acknowledgments | xvii
List of Abbreviations | xix

1. Introduction | 1

Part 1: Theoretical and Literary Research Approaches | 11

2. The Two-Fold Aspect of Narrative: Characterization through Discourse | 13
3. First-Century Characterization of Women and Bourdieu | 36
4. The Literary Pattern of Intercalation | 58
5. The Literary Pattern of the Sign-Sermon | 83
6. Four Roman Watches as Narrative Timestamps | 90
7. The Geographical/Chiastic Structure of the Gospel of Mark | 95

Part 2: Narrative Analysis of Passages Involving Women in the Gospel of Mark | 101

8. The Healing of Simon's Mother-in-Law (Mark 1:29–31) | 103
9. Jesus' Relatives (Mother) and the Beelzebul Controversy (Mark 3:20–35) | 112
10. Jairus' Daughter and the Woman with a Hemorrhage (Mark 5:21–43) | 124

Contents

11 Herodias, Her Daughter, and the Beheading of
    John the Baptizer (Mark 6:7–32) | 136

12 The Syrophoenician Woman (Mark 7:24–30) | 151

13 The Poor Widow Who Gave at the Temple (Mark 12:41–44) | 167

14 The Death Plot of the Leaders and the Anointing
    at Bethany (Mark 14:1–11) | 184

15 The Maidservant's Trial of Peter (Mark 14:53–72) | 196

16 The Women at Jesus' Crucifixion (Mark 15:40–41) | 210

17 The Women at the Tomb (Mark 15:42—16:8) | 224

18 Conclusion | 255

Bibliography | 265

List of Illustrations and Tables

FIGURES

Figure 1	Diagram of Narrative Text	19
Figure 2	Synoptic diagram of pertinent oppositions	41
Figure 3	The structure of the Gospel of Mark built around geographical locations	96
Figure 4	The structure of spiritual/physical healings in Mark 1:21—2:12	105
Figure 5	Responses to spiritual/physical healings in Mark 1:21—2:12	106
Figure 6	Comparison of "kingdom" and "house" in Mark 3:23–25	118
Figure 7	Diagram of the parable of the Sower in Mark 4	144
Figure 8	Three Controversies to Test Jesus and Three Teachings by Jesus	174
Figure 9	Comparison of giving by the "all" and the "widow"	181
Figure 10	Dramatized Irony	232
Figure 11	Chiastic Structure of Mark 3:20–35	113

TABLES

Table 1	Shepherd's list correlated with Downing's list	60
Table 2	Contrasting groups in the outer narrative of 2 Samuel 11 and the parable of 2 Samuel 12	72
Table 3	Parallels between the four Roman Watches in Mark 13 and the narrative in Mark 14	92

List of Illustrations and Tables

Table 4	Parallels between the threefold command in the parable of the Doorkeeper and the narrative of the Garden of Gethsemane	93
Table 5	Parable of the four soils in Mark 4	144
Table 6	Comparison of Herod with Pilate	148
Table 7	Contrasting the Galilee panel with the Jerusalem Panel	217
Table 8	Table comparing Galilee, On the way, and Jerusalem	218
Table 9	Comparison of Adam and Jesus as the new Adam	251n69
Table 10	Comparison of David and Jesus	251n69

Foreword

SEVERAL PUBLICATIONS ON WOMEN in the Gospel of Mark have already appeared. Several publications following a literary critical approach, with the characterization of women in this gospel as a focus, have also seen the light of day. It would also be fair to recognize the contributions and the value of inquiries in this field have, in a very real sense, advanced biblical scholarship—in particular exposing the possibility of alternative interpretations and yielding a critique of mainstream, in many cases a critique of "malestream" scholarship.

Yet few have accomplished what Dave Malick has set out to do and achieved. In both its theoretical approach, as well as in the analyses themselves, the objective is to bring to the surface, "what lies behind" not only of the Markan textual passages where women feature, but also of the literary critical category, characterization, the latter by making the "how of characterization" the leading question of the inquiry, and then by demonstrating how it has been integrated within a process of valorising womanhood within this gospel. The passion to provide contemporary women within a Christian, denomination environment with an enhancement of their status, from an early Christian writing, to provide them with something that infuses with value and worthiness, pervades this publication.

The work has been divided into two parts, but both parts are constructed from perspectives yielded by theoretical approaches that constitute the project. Although the first part has been entitled "Theoretical and Literary Research Approaches" and a second part "Narrative Analysis of Passages Involving Women in the Gospel of Mark," this division should not be taken as in a "chronological fashion" since the insights derived from the theoretical approaches constitute all chapters of the publication.

The theoretical approaches are presented as "Textual Criticism," "the two-fold aspect of narrative namely, story—discourse," then some appropriate insights derived from Bourdieu's notion of *habitus*, to be followed by literary techniques, such as, "intercalation," "sign-sermon," "narrative time stamps" as represented by the Roman watches, and "geographical markers" fitted within an overall chiastic structure. These approaches function to compose the first part, then to be followed by a second part of "close analytical readings" of Markan narrative passages. It is in this section that the "how" of women characterization is developed in detail, and Markan passages, referring to women, are selected for analysis. His close, analytical readings focus on how these narratives have been structured in terms of discourse, to be distinguished from story. This distinction enables the integration of a relevant variety of contextual settings. Although not absent from the chapters analysing specific Markan passages, a final theoretical approach, identified as "theological" concludes the study. It is argued that the theological dimensions shown by the relevant narratives provide us with a glimpse into a very subtle, but yet deliberate, attempt at subverting the rigidity of engendered, social structures that formed societies of the ancient Mediterranean world.

Analysing this writing from the perspective of discourse requires that narrative structure shifts into focus as analytical space where the interaction between the literary categories of actual author and implied audience can be deployed in inquiring the *modus operandi* of characterization. At the same time, it allows for an integration of appropriate elements from Pierre Bourdieu's rendering of *habitus* yielding the possibilities of recognizing the multi-dimensionality in Mark's construction of women characters. An implied audience, identified via the analysis of narrative structure, emerges here also as product of particular, first-century preunderstandings and practices concerning gender. It is precisely this type of multi-dimensionality that allows the contemporary reader to recognize and appreciate the manner in which Mark's presentation of women characters subtlely and subversively grinds against the manner of first century bodily habituation. As a matter of fact, it is in this tension, between the underlying engendered social structure of the Roman Empire within the context of the ancient Mediterranean world and Mark's way of constructing women characters, that a glimpse of a "going beyond" can be discerned. This is a theme functioning throughout this publication.

Taking into account the multi-dimensionality of his theoretical design proposes, the different categories appropriate to what will be used in the analytical section are specifically presented in different and separate chapters and explained in terms of their substance and function and how they will be implemented. As such, the reader is familiarized not only with the contents and strategies of the categories themselves but also what current research has done with them and how they will be utilized in this project itself. Pre-empting the analyses themselves, the reader has been acquainted with the current status of Gender Criticism on women in early Christianity, but also integrated within a Bourdieuan framework. This is then followed with separate chapters on the categories of intercalation, sign sermons as literary pattern, watches as indicators of temporality, as well as geographical markers as indicators of spatiality. The rather lengthy theoretical framework as presented in the first section is therefore anything but abstract and removed from the analyses, but serves to construct a reading-framework allowing the reader to ease into the second analytical section. At the same time, it serves to contextualize the specific categories deployed, not only within the context of the Markan Gospel itself, but also in the context of literary patterns used within antiquity.

Analysing the Markan passages where women characters have been constructed, Malick demonstrates how their characterisation performs as a mechanism for the valorisation of a womanhood that chips away at the solidified, rigidity of ancient Mediterranean constructions of gender. It would be going too far, and even to miss the point of his argument, to find a developing egalitarian structure within early Christianity in these analyses. Instead, how the characterization of women features in significant spaces within the narrative structure, how they are juxtaposed with constructions of masculinity, and how a "womanufacture" is made, is a contribution to biblical scholarship, even as it opens up possibilities of challenging a homogeneously engendered early Christian community. One cannot but think that his work also lends credibility to Leonard Cohen's "there's a crack in everything . . . that's how the light gets in"! And indeed the "light gets in" where the cracks have been disclosed by the author of this gospel.

From a theological perspective, what the project does is to challenge the privileging of masculinist perspectives performing as conditions for the creation of engendered socio-ecclesial hierarchies one-sidedly based on Pauline and Petrine biblical material. To respond to this situation of contemporary engendered unfairness, in a space where exactly the opposite should have been the point of departure, has been one of the main theological objectives for doing this work.

In conclusion, reference must be made to a recent study on the long ending of Mark, deliberately excluded from Malick's study on valid textual critical argumentation. What is remarkable is the similarity in conclusions reached. In her publication, entitled *Gospel Women and the Long Ending of Mark*, Kara J. Lyons-Pardue argues that the author of the long ending of Mark brings together several of the narrative trends present in the Gospel of Mark. What is of relevance here is how a female witness to the resurrection, Mary Magdalene, is brought back "onstage," how she is again brought back into a story line that at the same time again portray the failure of the eleven remaining male disciples. It is not even a remote objective of Lyons-Pardue to have the long ending restored as part of the Gospel, but rather to highlight the credibility of a second century interpretation of Mark's Gospel itself. At the same time, this can be deployed to highlight the validity of Malick's analysis of "how" the characterization of women has taken place in Mark's Gospel.

Professor Johannes N. Vorster,
Emeritus Professor and Academic Associate
of the Department of Biblical and Ancient Studies,
College of Human Sciences, University of South Africa

Acknowledgments

THIS WORK WOULD NOT have been possible apart from the patient, encouraging, and foreseeing counsel of my academic advisor, Professor Dr. Johannes N. Vorster at the University of South Africa. It is certainly because of you that this work exists.

This work also builds, with thanks, upon the foundation of years of training at Dallas Theological Seminary under professors who awakened me to the art of literary analysis in the Scriptures including Elliott E. Johnson, Allen P. Ross, Zane C. Hodges, and S. Craig Glickman.

I am also grateful to the many from Riverchase Baptist Church, Birmingham, Alabama, who participated in the Monday-evening studies on the Gospel of Mark. Our prolonged interaction provided the foundation for my understanding of the Gospel of Mark that appears in this work.

Finally, but mostly, I am grateful to my Lord, Jesus Christ, who pulled me from the roar of the night and graciously permitted me to comment, in a small way, on his Scripture.

χάριτι δὲ θεοῦ εἰμι ὅ εἰμι

(1 COR 15:10a)

List of Abbreviations

AD	*Anno Domini*
ASV	American Standard Version
b.	Babylonian Talmud
B. Bat.	Baba Batra
BC	Before Christ
BDAG	Bauer, Walter, Frederick W. Danker, W. F. Arndt, and F. W. Gingrich. *Greek-English Lexicon of the New Testament and Other Early Christian Literature*. 3rd ed. Chicago: University of Chicago Press, 2000.
BDB	Brown, Francis, S. R. Driver, and Charles A. Briggs. *Hebrew and English Lexicon of the Old Testament*. Oxford: Clarendon, 1907.
Ber.	Berakot
Bik.	Bekorot
C. Ap.	*Contra Apionem*
ca.	circa
D-R	Duay-Rheims Bible
ESV	English Standard Version
Git.	Gittin
HALOT	Koehler, Ludwig, Walter Baumgartner, and Johann J. Stamm. *The Hebrew and Aramaic Lexicon of the Old Testament*. Translated and edited by Mervyn E. J. Richardson. 4 vols. Leiden: Brill, 1994–1999.
HB	Hebrew Bible
Heb.	Hebrew
KJV	King James Version
LXX	Septuagint
m.	Mishnah

List of Abbreviations

NASB	New American Standard Bible
Ned.	Nedarim
NET	New English Translations
NIV	New International Version
NKJV	New King James Version
NT	New Testament
OT	Old Testament
Sabb.	Shabbat
Seqal.	Seqalim
Spec. Laws	*On the Special Laws*
y.	Jerusalem Talmud

1

Introduction

THE PROBLEM

A BASIC TENET IN the hermeneutics of theology is to build a doctrine upon the clearer, or less disputed, passages and then to interpret the more difficult passages in light of the clearer passages.[1] However, in evangelicalism,

---

1. It must be granted that a statement that there are "clearer" or "less disputed" passages is an assumption that could be questioned because of the multitudinous challenges to interpreting Scripture. Nevertheless, there are some passages that pose greater interpretive issues than others. It is the passages with less interpretive issues that are referred to here, and that are often used to form a foundation for a particular doctrine. "In the case of difficult or obscure passages, the interpreter should give precedence to biblical passages where the doctrine is clear" (Wilhoit and Ryken, *Effective Bible Teaching*, 126). Under the category of the analogy of scripture, Grant Osborne explained: "Milton Terry's dictum still stands: 'No single statement or obscure passage of one book can be allowed to set aside a doctrine which is clearly established by many passages.' . . . I would strengthen this by adding that doctrines should not be built on a single passage but rather should summarize all that Scripture says on that topic" (Osborne, *Hermeneutical Spiral*, 28). Millard Erickson set forth his method of theology in part under the subcategory of "unification of the biblical materials" as follows: "This means we are proceeding on the assumption that there are a unity and a consistency among these several books and authors. We will, then, emphasize the points of agreement among the Synoptic Gospels and interpret the rest in that light. We will treat any apparent discrepancies as differing and complementary interpretations rather than contradictions" (Erickson, *Christian Theology*, 73). Erickson applies this method to the issue of perseverance of the saints by harmonizing Hebrews 6 with what he considers to be the clear teaching of John 10:27–30 (Erickson, *Christian Theology*, 1003–5). An example of Wayne Grudem's use of this approach may be found in his chapter on "perseverance of

the ground of biblical gender studies is often broken on the rough terrain of the problem passages found in 1 Timothy 2, 1 Corinthians 11 and 14, or with the household codes of Ephesians 5–6, Colossians 3, and 1 Peter 2–3.[2] The evangelical approach to biblical gender studies uses the more disputed passages to form its theology of women. In other words, the evangelical approach to biblical gender studies is to focus on these passages to problematize the role of women in its theology of women.

Evangelicals are open to a literary analysis of the Scriptures that can substantiate theological findings that are exegetically bound by the text, and do not extrapolate beyond what can be textually supported. Usually an evangelical textual analysis is linear in that it deals with textual problems, lexicography, background issues, historical issues, sources, and perhaps redaction criticism.[3] However, a close reading of a text that is controlled by the book's narrative structure and substructures is rarely conducted in evangelical circles out of an abundance of concern for historicity, and a fear of being accused of allegorizing the text, or making-up conclusions not supported by the text itself. Therefore, there is a need for an evangelical evaluation of women in Mark employing literary criticism.

While the concern of this study will not be to respond directly to this problem within evangelical theological circles by an analysis of the debates, the objective will be to provide an alternative by an analysis of the characterization of women in a crucial early Christian writing, the Gospel of Mark. This author will argue that an analysis of women in the Gospel of Mark can yield significant contributions to the role of women and to early Christian realities that can be identified within evangelistic communities.

This study will point to many passages that portray women alternatively, in an exemplary position, and do not serve to maintain for them an inferior position within social hierarchies, as is sometimes claimed

---

the saints" where after discussing the emphasis of Hebrews 3:14, he states: "Attention to the context of Hebrews 3:14 will keep us from using this and other similar passages in a pastorally inappropriate way. We must remember that there are other evidences elsewhere in Scripture that give Christians assurance of salvation, so *we should not think that assurance that we belong to Christ is impossible until we die*" (Grudem, *Systematic Theology*, 793 [emphasis in original]).

2. See Grudem, *Evangelical Feminism*; Payne, *Man and Woman*; Westfall, *Paul and Gender*.

3. Ben Witherington III's works on women are a good example of a more typical evangelical approach to gender that focuses on source criticism and interpretive insights but does not deal with the narrative import of structure on the narrative texts. See Witherington, *Women in the Ministry of Jesus*; *Women and the Genesis of Christianity*; *Women in the Earliest Churches*.

with a focused reading of Pauline and Petrine material. The depth of the literary analysis will bring to the surface both strong, positive characteristics of women—even over men—and weak, fallible characteristics of women that make the studies foundational in a theological sense, and thus interpretative of the more difficult passages involving women. It is in this sense that it is believed that this study may have its greatest impact on an evangelical community which continually struggles over gender issues and appears to need a new way to think about the issue. It is hoped that this study will provide an open door to future narrative work in Matthew, Luke, and John that will reinvigorate the conversation regarding gender.

This writer has no deductive, predetermined outcome in view. Conclusions will be gathered through an inductive, literary analysis of all the passages in the Gospel of Mark that discuss women. The research problem is not that no one has addressed the narrative structure of Mark, intercalations in Mark, women in Mark, or characterization in Mark. The research problem is that no one has adequately and thoroughly addressed the import of narrative structure and substructures on Mark's presentation of women—especially in a way that evangelicals can hear.

THEORETICAL APPROACHES[4]

The theoretical approaches of this study will be working synchronically and not diachronically.[5] Since literary critical analysis is synchronic in its approach, this study will not venture into historical criticism which gives expression to a diachronic approach. This study will not follow the methods and goals of redaction criticism that examines the writer's alleged editing of sources in the Gospel to ascertain transparent representations of theological struggles in the original community that received the writing.[6] Redaction criticism has numerous concerns for the present study.

---

4. This writer prefers the qualification of "theoretical" instead of "methodology" because the former allows one to design an integrative framework where categories of interpretation can be used more appropriately to what is required by the narrative text itself.

5. A strictly diachronic approach studies the development of meaning of a text through time. Here the focus will be on how the portrayal of women in Mark is cast against a first-century engendered value system—how it either echoes or resists the valorization of women at one moment in time. This study will not discuss the development of the text of Mark, but will address underlying socio-political, or text-immanent, conditions and processes that are part of the surface of the text.

6. Lane, "Gospel of Mark in Current Study," 7–21; Kingsbury, "Gospel of Mark in Current Research," 101–7.

As Kingsbury observes: "The debate over the alleged creativity of Mark as a redactor is largely the result of the inability of scholars to reach a consensus on the vexing problem of separating tradition from redaction."[7] Joel Williams has properly observed that Mark is not a theology, but "a narrative, a narration of a series of events, and if the Gospel of Mark is to be understood, its narrative features must be recognized."[8] Continuing, Williams writes:

> If interpreters ignore the narrative features of Mark's Gospel, they will not adequately appreciate the potential impact of the story. In fact, removing the theology of the Gospel from its narrative setting may even cause us to misunderstand the theology of the Gospel itself. Theological themes exist within the developing plot of the narrative, and their place within this narrative may affect the way that we understand them. "Themes which, isolated from their narrative context, appear to be constant may actually shift significantly in meaning through some new development in the plot." Understanding the narrative of Mark's Gospel is necessary even for understanding the theology of Mark's Gospel.[9]

Accordingly, a literary approach to interpreting the Gospel of Mark will recognize the narrative form and features of the Gospel in its final form, emphasizing the contribution of the book in its entirety to the contextual setting of passages rather than focusing on selected "redacted" sections of Mark as clues to the message and theology of the work.[10]

---

7. Kingsbury, "Gospel of Mark," 104.

8. Williams, *Other Followers*, 18.

9. Williams, *Other Followers*, 19.

10. Williams writes: "In seeking to uncover the theology of the Evangelist, the redaction critic once again looks at something which stands behind the Gospel, the mind of Mark. Such studies have their place, but they present a problem if they claim to be an interpretation of Mark's text. In the end, redaction criticism focuses on material behind the text, not on the text in its final form" (Williams, *Other Followers*, 21). Kingsbury observes: "The attempt to achieve a viable description of the Marcan community by assuming that the text of the Gospel reflects directly and throughout the circumstances of Mark's own day will not do; clearly, a more differentiated approach is needed. Again, the endeavor to analyze Mark's Gospel literary-critically as a piece of narrative with plot and characters is a relative new venture" (Kingsbury, "Gospel of Mark," 105). Lane opines: "A second line of a approach has been informed by modern literary criticism, and it is committed to the exploration of a Gospel as a narrative story. Those who champion this approach insist that the text be respected as a literary text and that any aspect of the text be understood within the context of the story before a judgment is made on the theology of the evangelist or the historical realities of his community. Sustained

Furthermore, this analysis will not be canonical in scope. Despite the apparent benefit of reading accounts in Mark in the context of Matthew, Luke, and John, the downside of a synoptic reading of the gospels is that the audience will fill in gaps intentionally made by the implied author of Mark with material from the other gospels. For instance, the audience may be able to identify characters presented as anonymous in Mark by name through a synoptic reading/hearing of the canonical gospels, but this result may undo what the implied author is trying to do with what he is saying. Furthermore, a synoptic reading of the gospels may have a skewed effect on the audience's understanding of the end of the Gospel of Mark. By including information supplied in Matthew and Luke, conclusions may arise about who the women met at the tomb and what the women did following the announcement from the person at the tomb. By treating Mark as a narrative world unto itself, the implied audience of Mark will be asked to arrive at different conclusions than an audience might assume from a synoptic reading. Therefore, this analysis will stay within the parameters of the Gospel of Mark and the narrative world that the implied author created.

Narratives do not explicitly *tell* us, but *show* us, their theology.[11] For instance, in a Pauline epistle, the Apostle explicitly states that Adam was a type (τύπος) of Christ (Rom 5:14), but the Gospel of Luke shows the audience that Jesus is the "new Adam" by running its genealogy back to Adam, and then rearranging the order of the temptation account from that in Matthew, to match the temptation of Adam and Eve in the garden.[12] Luke shows the audience what Paul tells. So too when we encounter the narratives in Mark, we will look to how the narrative shows its theology of women rather than for explicit statements about women. The audience

---

reflection on Mark along these fruitful lines of research should result in an understanding of the evangelist and his message which is based not upon inference but upon an appropriation of the total statement of the gospel" (Lane, "Gospel of Mark," 20–21).

11. As Leland Ryken states: "To begin, literature is experiential. This means that the subject matter of literature is human experience. The approach to human experience, moreover, is concrete rather than abstract. Literature does not, for example, discourse about virtue but instead shows a virtuous person acting. We might say that literature does not tell *about* characters and actions and concepts but *presents* characters in action" (Ryken, *Literature of the Bible*, 13). An example of narrative that was later explicitly explained in didactic literature is Abram's encounter with Melchizedek (cf. Genesis 14:18–20; Hebrews 7:1–10). The narrative in Genesis showed what the writer of Hebrews later told. See the discussion in Malick, "Jesus' View of Women," 4–15.

12. See Glickman, "Temptation Account in Matthew and Luke," 407–24; Glickman, *Knowing Christ*, 49–60. See also Bock, *Luke 1:1—9:50*, 349, 360, 383.

needs to ask questions of the narrative like: How is Jesus portrayed as he interacts with women? What is the writer doing with the material to communicate his theological message? Is the arrangement of the material significant to its message? How the implied author communicates his message is as much a part of the message as what the writer says.[13]

Additional theoretical approaches employed in this study will be interdisciplinary. A first theoretical approach employed throughout this study will be to critically work in the Greek text of the Gospel of Mark as set forth in the 28th edition of the *Novum Testamentum Graece*. This approach includes the evaluation of textual variants, conducting Greek lexical studies, and analyzing Greek grammar. Textual criticism, which might be considered a diachronic approach because of its interest in the origins and development of the text, is only meant to demarcate the elements of the narrative—especially with respect to the ending of the Gospel.

A second theoretical approach will be to examine the two-fold aspect of narrative—story and discourse—and discuss how characterization occurs through the discourse of the narrative by means of narrative descriptions, a character's inner life, speech, actions, and point of view. An implied author uses these means to develop his discourse, create characterization, and enable an implied audience to create characterization.

A third theoretical approach will be to research first-century social custom and *habitus* in eastern Roman, Greek, and Jewish culture to determine if the portrayal of women in Mark accords or differs from the cultural expectations of the implied audience. One approach employed in developing a preunderstanding that an implied audience might have about first-century women will be to examine the work of French sociologist, Pierre Bourdieu, whose socio-analytical studies in the 1960s in Algeria among the Berbers of Kabylia provides suggestions for interpreting the social, interpersonal culture of the first-century Mediterranean world. Bourdieu's analysis will be followed by an overview of Greek and Israelite women in the first century, much of which agrees with Bourdieu's observations about women and men in the first-century Mediterranean world. This research approach will enable the actual reader to understand how characterization is developed by discourse in the narrative and understood by the implied audience. Characterization developed in the Gospel of Mark may align with historical, social values for men and women, or may oppose, or modify, such historical/social values.

---

13. As Adele Berlin has stated, "And we must look not only for *what* the text says, but also *how* it says it" (Berlin, *Poetics*, 20). This will be discussed more fully below.

A fourth theoretical approach will be to research sources prior to the Gospel of Mark that contribute to the literary techniques of intercalations and the sign-sermon to obtain a theoretical framework from which to analyze the use of these literary techniques in Mark. It will be shown that the implied author and implied audience understood the use of a literary technique like an "intercalation" that combines two distinct stories together into a cohesive whole. This narrative approach gives the implied audience insight about the characterization of women in the narrative. The implied author and audience will also understand the literary technique of a "sign-sermon," or "sermon-sign," where a speech in the narrative is clarified in terms of its scope and reference by a miracle or sign-narrative that is closely correlated with the speech. These ancient literary techniques will enable the implied author to develop his discourse in a way that the implied audience will grasp and from which the implied audience will be able to create characterization.

A fifth theoretical approach will involve arranging the many parts of the Gospel of Mark into a synthetic whole by employing the literary markers in the text as clues and guides to its architecture. It will be shown, for instance, that the telling of the gospel occurs around chiastic, geographical markers:[14]

>Wilderness
>>Galilee
>>>On the way (to Jerusalem)
>>Jerusalem
>Tomb

These geographical sections each have a theological emphasis that the implied author uses to develop the characterization of women for the implied audience. The wilderness and the tomb are similar terrain in which people enter into death but emerge alive. Galilee and Jerusalem are opposite in their responses to Jesus. In Galilee Jesus is active in his ministry and is generally received favorably. In Jerusalem Jesus limits his ministry and is ultimately killed. The way to Jerusalem defines the essential character quality of a follower of Jesus as someone who serves people rather than rules over others. Furthermore, the use of four Roman Watches as timestamps in Mark become cues for the implied audience to pay special attention to the characters being presented in the discourse

---

14. The basis of this geographical structure will be explained and substantiated more fully in chapter 7 below.

of the narrative to determine if they are acting in an "on guard" and alert way or acting as those who are metaphorically asleep when it comes to their relationship with the character Jesus.

A sixth theoretical approach will be to perform close, analytical readings in the Greek text of all the passages involving women in Mark employing the literary substructures of intercalation, sign-sermon, and characterization in an attempt to determine how women are portrayed in the discourse of the Gospel. These close, analytical readings will emphasize how the narratives are told, and the contextual settings of the narratives within the Gospel of Mark so that their meaning is not read in isolation but within the discourse that the implied author is creating. Sometimes these contextual settings are immediately evident to an implied audience upon its first exposure to the narrative in its development of the discourse. Sometimes the full meaning and significance of the narratives is only evident to an implied audience after a full exposure to the entire Gospel of Mark, or said differently, upon a subsequent reading/hearing of the narrative.

A seventh theoretical approach will be to develop a Markan theology of women based on the literary analysis of the passages involving women in the Gospel. This theology will be developed from the specific characterization of the women in the Markan narratives. It will be tied to how the narratives are told, how the implied audience created characterization of these women from its preunderstandings, and the rhetorical effect of Mark's portrayal of women on the implied audience.

These theoretical approaches will not be conducted in a chronological fashion as listed above but are the theoretical framework necessary to properly analyze the implied author's portrayal of women in the Gospel of Mark and the implied audience's creation of character.

STATEMENT OF THESIS

It is the thesis of this study that the use of narrative analysis and narrative characterization in passages involving women in the Gospel of Mark will show "how" the characterization of women has taken place. The characterization of women allows for several possibilities with which an implied audience could identify. The implied audience could identify both by accepting some characters and by rejecting other characters. As such, narrative characterization could invite an implied audience to identify with women characters that are portrayed as valuable, effective, modeling, discerning, correcting, serving followers of Christ. On the other hand, the implied audience could distance itself from those that have been depicted as fallible, resistant, hostile, and deadly opponents of Christ. The implied author's and implied audience's characterization of women may be both over and against male counterparts and similar to male counterparts in the Gospel. The determinative difference in every case will have to do with how well they respond, or fail to respond, to what God is saying and doing in their lives. All of this will be discovered through an analysis of the implied author's discourse and the implied audience's cultural preunderstandings that contribute to their creation of characterization of women in Mark.

Part 1

Theoretical and Literary Research Approaches

THE FIRST PART OF this work will address theoretical issues and literary structures employed in the second part of this study involving the narrative analysis of passages involving women in the Gospel of Mark. This section will discuss various issues including: the hermeneutics for the development of characterization through discourse; sociological expectation of women in first-century Israel; and the development of literary patterns employed in the Gospel of Mark. The literary patterns include: intercalations; the sign-sermon motif; the repetition of the four Roman watches as narrative markers; and the broad structure of the Gospel of Mark around geographical themes. Any of these topics are worthy of examination on their own. However, within the limited scope of this study, these discussions are meant to provide an interpretive foundation for the following analysis of the implied author's portrayal of women in Mark developed in Part 2 of this study. The theoretical and narrative issues discussed in this section enable an actual reader to understand what the implied author and the implied audience understood and thus be able to see how characterization is developed in the implied author's discourse and by the implied audience reception of that discourse.

2

The Two-Fold Aspect of Narrative
Characterization through Discourse

THE FIRST THEORETICAL ISSUE to be addressed is the two-fold aspect of narrative into categories of "story" and "discourse." After a distinction is made between the content, or "what," of a narrative (story) and the method, or "how," the actual author tells the story (discourse), the discussion will focus on the multifold means employed by the actual author to develop characterization in discourse through narrative descriptions, portrayals of a person's inner life, speech, actions, comparisons and contrasts, and point of view. The goal of this discussion is not to sort through all the possible permutations of these topics, but to describe them sufficiently so that the approach taken in the narratives of this study is clear.

NARRATIVE DESCRIPTIONS— STORY AND DISCOURSE

Because women are the focus of this thesis, "character" as a literary category requires attention. However, since character is a constituent of a narrative, narrative must first be explained before an examination of the "character" can be developed. Cornelis Bennema defines "narrative" as "those literary works that contain a story and a storyteller."[1] This definition

---

1. Bennema, *Theory of Character*, 28, relying on Scholes et al., *Nature of Narrative*, 283–336.

is broad enough to allow for fiction and nonfiction. One might question whether stories require a storyteller—especially with more modern stories like James Joyce's *A Portrait of an Artist as a Young Man* where every attempt is made to hide the narrator, but the definition still seems valid because even in Joyce's story there is an implied author telling the story.[2]

Narratives are often described as having two aspects, or a two-storied structure. Following French structuralists, Seymour Chatman categorizes the two tiers as "story" and "discourse."[3] "Story" consists of the *what* of the narrative including events, plot, and existents (character and setting). "Discourse" is the *way* of the narrative, or the "means through which the story is transmitted."[4] Said differently, discourse is how the story is told which is often in an order outside of a strict chronology of the events. Russian Formalists have a similar dualist model distinguishing *fabula* (story/tale—the sequence of events referred to in a narrative in their causal, chronological order) from *sjužet* (discourse—the sequence of events in the actual order in which they appear in the narrative).[5] The biblical storyteller uses the way he tells the story to have an impact on his implied reader/listener (hereinafter "audience").[6] The storyteller is not simply telling what happened but telling it in a way to marshal a response from the implied audience.[7] As Abraham Kuruvilla explained: "Rather

---

2. See Booth, *Rhetoric of Fiction*.
3. Chatman, *Story and Discourse*, 9.
4. Chatman, *Story and Discourse*, 9.
5. Tomashevsky opines: "In brief, the story is 'the action itself,' the plot, 'how the reader learns of the action'" (Tomashevsky, "Thematics," 66, 67n5, 68). See also Resseguie, *Narrative Criticism*; Rhoads and Michie, *Mark as Story*, 9. Tzvetan Todorov distinguishes between *histoire* (story—a reality of events that would have passed—events reported) and *discours* (the manner in which the narrator makes events known to us) (Todorov, "Categories of Literary Narrative," 383–84). Mieke Ball follows a three-layer distinction of narrative text (a finite, structured whole composed of language signs that tells a story), story (the sequence of events), and *fabula* (a series of logically and chronologically related events that are caused or experienced by actors—the way in which events are presented) (Bal, *Narratology*, 5–6). See also Rimmon-Kenan, *Narrative Fiction*, 152n2.
6. Sternberg, *Poetics of Biblical Narrative*, 482.
7. Even though a work may have a real, historical "author" and "audience," under the literary critical analysis adopted in this study, the historical author and audience are not in view, and the complexities of the historical author and audience will not be addressed. Instead, the literary categories of "implied author" and "implied audience" (reader/listener) will be employed. The actual author (even if a group of people over time, as in a folk ballad) decides (wittingly or unwittingly) how to encode or represent her/himself, whether negatively or positively, through expressions in the text and through common reservoirs of knowledge between him and the audience he has in

than being simply *presented* by a text, life is *represented* as something, inviting the reader to see the world in one way and not another, and to respond by complying with the demands of that world."[8] For ease of reference and clarity, this writer will use Chatman's categories of "story" and "discourse" in this discussion.

Within these categories, the analysis of character is often developed under the category of "story."[9] Character is seen as part of the "what" of story because it is a "form of content" and thus a subcategory of "existents." But Chatman also recognizes the interdependence of story structure and discourse structure.[10] Because characterization is also a discussion of *how* characters are developed in a narrative, it seems appropriate to identify characterization with "discourse."[11] While character may be described, in the abstract, as a compilation of motifs, or a cluster of traits of someone in the narrative, and in that sense fall under the umbrella of "story," characterization is built from *how* the account is told—the storyteller's presentation as found in the discourse of the work. Many see characterization occurring through discourse. Boris Tomashevesky describes characterization as a function of discourse through the means of direct

---

mind to create an implied author for the implied reader/listener. The implied audience is created by the actual author through selected means and material (including socially conventional and acceptable language, cultural codes, compositional levels of design, selection and arrangement or design of material) deemed suitable to enable the implied audience to interpret a text whether it is read, heard, or performed. The implied reader does not produce the text but does determine the production of the text in terms of what is appropriate and what is not. The success of a communication encapsulated in narrative form is relative to the degree of identification that is established between implied author and implied audience. See Booth et al., *Rhetoric of Fiction*, 70–75, 137–38, 157, 422–31; Abrams, *Glossary of Literary Terms*, 288; Resseguie, *Narrative Criticism*, 39; Bal, *Narratology*, 18; Chatman, *Story and Discourse*, 148–51.

8. Kuruvilla, *Privilege the Text!*, 41.

9. Chatman, *Story and Discourse*, 107–38; Rhoads and Michie, *Mark as Story*, 101–36; Culpepper, *Anatomy of the Fourth Gospel*; Kingsbury, *Conflict in Mark*; Todorov, "Categories of Literary Narrative," 393–402; Bal, *Narratology*, 114–31.

10. Chatman, *Story and Discourse*, 137.

11. As Stephen Moore wrote: "When we come to read or analyze a concrete narrative text, for example, Mark, everything in that text is encountered as discourse-rhetoric" (Moore, *Literary Criticism and the Gospels*, 61). Rimmon-Kenan also observes that in the text: "The events do not necessarily appear in chronological order, the characteristics of the participants are dispersed throughout, and all the items of the narrative content are filtered through some prism or perspective ('focalizer')" (Rimmon-Kenan, *Narrative Fiction*, 5). Adele Berlin seems to approach characterization as discourse in that the implied reader "reconstructs a character from the information provided to him in the discourse" (Berlin, *Poetics*, 33–42).

characterization (through a direct report, or the character's own words) and indirect characterization (where the character shows himself to the audience through his or her actions).[12] Similarly, Shlomith Rimmon-Kenan argues that character is a construct put together by the audience from how the text is told.[13] Both direct and indirect characterization look to how the actual author presents the character in the narrative. Marianne Thompson argues that the audience develops characters by mining the text for its rhetorical and literary strategies in presenting characters.[14]

Character should be differentiated from broader, related categories even though it is constituted by its own elements that need to be considered in an analysis. For instance, the term "character" is narrower than the term "actor." "Character" refers to anthropomorphic figures the narrator tells us about. The term "actor" can describe anyone, or thing, that acts as an anthropomorphic figure—a dog, a machine, God, etc.[15] Characters resemble people who are created in the implied audience's imagination from sources like "fantasy, imitation, memory: paper people, without flesh and blood."[16] As narratives provide a *"form of representation,"*[17] they present characters that may refer to real people, but are actually people created from a vast repertoire of sources in the implied audience's

12. Tomashevsky, "Thematics," 88.
13. Rimmon-Kenan, *Narrative Fiction*.
14. Meye, "God's Voice You Have Never Heard," 180.
15. Bal, *Narratology*, 114.
16. Bal, *Narratology*, 114.

17. Berlin writes: "This is not a judgment on the existence of a historical Abraham any more than it is a statement about the existence of apples. It is just that we should not confuse a historical individual with his [Abraham's] narrative representation. . . . Somehow we have no problem with paintings of apples. We know they represent apples even though they are two-dimensional, and not always true to life in size or color. Conversely, we know that paintings of apples are not real; if we cut them no juice will run out, if we plant them they will not grow. We can make the transfer from a realistic painting to the object that it represents—i.e., we can 'naturalize' the painting—because we know (either intuitively or from having learned them) the conventions of the medium" (Berlin, *Poetics,* 13). Likewise, Resseguie explains: "An author is selective in what he or she writes in a narrative, for only some events and speeches can be narrated. No author can give a complete record of everything that happens in a person's life, . . . literary characters, whether real life or fictional, are given life by an author and re-created in the reader's imagination" (Resseguie, *Narrative Criticism*, 121). This is not to deny that a representation may be referential (built upon a memory of a person), but to affirm that the narrative representation is not the actual person. As Cornelis Bennema states: "While characters may resemble people, they only exist within the story world of the text even when they represent real people in the real world" (Bennema, *Theory of Character*, 29).

imagination, such as hero, villain, master, servant, loyal, disloyal, wise, foolish, religious, etc. Bennema defines "character" as referring to "a human actor, individual or collective, imaginary or real, who plays a role in the story of a literary narrative."[18]

As with the category of "actor," there are distinct characteristics to "character." Character refers to "the anthropomorphic figures the narrator tells us about."[19] E. M. Forster distinguished between flat and round characters.[20] Berlin describes flat characters as having a "single quality of trait."[21] Bal discusses flat characters based on psychological criteria stating that they are "stable, stereotypical characters that exhibit/contain nothing surprising."[22] Often flat characters function as types—or something outside of the character himself. He or she represents others in the narrative as well as himself or herself including religious types, psychological types, intellectual types, social types, and geographical types.[23] Mary Ann Tolbert stresses the typological nature of characters in the Gospel of Mark as illustrative of the four types of responses to Jesus presented in the parable of the "sower" in Mark 4. Jesus' opponents are the soil along the path; the disciples are the rocky soil; Herod and the rich young ruler are the thorny soil; and many, anonymous, minor characters represent the good soil.[24] Each character in the parable has a simple focus that can be projected by typology on other characters in the narrative.

By way of contrast, "round characters are like 'complex' persons, who undergo a change in the course of the story and remain capable of

---

18. Bennema, *Theory of Character*, 29. For this definition, Bennema relies upon Uri Margolin's definition of "Character." See Margolin, "Character," 66–69.

19. Bal, *Narratology*, 114.

20. Forster, *Aspects of the Novel*, 67. See also the discussion by Chatman, *Story and Discourse*, 132–33.

21. Berlin, *Poetics*, 23. See also Tomashevsky's distinction between "the *static character*, who remains exactly the same throughout the development of the story; and the *dynamic character*, whose characteristics change throughout the course of the story" (Tomashevsky, "Thematics," 89).

22. Bal, *Narratology*, 117. However, Bal continues to argue that traditional psychological criteria for flat and round characters exclude other forms of characterization in other genres like fairy tales, detective fiction, and popular fiction.

23. Scholes et al., *Nature of Narrative*, 204.

24. Tolbert, *Sowing the Gospel*, 165–72.

surprising the reader."²⁵ As Berlin explains: "Round characters ... are much more complex, manifesting a multitude of traits, and appearing as 'real people.'"²⁶

Characters in ancient works were once thought to be "flat."²⁷ However, several biblical scholars have argued that round characters are found in the Bible.²⁸ Picking up on Forester's statement that when there is more than one factor in a character, we get the beginning of the curve towards the round, Rimmon-Kenan suggests that characters should be viewed as points on a continuum with "infinite degrees of complexity."²⁹

The implied audience's construction of character relies in part on discourse. The actual author's construction of character (characterization) is the focus of discourse and of this study in particular.³⁰ The actual, flesh-and-blood, author is the one who does the work of construction, who creates the account. S/he writes with assumptions about his/her hypothetical, implied audience's beliefs, knowledge, and familiarity with literary conventions.³¹ The implied author, like the implied audience, is an invention in the hand of the actual author, whether or not the actual author is aware of what s/he is doing.³² The implied author is created in

---

25. Bal, *Narratology*, 117.

26. Berlin, *Poetics*, 23.

27. Scholes et al. state: "Characters in primitive stories are invariably 'flat,' 'static,' and quite 'opaque.' The very recurring epithets of formulaic narrative are signs of flatness in characterization. ... The concept of the developing character who changes inwardly is quite a late arrival in narrative. ... The inward life is assumed but not presented in primitive narrative literature, whether Hebraic or Hellenic" (Scholes et al., *Nature of Narrative*, 164). See also Moore, who states, "Characterization in the Gospels tends toward the 'flat' and 'static' end of the spectrum" (Moore, *Literary Criticism*, 15). Likewise, see Tolbert, *Sowing the Gospel*, 76–77.

28. Berlin, *Poetics*, 23. See also Sternberg, *Poetics of Biblical Narrative*, 322–64; Alter, *Art of Biblical Narrative*, 114–30; Malbon and Berlin, *Characterization in Biblical Literature*. Bennema surveys narratives in both the Hebrew Scriptures and Greco-Roman literature that predates and post-dates the canonical Gospels to convincingly show that character in these ancient writings was not always flat, static or typecast, but fuller than commonly thought by biblical scholars. Bennema, *Theory of Character*, 33–44. See also Bal, *Narratology*, 115–16.

29. Rimmon-Kenan, *Narrative Fiction*. Later, Bennema will make the same claim for characters in New Testament narratives. See Bennema, *Theory of Character*, 46–49, 58, 59.

30. Bennema, *Theory of Character*, 28.

31. Rabinowitz, "Truth in Fiction," 126.

32. James Phelan discusses the complexity of narrative theory in modern, nineteenth- and twentieth-century works, and especially second-person fictional narrative as he distinguishes between Gerald Prince's narratee and narrative audience, and Peter

the work and may or may not have any correlation with the actual author. The implied author is who the actual author projects as the teller of the narrative. Booth describes this as the masking of the actual author into who the author wants to appear to be.[33] The actual author also guides in the selection of the appropriate medium of communication, language, and detail that will create an implied audience and enable the implied audience to identify with his or her message. The implied audience may be able to construct an image of character as a male, female, impetuous, contradictory, or adversarial person. The implied audience's understanding of character comes from the storyteller's presentation of character through discourse, and from the implied audience's values, norms, socio-cultural world. Seymore Chatman offers the following narrative-communication diagram:[34]

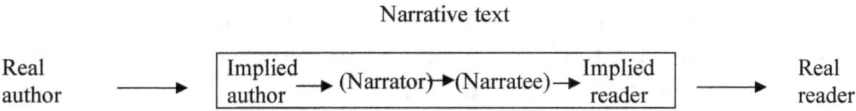

The real author and real reader stand outside of the narrative. The implied author and implied reader are part of the narrative, and the parentheses around narrator and narratee indicate that they are optional to the narrative.[35]

Rabinowitz's categories of actual audience, the authorial audience, the narrative audience, and the ideal narrative audience. Phelan, *Narrative as Rhetoric*, 135–53; Prince, "Introduction of the Study of the Narratee," 213–33; Rabinowitz, "Truth in Fiction," 121–41. As stated above, because this analysis is of the ancient work, the Gospel of Mark, and not an analysis of a modern fictional work, this discussion will limit itself to the rhetorical categories of the actual author's creation of an implied author and implied audience. Furthermore, narrative discussions of an unrealizable narrator in modern and post-modern works, who does not speak or act in accordance with the norms of a work or the audience's world values and standards of normalcy, are not an aspect of the ancient work, the Gospel of Mark, where the narrator aligns himself with the implied author and the discourse is not so contrary to the audience's common sense and ethical standards that it creates dissonance with the narrator. Accordingly, the rhetorical device of an unreliable narrator will not be examined. See Nünning, "Reconceptualizing Unreliable Narration," 89–107.

33. Booth, "Resurrection of the Implied Author."

34. Chatman, *Story and Discourse*, 151. This writer would broaden Chatman's category of "reader" to "audience." Chatman's diagram is further discussed in Shaw, "Why Won't Our Terms Stay Put?," 299–311.

35. Chatman, *Story and Discourse*, 151.

As a character is developed in the narrative, he or she acts a certain way and may undergo change. The implied audience may include that change in its construction of the character, but it was the actual author's presentation of the character through what the character did, said, and/or thought that was portrayed in the progress of the narrative that contributed to the creation of the character which the implied audience was later able to create.[36] The implied audience also brings its preunderstandings about social habits, customs, and expectations to its reconstruction of character in combination with the discourse presented by the actual author.

CHARACTERIZATION

Henry James aptly observed: "What is character but the determination of incident? What is incident but the illustration of character."[37] This narrative anagram is a way of saying more than how characters function in narratives; it is an indication of how characterization is developed in the narrative—through discourse.[38] As Berlin explains, the audience constructs character from the discourse of the narrative: "He is told by the statements and evaluations of the narrator and other characters, and he infers from the speech and action of the character himself."[39] For the audience, the construction of character is similar to the inductive, real-life process of determining who a person is.

> The reader grasps and assesses these characters by interpreting the whole characterization. That is, the reader reconstructs what kind of "persons" the characters are in the same way that we

---

36. See Resseguie, *Narrative Criticism*, 39.

37. James, "Art of Fiction." Aristotle understood character to be subordinate to action: "Thus tragedy is the imitation of an action, and of the agents mainly with a view to the action" (Aristotle, *Poetics*, 149–50). Following Henry James's lead, Rimmon-Kenan believes: "Instead of subordinating character to action or the other way round, it may be possible to consider the two as interdependent" (Rimmon-Kenan, *Narrative Fiction*, 566–67). Sternberg believes the audience fills gaps in the narrative and indirectly discovers characterization (i.e., "Mephibosheth's lameness evokes the characteristic mixture of David's motives"). See Sternberg, *Poetics of Biblical Narrative*, 342–46. Williams states, "Characters in Mark's Gospel are analyzed according to their qualities as well as their actions" (Williams, *Other Followers*, 58).

38. For instance, Alice Bach argues persuasively that Bathsheba should be treated as an autonomous being, and not merely as a plot function. Bach, "Signs of the Flesh, 61–79; Malbon and Berlin, *Characterization in the Bible*, 63, 70–76.

39. Berlin, *Poetics*, 34. See also Burnett, "Characterization," 5.

evaluate people, observing what they say and do and how others react to them. The reader also takes note of the characters' participation in the events of the story, their interactions with others, the motives assigned or suggested by the story, the ways in which the characters live up to the standards of judgment in the story, and how they compare with other characters.[40]

The implied audience also brings her/his own values, norms, and social-cultural understandings and uses them together with the text or presentation to construct character.

Robert Alter proposes a scale of certainty through the multitudinous means of characterization. Character revealed through actions or appearance leaves the implied audience with having to make inferences. Direct speech by a character or others leads the implied audience to weigh the claims made, statements of what the character feels or intends and leaves the implied audience with increased certainty.[41] However, since all the elements of Alter's proposed scale are created by the storyteller, one wonders if it is proper to posit such a hierarchy of certainty. It seems better to view all the ways in which the story is told to comprise the actual author's presentation of the story and characterization of participants rather than to consider some elements to be more or less certain. The search for certainty may be a resistance to representation in narrative; it may be part of the untiring pursuit of historical or referential meaning.

Narrative Descriptions

One means by which implied audiences construct character is through narrative descriptions. The audience is given some detail about a character's appearance or dress, or a character is described as being a king, a widow, a Pharisee, wealthy, old, or through distinctive physical features, like "John was dressed in camel's hair and a leather belt around his waist and eating locust and wild honey" (Mark 1:6).[42] In a prologue full of foreshadows to the following narrative, this description not only says something about the story, namely, that John functions as a prophesized Elijah figure, but also describes John himself as one who is primitive,

---

40. Rhoads and Michie, *Mark as Story*, 102.
41. Alter, *Art of Biblical Narrative*, 116–17.
42. See Berlin, *Poetics*; Williams, *Other Followers*, 65.

from the wild, and not from the political, social establishment of the day.⁴³ The implied audience brings with it preunderstandings that align, or do not align, with those the implied author seeks to evoke from an implied audience in its first reading/hearing of a story. These characteristics of John may only be grasped upon a second or third hearing of the Gospel. They are still the actual author's selected presentation of character, but their significance may, or may not, be immediately evident to the implied audience because of their preunderstandings.

Similarly, on a high mountain, Jesus is described as wearing clothing that was beyond an earthly description: "His garments became radiant white, exceedingly (στίλβοντα λευκὰ λίαν), which a cloth refiner on earth is not able thus to make white" (Mark 9:3). This description of Jesus' clothes helps the audience identify him as being outside of the normal social circles in the sense that he is otherworldly. While the implied audience may have a preunderstanding that a white garment signified social status, and a character clothed in white would have indicated high status, the description in the narrative goes further than social preunderstandings signifying an exceptional status for Jesus. Through the means of discourse, the implied author has created characterization by showing Jesus to be beyond what the implied audience may have understood by alluding to a whiteness beyond the capacities of an earthly cloth refiner. The form of expression of an exaggerated whiteness beyond the capacity of existing possibilities leads the implied audience in their characterization of Jesus. Likewise, when the women enter the tomb, the narrator explains that "they saw a young man, sitting to the right, wearing a white robe" (Mark 16:5). The person is described as a young man (νεανίσκος), but his clothing is reminiscent of Jesus' clothing on the mountain in that it is white (λευκός). This description suggests to the implied audience that the youth may also be otherworldly. The structure of the narrative, its discourse, transmits information to the implied audience that contributes to its ability to construct character.

---

43. Booth states: "Modes of dress and hair style, types of gentlemanly behavior, sexual conduct—all areas of life where convention operates—can be used to establish character, but only within limits of time and place carefully defined and controlled by the author" (Booth, *Rhetoric of Fiction,* 113). One might also add, and understood by the implied audience.

Inner Life

Audiences can construct character through a description of a character's inner life.[44] Scholes, Phelan, and Kellogg explain that an inner life can be developed in a narrative through: (1) direct narrative statements and (2) interior monologues including thoughts and self-expressions.[45] Inner life pertains to emotions such as "fear" or cognitive activity, such as "thinking."

In Mark, the narrator often describes a character's inner life. For instance, the audience is told that "Herod *feared* John *knowing* he was a righteous and holy man" (Mark 6:20). The audience is told that Pilate "*knew* the chief priests handed Jesus over on account of *jealousy*" (Mark 15:10). The narrator tells the audience that after Jesus calmed the storm, the disciples in the boat were "*afraid*" (Mark 4:41).[46] After Jesus fed the five thousand and walked on the water, the narrator tells the implied audience about the inside thoughts of the disciples: "They were *utterly astonished* because they *did not understand* the bread, but their *heart was hardened*" (Mark 6:52). Also, when Jesus is transfigured, the implied audience is told that Peter did not *know* what to say, and that Peter, James, and John were *afraid* (Mark 9:6). What the implied audience learns of a character's inner life contributes to its creation of characterization.

Speech

Implied audiences will construct character through speech.[47] John the Baptist's first words not only contribute to the development of the plot of the Gospel but show the implied audience John's perception of himself with respect to Jesus: "The one who is stronger than me comes after me of whom I am not worthy, bending down, to loose the strap of his sandals. I baptized you with water, but he will baptize you with the Holy Spirit" (Mark 1:7). At his baptism, Jesus himself is characterized by words spoken

---

44. Scholes, Phelan, and Kellogg denied this method of characterization for ancient Hebrew biblical writing, stating: "The inward life is assumed but not presented in primitive narrative literature, whether Hebraic or Hellenic" (Scholes et al., *Nature of Narrative*, 166). However, they also believed that the inward life became prominent with the Christian Scriptures (167). Berlin corrects their misapprehension with the Hebrew Scriptures (Berlin, *Poetics and Interpretation of Biblical Narrative*, 37–38). See also Rhoads and Michie, *Mark as Story*, 37–38; Williams, *Other Followers of Jesus*, 63–64.

45. Scholes et al., *Nature of Narrative*, 171–201.

46. The words above in *italics* all depict the inner life of a character.

47. Williams, *Other Followers*, 64–65.

from heaven: "You are my loved son. In you I am well-pleased" (Mark 1:11). Demons show their unclean character by saying: "Send us into the pigs in order that we may enter into them" (Mark 5:12). The disciples show themselves to have limited perception and perhaps impatience with Jesus when Jesus asks who it was that touched him, and they answer: "You see the crowd pressing upon you, and you say, 'Who touched me?'" (Mark 5:31). This limited, physical perspective is repeated in Mark 6:37 when Jesus instructs the disciples to feed the multitude and they respond: "Going should we buy bread for two hundred denarii and give them to eat?" The disciples' speech often shows that they do not understand the parables that Jesus speaks (Mark 4:10–13; 7:17; 8:15–16). Implied audiences use the discourse of speech to construct characterization.

Actions

Implied audiences also construct character through actions.[48] The portrayal of the value of an act in narrative structure illustrates how a character is to be formed by the implied audience. Actions serve the "how" of characterization. They bestow a particular quality on a particular character. As Aristotle stated, "Character comes in as subsidiary to the actions."[49] In the calling of Simon and Andrew, the disciples do not speak, but leave their nets and follow Jesus (Mark 1:16–18). In the calling of James and John, the disciples do not speak but leave their father in the boat and follow Jesus (Mark 1:19–20). In the calling of Levi, Levi does not speak, but rises from his tax booth and follows Jesus (Mark 2:13–14). These initial disciples are shown to be the kind of people who are willing to give up their livelihood in their pursuit of Jesus. However, when Jesus invites a rich man to sell all his possessions and follow him, the narrator tells the audience that the man went away distressed, unwilling to give up that which sustained his life to follow Jesus (Mark 10:20–22). By immediate contrast, blind Bartimaeus leaves his cloak and immediately follows Jesus (Mark 10:50–52). It is the actions of these characters that form and distinguish them for the implied audience. As the narrative develops, the disciples may say that they are willing to follow Jesus to the point of death (Mark 14:27–31), but they show their fickle character by scattering upon Jesus' arrest (Mark 14:50). This vacillation may be understood by

---

48. Williams, *Other Followers*, 64.
49. Aristotle, *Poetics*, 140.

the implied audience as an indication that the disciples are less "male" through the social-cultural gender value system. As another example, Jesus shows himself to be like Moses by feeding the five thousand Israelites in the wilderness (Mark 6:35–44). He then shows himself to be greater than Moses by not walking through the water on dry ground (see Exod 14:22), but on the water (Mark 6:48), and to be Yahweh himself by passing by the disciples in the boat as Yahweh passed by Moses on the mountain (Mark 6:48; see Exod 33:19–23). It is through actions that character is inferred for the implied audience.

An implied audience constructs character through comparisons and contrasts, providing the implied audience an opportunity to fill in gaps by implication.[50] This parallel means of characterization causes traits to stand out in characters.[51] Often it is through comparison that the audience discovers the contrast. Furthermore, it is through comparison that a character is often developed throughout a narrative.[52] Characters are not so much "individuals" as "interdividuals" in that they are seen, compared, and contrasted, in relationship to others.[53]

A Combination

Rarely is characterization developed through a single technique but through a combination of techniques.[54] As discussed above, Jesus shows himself to be greater than Moses through his acts of feeding the five

---

50. Berlin focuses on "contrast," noting that characterization is developed through, "three types of contrast: (1) contrast with another character, (2) contrast with an earlier action of the same character, and (3) contrast with the expected norm" (Berlin, *Poetics*, 40). Alice Bach provides a good example of comparing and contrasting an earlier presentation of Bathsheba as an object in 2 Samuel 11–12 with the later transformation of Bathsheba as queen mother in 1 Kings 1–2 (Bach, "Signs of the Flesh," 70–77). Laura Donaldson also provides a good example of comparison between Joseph and Potiphar's wife to show that Potiphar's wife "uses her sexuality as a weapon to prevent the household's passing from man to man (from Potiphar to Joseph) rather than from man to woman (from Potiphar to Potiphar's wife)" (Donaldson, "Cyborgs, Ciphers, and Sexuality," 90). See also Williams, who states that: "The narrator may highlight the traits of a character through the use of an analogy" (Williams, *Other Followers*, 65–66).

51. Berlin, *Poetics*, 40.

52. Marianne Thompson argues that characters are presented and developed in biblical narratives (Thompson, "God's Voice You Have Never Heard," 179). See also Scholes et al., *Nature of Narrative*, 169.

53. McCraken, "Character in the Boundary," 36.

54. Berlin, *Poetics*, 41. See also Williams, *Other Followers*, 67.

thousand, as God fed Israel in the wilderness (Mark 6:35–44), walking on the water, surpassing the provision of Israel passing through the water in escape from the Egyptians (Mark 6:48; see Exod 14:22), and walking past the disciples in the boat as Yahweh passed Moses on the mountain (Mark 6:48; see Exod 33:19–23). However, the disciples do not correlate Jesus on the water with either Moses or Yahweh. The actual author gives the implied audience an inside view of the disciples: "Seeing him walking upon the sea, they thought that he was a ghost, and they cried out because all saw him, and they were terrified" (Mark 6:49–50). Then, when Jesus enters the boat with the disciples and the wind calms down, the narrator explains: "For they did not understand from the bread" (Mark 6:54). In other words, while Jesus is being shown to be greater than Moses by what he does, even as being Yahweh himself, the disciples do not gain any understanding because they did not understand the first miracle of feeding the five thousand. If the greater-than-Moses imagery is not comprehended from the first, most obvious act of Jesus, then the following acts are also incomprehensible to the disciples. Then the narrator provides an evaluative, inside look at the disciples when he explains, "Their heart had been hardened" (Mark 6:52). The action that reveals to the audience the Moses/God-like character of Jesus also demonstrates the fallible character of the disciples by showing their inner life, fearful response, and giving the inside view that they lack understanding and are hard-hearted. Literary criticism is a process that teases out these different techniques in how a character is created by the actual author and the implied audience.

Point of View

Another means by which an actual author and an implied audience construct character is through point of view, or the way a story gets told.[55] As Berlin explains:

> It is impossible to discuss character without reference to point of view, for, after all, a character is not perceived by the reader directly, but rather mediated or filtered through the telling of

---

55. See also Resseguie, *Narrative Criticism*, 167–73. Others refer to this literary technique as "focalization," meaning the angle of vision which is formulated by the author. Rimmon-Kenan, *Narrative Fiction*; Bal, *Narratology*, 100. An actual or implied author's point of view or focalization is a way of presenting a character to the implied audience, and that presentation may form the character.

the (implied) author, the narrator, or another character. For the reader is shown only what the author wishes to show. Never can the reader step behind the story to know a character other than in the way the narrative presents him. The purpose of a discussion of point of view is to understand whose telling or showing we are receiving, and how these types of presentations are made.[56]

Seymour Chatman distinguishes between point of view and narrative voice:

> Point of view is the physical place or ideological situation or practical life-orientation to which narrative events stand in relation. Voice, on the contrary, refers to the speech or other overt means through which events and existents are communicated to the audience. Point of view does *not* mean expression; it only means the perspective in terms of which the expression is made. *The perspective and the expression need not be lodged in the same person.*[57]

Through a review of Russian literature, Boris Uspensky identified four kinds of point of view: (1) ideological; (2) phraseological; (3) spatial and temporal; and (4) psychological.[58] Uspensky observed that "the use of several different points of view in narration may be noted even in relatively ancient texts."[59] In Mark's Gospel the point of view is most often expressed by the implied author/narrator and Jesus. However, even with that limitation, the narrator can speak through selected points of view.

---

56. Berlin, *Poetics*, 43. See also Abrams, *Glossary of Literary Terms*, 301–6. Bennema argues that audiences of non-fictional narratives should reconstruct character based not only on what a narrator reveals, but on whatever extra-textual information the readers have on a character. In this case, it would be a synoptic reading of the Gospels. He identifies this as "historical narrative criticism." However, Bennema's emphasis is upon the reconstruction of character as a function of "story," rather than the emphasis on the implied author's creation of character (characterization) through "discourse" (Bennema, *Theory of Character*, 28). Bennema also appears to be inconsistent with his approach in that he does not view the need to interpret Pilate through Mark's presentation, but only through John's presentation (Bennema, *Theory of Character*, 65n10). Therefore, within the confines of a narrative, Berlin seems to be correct in focusing on the way the narrative presents a character. This is especially essential when the audience is solely relying on the narrative world of a particular book, like Mark.

57. Chatman, *Story and Discourse*, 153.
58. Uspensky, *Poetics of Composition*, 6.
59. Uspensky, *Poetics of Composition*, 171.

Ideological point of view

By ideological point of view, Uspensky is describing the point of view the author (or implied author, narrator, or a character) assumes when he describes the narrative world in the story.[60] This is the plane of the narrator's norms, values, and worldview.[61] This appears to align with what Chatman describes as conceptual point of view, the perspective of attitudes, concepts, and worldview or *Weltanschauung*.[62]

In Mark, the ideological plane is that of the implied author/narrator. Jesus is also presented in the narrative with knowledge similar to the narrator.[63] All characters in Mark are evaluated by how they align, or misalign, with the narrator's and Jesus' ideological perspective. The narrator describes the disciples as hard-hearted because they do not understand the significance of Jesus feeding bread to the five thousand (Mark 6:52). Jesus also describes the disciples as hard-hearted because they do not understand the significance of Jesus feeding bread to the five thousand and the four thousand (Mark 8:15–21). These evaluative statements by the narrator and Jesus provide clues for the implied audience on how to construct the characters of the disciples and Jesus, even as it simultaneously allows for an identification between the character Jesus and the narrator.

Phraseological point of view

Point of view on the phraseological plane describes "cases where the author uses different diction to describe different characters or where he makes use of one form or another of reported or substituted speech in his description."[64] Resseguie provides a list of questions that help to identify phraseological point of view:

> What names, titles, and epithets are used for a character by their narrator or by other characters? What tone is expressed in their speech? Is it affirming or disparaging? What are a character's

---

60. Uspensky, *Poetics of Composition*, 8.
61. Resseguie, *Narrative Criticism*, 169; Berlin, *Poetics*, 55.
62. Chatman, *Story and Discourse*, 151–52.
63. See Berlin, *Poetics*, 55–56; Petersen, "Point of View in Mark's Narrative," 100, 102.
64. Uspensky, *Poetics of Composition*, 17–56; Berlin, *Poetics*, 56. This appears to align with what Chatman describes as "narrative voice" (Chatman, *Story and Discourse*, 153).

first words? Does a character's speech change in a narrative or remain the same? Does the narrator comment on a character or evaluate an action? Does the narrator offer asides such as explanations or parenthetical comments? Does the narrator provide an interpretation or evaluation of characters or events?[65]

This use of diction is part of the discourse of narrative. The phraseological point of view is a category that belongs to the domain of discourse because it prompts the implied audience to analyze how the "dictions" of characters elaborate their "persons" in the making of a character. It concurs, therefore, with Chatman's view of what a form of expression entails that may be found in the structure of a narrative's transmission.

For instance, in Mark 6, Jesus visits his hometown and teaches in the synagogue (Mark 6:2). When the people respond to Jesus teaching, he is not even named by people in his home town who knew him, but is called "this one." "Where did this one (τούτῳ) get these things" (2 times in 6:2; 1 time in 6:3). Then in Mark 6:3, they ask a question that may have a derogatory implication: "Isn't this Mary's son?" In the Hebrew tradition, and in Mark, children are usually identified with a patronymic name, like James the son of Zebedee (Mark 1:19; 3:17), Levi the son of Alphaeus (Mark 2:14), James the son of Alphaeus (Mark 3:18), Simon, the father of Alexander and Rufus (Mark 15:21). By referring to Jesus as the son of Mary, they may be making a slur against Mary.[66] Those in Nazareth refer to Jesus in disparaging ways, and the narrator tells us that they were offended/scandalized by him (Mark 6:3). This substitutionary diction to describe Jesus is an example of the use of a phraseological point of view.

Spatial and temporal point of view

These are actually two separate but related perspectives. As Uspensky explains: "In some cases, the point of view of the narrator may be more or less clearly specified in space or in time, and we may be able to guess the position, defined in spatial or temporal coordinates, from which the narration is conducted."[67] Uspensky illustrates this latter technique well through an excerpt from Tolstoy's *War and Peace* where the narrator

---

65. Resseguie, *Narrative Criticism*, 170–71.

66. Lynn Cohick questions this reading of Mark 6, suggesting that the town's people were not commenting on Jesus' illegitimacy but emphasizing that his mother's family had more prestige than Joseph's family (Cohick, *Women in the World*, 154).

67. Uspensky, *Poetics of Composition*, 57.

shifts focus sequentially from one person to another at a dinner party in the Rostovs' home.[68]

Resseguie clarifies the *spatial point of view* with the following description:

> Spatial point of view refers to the narrator's relationship to the narrative in terms of space. From what vantage point does the narrator view the actions? Does a narrator see events from one character's perspective, moving with that character throughout the narration? Or is the narrator an invisible, roving presence similar to a moving camera and montage? The roving narrator has the advantage of moving freely from character to character, stopping long enough to focus on certain details and then moving on to another character or series of events.[69]

Resseguie also illustrates the use of spatial point of view in Mark with the description of the trials of Jesus and of Peter:

> In Mark, the narrator moves seamlessly from Jesus' trial before the chief priests and the council to Peter's "trial" in the courtyard below that culminates in his denial of Jesus. The narrator is not limited by one spatial perspective but views Jesus and Peter simultaneously. The roving perspective thus allows the reader to compare and contrast Jesus' trail with Peter's "trial."[70]

A bird's-eye, or panoptic, view is another example of spatial point of view. Uspensky describes it as follows:

> When there is a need for an all-embracing description of a particular scene, we often find neither the sequential survey nor the moving narrator, but an encompassing view of the scene from some single, very general, point of view. Because such a spatial

---

68. Uspensky, *Poetics of Composition*, 60–61.

69. Resseguie, *Narrative Criticism*, 171. Berlin further explains: "This refers to the location of time and space of the narrator in relation to the narrative. The narrator may be telling the story as it happens or long afterwards. He may be attached to one character (as he is to Abraham in much of Gen 22), in which case he would tell things as that character saw them; or he may jump from character to character, from scene to scene, or give a panoramic view of things" (Berlin, *Poetics*, 56).

70. Resseguie, *Narrative Criticism*, 171. Again, Uspensky explains how this shifting position works: "The description tends to fall into separate scenes, each described from a different spatial position; only when they are joined together is the illusion of movement produced—in the same way that the movement in film is the result of the projection of a sequence of still frames" (Uspensky, *Poetics of Composition*, 62).

position usually presupposes very broad horizons, we may call it the bird's-eye point of view.

He continues:

> Frequently, the bird's-eye view is used at the beginning or the end of a particular scene, or even at the beginning or the end of a whole narrative. For example, scenes which have a large number of characters are often treated in the following way: a general summary view of the entire scene is given first, from a bird's-eye viewpoint; then the author turns to descriptions of the characters, so that the view is broken down into smaller visual fields; at the end of the scene, the bird's-eye view is often used again. This elevated viewpoint, then, used at the beginning and the end of the narration, serves as a kind of "frame" for the scene, or for the work as a whole.[71]

An example of the bird's-eye-view perspective may be seen in the narrator's description of Jesus' crucifixion in Mark 15:22–41. The narrator is present at the crucifixion but describes the events taking place and the people looking-on in general terms as an onlooker. At the third hour, Jesus is brought to Golgotha and crucified with two other criminals with the inscription, "The King of the Jews." Passers-by hurl abuse at him. The religious leaders mock him. At the sixth hour, darkness falls over the land. The narration then moves in closer so that we can hear the words of Jesus at his death. When he dies at the ninth hour, the narrator moves away to report that the veil of the temple is torn, the centurion's confession, and the presence of women watching at a distance.

Temporal point of view refers to the narrator's temporal relationship with the narrative:

> The author may count time and order the chronological events from the position of one of the characters (then authorial time coincides with the subjective timing of events belong to a particular character); or he may use his own time schema. . . . Thus, the narrator may change his positions, borrowing the time scene of first one character, then another—or he may assume his own temporal position and use his own authorial time, which may not coincide with the individual time sense of any of the characters.[72]

As Resseguie summarizes:

---

71. Uspensky, *Poetics of Composition*, 63–64.
72. Uspensky, *Poetics of Composition*, 65–66.

> Temporal point of view refers to the pace of the narration or the temporal distance between the time of narration and time of the story. Does the narration take place prior to the events? . . . Or does the narration take place simultaneously with the events as they unfold? Or have the events of the narrative already taken place?[73]

In the example above from Mark's description of the crucifixion, the narrator follows a close, chronological, hour-by-hour telling of the event from the third, to the sixth, to the ninth hour. Therefore, the narration is taking place simultaneously with the events as they unfold. However, from the broader perspective of the Gospel as a whole, the crucifixion account is slowing down the narrative pace. The bulk of the narrative has moved at an unspecified pace from Galilee to Jerusalem. The story has taken place over days, weeks, perhaps even years which corresponds with the narrator's own time schema as he describes only one journey from Galilee to Jerusalem. Chronology is generally not distinguished. However, when Jesus and the disciples reach Jerusalem, narrative time begins to slow down to two days before the Passover and the Feast of Unleavened Bread (Mark 14:1), to the first day of Unleavened Bread (14:12), to the Passover, or the night before Jesus' crucifixion (14:16—15:21), and then hours during Jesus' crucifixion (15:22–41).[74] The pace of the narrative then picks up again with Jesus' burial (15:42–47), and leaps to the first day of the week after his burial, "When the Sabbath was over" (16:1–8).

In Mark, the narrator can also speak before events occur through the character of Jesus (Mark 8:31; 9:1, 31; 10:33–34; 11:1–8; 12:1–12; 13:1–32; 14:13–16, 18–21, 27–31), and after events occur (6:14–29).

Psychological point of view

Point of view on the psychological plane describes how the author constructs his narration. As Uspensky explains, the actual author

> usually has two options open to him: he may structure the events and characters of the narrative through the deliberately subjective viewpoint of some particular individual's (or individuals') consciousness, or he may describe the events as objectively as possible. In other words, he may use the *données* of the

---

73. Resseguie, *Narrative Criticism*, 171.
74. See Tolbert, *Sowing the Gospel*, 272.

perceptions of one consciousness or several, or he may use the facts as they are known to him. Different combinations of these two techniques are possible; the author may alternate between them or may combine them in various ways.[75]

Berlin further explains:

> This refers to the viewpoint from which actions and behaviors are perceived or described. The viewpoint may be objective, or external—i.e., only those things that could be seen by an observer are presented. Or the viewpoint may be subjective, or internal. This is accomplished either by presenting the viewpoint of a character, or by the words of an omniscient narrator who has entered the mind of a character.[76]

The psychological plane appears to correspond to Chatman's perceptual point of view.[77] The psychological plane can correspond to the discussion above under "narrative descriptions" where the narrator tells his story by giving an "inside view" of characters.

For instance, in Mark 2:6–7, Jesus tells the paralytic that his sins are forgiven. Then the narrator tells the implied audience: "But certain ones of the scribes were sitting there and dialoging in their hearts: 'Why does this one speak thus? He blasphemes. Who is able to forgive sins except one, God?'" By providing an inward view into the thoughts of the scribes, the narrator is developing the story by showing the actual conflict between the thoughts of the religious leaders and Jesus. The narrator then hands-off his omniscience to Jesus by stating: "And immediately, Jesus knowing in his spirit that they were dialoging thus in themselves says to them: 'Why do you dialogue these things in your hearts?'" (Mark 2:8). It is the psychological plane that provides the conflict that moves the story forward as Jesus heals the paralytic as a sign to the religious leaders that he has authority to forgive sins (Mark 2:9–12). In verse 12, the narrator's voice reappears objectively summarizing the effects of Jesus' words: "And he [the paralytic] arose, and immediately taking the pallet, he went out before all, so that all were astonished and glorified God saying that, 'not once have we seen this.'"

---

75. Uspensky, *Poetics of Composition*, 81.
76. Berlin, *Poetics*, 56.
77. Chatman, *Story and Discourse*, 151–52.

CONCLUSION

Characterization in the Gospel of Mark is determined by a combination of the actual author's construction of the text and the implied audience's construction by its careful attention to how the narrative is presented together with the preunderstandings that the implied audience brings to their reading/hearing of the account. The author lays out discourse, but the audience must actively process how the story is told—including filling-in gaps in the narratives from their own understanding and comparing and contrasting parallel, and/or contextual narratives in the text. Although Chatman understands "characters" to be a sub-section of "existents," this writer has demonstrated that characterization better fits as a feature of discourse since it is a form of expression that is part and parcel of the structure of narrative transmission. The actual author indeed lays out the course of the narrative, but the implied audience brings their preunderstandings to its reading/performance of the text to construct characterization. Rabinowitz suggests that one reason an actual audience finds an older work hard to understand is because the actual audience does not share the knowledge base needed to align itself with the implied audience.[78] The first part of this thesis will explicate some of the knowledge base understood by the actual author and the implied audience.

Contrary to Brennema who argues for a historically informed audience who recreates character from *sources* available to them from outside of the text, a literary approach, and the approach of this study, limits the construction of character to the presentation in the text and the audience's social-cultural preunderstandings.[79] The use of *sources* from outside of the narrative to fill-in gaps leads to a reconstruction of character that is beyond, if not foreign, to the narrative of Mark. Many have pursued this approach in synoptic readings of the gospels only to construct synthetic composites of character that cannot be found in any particular narrative.[80] Even if an implied audience, whether ancient or modern, knows of other sources about a character, a true literary reading of a work must allow for the actual author to make his own construction of a character and perhaps even challenge an implied audience's preunderstandings.[81]

---

78. Rabinowitz, "Truth in Fiction," 127.
79. Bennema, *Theory of Character*, 67–72.
80. See Pentecost and Danilson, *Words and Works*; Edersheim, *Life and Times*.
81. A modern-day example of this dilemma occurred with the recent publication of Harper Lee's *Go Set a Watchman*. In Lee's previous work, *To Kill a Mockingbird*, attorney

Close attention to the actual and implied author's presentation through discourse of character will be one tool that enables an implied audience to construct the character of women in the Gospel of Mark. This chapter has focused on the use of discourse to construct characterization. The next chapter will focus on first-century preunderstandings that contribute to the actual author and the implied audience's construction of characterization.

Atticus Finch was portrayed as a champion of civil rights. However, in her more recent novel, he is portrayed as one who struggles with personal and political issues surrounding race in the South. This new portrayal of Finch has caused distress for readers of the previous work. Lee's more recent characterization of Finch is thought to conflict with her previous characterization. However, the fact remains that each work has its own characterization. Knowledge of other characterizations may cause readers to attempt to reconcile differences so as to develop a kind of "systematic" character from "every and any source," but this does not deny that the actual characterization of Finch is unique to each work. This writer has previously attempted to fill-in the gaps regarding Mary in Mark 3:20–35 through a reading of other gospel accounts involving Mary in "Examination of Jesus' View of Women," 5–6. While there is theological value to a synthetic study, it moves the audience away from the emphasis on character being made in a particular work. Accordingly, the goal of this literary analysis of Mark will be to attempt to fill-in gaps from within the contextual constraints of Mark and the actual author's and implied audience's preunderstandings.

3

First-Century Characterization of Women and Bourdieu

THE SECOND THEORETICAL ISSUE in this study is the nature of first-century women. This analysis is needed to obtain a concurrent base of social/cultural knowledge with the actual author and the implied audience, and thereby lessen the gap in understanding between an actual audience and the actual author/implied audience. Characterization in the Gospel of Mark requires a base understanding about first-century women. Even though the actual author is not bound by the social understanding of women in his/her day, those receiving the narrative would be aware of society's expectations for women and would use that preunderstanding to create characterization from the Markan narrative. Plausibility for the recipient often depends on conformity with social expectations. Deviations from social expectations would not only be noticed by the recipient but contribute to what the actual/implied author is saying to the audience. Accordingly, a brief survey of first-century women follows. This discussion will first examine the work of French sociologist, Pierre Bourdieu whose socio-analytic studies in the 1960s in Algeria among the Berbers of Kabylia provides suggestions for interpreting the social, interpersonal culture of the first-century, Mediterranean world. Aspects of Bourdieu's work can be used to analyze how characters are infused with values that are different for men and for women in the first-century

Mediterranean world. Bourdieu's analysis will be followed by an overview of Greek and Israelite women in the first century. As will be discussed below, this overview of first-century women will not address women in the western, Roman Empire or northern Africa because of their limited influence on social customs for women in Israel located in the eastern Roman Empire.[1] It is essential for the actual, present-day reader to be educated on the first-century's valorization of characterization to understand *how* characterization is developed by discourse in the narrative and understood by the implied audience. Characterization developed in the narrative may align with historical, social values for men and women or may oppose, or modify, such historical/social values.

FIRST-CENTURY WOMEN AND PIERRE BOURDIEU

Identifying the social patterns and habits of women in first-century Galilee and Judea is difficult not only because of the multiplicity of cultures present in this geographical area (Jewish, Greek, Roman), but because of the difficulty in discerning how men and women interacted in society through written texts and archeology alone.[2] Although material from the Old Testament and rabbinic writings offer some help, they often talk more about "how the lawgivers, prophets and rabbis said one ought to live" than about how people actually did live.[3] Bruce Malina observed that meanings include models of society and social science.[4] Accordingly, Carol Meyers acknowledges the need to depend on extrapolations from current sociological and anthropological studies to arrive at ancient people's roles and interactions.[5]

---

1. This will be discussed more fully in the historical analysis of first-century women below.

2. Downing, "In Quest of First-Century CE Galilee," 86; Pomeroy, *Goddesses, Whores, Wives, and Slaves*, 21.

3. See Finley, "Review of Henri Daniel-Rops's Daily Life," 47–48; Corley, *Private Women, Public Meals*, ix. However, Corley herself basis her analysis of women from written sources.

4. Malina, "Social Sciences and Biblical Interpretation," 233. See also Downing, "In Quest of First-Century CE Galilee," 93.

5. Meyers, *Discovering Eve*, 18–20, 139–64. See also Sarah Pomeroy, who states: "It is impossible to draw any conclusions about social systems in prehistory in the absence of written documents from the time" (Pomeroy, *Goddesses, Whores, Wives, and Slaves*, 15).

Anthropological and social studies of twentieth-century peasant communities have provided helpful suggestions for interpreting the social, interpersonal culture of the first-century, Mediterranean world.[6] French sociologist, Pierre Bourdieu, conducted socio-analytic studies in the 1960s in Algeria among the Berbers of Kabylia, the Kabyle peasants.[7] Regarding the relevance of the Kabyle to Mediterranean studies, Bourdieu argues that the cultural tradition among the Kabyle is paradigmatic of the Mediterranean tradition.[8] Bourdieu describes the Kabyle as a relatively untouched social system because of its lack of a written tradition.[9]

Broadly speaking, Kabayle society adheres through family relationships, and these relationships run through the father. The father is the patriarch—the leader, priest, and judge—with power over family life and organization. He decides and presides over family ceremonies, marriage, and counsels.[10] A woman remains subject to paternal authority throughout her life. She transitions from her position under her father to a position under her husband, but the entire goal of the marriage is to strengthen family ties.[11] The mother supervises the domestic tasks and helps the father in his management of the family. She also represents the power of the father in female society.[12]

In his study, Bourdieu sought to resolve the antinomy of objectivism and subjectivism through the concept of *habitus*—a "system of durable, transposable dispositions."[13] By "dispositions," Bourdieu is describing: "the result of an organizing action, with a meaning close to that of words such as structure; it also designates a way of being, a habitual state (especially of the body) and, in particular, a predisposition, tendency, propensity, or inclination."[14] These dispositions are not determined by the future in the sense that they are outcome oriented but

> are determined by the past conditions which have produced the principle of their production, that is, by the actual outcome

---

6. Neyrey, *Social World of Luke-Acts*; Malina, *New Testament World*.

7. See Bourdieu, *Algerians*; "Sentiment of Honour in Kabyle Society," 191–231; *Masculine Domination*, 5.

8. Bourdieu, *Masculine Domination*, 6. See Peristiany, *Honour and Shame*.

9. Bourdieu, *Masculine Domination*, 6.

10. Bourdieu, *Algerians*, 3–4.

11. Bourdieu, *Algerians*, 8.

12. Bourdieu, *Algerians*, 6.

13. Bourdieu, *Outline of a Theory of Practice*, 72.

14. Bourdieu, *Outline of a Theory of Practice*, 71n1.

First-Century Characterization of Women and Bourdieu

of identical or interchangeable past practices, which coincides with their own outcome to the extent (and only to the extent) that the objective structures of which they are the product are prolonged in the structures within which they function.[15]

An example of *habitus* is observed in the division of labor between men and women of the Kabyle. Men's work is primarily outdoors as they take goats and sheep to the market, work in the fields plowing, sowing, harvesting, winnowing, transport dung fields on the back of animals, knock down trees, build roofs for houses, create utensils from wood, and slaughter animals. Indoors, men only feed cattle at night, and the broom was prohibited to a man. Women's work was primarily indoors. They brought supplies into the house, tied up cattle brought back to the house from the fields, cooked, wove, milled, kneaded clay, cared for the garden, transported seed-corn, dung (on back), water, wood, stones for house building, gathered olives, figs, acorns, twigs, and kneaded by hand clay for the house and the threshing floor.[16]

Discussing this division of labor, Bourdieu emphasized how it manifests more than tasks, but global, "homologous oppositions—up/down, above/below, in front/behind, right/left, straight/curved (and twisted), dry/wet, spicy/bland, light/dark, outside (public)/inside (private)."[17] More particularly, Bourdieu explains:

> The distribution of activities between the sexes . . . can be accounted for by combining three cardinal oppositions: the opposition between movement inwards (and, secondarily, downwards) and movement outwards (or upwards); the opposition between the wet and the dry; and the opposition between continuous actions, aimed at maintaining and managing the united contraries, and short, discontinuous actions, aimed at uniting contraries or separating united contraries. There is no need to dwell on the opposition between the inside, the house, cooking, or inward movement (storing provisions), and the outside, the field, the market, the assembly, or outward movement, between the invisible and the visible, the private and the public, etc. The opposition between the wet and the dry, which partly overlaps with the former, assigns to woman everything that has to do with water, green things, grass, the garden, vegetables,

15. Bourdieu, *Outline of a Theory of Practice*, 72–73. See also Downing, "In Quest of First-Century CE Galilee," 84.

16. Bourdieu, *Logic of Practice*, 217.

17. Bourdieu, *Masculine Domination*, 7.

milk, wood, stone, earth (women hoe barefoot and knead the clay for pottery or the inner walls with their bare hands), But the last opposition, the most important one in terms of ritual logic, distinguishes male acts, brief, dangerous confrontations with the liminal forces—ploughing, harvesting, slaughter of the ox—which use instruments made with fire and are accompanied by prophylactic rites, and female acts of gestation and maintenance, continuous attention aimed at ensuring continuity—cooking (analogous to gestation), rearing children and livestock (which implies cleaning, sweeping, carrying away dung, the smell of which causes livestock and children to fade away), weaving (seen from one standpoint as bringing up a life), managing the reserves, or mere picking and gathering, all these activities being accompanied by simple propitiatory rites. Supremely vulnerable in herself, that is, in her life and her fertility ("a pregnant woman has one foot in this world and one foot in the other"; "her grave is open from conception to the fortieth day after confinement") and in the lives for which she is responsible, those of the children, the livestock and the garden, woman, the guardian of the united contraries, that is, of life itself, must manage and protect life, both technically and magically.[18]

These oppositions also show themselves in the structure of the Kabyle house which itself is an inverted microcosm of the world.[19] The following chart is a "synoptic diagram of pertinent oppositions" in the Kabyle world:[20]

---

18. Bourdieu, *Logic of Practice*, 216–17.
19. Bourdieu, *Logic of Practice*, 316–17n1; 271–83.
20. Bourdieu, *Logic of Practice*, 215.

First-Century Characterization of Women and Bourdieu 41

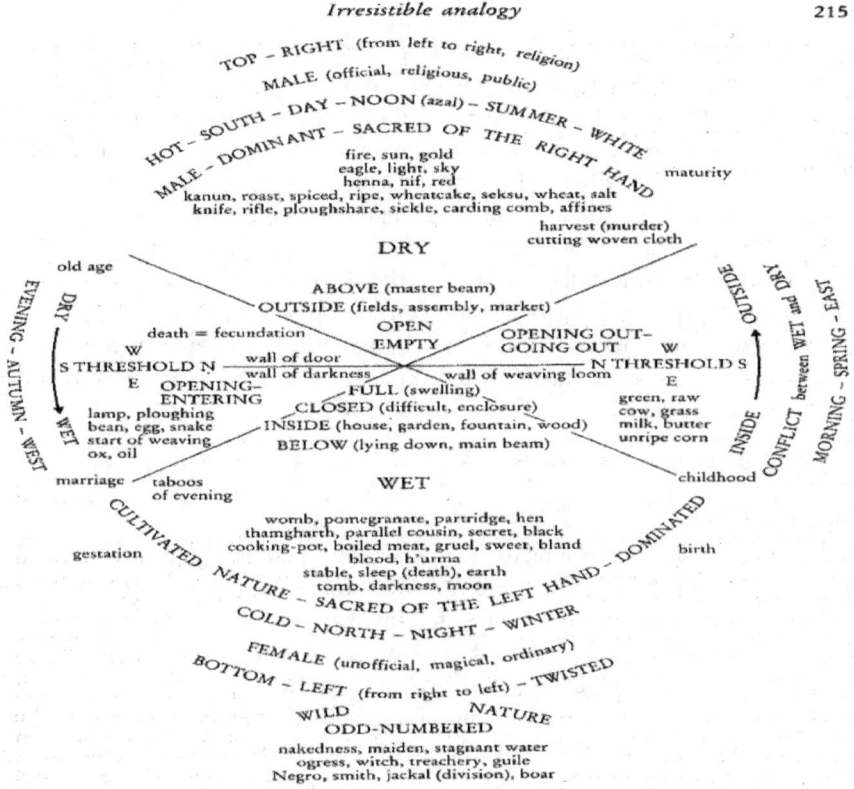

Bourdieu explains:

> This table can be read either in terms of the vertical oppositions (dry/wet, top/bottom, right/left, male/female, etc.) or in terms of the processes (e.g., those of the cycle of life: marriage, gestation, birth, etc., or of the arming year) and movements (opening/closing, going in/coming out, etc.).[21]

Bourdieu further explains:

> The social order functions as an immense symbolic machine tending to ratify the masculine domination on which it is founded: it is the sexual division of labour, a very strict distribution of the activities assigned to each sex, of their place, time and instruments; it is the structure of space, with the opposition between the place of assembly or the market, reserved for men, and the house, reserved for women, or, within the house,

---

21. Bourdieu, *Masculine Domination*, 12.

between the male part, the hearth, and the female part—the stable, the water and vegetable stores; it is the structure of time, the day and the farming year, or the cycle of life, with its male moments of rupture and the long female periods of gestation.

The social world constructs the body as a sexually defined reality and as the depository of sexually defining principles of vision and division. This embodied social programme of perception is applied to all the things of the world and firstly to the *body* itself, in its biological reality. It is this programme which constructs the difference between the biological sexes in conformity with the principles of a mythic vision of the world rooted in the arbitrary relationship of domination of men over women, itself inscribed, with the division of labour, in the reality of the social order.[22]

The Kabyle house is a microcosm of the universe reflecting the place of a woman and a man in the world:

> Considered in relation to the male world of public life and farming work, the house, the universe of women, is *haram*, that is to say, both sacred and illicit for any man who is not part of it (hence the expression used in swearing an oath: "May my wife [or, my house] become illicit [*haram*] to me if . . ."). . . .
>
> The woman can be said to be confined to the house only so long as it is also pointed out that the man is kept out of it, at least in the daytime. A man's place is outside, in the fields or in the assembly; boys are taught this at a very early age. . . . As soon as the sun has risen, in summer, a man must be out in the fields or at the assembly; in winter, if he is not in the fields, he must be at the assembly or on the benches set in the shelter of the pentroof over the door to the courtyard. Even at night, at least in the dry season, the men and the boys, as soon as they are circumcised, sleep outside the house, either near the haystacks, on the threshing floor, beside the shackled mule and donkey, or on the fig-drying floor, or in the fields, or more rarely in the assembly house. . . .
>
> It is understandable that all biological activities, sleeping, eating, procreating, should be banished from the external universe . . . and confined to the house, the sanctuary of privacy and the secrets of nature, the world of woman, who is assigned to the management of nature and excluded from public life. In contrast the man's work, which is performed outdoors, woman's work is essentially obscure and hidden. . . . "Inside the house,

---

22. Bourdieu, *Masculine Domination*, 9–11.

woman is always on the move, she bustles like a fly in the whey; outside the house, nothing of her work is seen."[23]

It becomes clear from Bourdieu's notion of *habitus* how bodies are habituated in terms of space, time, and activities besides what can be seen as the "natural." These embodied acts of being and doing are not conscious choices but enculturated ways of being memorized in the body that determine how someone walks, how someone eats, and the very posture of their bodies.[24] Even though daily activities necessitate that the household cannot retain men, this is the structure that would be associated with what womanhood constitutes. Anne Carson suggests that in antiquity, women were isolated from society because of their association with defilement.[25] As such, producing the character of a woman will probably in some way or other use the institution of the household as building material. This implies then that characterization of women will in some way or other connect with the household and with those events, activities, and persons that constitute the household, in addition to the space of the household itself.

Jennifer Glancy relies on Bourdieu's discussion of *habitus* to describe embodied history that has application beyond the scope of first-century women as people carry knowledge in their bodies.[26] The sexual habitation of a free woman would be distinct from the sexual habitation of a slave woman.[27] In Glancy's earlier work, *Corporal Knowledge: Early Christian Bodies,* she examined how social location is known in the body from the first century through the time of St. Augustine (ca. AD 430), and even into the present.[28] Glancy is an example of someone who has applied the research of Bourdieu well beyond a first-century ancient Mediterranean world affirming that "we know the world [Christian antiquity] as mediated through our own corporal narratives."[29] This implies that an actual reader may have some corresponding corporate experience with an ancient actual author and implied reader through the common experience of the body. Bourdieu himself argues that some aspects of *habitus*

23. Bourdieu, *Logic of Practice,* 275–76.
24. Bourdieu, *Logic of Practice,* 65–70.
25. Carson, "Dirt and Desire," 78.
26. Glancy, "Early Christianity, Slavery, and Women's Bodies," 143–58.
27. Glancy, "Early Christianity, Slavery, and Women's Bodies," 148–49.
28. Glancy, *Corporal Knowledge,* 4–7, 10–11.
29. Glancy, *Corporal Knowledge,* 7, 9.

between the sexes continues in modern, advanced societies.[30] Since Bourdieu's theories can reach across time and national/cultural boundaries, they should be considered in the examination of a first-century Mediterranean people.[31]

If Bourdieu is taken seriously on the categories that he has typified in the making of social order and how these also perform in the making of cosmic order, then the differentiations in "above" and "below," "right versus left," "wet versus dry," "hot versus cold," "in versus out," etc., should also be considered in the *how* of characterization. As such, character construction is the product of how these categories have become the driving forces of habituation. The habituation of bodies happens via the constant deployment of these categories in a vast range of discursive practices, and to such an extent that their constant and continued reiteration infuse them with the status of objectivity. When related to gender, it becomes taken-for-granted that a man would be allocated to the position of "above," would be seen as "hotter" than a woman, would rather be "dry" whereas a woman could be cast in the role of a "leaking vessel."[32] And these categories all contribute to a social hierarchy in which women are seen as inferior, their bodies as defective, their virtue-potential as lacking, and always in need of control and guidance by men.

Bourdieu's habitation of men and women and of their bodies must be considered in the development of characterization in a first-century narrative like the Gospel of Mark. If the objective structures, reflected in the institution of marriage for example, dictate an engendered differential of power, and this then habituate gendered bodies in a strict

---

30. Bourdieu, *Masculine Domination*. See also Bourdieu's statement: "The opposition between the centrifugal male orientation and the centripetal female orientation, which is the principle of the organization of the internal space of the house, no doubt also underlies the relationship that the two sexes have to their own bodies, and more specifically to their sexuality. As in every society dominated by male values—and European societies, which assign men to politics, history or war, and women to the hearth, the novel and psychology, are no exception to this—the specifically male relationship to the body and sexuality is that of sublimation" (Bourdieu, *Logic of Practice*, 77).

31. See Hallett, "Women's Lives in the Ancient Mediterranean," 33–34, which describes the constant distinction of men and women and the association of women of all classes with wool-working and the home from Homer through the Romans.

32. Hippocrates aligns with Bourdieu about women being associated with "wet" and men being associated with "dry" when he states: "The female flourishes more in an environment of water, from things cold and wet and soft, whether food or drink or activities. The male flourishes more in an environment of fire, from dry, hot foods and mode of fire" (Hippocrates, *Nature of Man*, 27). See also Carson, "Dirt and Desire," 78–87.

hierarchy, characterization will also proceed from this dictate, even if that characterization does not completely align with the *habitus* of society. If a social order of a society promotes, cultivates, and maintains a *habitus* that produces a hierarchy of bodies, and accordingly also structures its demarcation of space and time, as well as practices according to this, characterization will operate to present this *habitus*. What is taken as "natural" concerning bodies and "natural bodily hierarchies" will be invested in how a character is portrayed. Where manhood or manliness, for example, is seen as the perfected natural body, masculine perfection will also perform in the making of a character, and even where the objective may be to give recognition to womanhood in a narrative. The female character will be constructed either to align with this perfection or not to align owing to a socially resisting motivation. Just as values are "embodied" via habituation, values will also be given character, or to put it differently, values will produce, guide, constitute characters. Consequently, the characterization of women in the ancient Mediterranean world will be constituted by the gendered values of this environment. As such, characterization takes place within the social hierarchies in place, thereby allocating a woman character a specific subordinate position to a man. However, habituation may also allow the production of a woman character that could signify subversion.

In some way, the *act* of characterization draws upon these habituated resources. It could be argued that Bourdieu's work, as an interpretive analytic, points us to look for fixed norms that function as ready-made, fixed, unquestionable knowledge within a society. The making of characters in a literary work can hardly avoid creating them from this reservoir of already existing knowledge since it would be impossible for its implied audience not to identify this existing knowledge in the reading/listening process. There is a gap between the implied audience's knowledge, and the knowledge of an actual twenty-first-century audience of an ancient work like the Gospel of Mark. Some of the categories provided by Bourdieu point to ways of living that can be taken up in an analysis of women characters in antiquity. Using Bourdieu's categories could help the actual reader to determine whether the characters who have been created were in sync with the norms that were at work during the time of writing or in confrontation with those norms in the Gospel of Mark.

Finally, it must be conceded that Galilean peasants in Jesus' day may not have followed all the *habitus* described in Bourdieu's study of the Kabyle. However, just as Mediterranean themes of honor and shame are present in first-century Galilee, it may be that an examination of the Gospels, and especially Mark in this case, is enhanced by reading the narratives in the light of Kabyle *habitus*—especially with respect to gender significance.

GREEK AND ISRAELITE WOMEN

Many of Bourdieu's descriptions of women among the Kabyle find parallels in writings about historical Greek and Israelite women. There are less similarities between the life of Roman women in the western Roman Empire and in northern Africa than between Israelite women living in the eastern Roman Empire.[33] The effects of Roman life on women is more pronounced in the letters of the Apostle Paul who ministered among and wrote to churches living in the western Roman Empire than with Israelite women living in the eastern Roman Empire. Even if the Gospel of Mark was originally delivered to a Roman audience, the women described in its narrative are those living in the eastern Roman Empire. Therefore, they are generally described in the Markan narrative within the context of more conservative eastern Roman Empire cultural settings. The implied author of Mark does provide a broader description of a woman's right to divorce her husband (Mark 10:12) than was the experience of most women in Israel, but this more-inclusive language may be due to the narrative world of Mark where Herodias divorced her husband Herod Philip to marry Herod Antipas, the brother of Herod Phillip (see Mark 6:18–19).[34] Even though the Herods lived in and around Israel, they were royalty, in power by Roman decree, and lived lives affiliated with the western Empire and not the standards of the general, common populace of Israel.

Sarah Pomeroy wrote a social history of women in the Greek world (from 1184 BC through the Hellenistic period) and in the Roman world (from the Roman Republic through the Empire to the death of Constantine in AD 337). Pomeroy broadly concluded that even though Roman women were not excluded from social, political, and cultural life to the same extent as Greek women, "Roman society never encouraged women to engage in the same activities as men in the same social class."[35]

---

33. See the discussion by Cynthia Long Westfall, who describes a continuum from more restrictive to less restrictive roles for women in the following geographical order: Athens, Jerusalem, Rome, and Alexandria (Westfall, *Paul and Gender*, 16).

34. Josephus, *Jewish Antiquities*, 7:133.

35. Pomeroy, *Goddesses, Whores, Wives, and Slaves*, 129.

Pomeroy also summarized the patriarchal attitude toward women in Greece and Rome:

> A chasm gapes between the beastlike women in the verses of Semonides and the female watchdogs of Plato's Republic; yet, upon closer analysis, the attitudes of one of the most celebrated misogynists and one of the greatest philogynists of antiquity show more similarities than differences. Even Plato—of ancient authors one of the most sympathetic to women—found that the one sex was in general inferior to the other, although he allowed for exceptions. Plato had strayed far from the mainstream of Greek thought. The views of Aristotle were more representative: he elucidated in detail the range of woman's inferiority, from her passive role in procreativity to her limited capacity for mental activity. Serious intellectual thought about women continued: Stoicism, the most popular of the Hellenistic and Roman philosophies, directed women's energies to marriage and motherhood. The argumentation is brilliant and difficult to refute. And this rationalized confinement of women to the domestic sphere, as well as the systematization of anti-female thought by poets and philosophers, are two of the most devastating creations in the classical legacy.[36]

Hennie Marsman studied women in Ugarit, a polytheistic kingdom situated on the coast of Syria at the latitude of Cyprus during the Bronze Age (ca. 1400–1185 BC) and monotheistic Israel as revealed in the canonical Hebrew Scriptures, extra-biblical texts, and data from Mesopotamia, Egypt, and Hatti to determine if there was any difference in the position of women in the Ugarit and Israeli cultures.[37] After examining documents addressing the social position of women in the family, society, the court, property, business, professions, domestic activities, and slavery, Marsman concluded:

> I have demonstrated that by and large, leaving aside minor differences, the social and religious position of women was the same in Ugarit and Israel, and as far as I was able to ascertain, in the ancient Near East as a whole. Everywhere women were subordinated to men, even though women belonging to the upper classes often enjoyed somewhat more freedom than other women. Already in Antiquity this inequality between men and

---

36. Pomeroy, *Goddesses, Whores, Wives, and Slaves*, 230. See also Stewart, "Masculinity in the New Testament," 94.

37. Marsman, *Women in Ugarit and Israel*.

women was presented by men as being in accordance with the will of the gods or God. However, this line of reasoning is questionable when we take into account that adherents of totally different religions, both polytheists and monotheists, have made the same claim.[38]

Greek Women

As Froma Zeitlin explained, when one looks at gods in the eras of Archaic (eighth to sixth centuries BC) and Classical (fifth and fourth centuries BC) Greece, often the categories of male and female are not limited to anatomical and physiological characteristics but are associated with "socially prescribed traits, roles, and obligations"[39] or *habitus* as Bourdieu would describe. Those in ancient Greece lived in a divided world emphasizing distinctions between the roles, attributes, spaces, and spheres of influence for the male and female.[40] As with the Kabyle, men were associated with the hot and dry, while women were associated with the cold and wet.[41] Aristotle understood women to be deformed men noting that men were hotter than women.[42] Furthermore, female gods had limitations even when they had some measure of "control" over male gods. For instance, they may be able to seduce male gods, but it was the male god who could give immortality.[43] A goddess was subject to the all-too-human experiences of pregnancy and giving birth.[44] Athena was a masculine woman who found success as the goddess of wisdom and as a warrior often denying her own femininity and sexuality.[45]

For the ancient Greeks, men were thought of as stable both in the house and in the city, but women were considered mobile.[46] This mobility, when joined with issues of pollution and defilement, led to social policies

---

38. Marsman, *Women in Ugarit and Israel*, 738.
39. Zeitlin, "Reflections on Erotic Desire," 52.
40. Zeitlin, "Reflections on Erotic Desire," 58.
41. Zeitlin, "Reflections on Erotic Desire," 75n24.
42. Aristotle, *Generation of Animals*, 25 (174). See also Downing, "Nature(s) of Christian Women and Men," 179; Stewart, "Masculinity in the New Testament," 94.
43. Hesiod, *Theogony*, 1:218–38.
44. Zeitlin, "Reflections on Erotic Desire," 69.
45. Pomeroy, *Goddesses, Whores, Wives, and Slaves*, 4.
46. Carson, "Dirt and Desire, 77–78.

that isolated the female from society.⁴⁷ Women were also considered to be wet both physiologically and psychologically while men were associated with dryness:

> Males and females would be formed, so far as possible, in the following manner. Females, inclining more to water, grow from foods, drinks and pursuits that are cold, moist and gentle. Males, inclining to fire, grow from foods and regimen that are dry and warm.⁴⁸

In the Bronze and Homeric eras (ca. eighth century BC) men served as warriors and women were expected to marry and give birth to future warriors.⁴⁹ Women were property over whom men were dominate—often the spoils of war.⁵⁰ Women, especially wives, were to be monogamous, but men were polygamous.⁵¹ The duties of women revolved around the household—making clothing, weaving, bathing and anointing men, fetching water, grinding corn, and reaping.⁵² Even though wives were not secluded, they were expected to be modest.⁵³

During the Archaic period (800–500 BC) women were primarily the bearers of children and warriors. They were likened to a "field to plow."⁵⁴ Politically, wives became the bond between families.⁵⁵ In Sparta and Gortyn, Dorian women had more rights to property—especially their dowries and inheritances. Housework and clothing were prepared by women of inferior classes while citizen women engaged in gymnastics, music, household management, and of course, childrearing.⁵⁶ However, Ionian women in Athens continued to perform the work in the household.⁵⁷ While men spent most of their days in public areas like the marketplace or the gymnasium, respectable women stayed at home and sent

---

47. Carson, "Dirt and Desire," 78.
48. Hippocrates, *Nature of Man*, 4:27.
49. Pomeroy, *Goddesses, Whores, Wives, and Slaves*, 18.
50. Pomeroy, *Goddesses, Whores, Wives, and Slaves*, 25–27.
51. Pomeroy, *Goddesses, Whores, Wives, and Slaves*, 27.
52. Pomeroy, *Goddesses, Whores, Wives, and Slaves*, 29–30.
53. Pomeroy, *Goddesses, Whores, Wives, and Slaves*, 30.
54. Pomeroy, *Goddesses, Whores, Wives, and Slaves*, 99. Men were the "phallus/plow" and women were the "furrow."
55. Pomeroy, *Goddesses, Whores, Wives, and Slaves*, 32–35.
56. Pomeroy, *Goddesses, Whores, Wives, and Slaves*, 35.
57. Pomeroy, *Goddesses, Whores, Wives, and Slaves*, 43.

their servants to conduct errands.[58] Women would go out for festivals and funerals. They also prepared a human body for burial and mourned at funerals.[59] However, "Only women over sixty years of age or within the degree of children or cousins were permitted to enter the room of the deceased and to accompany the dead when the corpse was carried to the tomb, following the men in the funeral procession."[60] Women were always under the guardianship of a man—father, brother, husband.[61] With the growth of urbanization, women's activities were moved indoors to make them less visible. Women of the upper class supervised household activities, but many women did the work of slaves in the household creating clothing and preparing food. To protect women, they did not go to the marketplace.[62] Women did not participate in governmental or public affairs; therefore, their education was limited to domestic matters.[63] When a woman acted in a way that was not characteristic of submissiveness and modesty, they were often characterized as "masculine."[64]

Hellenistic women (ca. 323–30 BC) had more freedom, depending on their social class, than women during the Archaic period. Women were more involved in the political activities of men and in economic affairs. They also had more options regarding marriage, public roles, education, and their private lives.[65]

Israelite Women

Much of what is known about Israelite women is found in rabbinic works of oral law which were later written down including the Mishnah (teaching of scholars and sages prior to AD 220) and the encyclopedic commentary on the Mishnah known as the Talmud, whether Babylonian or

58. Pomeroy, *Goddesses, Whores, Wives, and Slaves*, 79. Women usually lived in rooms away from the street, or upstairs.

59. Pomeroy, *Goddesses, Whores, Wives, and Slaves*, 43.

60. Pomeroy, *Goddesses, Whores, Wives, and Slaves*, 79.

61. Pomeroy, *Goddesses, Whores, Wives, and Slaves*, 62–63.

62. Pomeroy, *Goddesses, Whores, Wives, and Slaves*, 71.

63. Pomeroy, *Goddesses, Whores, Wives, and Slaves*, 74.

64. Pomeroy, *Goddesses, Whores, Wives, and Slaves*, 98. This is also true in the Old Testament. The adjective sometimes translated as "excellent" for a wife in Proverbs 31:10 (see NAS and NASB) is חַיִל in Hebrew, meaning "strong" or "powerful," HALOT s.v. "חַיִל," and "ἀνδρείαν" in the LXX meaning "manly" or "courageous, BDAG s.v. "ἀνδρεῖος."

65. Pomeroy, *Goddesses, Whores, Wives, and Slaves*, 120.

First-Century Characterization of Women and Bourdieu 51

Jerusalem (ca. 450 BC to AD 600).[66] Ross Kraemer discusses some of the difficulties of using these written materials including their late dates.[67] But as Deborah Sawyer observes, much of the material within the Mishnah and Talmudim dates back to and prior to the first century.[68] The writers of the Mishna, Tannaim, and Gemara, Amoraim, were male, so the writings contain androcentric views of who women are and how they ought to act.[69] However, not all history is lost behind the veil of these male writings. The hermeneutics of suspicion that questions objectivity of an author's description of women does not mean that nothing about women's lives is recoverable from this data. As Lynn Cohick explains: "Because texts were written by men, often with agendas far different from our purpose here (which is to fairly and accurately describe women's lives), we must tread carefully through the maze of misdirection that ancient authors configured along the way" and give "special attention to the genre of the evidence."[70] Ross Kraemer argues that agricultural finds should also be examined in additional to literary sources.[71]

In addition, even though Jewish people were exposed to a wider Greco-Roman culture, there is evidence that, at least in some areas, the Jews remained distinct in their culture from the western Roman Empire.[72] For instance, under Roman law, it was common for fathers and mothers to decide whether to reject a child at birth and abandon a child to exposure or infanticide.[73] However, infanticide and exposure of infants was uniformly condemned in Jewish literature.[74] Also, Roman law allowed a daughter to inherit property, but there is some evidence that the Pharisees prohibited a father's daughter from inheriting property even though the Sadducees allowed it.[75] Unlike the Roman focus of marriage

66. Kolatch, *Who's Who in the Talmud*, 5–7.

67. Kraemer, "Jewish Women and Christian Origins," 37.

68. Sawyer, *Women and Religion*, 163n71.

69. Schüssler Fiorenza, *In Memory of Her*, 106. See also Neusner, "Formation of Rabbinic Judaism," 19–20.

70. Cohick, *Women in the World*, 27.

71. Kraemer, "Jewish Women and Women's Judaism(s)," 53–54.

72. Sawyer repeatedly observes that the concerns and practices of women in first-century Israel were distinct from surrounding cultures. Sawyer, *Women and Religion*, 32.

73. Cohick, *Women in the World*, 35–41.

74. Cohick, *Women in the World*, 41–42, citing Josephus, *C. Ap.* 2.202; Tacitus, *Historae*, 5.5; Strabo, *Geographica* 17.2.5.

75. Cohick, *Women in the World*, 55–56. See b. B. Bat. 115b–116a.

around matters of status and rank, Jewish marriages were concerned with endogamy, or limiting marriage to other Jewish relatives rather than Gentiles.[76] Finally, there is some evidence that polygamy was practiced by some Jewish people. However, a polygamous marriage was illicit under Roman law.[77]

There is some evidence that younger, upper-class women were restricted to the house prior to marriage out of a desire to protect their purity.[78] Similar to the practice of the Kabyle, Philo (ca. 20 BC to AD 50) stated, in a prescriptive rather than a descriptive manner, that it was suitable for men to be found in the market, council-halls, law courts, gatherings, and meetings where a large number of people were gathered. "The women are best suited to the indoor life which never strays from the house, within which the middle door is taken by the maidens as their boundary, and the outer door by those who have reached full womanhood."[79] Further, Philo states: "The harmonious coming together of man and woman and their consummation is figuratively a house. And everything which is without a woman is imperfect and homeless. For to man are entrusted the public affairs of state; while to a woman the affairs of the home are proper."[80]

There is evidence that first-century Jewish women followed the Greco-Roman custom of participating in public meals with men at birthdays, weddings, and especially religious festivals.[81] Although in ancient Greece, the meals were only for men who also had prostitutes participate in the symposium that followed the meal, by the second century BC men were known to bring their wives to public meals and to the symposium that followed the meal.[82] The evidence is mixed regarding the dining posture of women. When women reclined at a meal, they were considered sexual

---

76. Cohick, *Women in the World*, 81–83. See also Tob 3:15; 4:12–13; 6:11; 7:10, 12.

77. Cohick, *Women in the World*, 117–19. Cohick discusses evidence from second-century AD documents that the Jewish woman Babatha, after her husband's death, remarried a man who was also married to another woman at the time. Cohick suggests that the marriage contract may have been written in Aramaic because it would not be recognized under Roman law.

78. Cohick, *Women in the World*, 54–55. See also 2 Macc 3:19; 3 Macc 1:18; Tobit; Judith, *Joseph and Aseneth*; *Liber Antiquitatum Biblicarum*; Kraemer, "Jewish Women and Women's Judaism(s)," 60–61.

79. Philo, *On the Decalogue* 3.169–70.

80. Philo, *Questions on Genesis* 1.26. See also Sawyer, *Women and Religion*, 36.

81. Cohick, *Women in the World*, 87–88; Corley, *Private Women, Public Meals*, 66–75.

82. Cohick, *Women in the World*, 88; Sir 9:9.

First-Century Characterization of Women and Bourdieu 53

partners with the men with whom they shared the couch. This was not a problem for married women who were assumed to be sexual partners of their husbands. In the alternative, women would sit in chairs at table to emphasize their chasteness.[83] Philo describes men dining by themselves on the right side and women reclining by themselves on the left side.[84]

Shmuel Safrai argues that during the first century AD, women were active in the religious life of the community alongside of men. They could be counted as part of the ten people required to constitute a congregational quorum in m. Megillah 4:3.[85] Women were participants with men in synagogue worship and attended public baths (y. Ber. 9D).[86] Like men, women were obligated to say the synagogue prayer of the "Eighteen Benedictions" even if done privately (m. Ber. 3:3, 4:3). Safrai argues that the archeological discoveries of the synagogue at Dura-Europos (mid-third century AD) and the first-century synagogue at Masada do not show any physical structures that separated men and women in the synagogues.[87] Women were also not segregated in the Second Temple even though there was an outer court called the Women's Court.[88] Men and women mingled in this court, and men had to pass through this court to reach the Israelites' court.[89] Public assemblies took place in the Women's Court including the reading of the Torah by the High priest on the Day of Atonement (m. Yoma 7:1; b. Yoma 69b).[90] The assembly of "men, women, children and aliens" was held every seven years during the Feast of Tabernacles for the public reading of Torah (Deut 31:10–12;

---

83. Cohick, *Women in the World*, 89–90.

84. Philo, *On the Contemplative Life*, 69. See also Corley, *Private Women, Public Meals*, 71–72.

85. Safrai, "Place of Women," 9.

86. Safrai, "Place of Women," 9. However, this writer has not seen evidence that Jewish women participated in public baths. Of course, the public baths were probably separate for men and women. See Balsdon, *Roman Women*, 265–70.

87. Safrai, "Place of Women," 10. See also Kraemer, "Jewish Women and Women's Judaism(s)," 64; Sawyer, *Women and Religion*, 77–79. Philo differs, stating: "This common sanctuary in which they meet every seventh day is a double enclosure, one portion set apart for the use of the men, the other for the women. For women too regularly make part of the audience with the same ardor and the same sense of their calling" (Philo, *On the Contemplative Life*, 131).

88. Safrai, "Role of Women," 5–6; "Place of Women," 10–11.

89. During the water-drawing ceremony on the Feast of Tabernacles, women watched men dancing in the Women's Court in elevated galleries. See m. Middot 2:5p; Safrai, "Place of Women," 11; Sawyer, *Women and Religion*, 73.

90. See also Kraemer, "Jewish Women and Women's Judaism(s)," 63.

m. Sotah 7:8; b. Sotah 41b).⁹¹ Furthermore, women passed through the Israelites' Court into the Priests' Court to offer sacrifices (m. Bik. 1:5, 3:6, 20; cf. m. Middot 2:5).⁹²

More recent scholarship suggests that women were active members of the Essene community.⁹³ There is also evidence from rabbinic literature that some women studied and interpreted the law (See m. Ned. 4:3E).⁹⁴ Apparently, Jewish mothers, like Greco-Roman mothers, were educated sufficiently to educate and/or train their children (see Tob 1:8; Sus 1:3; 2 Macc 2:27).⁹⁵ If the *Therapeutrides* of first-century Alexandria, Egypt were in fact real women, and not a myth or legend as some assert, there is evidence that upper-class Jewish women joined with Jewish men in the study of philosophy and the allegorical method of interpreting the Scriptures.⁹⁶ Lynn Cohick argues that average, poorer women participated in the same work performed by men (other than being solders or politicians). She argues that they worked in the fields, were blacksmiths, weavers, tailors, fullers, money lenders, merchants, vendors, and artisans. However, most of her evidence is derived from the western Roman Empire rather than eastern, Jewish settings.⁹⁷ She further argues that women drew their social status from character (being a faithful wife, working hard, and caring for the home) rather than their work. She admits that this may have been due in part to the fact that slaves did much of the same work as free women, but this was also true of men.⁹⁸ She states, without much support, that the descriptions of women as working with fabric are allegorical or mythical rather than statements of a woman's occupation.⁹⁹ One wonders whether this was the case for an average, first-century,

---

91. Kraemer, "Jewish Women and Women's Judaism(s)," 63.

92. Safrai, "Place of Women," 12. See also Kraemer, "Jewish Women and Women's Judaism(s)," 63; *contra* Sawyer, except for perhaps in Egypt, *Women and Religion*, 74.

93. Cohick, *Women in the World*, 201–4. See also Rule of the Congregation (1Q28a or 1QSa) and 4QInstruction (4Q415 2 II).

94. Cohick, *Women in the World*, 209.

95. Cohick, *Women in the World*, 143–44; Sawyer, *Women and Religion*, 82.

96. Philo, *On the Contemplative Life*, 21. See also Cohick, *Women in the World*, 251–54.

97. See also Kraemer, "Jewish Women and Women's Judaism(s)," 61–62.

98. Cohick, *Women in the World*, 255.

99. Cohick, *Women in the World*, 238. However, Percy and Balsdon explain: "The Romans being for the first centuries of their existence an agricultural people, their houses, large or small, were country houses, and while the husband took care of the land, his wife took care of the household" (Percy and Balsdon, *Roman Women*, 27).

First-Century Characterization of Women and Bourdieu 55

eastern, Jewish woman. Again, Philo claims that Jewish women lived within the home and were rarely involved in public life.[100]

Cohick devotes an entire chapter to women as benefactors and patrons in the Roman Empire.[101] Her evidence primarily comes from the western Roman Empire as she describes Empress Livia, the second wife of Caesar August, Eumachia, Mamia and Metrodora from Pompeii and Julia Severa, Tation of Phocaea of Ironia, Fulvia and Helena, Queen of Adiabene or northern Mesopotamia, Phoebe and Julia Theodora from Corinth, Phoebe of Cenchrae, Lydia of Thyatira, and elite women of Thessalonica, Beroea, and Athens.[102] Cohick tries to argue for Israelite honoring of Empress Livia because she was a beneficiary in the wills of Herod the Great and his sister, and because she gave personal, marital counsel to Salome,[103] however, the elite Herodian family was closely tied to western Rome having been appointed rulers over the Jews by Roman emperors. The Herodians did not reflect the actions and customs of average and poor first-century Israelites.

There is evidence of Israelite women, including Mary Magdalene, Joanna the wife of Chuza, Herod's steward, and Susanna providing for Jesus in his itinerate ministry out of their own wealth (Luke 8:1–3). That said, these women were not honored in the same way that Roman patrons were honored with inscriptions, statutes, and buildings dedicated to them for their beneficial acts. Cohick posits interesting speculation about the extent of the influence of the women who financially provided for Jesus, but her speculations have not been substantiated by evidence.[104] Nevertheless, the women identified in Luke 8:1–3 are an example of Israelite women using their wealth to support the work of another. One does not know how pervasive this practice was in first-century Israel.

---

100. "Market-places and council-halls and law-courts and gatherings and meetings where a large number of people are assembled, and open-air life with full scope for discussion and action—all these are suitable to men both in war and peace. The women are best suited to the indoor life which never strays from the house, within which the middle door is taken by the maidens as their boundary, and the outer door by those who have reached full womanhood" (Philo, *Spec. Laws* 3.174). Philo also states that women were to manage the household, should seek a life of seclusion, and should only go to temple when most people have gone home (Philo, *Spec. Laws* 3.172).

101. Cohick, *Women in the World*, 285–320.

102. Cohick, *Women in the World*, 291–309.

103. Cohick, *Women in the World*, 293.

104. Cohick, *Women in the World*, 314–17.

CONCLUSION

It appears that the life of first-century women in the eastern portion of the Roman Empire was more limited than their counterparts in the western Roman Empire. If anything, the lives of women in Israel were similar to the life of Greek women that preceded them and the Kabyle peasants described in the sociological studies of Pierre Bourdieu. Israelite women, like most women in the ancient and later Greco-Roman world, were in some manner dominated by men in an androcentric society. Israelite women were primarily identified with the home and overseeing or doing the work of the home rather than the outside world which was the domain of men. Israelite women may have also shared the Kabyle and Greek concepts of coldness and wetness while men were associated with dryness and heat, making women inferior to men because they deviated from the masculine perfection of dryness and stability. This perceived instability resulted in the need to confine women to the more private world of the home. In marriage, women were to preserve the family and the state by creating necessary warriors. When Israelite women joined their husbands in worship or at a celebration, they were not segregated, but maintained propriety in how they sat, or reclined, at the social gathering.

More freedom was available to women of higher financial and social status, than that of lower status in Israel, Greece, and even Rome. Some Jewish women had the privilege of intensive study of the Scriptures or education, but it appears that all women were educated on some level because they became the instructors of their children.

Life for Israelite women in the first century AD was generally not characterized by equality with men. Their domains and spheres of influence were distinct because their essence was considered to be distinct. Private home and domestic work were considered to be the proper measure of life for a first-century Israelite woman in the eastern Roman Empire. Exceptions to the norm existed but were few and for the elevated women of social status and/or wealth.

The implied audience of the Gospel of Mark would possess social and cultural preunderstandings about first-century, Mediterranean women as described by Bourdieu and in historical writings and archaeology. The actual author and implied audience of Mark would use this understanding to construct the characterization of women through discourse in the narrative. A present-day reader would need to share first-century understandings of *habitus* and culture with the original author and implied audience to lessen the gap between their world and the Markan narrative world of women.

4

The Literary Pattern of Intercalation

THE THIRD THEORETICAL ISSUE and research approach to be discussed is the narrative pattern known as "intercalation." It is also called "interpolation" (focusing on a redactional insertion of a story into another story), "framing" or "bracketing" (focusing generally on the outer story around an inner story or stories), and "sandwiching" (focusing on an inner story sandwiched between two episodes of an outer story).[1] It is a form of duality which permeates Mark's gospel.[2] The pattern of an intercalation is that a first story is begun, then the first story is interrupted by a second, inner story which is told to its conclusion, whereupon the first story resumes and is told to its completion.[3] The purpose of this section is to identify the narrative characteristics of Mark's intercalations and then survey both Greek and Hebrew literature prior to Mark in an attempt to identify the potential influence of other literature on Mark's use of the narrative pattern.

---

1. Shepherd, *Markan Sandwich Stories*, 1–2n2, 4–7; Wright, "Markan Intercalations," 14–15.

2. Neirynck, *Duality in Mark*, 133.

3. Shepherd, *Markan Sandwich Stories*, 2. F. Gerald Downing offers the following definition of Mark's intercalations: "He [Mark] repeatedly 'sandwiches' one narrative that would seem able to stand on its own within another that would seem entirely coherent without it, 'cutting' sharply from one to the other and back again: a1-b-a2. Yet, independent as they seem, each narrative, inner and outer, would seem to illuminate the other" (Downing, "Markan Intercalation," 118).

The actual author of Mark uses intercalations as a means of telling his/her story (discourse). This use of a literary pattern would only be an effective means of characterization if it was also known or recognized by the implied audience. Similarly, an actual, present-day audience will only understand what the author is doing, and what an implied audience would perceive, if an actual audience is aware of this literary pattern employed to tell the narrative of Mark. The actual author of Mark need not explicitly rely on other, earlier literature that employed this narrative pattern, or specifically use the narrative pattern in precisely the same way that it is used by prior writers so long as the pattern is recognizable. The actual author of Mark can take a known pattern and adapt it to his purposes as long as his/her implied audience can perceive what he is doing.

CHARACTERISTICS OF MARKAN INTERCALATIONS

Tom Shepherd identifies eight characteristics present in Markan intercalations:

1. Apart from initial focalization, the outer story is the temporal border of the inner story.
2. There is a unique pattern of focalization and defocalization of the two stories which includes incomplete defocalization of the outer story at the point where breakaway occurs to the inner story. This creates a "gap" for the outer story across the inner story.
3. A new character or newly named character is noted at the reentry into the outer story.
4. Active character crossover does not occur between the two stories, except for Jesus.
5. Parallel actions are done by contrasting groups or contrasting actions are done by parallel groups in the two stories.
6. The outer story has an elliptical action which crosses the inner story and contrasts with the actions of the inner story.
7. The plots of the two stories interlink following a turn—return pattern.
8. An ellipsis of the outer story occurs across the inner story.[4]

---

4. Shepherd, *Markan Sandwich Stories*, 327.

Similarly, F. Gerald Downing identifies five characterizations present in Markan intercalations which he symbolizes using an "a1-b-a2" pattern:

1. Some distinct or entirely distinct character(s) [item(s)] in the middle sequence (b),
2. A distinct even if neighboring locality for the middle sequence (b).
3. An a1-b-a2 time sequence (even a1-b1-a2-b2, as at Mark 11:25) *or* contemporaneity (but not 'a' complete before 'b' starts).
4. There are similarities and contrasts in characters and actions.
5. We may well discern a dramatic irony—as hearers we know more than do the actors.[5]

One might correlate Downing's list with Shepherd's in the following table:

Shepherd's List	Downing's list
3	1
1	3
3, 4, 5	4
5	4

Accordingly, a composite list identifying characteristics of Markan intercalations would include Shepherd's list and numbers 2 and 5 of Downing's list, as follows:

1. Apart from initial focalization, the outer story is the temporal border of the inner story;
2. There is a unique pattern of focalization and defocalization of the two stories which includes incomplete defocalization of the outer story at the point where breakaway occurs to the inner story. This creates a "gap" for the outer story across the inner story;
3. A new character or newly named character is noted at the reentry into the outer story;
4. Active character crossover does not occur between the two stories, except for a main character (in Mark, it is Jesus);
5. Parallel actions are done by contrasting groups or contrasting actions are done by parallel groups in the two stories;

5. Downing, *Doing Things with Words*, 121.

6. The outer story has an elliptical action which crosses the inner story and contrasts with the actions of the inner story;
7. The plots of the two stories interlink following a turn—return pattern.
8. An ellipsis of the outer story occurs across the inner story;
9. A distinct even if neighboring locality for the middle sequence (b); and
10. We may well discern a dramatic irony—as hearers we know more than do the actors.

These ten categories will be used to evaluate narratives prior to Mark that use a similar narrative technique of breaking-off an outer story to tell an inner story to completion, to resume the outer story. By comparing Mark's intercalating technique with that used by earlier writers in both Greek and Hebrew literature, one may be able to discover patterns present in the Gospel of Mark, and ways in which the implied author of Mark is distinct in his use of the technique.

SURVEY OF LITERATURE PRIOR TO MARK FOR INTERCALATIONS

The literary technique of interrupting a present story to tell a related backstory, or concurrent story in another location, or an otherwise related story before resuming the initial story is ancient, and well represented in Greek and Hebrew narratives.

Classical Greek

Homer's Iliad (ca. 800–700 BC)

In book 16 of Homer's *Iliad*, the Greek ("Achaean") army is near the end of the long Trojan War. Achilles has determined to no longer fight with the Achaeans in the war after Agamemnon took the beautiful maiden, Briseis, from him. Achilles seeks the services of Zeus to destroy the Achaeans. Zeus supports the Trojans and the Achaeans suffer great losses. The Trojans push the Achaeans behind the ramparts that protect their ships, break through the ramparts, and set fire to one of the ships. In book 16,

Achilles is concerned for his friends but refuses to fight. However, he agrees to allow his friend Patroclus, son of Zeus, to take Achilles place in the battle wearing Achilles's armor.[6]

In 16.155–65 the outer story is suspended to tell of Patroclus in Achilles's armor rousing the Myrmidons to fight. The Myrmidons are likened to ravening wolves under Achilles's (Patroclus's) leadership. Additional background is given to describe the five leaders appointed by Achilles to give orders under him.[7] Then a description is given of the cohesiveness of Myrmidons's battle array as they prepared for war against the Trojans.[8] Finally, Achilles is described in his hut, opening the chest given him by his goddess mother, Thetis, and changing his prayer to Zeus for the victory and protection of Patroclus and the Myrmidons over the Trojans.[9]

The outer story resumes with details of the battle describing how Patroclus and the Myrmidons routed the Trojans all the way back to Troy's city wall,[10] and how Patroclus dies at the hands of Apollo and Hector.[11]

Unlike Markan intercalations, it does not appear that the outer story is the temporal border of the inner story. Time may well be contemporaneous and continuous as Patroclus rouses the Myrmidons to enter into battle and as Achilles prays. There is a gap from the outer story over the inner story as the preparations for battle are recounted. However, there is not a new character, or newly named character, at the reentry into the outer story. There is character crossover of Patroclus in both stories. There are no parallel actions done by contrasting groups or contrasting actions done by parallel groups in the two stories except for perhaps by Achilles who earlier prayed to Zeus for the defeat of the Achaeans by the Trojans but now prays for the defeat of the Trojans by the Achaeans. The elliptical action of the outer story crosses the inner story, but it is not contrary to it. The plots of the two stories interlink following a turn and return pattern. There is an ellipsis of the outer story across the inner story but only so the inner story can provide background for the continuation of the outer story. As James Edwards explained, it appears that the breakaways from the outer story function "to create suspense as well as to provide

---

6. Homer, *Iliad* 16.1–154.
7. Homer, *Iliad* 16.168–209.
8. Homer, *Iliad* 16.210–20A.
9. Homer, *Iliad* 16.220B–256.
10. Homer, *Iliad* 16.257–711.
11. Homer, *Iliad* 16.712–867.

information which he [Homer] felt necessary."[12] The location of the outer story eventually changes from the ramparts of the Achaeans' ships to the outer wall of Troy, but the location is the same at the beginning of the outer and inner stories. Finally, there is some dramatic irony between the two stories. The narrator tells the audience at the end of Achilles's prayer that Zeus granted part of his petition but refused another part: "That Patroclus should thrust back the war and battle from the ships he granted; but that he should return safe out of the battle he refused."[13] The audience knows that Patroclus is going to die in the upcoming battle. Patroclus does not know that his demise is determined by Zeus. This dramatic irony creates suspense for the audience who looks to see *how* the prediction will occur. The ironic twist increases in the narrative as Patroclus, the leader of the victorious Greeks over the Trojans, is slain at the hands of the god, Apollo, and Hector, the leader of the Trojans.

The breakaway pattern in the midst of a narrative to a second narrative is an ancient story-telling technique that would be familiar to later audiences. However, often the function of the inner story is to provide background for the outer story, and the stories can run contemporaneously or at least in continuous time. The outer stories are much longer than Mark's outer stories, and the inner stories are not as distinct from the outer stories in Homer's *Iliad* as they are in Mark's Gospel. Nevertheless, this breakaway pattern provides a narrative technique that later writers, like Mark, would be able to incorporate and adapt to their particular narratives.

Homer's Odyssey (ca. 800–700 BC)

In book 19 of Homer's epic poem, the *Odyssey*, Odysseus returned home after the fall of Troy, incognito as an elderly beggar, to view the situation regarding the suitors of his wife, Penelope. Being well received by Penelope, as the "stranger" who tells of his encounter with Penelope's husband on the Island of Crete and knowledge that he is alive and returning home within a month, Penelope instructs her maidens to wash his feet.[14] The old woman whom the stranger allows to wash his feet is his former nurse, Eurycleia, who notices similarities between the beggar and

---

12. Edwards, "Markan Sandwiches," 200.
13. Homer, *Iliad* 6.250–54.
14. Homer, *Odyssey* 19.70–359.

Odysseus.[15] Then, while washing his feet, Eurycleia recognizes who the stranger is by a scar on his thigh which Odysseus received in his childhood while hunting wild boar on a visit to his Grandfather, Autolycus.[16] When the scar is discovered, the poet inserts a digression, or flashback, relating the accident that caused the scar with all of its particulars.[17] Then the narrative resumes in the present story time with Eurycleia allowing Odysseus's left leg to drop into the basin of water as she recognizes "with joy and grief" that he is Odysseus.[18] Eric Auerbach correctly comments on the structure of the unit: "There are more than seventy of these verses [in the interruption, 19:396–466]—while to the incident itself some forty are devoted before the interruption [19:349–95] and some forty after it [19:467–507]."[19]

Points 2, 3, 7, and 8 of the composite list above are present in the story of Odysseus with Eurycleia, but many characteristics of Markan intercalations are absent. There is a focalization and defocalization of the two stories at the point where a breakaway occurs from the outer story of Eurycleia preparing to wash Odysseus feet, to the inner story where the cause of Odysseus's scar is recounted, creating a gap for the outer story across the inner story that is picked up with the resumption of the outer story. A "new" character, or at least a newly-named character to the other characters in the narrative, is noted on reentry into the outer story as Eurycleia now understands that the beggar is "Odysseus." The plots of the two stories interlink following a turn—return pattern, and an ellipsis of the outer story occurs across the inner story recounting the cause of Odysseus's scar. However, the story time does not move continuously through both stories. Story time changes as the inner story provides a flashback to the time and events causing Odysseus's scar. Nevertheless, there may be a similarity between Homer's account and the intercalation in Mark 6:7–32 as the inner story provides a "flashback" to the circumstances surrounding the beheading of John the Baptizer. Unlike Mark's intercalations, there is active character crossover between the two stories. In addition to Odysseus, Eurycleia appears as a character in the inner story at the naming of the baby, Odysseus, by his grandfather, Autolycus.[20]

15. Homer, *Odyssey* 19.360–80.
16. Homer, *Odyssey* 19.386–95.
17. Homer, *Odyssey* 19.396–466.
18. Homer, *Odyssey* 19.467–79.
19. Auerbach, *Mimesis*, 4.
20. Homer, *Odyssey* 19.400–410.

There are no parallel actions done by the characters in the two stories. The locality is distinct between the two stories, and there is no dramatic irony for the hearer/audience. Both of the characters, Odysseus and Eurycleia, know more than the audience knows when the inner story is told. Clear similarities exist between Homer's flashback and Mark's intercalations, but the function of Homer's flashback is to bring the audience up-to-speed on the reason Eurycleia recognizes Odysseus when she sees his scar. Although there is a disruption in story time, the logic appears to be linear rather than interactive between the narratives. Homer's stories fill a gap for the audience, rather than Mark's stories which create gaps that the audience must fill by comparing the stories.

Hebrew Scriptures / Old Testament

James Edwards suggests that there are not many examples of intercalations in the Hebrew Scriptures (Hos 1–3; 2 Sam 11:1—12:25).[21] However, there may be more than those identified by Edwards, and some of those identified by Edwards may not actually be intercalations like the David-and-Bathsheba story (2 Sam 11:1—12:25). The following is a survey of proposed intercalations in the Hebrew Scriptures.

Genesis 37, 38, and 39 (ca. 1450–1500 BC)

Genesis 38 provides an early example of an outer story being interrupted by an inner story. The outer story concerns the testing of Joseph (Gen 37; 39). It is interrupted by an inner story spanning the life of Joseph's older brother, Judah (Gen 38). Time extends in the inner story through Judah's marriage, children, and grandchildren. However, time in the outer story is arrested only to be resumed again at the very same moment, after the completion of the inner story, with Joseph being taken down to Egypt and sold to Potiphar, Pharaoh's officer, the captain of the bodyguard (cf. Gen 37:36 with Gen 39:1). This structure, though larger in size than Mark's intercalations, contains all ten points of the composite list above.

For instance, there is a distinct locality for the inner story from the outer story. Joseph is in Egypt, and Judah remains in the land of Canaan. The outer story is the temporal border of the inner story. The first verse of the inner story states, "And it came about at that time," alluding to the

---

21. Edwards, "Markan Sandwiches," 125.

time when Joseph was sold into slavery in Genesis 37. Through Genesis 38:1, the narrator explicitly links the inner story to the outer story chronologically. The narrator then resumes the chronology of the outer story by repeating Joseph's situation in Egypt after the completion of the inner story in Genesis 39:1. This focalization and defocalization of the two stories creates a gap for the outer story across the inner story. As the story of Judah develops, the audience wonders about what happened to Joseph during these years.

Because the outer story with Joseph extends throughout the end of the book of Genesis, there are multiple new characters introduced when the outer story resumes, but the most immediate characters are Potiphar and his wife in Genesis 39. Contrasting actions are done by Joseph and Judah in the two stories. Joseph's response to the approach of Potiphar's wife is opposite of the response of Judah and his sons toward Tamar in Genesis 38. Joseph resists satisfying his own desires at the expense of his master's family life, while Judah and his sons only satisfy their desires with Tamar at the expense of their family life. Judah is being compared to Joseph by the juxtaposition of the stories. The Judah story in Genesis 38 helps the audience understand why it was that Joseph was chosen as the heir apparent in Genesis 37, rather than Judah. Rueben was the firstborn son of Leah, who disqualified himself from being the heir by attempting to usurp his father's position in the family through having relations with Bilhah, the servant of Rachel (see Gen 35:22). Simeon and Levi were disqualified by their use of the sign of the covenant to slay the men at Shechem for the defilement of their sister, Dinah (Gen 34). Judah is the next in line but is not chosen to be the heir by Jacob. Jacob chooses Joseph, the first son of Rachel and provides him with a robe that telegraphed to all that he was the heir apparent. Genesis 38 shows the audience the kind of person that Judah is—irresponsible, self-gratifying, crass, immoral, unconcerned about preserving the family, and self-righteous. However, by the end of the inner story, the scene is set for change in Judah through God's persistent pursuit of Judah through Tamar, and the sovereign birth of twins where the younger (Perez) creates a "breach" and is born before the elder (Zerah) who "flashed" his hand out of the womb first. The confluence of events, not dissimilar to the birth of Judah's father Jacob and Esau, provides the opportunity for change in Judah at the close of Genesis 38. Allen Ross comments: "God's design for Joseph's prominence could not be set aside as easily as Judah thought. In his own family, and in spite of his own indifference to Tamar, Judah saw the strange outworking of the plan whereby the younger gained priority in the family."[22] Judah will show himself to be a different man when the narrative takes up his story in Genesis 42–44.

This change in Judah provides dramatic irony for the audience because Joseph in the outer story knows nothing about what has transpired in Judah's life, but the audience does. Therefore, when Judah offers himself on behalf of Benjamin for the sake of his family and especially his father (see Gen 44:18–34), the audience knows how this transformation occurred over the years, whereas Joseph is only able to see that a transformation has occurred (Gen 45:1–15).

There is active character crossover between the two stories in the person of Judah. He only appears in a minor way in the first part of the outer story at 37:26–27, and in a much more substantial way in the later narratives of Genesis 42–44. None of the other characters in the inner story carry over into the outer story once it resumes except for Judah. As in the Markan intercalations where Jesus is the only active character to crossover between the two stories, Judah functions as the only active character to crossover between the two stories.

Therefore, even though the size of the Genesis stories is much larger than any of Mark's intercalations, the displacement of the Judah story appears to provide a pattern that those familiar with the Hebrew Scriptures would have known.

1 Samuel 17 (ca. 913–722 BC)

J. P. Fokkelman identifies 1 Samuel 17–19 as act five of fifteen acts in 1 Samuel 1—2 Samuel 24.[23] Recognizing that chapter 17 has "one distinct plot," Fokkelman divides the account into six *scene parts*: 1–11, 12–22, 23–31, 32–40, 41–54, 55–18:5.[24] For the purposes of this study, the second "scene part" in 1 Samuel 17:12–22 interrupts the flow of the main narrative begun in 17:1–11 with a back story regarding the shepherd David. The outer story begins in 17:1–11 with the armies of the Philistines and Israel drawn up in battle array to fight in the valley of Elah (1 Sam 17:1–3). The narrative then progresses by recounting how a terrible

---

22. Ross, *Creation and Blessing*, 612. See also Wenham, *Genesis*, 2:363–65.

23. Fokkelman, *Narrative Art and Poetry*, 1:20, 23, 27, 31. The Old Greek codices (LXXB) omit verses 12–31.

24. Fokkelman, *Narrative Art and Poetry*, 2:145.

fore-fighter named Goliath from Gath came forward from the armies of the Philistines in formidable military stature (1 Sam 17:4–8) and taunted the Israelites to choose a man (אִישׁ) to come forward and fight him to decide the battle between the two armies (1 Sam 17:8–11).

The outer story then breaks away to an inner story in 1 Samuel 17:12–22 that takes the audience to Bethlehem to meet David, the son of a man (אִישׁ) named Jesse. Moreover, David was previously identified in 1 Samuel 16:18 as a "man of war" (וְאִישׁ מִלְחָמָה). In the inner story, the audience is told that Jesse is old, and his three older sons (Eliab the firstborn, Abinadab the second born, and Shammah, the third born) had followed after Saul to war (1 Sam 17:13–14) whom the audience knows from the outer story is terrified before Goliath (cf. 1 Sam 17:11). The narrator does not say that David followed after Saul, but that he went back and forth from Saul to tend his father's flock at Bethlehem (1 Sam 17:15). Narrative time continues from the outer story into the inner story as the narrator reports that the Philistine came forward for forty days and took his stand (1 Sam 17:16). The statement in 17:16 is the narrator's way to pair, and thus preview, David and Goliath. David is the shepherd who will "leave the sheep, but will be given a new flock, which he discovers at the time when, as a shepherd and with the means of a shepherd, he delivers his flock from a terrible beast in scale armor."[25] David then leaves his flock with a keeper and goes to the battle front, not at the command of Saul, but from his father with food for his brothers and their commander (1 Sam 17:17–22).

When the outer story resumes, the audience is at the same time in the story that it was when the outer story broke off—with the terrible fore-fighter, the Philistine, Goliath, from Gath, coming up from the army of the Philistines speaking the same words as he previously spoke (1 Sam 17:23 cf. 17:4–11). The new element that arises in the resumption of the outer story is that the narrator reports David heard what Goliath was saying and responded (1 Sam 17:23–27). The outer story then moves forward without any additional narrative disconnect to David's defeat of Goliath, the routing of the Philistines, and the acceptance of David into Saul's court and by the heir apparent, Jonathan (17:23—18:5).

Points 1 through 10 of the composite-list above for Markan Intercalations are present in the of stories of David and Goliath. The outer story is the temporal border of the inner story. The outer story breaks

---

25. Fokkelman, *Narrative Art and Poetry*, 2:154.

off with Goliath coming forth to challenge the Israelites (1 Sam 17:1–11) and resumes with Goliath coming forth to challenge the Israelites (1 Sam 17:23). Even though the inner story has a reference to Goliath coming forward over a period of 40 days (1 Sam 17:16), the time in the statement includes and extends beyond the time stated in 17:23 when the outer story resumes; its purpose is to juxtapose David with Goliath to foreshadow the upcoming match between the warrior and the shepherd. Furthermore, time in the inner story appears to extend prior to the time of the outer story as David is reported in the inner story having gone back and forth between his father's house and Saul (1 Sam 17:15). The defocalization of the outer story with the inner story creates a gap for the audience who does not know the outcome of the conflict between the Philistines and Israel. The only active character crossover between the two stories is David. He is described and spoken to in the inner story but is active and speaks in the resumption of the outer story. The parallel actions done by contrasting groups include David's older brothers who "followed after Saul" (הָלְכוּ אַחֲרֵי שָׁאוּל) in conventional, military array against the Philistines (1 Sam 17:14) and David who returned from Saul (וְשָׁב מֵעַל שָׁאוּל) (1 Sam 17:15) to shepherd his father's flock (לִרְעוֹת אֶת־צֹאן אָבִיו), who then battled the Philistine, not with the armor of Saul, but with the tools of a shepherd—stones and a sling (1 Sam 17:38–40). Contrasting actions also occur between these parallel groups. David's elder brothers are part of the Israelites who are fearful before Goliath (1 Sam 17:11, 24), but David, the younger brother and shepherd, is outraged at Goliath's words and steps forward to fight him in the name of Israel's God as he would a bear or a lion, or in this case a "dog" (הַכֶּלֶב) in protection of the sheep (1 Sam 17:26, 36–37, 43). The outer story has an elliptical action in that the battle with the Philistines is staged in Elah, while David and his father are in the agricultural, shepherding setting of Bethlehem. But the outer story leaks into the inner story by the reference of Jesse's older sons following after Saul, David going back and forth between Saul and his father's flock, and the singular mention of the Philistine coming forward morning and evening for forty days to take his stand. Then when David enters the outer story, he brings his shepherding resources from the inner story with him to silence the taunts of the Philistine. This interplay between the outer and inner stories interlink them as the narrative turns from Elah to Bethlehem, and then returns to Elah with the shepherd from Bethlehem. The distinct localities of the two stories also plays a role as the shepherd from the "house of bread" (בֵּית לֶחֶם) brings nourishing life to the battle at Elah both literally and metaphorically. Finally, there is dramatic irony for the audience who knows that this shepherd is a "man" of war that Goliath is calling for, even though he appears to be a young, ruddy youth, and the audience comes to understand that what the nation needs as its leader is not a warrior but a shepherd.

The inner and outer stories in 1 Samuel 17 are interconnected in many of the ways Mark connects his intercalations. First Samuel 17 provides an ancient example, available to the original author of Mark as one familiar with the Scriptures, of how to break away from a main story to tell an inner story that has an impact on the outer story. However, the inner story in 1 Samuel 17 is distinct from Mark's intercalations in that it logically functions as background for the forward movement of the outer story. The two stories are not as distinct as the Joseph and Judah stories. Nevertheless, the breakaway pattern in Genesis 38 and 1 Samuel 17 may be examples of a compositional technique that was generally known containing distinct stories that interrelated to one another to create a greater whole.

2 Samuel 11:1—12:25 (ca. 913–722 BC)

Chapters 11 and 12 of Second Samuel function as a hinge within the book. In chapters 1–10 David triumphs. God establishes the monarchy bringing David out from exile as the sole ruler over a secure and united Israel (2 Sam 1:1—8:18). Then David's rule is marked by loyal love, justice, and brave conquest (2 Sam 9:1—10:19). Chapters 11–12 recount a double breach of the covenant by David which leads to God's judgment on David's family, but not the loss of the kingdom (due to the promise in 2 Samuel 7). In chapters 13 through 20 there is a downward destabilization of David's family unfolding the consequences of David's sin, through which the monarchy barely survives. The alleged intercalation at issue in this study occurs in the central section of the book, the well-known account of David and Bathsheba where the narrative progress of the outer story is supposedly interrupted in 2 Samuel 12:1–6 by an inner story/parable told to David by Nathan the prophet.[26]

The book's pivot in chapters 11 through 12 is bracketed by a reference to war with the Ammonites (2 Sam 11:1; 12:26–31). The initiation of the war forms the backdrop for the action in the outer story. David

---

26. Edwards, "Markan Sandwiches," 202.

remained at home while Israel went to war (2 Sam 11:1). Bathsheba's husband was away, fighting the war, when David pressed himself upon her (11:2–5). Uriah the Hittite (not even an Israelite) is brought home from the war in an attempt to cover David's sin (11:6–13). Uriah shows himself to have more integrity than David by refusing to be with his wife while Israel is at war (11:8–13). Then Uriah is returned to the front lines to die in the war at David's command to his general, Joab (11:14–25). After Bathsheba mourned the death of her husband, David brought her to his house, married her, and she bore him a son (11:26–27). After the alleged inner story (12:1–6) and the supposed resumption of the outer story, the narrative ends with a report of final victory over the Ammonites at Rabbah (12:26–31). David is still away from the battle and has to be cajoled by his general, Joab, to join him by threatening to capture Rabbah and name it after himself (Joab) if David does not engage in the battle (12:26–28). David responds by entering the war once again as Israel's warrior king, capturing Rabbah, being crowned with the King of Ammon's crown, and subjugating the captives as he had done previously (12:29–31; cf. 10:1–19).

J. P. Fokkelman summarizes the outer story's concentric structure when he observes that there are "two scenes of normal proportions . . . surrounded by two short paragraphs":

11:2–4   David-Bathsheba: adultery
  11:5–13   David-Uriah: unsuccessful concealment
  11:14–25   David-Uriah-Joab: murder as concealment
11:26–27   David-Bathsheba: marriage[27]

The outer story breaks away with the narrator bringing in a new character, YHWH, with an evaluative comment: "The thing which David did was evil in the eyes of the Lord" (2 Sam 11:27e).[28] The Lord then sends his envoy, Nathan the prophet, to the king with a parable. The genre of the narrative changes, but one wonders if the parable actually functions as an "inner story." It does appear to break the narrative progression of the outer story, but its function may be different than that of an inner story. It is not clear where the inner story ends and the outer story resumes. James Edwards correctly observes that Nathan's parable "breaks the continuity of the narrative yet provides the key to its understanding, for the parable allows David to see his action from God's perspective."[29]

---

27. Fokkelman, *Narrative Art and Poetry*, 1:70.

28. Fokkelman, *Narrative Art and Poetry*, 1:71.

29. Edwards, "Markan Sandwiches," 202. See also Fokkelman, *Narrative Art and Poetry*, 1:70–71.

Accordingly, Nathan's parable does not appear to function as an inner story but as a progression of the outer story using a means that will disarm David to think as a righteous judge and then apply God's righteous judgment to himself.

The outer story does not appear to be the temporal boarder of the inner story. While Nathan's parable may suggest a defocalization from the outer story, it is a means of communicating what the narrator has stated in 11:27e that what David did was evil in the eyes of YHWH. Even though it is difficult to identify the reentry of the outer story (outside of the change in genre), there is no new character that is noted at a point of reentry. Active character crossover occurs not only with David, but with Nathan who speaks the parable to David and then applies the judgment to David. Parallel actions may be said to occur by contrasting groups in the initial outer story and the parable:[30]

The Outer Narrative	The Parable
David	Rich man
Uriah	Poor man
Bathsheba	Lamb
Harem	Herds

However, when the proposed inner story resumes after the parable, the parallels do not continue. This observation supports a more linear development of the story than a cyclical one. There is no elliptical action that crosses the inner story and contrasts with the actions of the outer story. On the contrary, the inner story (parable) is parallel with the outer story. There is not a turn-and-return pattern between the outer and inner stories. There is no distinct locality for the middle sequence, and there is no dramatic irony. When the parable is told, we know no more than David about its application other than the hint provided in the summary of 11:27e and the audible play off of the name Bathsheba (בַּת־שֶׁבַע) ("daughter" of Sheba) and the statement in the parable that the poor man's lamb was like a "daughter" (כְּבַת) to him (12:3).

Therefore, it does not appear that the parable told by Nathan the prophet in 2 Samuel 12:1–6 functions in the narrative as an inner story, even though it is a different genre than the rest of the narrative in chapters 11 through 12. The parable is a means used by Nathan and the Lord to

---

30. Fokkelman, *Narrative Art and Poetry*, 1:78.

The Literary Pattern of Intercalation 73

raise up the righteous aspect of David's character so that David can hear and receive the forthcoming judgment against him and his household. All of chapters 11 through 12 appear to be apprehended as a continuing, single story.

2 Kings 8:1–8 (ca. sixth century BC)

On a smaller scale, a breakaway pattern exists in 2 Kings 8:1–6. This unit makes reference to the prophet Elisha's healing of the Shunamite woman's son told in 2 Kings 4:8–37. In verses 8:1–3, an outer story begins where Elisha tells the Shunamite woman to go with her household to sojourn in the land of Philistia for seven years because the Lord is going to bring a famine on the land of Israel for seven years (cf. 2 Kgs 4:38; 6:25; 7:4); the woman and her household obey the word of God and go to Philistia. After seven years, the woman returns from the land of Philistia and cries out to the king (Joram, of the northern kingdom of Israel; cf. 2 Kgs 8:16) for her house and her field to be returned to her.

The inner story begins in 2 Kings 8:4 and is out of chronological sequence with verses 1–3 in that it takes place prior to the Shunamite women coming to the king. The narrator tells the audience that the king was talking with Elisha's servant, Gehazi (cf. 2 Kgs 4:12–13; 5:20–25), asking that Gehazi tell him of the great things Elisha had done (2 Kgs 8:4). In 2 Kings 8:5 the narrator explains that as Gehazi was telling the king of how Elisha had restored to life one who was dead, the Shunamite woman appeared and appealed to the King for her house and her field. Gehazi then said to the King: "My lord, O king, this is the woman, and this is her son whom Elisha restored to life." Time in the inner story is thereby brought back to the present time of verse 3 in the outer story.

The outer story then resumes with the Shunamite woman confirming the work of Elisha in raising her son, and the king granting the woman her request for her home and her field and ordering that the proceeds from the woman's land be paid to her from the time she left the land to the present (2 Kgs 8:6). The outer story, broken off in verse 3 is now completed in verse 6.

Points 1, 2, 6, 7, 8, and 10 of the composite list for Markan intercalations above are present in the story of the Shunamite woman and the king, but many characteristics of Markan intercalations are absent. It appears that the outer story is the temporal boarder of the inner story as the woman comes to the king. The inner story is defocalized as the king speaks with Gehazi at a time prior to the arrival of the Shunamite woman. Nevertheless, the prior acts of Elisha for the Shunamite woman are told to the king bringing her into the inner story. The outer story has an elliptical action which crosses the inner story. We are told at the end of the outer story that the woman appealed to the king for her house and her field (2 Kgs 8:3). However, we do not know the king's response. The inner story forms a background or setting for the king to respond favorably to the woman's request when she arrives. Clearly the plots of the two stories interlink as the woman who went to the king turns out to be the woman whose son was raised from the dead by Elisha, and now comes to the king in the time of the inner story exactly where the outer story left off. There is also dramatic irony because the audience knows what the king does not know about the identity of the woman. The audience knows about what Elisha did for the Shunamite woman even though the king does not. The audience also knows what the woman is seeking when she arrives in the inner story even though the king does not know until she asks him for relief. The merging of these two stories, however, provides insight for the audience to understand why this ungodly king would grant a request to this woman—he is impressed by Elisha. This background information in the inner story is similar to the way the account in Homer functions in that it gives the audience insight rather than functioning as dramatic irony.

Unlike Markan intercalations, these two stories do not provide a new character or newly named character at the reentry into the outer story. The king and the woman are present in both stories. Also, active character crossover exists between the two stories in the person of the Shunamite woman and the king. There do not appear to be parallel actions that are done by contrasting groups, or contrasting actions done by parallel groups in the two stories. The inner story appears to provide an explanatory background to the king's grant of the woman's request. There is also not a distinct event in a neighboring locality for the middle story. The woman goes to the king in the outer story and comes again to the king in the inner story. Gehazi is also with the king in the inner story. The location appears to be the same at all times—the location of the king.

Even though this short unit is not identical to Markan intercalations, it does show a pattern of breaking away from one story to provide background in a second story to bring about a comprehensible resolution of the first story.

Hosea 1–3 (ca. 790–686 BC)

James Edwards believes that the interchange in Hosea 1–3 resembles Mark's sandwich technique.[31] However, the similarities may be limited. In 1:1—3:5, the Lord's loyal love for the idolatrous, northern kingdom of Israel is demonstrated through Hosea's marriage to Gomer. The biographical information of Hosea and his family is placed at the front of the book to function as an introduction to the book's message, as a picture which will illumine the remainder of the book (4–14). Every element of the remainder of the book can be found in this illustration (i.e., the nation's faithlessness, God's faithfulness, the nation's coming judgment, future repentance, and hope of restoration). Chapters 1–3 illustrate the content of the rest of the book and encourage the nation on an emotional level to repent to their loving God.

The outer story is found in Hosea 1:1–9. The Lord told Hosea to take a wife of harlotry and have children of harlotry in order to picture the Lord's relationship to Israel who have forsaken their covenant with the Lord (Hos 1:2). The image of harlotry for idolatry is meaningful for Israel's activity in Baalism, a fertility cult, as a means to obtain fertility of their crops, animals, and children. Hosea obeyed and married Gomer the daughter of Diblaim (Hos 1:3a). Hosea's wife then gave birth to three children: (1) a son named *Jezreel* (יִזְרְעֶאל) to picture the coming judgment the Lord is going to bring upon the house of Jehu at Jezreel for Jehu's murder of the sons of Ahab (Hos 1:3b–5); (2) a daughter named *Lo-ruhamah* (לֹא רֻחָמָה) to picture the nation's plight because the Lord was not going to have compassion upon Israel as he would upon Judah (Hos 1:6–7); and (3) a son named *Lo-ammi* (לֹא עַמִּי) to picture the broken covenant relationship with Israel and the Lord.

An inner story begins in 1:10 and continues through 2:23 (Heb 2:1–25). Whereas the outer story is in prose, the inner story is in poetry. Whereas the outer story is biographical, the inner story is a discourse. Whereas the outer story functions metaphorically, the inner story functions as an explicit indictment. The Lord first speaks of a time after judgment when the brokenness of Israel's relationship with Him will be restored—they will be his people and receive compassion taking the negatives away from the names *Lo-ammi* and *Lo-ruhamah* (Hos 1:10—2:1; Heb 2:1–3). However, the Lord then indicts the nation for its faithlessness toward him requiring that he bring difficulty until she turns back to him

---

31. Edwards, "Markan Sandwiches," 201–2.

(Hos 2:2–7 [Heb 2:3–9]). Because the nation did not realize that it was the Lord who gave her what good she had, the good will be taken away from her in discipline (Hos 2:8–13 [Heb 2:10–15]). Then, rounding out the inner story as it began, the Lord declares that after judgment he will bring his faithless wife back to him in a time of blessing with a restored covenant (Hos 2:14–23 [Heb 2:16–25]).

The outer story resumes in 3:1–5 with an emphasis on the image of restoration through a resumption of prose showing Hosea's redemption and seclusion of his wife Gomer. Hosea's activity symbolizes the Lord's redemption and captivity of the nation Israel in order to turn her back to him. The Lord tells Hosea to go and love Gomer even though she is an adulteress to picture the Lord's love for Israel who are an idolatress people (Hos 3:1). Hosea redeems Gomer (from whoever owns her at the time) for fifteen shekels of silver and some barley (Hos 3:2). Hosea was then to prohibit Gomer from any relations with a man as a picture of the coming captivity of the nation Israel so that the nation will return with a desire for the Lord (Hos 3:3–5).

The two stories are distinct with the inner story interrupting the outer story. However, they do not align with many of the elements in the composite list identifying characteristics of Markan intercalations. The outer story is not a temporal boarder of the inner story. The outer story takes place in the lifetime of Hosea, but the inner story extends beyond the lifetime of Hosea through the exile of the northern nation and its subsequent return to the land. When the outer story resumes, it is at a future time in the life of Hosea and functions metaphorically once again to picture the future redemption, captivity and return of the nation through Hosea's acts toward Gomer. There is not a unique pattern of focalization and defocalization of the two stories; they bleed into one another, so that there is not a gap for the outer story across the inner story. The correlation of the two stories is explicit and is often expressed through the repetition of words like *Lo-ammi* and *Lo-ruhamah* (Hos 1:10 [Heb 2:1]) or through an interchange where in the outer story Hosea's actions are explicitly compared to the acts of the Lord toward the nation (Hos 3:1, 4–5). There is not a new character at the reentry of the outer story. Active character crossover does not occur between the two stories except for the Lord. Parallel actions are done by Hosea/the Lord and Gomer/the nation in the two stories. However, the outer story does not have an elliptical action which crosses the inner story and contrasts with the actions of the inner story. The two stories are in parallel in that Hosea's story illustrates the Lord's actions toward the nation. There is a turn and return pattern to the story of Hosea in the outer story, and the themes in the two stories interlink. There is no distinct locality for the middle story, and dramatic irony does not exist in the two narratives. Edwards correctly observes that the inner story is an intentional commentary on the flanking outer stories.[32]

Even though Hosea 1–3 contains a breakaway technique between the actions of Hosea and the indictment of the Lord, the stories appear to be more explicitly integrated with one another and emphasize a common message than the sandwich stories in Mark. They provide a literary example of interrupting an outer story with an inner story to be followed by the resumption of the outer story, but the two stories have more in common with one another than Mark's sandwiches.

Apocrypha and Septuagint

2 Maccabees 6–7 (ca. 180–161 BC)

Second Maccabees (ΜΑΚΚΑΒΑΙΩΝ Β), by a certain Jason of Cyrene, is a theological reading of Jewish history narrating events "from the time of the high priest Onias III and Syrian king Seleucus IV to the defeat of Nicanor's army."[33] This Greek writing was probably composed sometime during the first century BC.[34]

In chapters 4–5, Antiochus IV (also called Epiphanies because he was to be the manifestation of the Olympian Zeus on earth)[35] and the Seleucid army invaded the land of Judah and went into Egypt. Jason, the corrupt brother of Onias (2 Macc 4:7) and a pro-Egyptian, thought that Antiochus IV was dead and led an unsuccessful revolt in Jerusalem in an attempt to recover the high priesthood (2 Macc 5:1–10). Antiochus, thinking that all Judea was in revolt, returned and overtook Jerusalem, slayed eighty thousand people, and desecrated the temple (2 Macc 5:1–20). Antiochus fled to Antioch with eighteen hundred talents from the temple and left leaders to afflict the people, including Phrygian-born Philip, Menalaus who Hellenized his people, and Apollonius, Captain of the Mysians, who attacked the Jewish observers in Jerusalem (2 Macc

32. Edwards, "Markan Sandwiches," 196, 121.
33. Metzger, *Annotated Apocrypha*, 263.
34. Metzger, *Annotated Apocrypha*, 263.
35. Bruce, *New Testament History*, 3–4.

5:21–27). Judas Maccabeus and nine others escaped the city from Apollonius's attack.

The passage that is the focus of this study begins in chapter 6:1 with the continuation of Antiochus's harsh treatment of the Jews. The outer story, in verses 1–11, describes the enforcement of Hellenized cultural and religious customs on the Jews. These customs were not only contrary to Jewish law but banned Jewish practices and turned the temple over to the cult of Olympian Zeus. Forced Hellenization was imposed upon the Jews in Jerusalem and the Jews in nearby Greek cities by an Athenian senator appointed by Antiochus. The outer story is told in a third-person narrative.

An inner story interrupts the outer story in verses 12–17 and is told in the first-person. It provides a theological perspective to the suffering the Jews are experiencing at the hands of the Seleucids. The inner story encourages the audience[36] not to despair over their calamities which are not meant to destroy the Jewish people. The Lord allows the full measure of sin to build up in other nations so that they might be destroyed, but not Israel. Instead, the narrator explains that the Lord is disciplining the Jewish people along their journey so that the Lord will not have to destroy them.

The outer story resumes in 6:18—7:42 through third-person narrative. It details the continued martyrdom of the Jews under the Seleucids. Specifically, the martyrdom of elderly Eleazar (2 Macc 6:18–31), a scribe, and the martyrdom of seven brothers and their mother (2 Macc 7:1–42). In both examples, martyrdom arose out of the Jewish people's refusal to eat swine's flesh (ὔειον κρέας) in violation of God's dietary laws. In all cases, their martyrdom was a testimony of courage and faithfulness to others, and the martyred spoke words of faith during their suffering.

In this narrative, the outer story is the temporal boarder of the inner story in that the progress of the narrative is suspended while the narrator directly speaks to the audience in the inner story. There is a pattern of focalization and defocalization of the two stories creating a gap in the narrative as the admonition is given in the inner story. At the reentry of the outer story, a new character is introduced as the martyrdom of Eleazar is recounted; the narrative then continues with the detailed telling of martyrdom of the woman with seven sons. There is no active character cross over between the two stories other than the narrator who

---

36. The participial phrase τοὺς ἐντυγχάνοντας allows for audiences with the more generic sense of "those encountering" the book.

moves from third person to first person and then third person again. The resumption of the outer story includes echoes of the narrator's perspective in the words of the martyred, but there are not parallel actions done by contrasting groups or contrasting actions done by parallel groups in the two episodes. The elliptical action that crosses the inner story does not contrast with the actions, or in this case admonitions, of the inner story. Although the inner story does not have a plot, there is a turn and return pattern between the two stories. There is no distinct locality for the inner story. And there is no dramatic irony with the stories. Actually, the opposite occurs in that the audience is brought up to speed on the proper attitude to have while hearing about the atrocities being carried out against the Jews by the Seleucids.

Many of the elements of Markan intercalations are present in 2 Maccabees 6–7, but the narrative of the outer story is much longer than Mark's narratives, and the function of the two stories is not parallel. Mark's stories provide dramatic irony for the audience. These stories provide a perspective for the audience to hold onto as it continues to hear about the calamity brought upon the Jewish people in Jerusalem during the reign of Antiochus IV. Nevertheless, this kind of narrative would provide a pattern for the actual author of Mark to assimilate and modify as he put together his sandwich stories and the implied audience would recognize the pattern.

Hellenistic and Roman Histories, Theatrical Comedies, and Romances

Downing surveys literary parallels among Hellenistic and Roman histories like Josephus (ca. AD 37–100), Lucian (ca. AD 125–after 180), Dionysius of Halicarnassus (ca. 60–after 7 BC), Thucydides (ca. 460–400 BC), and Plutarch's *Lives* (ca. AD 46–120) and does not find the literature rewarding in terms of the use of intercalations. The writing is usually done in a topical, sequential arrangement of material without interruptions or digressions.[37] There is an intercalation in Plutarch's *Lives*, *Solon* with an exchange with Aesop and Salon as an inner story[38] to the account dealing with Salon and King Croesus of Lydia.[39] This passage does have a slight interruption in

---

37. Downing, "Markan Intercalation," 122–23.
38. Plutarch, *Lives*.
39. Plutarch, *Lives* (Solon 27–28); Downing, "Markan Intercalation," 124.

the narrative with a conversation between Aesop and Solon before the narrative continues in a way which affirms Solon's wisdom about a happy man being one who ends his life with valor and free of distress. The inner story confirms the status of Solon in the eyes of Aesop after King Croesus has diminished Solon's definition of a happy man, but it is related to the outer story as an aside rather than as a distinct narrative.[40] Plutarch's writing postdates Mark, but reflects a widespread, literary, discursive practice of storytelling that was performed in oral cultures, perhaps to maintain attention, and perhaps to emphasize a message.

Downing also surveys theatrical comedies like Plautus's *The Two Bacchises* (*Bacchides*) (ca. 254–184 BC). It appears that the Latin *Bacchides* was based upon an earlier Greek work, *Dis Exapation* (The Double Deceiver).[41] This may have made the work accessible to Mark. Downing also notes that this romantic comedy was "read but not performed in the first century CE."[42] The play has scene changes which tell different parts of the story to the audience. In relating these theatrical writings to Mark, Downing concludes:

> The Markan intercalations are certainly "dramatic" in a theatrical sense; it must remain possible, but no more, that these conventions, or similar stage devices contemporary with Mark, could have had some influence on Mark's way of telling his stories.[43]

Finally, Downing finds Hellenistic romances like Chariton's *Chaeraes and Callirhoe* (first to second century AD), Zenophon of Ephesus's *An Ephesian Tale* (second to third century AD), Achilles Tatius's *Leucippe and Clitophon* (second century AD) to be closer to Mark's intercalations.[44] However, all of the romances reviewed by Downing are later than Mark. They may have been told orally prior to being placed in written form, and the actual author of Mark could have heard them. However, it is just as possible that Mark's intercalations contributed to what appears to be a conventional literary pattern and/or narrative technique. Downing posits that these romances may have influenced Mark.[45] While this is a possible

---

40. Downing, "Markan Intercalation," 125.
41. Plautus, *Amphitryon*, 356–57.
42. Downing, "Markan Intercalation," 123.
43. Downing, "Markan Intercalation," 126.
44. Downing, "Markan Intercalation," 118–32.
45. Downing, "Markan Intercalation," 131–32.

explanation for Mark and his hearers to understand the pattern of cutting from one story to another story and back to the first story from theatrical works and romances, there are many other written examples that predate the time of Mark that could have been an influence on his method of storytelling.

CONCLUSION

The pattern of storytelling where an initial story is broken away from to tell an inner story to conclusion before the outer story resumes, is ancient, reaching at least as far back as the fifteenth century BC in the Hebrew Scriptures and the seventh century BC in ancient Greek writings. However, what writers are doing with what they are saying with this narrative pattern often varies. Homer often employs this breakaway technique to tell background information in the inner story that helps the audience better understand the outer story. In 1 Samuel 17, the inner story is also used to provide the audience with background to the forward movement of the outer story. Likewise, in 2 Kings 8:1–8, the inner story provides a background or setting for the king to respond favorably to the woman's request when she arrives. Furthermore, the outer and inner stories are directly related to one another in Homer's *Iliad* and *Odyssey*, 1 Samuel 17, 2 Samuel 11:1—12:25 (if 2 Sam 11:27e—12:6 is even an inner story), 2 Kings 8:1–8, Hosea 1–3, 2 Maccabees 6–7, and Plutarch, *Lives, Solon*. The inner stories are not so different in nature that they could stand on their own; they are related narratives that directly aid the audience in better understanding the outer story. Accordingly, dramatic irony rarely arises for the audience by reading the stories together. The author is bringing the audience up-to-speed rather than providing the audience and the implied author information that is unknown to the characters in the narratives.

One significant exception is the narrative in Genesis 37, 38, and 39. The inner story of Judah is very distinct from the outer, Joseph story. The narratives also provide the audience with dramatic irony since they, unlike the brothers or father in the story, know about the inner awaking that has transpired in Judah through the persistence of his daughter-in-law, Tamar. Of all of the examples discussed above, the Joseph/Judah stories are the most similar to Mark's intercalations, even if the accounts in Genesis are much longer than Mark's intercalated stories.

It seems clear from this limited review of literature that predates Mark's gospel that a breakaway pattern in storytelling was common. Intercalations functioned so frequently in the way stories were told that it was a type of a habituated literary practice that would have functioned in the production of narratives and would have been familiar to both authors and audiences. No formal training was required because a person grew up with the practice of storytelling, and this practice so frequently deployed intercalations that it became part-and-parcel of the way in which stories were told in an oral culture. The technique assisted in memorizing, making a story alive, and ensuring that a particular point would reach an audience. Accordingly, what the actual author of Mark does in his intercalated stories is not so unique that no one would understand how to read or listen to the paired narratives. Mark's intercalated narratives will be more concise and require greater audience participation since the inner story is doing more than providing the audience with related, background information. The author of Mark appears to have adapted and refined a ubiquitous tradition in storytelling to suit his purposes and engage his audience in the gospel. The literary pattern of intercalation will be discussed and applied in the following Markan passages: (a) Jesus' Relatives and the Beelzebul Controversy in Mark 3:20–35; (b) Jairus's daughter and the woman with a hemorrhage of blood in Mark 5:21–43; and (c) the death plot by the religious leaders and the anointing of Jesus at Bethany in Mark 14:1–22. Even though the account of Herodias and her daughter is part of an intercalation in Mark 6:7–32, it will not be developed under this narrative structure for reasons discussed in that analysis. An awareness of this literary technique gives a present-day actual audience the ability to understand what the actual author of Mark was doing in developing his discourse, and what the implied audience of Mark understood in its creation of character from the Markan discourse.

5

The Literary Pattern of the Sign-Sermon

THE FIFTH THEORETICAL ISSUE to be discussed is the narrative, sign-sermon pattern that is used by the actual/implied author of Mark to develop the discourse of the narrative discussed in chapter 7 of this work. An examination of this literary approach to the narrative is essential for an understanding of what the actual/implied author is doing with what he is saying in the discourse of the narrative. It will be argued that the implied audience probably had an awareness of this approach to arranging material in a narrative and would use this understanding to construct characterization in the Gospel of Mark. Furthermore, without an understanding of the sign-sermon architecture of a narrative discourse, a present-day audience will miss clues to the construction of argument and character that the actual author and implied audience understood and relied upon.

This arrangement of material in a sign-sermon involves a miracle, or "sign," that is followed by an explanation that is logically and intricately related to the sign. The order can be inverted, sermon/sign, but the narrative pattern connects what might otherwise be considered to be separate and distinct material in the narrative. While characterization might be more directly developed from the content of a sermon, the sign, or miracle, often crystallizes for the implied audience the meaning, significance, and scope of the sermon. This study will show that the literary pattern arises from Hebrew parallelism—especially emblematic parallelism—and is used extensively in the Hebrew Scriptures, as seen in Genesis 9 and Jeremiah chapters 13 and 19, the book of Hosea, and New Testament narratives such as the Gospels and the Acts of the Apostles.

EMBLEMATIC PARALLELISM

Although not as developed as Robert Alter's "type scenes,"[1] the implied author of Mark uses a convention of typological symbolism which this writer identifies as a "sign-sermon" pattern to unify smaller units, develop narrative logic, and crystallize characterization. Its source may well reach back into Hebrew, emblematic parallelism where the author uses images to convey the poetic meaning. While one line conveys the main point in a direct fashion, the second line illuminates it by an image. There is a movement from point-to-picture or picture-to-point (see Pss 23:1, 2, 4; 103:13; 113:5, 6; 57:1).[2]

HEBREW AND GREEK SCRIPTURES

This poetic device was artfully applied to miracles that were joined with other narratives in the Hebrew and Greek Scriptures.[3] As Raymond Brown observes: "Miracles are important external signs of revelation."[4] Revelation seems to be precisely the function of miracles, but not in terms of expressing new content but in terms of affirming, in almost an existential sense, the truth expressed in the sermon (whether the sermon precedes or follows the sign).[5] This interplay of sign and sermon allows an implied audience to more fully understand the scope of a sermon, and apply that scope in its construction of characterization. This correlation of sign-to-sermon can be seen in a brief examination of several passages.

---

1. Alter, *Art of Biblical Narrative*, 47–62.
2. See Ross, *Commentary on the Psalms*, 1:88.
3. Kurz, *Reading Luke-Acts*, 78.
4. Brown, "Gospel Miracles," 185.
5. Brown, "Gospel Miracles," 199.

The Literary Pattern of the Sign-Sermon

Genesis 9

After the floodwaters receded and Noah sacrificed a thank offering (Gen 8), God blessed Noah and made a covenant not to destroy the earth again by flood (Gen 9:8–11). He then gave a *sign* of the covenant in his "bow" which was to be seen in the cloud (Gen 9:12–17). This sign graphically portrayed the message (covenant) in that it was called a קֶשֶׁת which referred to a hunter's bow as in Genesis 27:3; 48:22.[6] As a picture of God's promise never to destroy the earth again by water, God hung his weapon in the sky. One effect of this construction of the narrative discourse is for the implied audience to visually perceive the enormity of God by the physical size of his weapon, the dangerousness of God as a hunter of humanity, and the beneficence of God as one who limits himself for the sake of humankind. These are all character qualities explicitly shown through the image of the bow.

Jeremiah 13 and 19

Though neither of these events are "miracles," they are signs to support the prophet's messages of judgment to Judah.

In Jeremiah 13 the pattern is "sign-sermon." Jeremiah was told by the Lord to purchase a new waistband, wear it, and place it among the rocks along the Euphrates. Then Jeremiah was told to dig it up. It was naturally ruined and totally worthless (Jer 13:1–7). Then the Lord compared Judah to the waistband in that they were to cling to God as a waistband clings to a waist; but since they did not, God would destroy them because they went after other gods (symbolized by placing the waistband along the Euphrates) and became totally worthless (Jer 13:8–11).[7] Although the sign was given first, its significance was not ascertained until the sermon was spoken. It was the sermon that contained the revelation; the sign provided an emotional illustration of the sermon's message that vilified Judah and its actions. The sign works with the sermon to enable the implied audience to develop its characterization of the nation.

In Jeremiah 19, the form is "sermon-sign-sermon." Verses 1–9 proclaimed the destruction of the nation. Jeremiah was then told to break

---

6. BDB s.v. "קֶשֶׁת." See also Ross, *Creation and Blessing*, 209; Waltke and Fredricks, *Genesis*, 134; Von Rad, *Genesis*, 134; Sarna, *Genesis*, 63.

7. See Chisholm, *Handbook on the Prophets*, 91; Thompson, *Book of Jeremiah*, 364.

a jar in verse 10. He consequently proclaimed that the destruction of Judah would be a shattering which could not be repaired (11–13).[8] Once again the supportive nature of the sign is understood in terms of its visceral confirmation of the message through the image of the broken jar. Through these sign-sermons, the implied author is able to once again characterize the nation of Judah and the powerful working of God.

Hosea

The first half of Hosea is built around the "sign-sermon" motif. From the start, Yahweh tells Hosea that his wife is a symbol of the relationship that the northern kingdom has with Yahweh (Hos 1:1—2:1).[9] Then using the figure of a faithless wife, Yahweh indicts the northern kingdom for its faithlessness against Him (Hos 2:2–23). Finally, Hosea's redemption of his wife, Gomer, is symbolic of Yahweh's redemption of Israel (Hos 3:1–5). This interweaving of the sign with the sermon provides an emotional charge to the revelation of the prophet and is central to revealing the heart of God's work for the nation as the implied audience constructs the character of God and the nation from the longsuffering acts of Hosea with his faithless wife.

The Gospels

Jesus' healing of the paralytic in Mark 2:1–12 (= Matt 9:1–8 = Luke 5:17–26) provides a concise, gospel example of a miracle designed to *picture* the words of Jesus. At first Jesus does not heal the lame man but proclaims that his sins are forgiven (a *sermon*, Mark 2:5). But when the scribes and Pharisees reason that Jesus is blaspheming because only God can forgive sins (Mark 2:6–7), Jesus heals the man as a *sign* in the physical realm that confirms his words in the spiritual realm, saying:

> Which is easier: to say to this paralyzed man, "Your sins are forgiven"; or to say, "Get up, pick up your pallet and walk"? "But so that you may know that the Son of Man has authority on earth to forgive sins."—He said to the paralyzed man, "I say to you, get up, pick up your pallet, and go home." And he got up, and immediately picked up his pallet and went out in the sight

---

8. See Chisholm, *Handbook on the Prophets*, 141; Thompson, *Book of Jeremiah*, 458.
9. See Chisholm, *Handbook on the Prophets*, 336; Wolff, *Hosea*, 16.

everyone, so that they were all amazed and were glorifying God, saying, "We have never seen anything like this!" (Mark 2:9–12 NASB 2020)

Throughout the book of Acts and much of the New Testament, the lame function as a physical metaphor for the spiritual condition of a contextual people (cf. John 5:1–9; Acts 9:32–34). The dead also play a similar role in Acts (9:36–42; 20:6–12).[10] In this particular case, the miracle of healing the lame man vilifies the religious leaders in the eyes of the implied audience, and vindicates Jesus as a truth teller with omniscient power to know the thoughts of characters in the story with as much accuracy as the implied author/narrator (cf. Mark 2:7 with 2:8).

The Acts of the Apostles

The healing of the lame man in the temple at Acts 3:1–26 pictures (*sign*) the spiritual salvation that Peter will proclaim for Israel. The miracle offers symbolic elements which transfer to the sermon which follows.[11] Comparisons between the man and the people are significant. The man is lame. In the Hebrew Scriptures, "walking" symbolizes a moral lifestyle (Psalm 1:1),[12] and the setting of Acts 3 is very Jewish. The beggar's condition appears to represent the nation's inability to walk with God. Like the man, Israel is lame.[13] The man in Acts 3 is a beggar in need of a physical

---

10. In the Gospel of John, all miracles are specifically identified as "signs" (σημεῖον). See John 2:11, 23; 3:2; 4:54; 6:2, 14, 26; 7:31; 9:16; 11:47; 12:18, 37; 20:30.

11. Leo O'Reilly writes: "We shall see that the healing is a sign of salvation and that it bears witness to the power of the word to effect the salvation which it proclaims" (O'Reilly, *Word and Sign*, 88). Darrell Bock writes: "The miracle is a visual act that points to a deeper reality" (Bock, *Acts*, 144). M. Dennis Hamm asserts, "Indeed, not only is the healing the *occasion* of the speeches, but the healed man's physical presence is a dramatic part of the narrative and becomes, as it were, part of the dialogue (3, 11; 4, 10.14)" (Hamm, "Acts 3:1–10," 305).

12. Commenting on the verb "walks" in Psalm 1:1, Allen Ross states: "The first [verb] is 'walks' (הָלַךְ, an implied comparison that becomes an idiom), which signifies how one lives, whether morally and ethically or not; here it would refer to living according to the advice of the ungodly" (Ross, *Psalms*, 1:12).

13. The correlation of the salvation of the lame man with the salvation of Israel is more explicitly made in Acts 4:9–12 where the lame man's salvation is offered to the leaders of Israel. See also Bede the Venerable, who identified Israel with the lame man in his *Commentary on the Acts of the Apostles* 3.2A, 5:38; Mikael C. Parsons also notices the symbolic nature of this miracle when he writes: "Just as the blind man who sees in John 9 is the ideal disciple in the Fourth Gospel where believing is symbolized as a kind of seeing, so the lame man who walks of Acts 3 is the symbol of salvation in a story

provision,[14] so too the nation is in need of spiritual provision.[15] The beggar is located outside of the temple suggesting that the nation, though injured and impoverished sits at the threshold of the kingdom of God.[16] After being healed, the beggar enters the temple leaping (ἐξαλλόμενος) and praising God (see the LXX of Isa 35:6, "Then shall the lame one leap [ἅλομαι] as a deer"). This physical picture suggests the arrival of the Messianic salvation which Peter is about to offer the nation.[17] The miracle is a demonstration of the power of Christ's name (Acts 3:16) to meet the nation's salvation, even for each individual since the nation's need includes individual needs (see Acts 3:26, "every one of you," "ἕκαστον").

The sermon explains and applies the miracle of healing to the Jews in the temple. It has a simple structural divider at the beginning of 3:17 (Καὶ νῦν, ἀδελφοί). The first section argues that what has happened was not of Peter and John, but of God (3:12–16); the second section tells what the hearers should do in response to the miracle (3:17–26).[18] In this sermon, Peter offers spiritual, kingdom blessings to his audience just as the lame man received physical, kingdom blessings. The physical healing of the lame man pictured and foreshadowed the spiritual healing available

---

where journey narratives occupy much narrative space, and where the Christian movement is referred to simply as the 'Way' (see 9:2; 19:9, 23; 22:4; 24:14, 22)" (Parsons, "Christian Origins and Narrative Openings," 25). See also Hamm, "Acts 3:1–10," 305.

14. The expression of faith is not explicitly recounted as part of the miracle. Peter states that the man was healed by faith in Acts 3:16. However, the owner of that faith is not clear; Talbert suggests that Peter is describing the faith of the apostles rather than the lame man (Talbert, *Reading Acts*, 33; see also Wall, *Acts of the Apostles*, 32n5). However, the lame man's response of "praising God" and "clinging to Peter and John" reflects his faith and is certainly different from that of the healed man in John 5 who turns over Jesus to those who wish to harm him.

15. These concepts are interrelated. Talbert argues, "In Luke-Acts salvation encompasses the whole person. . . . The physical healings of the bodies of the afflicted are foretastes of the resurrection of the dead, just as one's conversion is a foretaste of the ultimate redemption from all sin. There is in Luke-Acts no reduction of salvation to a purely spiritual transaction any more than there is a reduction of it to a purely physical or political reality. The whole person is affected" (Talbert, *Reading Acts*, 35).

16. Hamm, "Acts 3:1–10," 309–12.

17. O'Reilly confirms: "The allusion to Is 35 implies that Luke sees in Peter's first miracle a fulfillment of this scriptural prophecy. It is a concrete realization of the messianic salvation promised for the last times" (O'Reilly, *Word and Sign*, 39). See also Talbert, *Reading Acts*, 222; Hamm, "Acts 3:12–26," 333.

18. Talbert holds to a similar structure of (1) "how the healing happened" in vv. 12–16, and (2) "what the healing demands and why" in vv. 17–26 (Talbert, *Reading Acts*, 52). See also Parsons, "Christian Origins and Narrative Openings," 22; Bock, *Acts*, 165.

for the Jews upon their reception of Peter's word about Jesus.[19] The correlation between the physical and spiritual kingdom blessings is implied in Acts 3:16, and later made textually explicit before the religious leaders through the terms σέσωται and σωτηρία.[20]

The sign functions for the implied audience to both vilify the people addressed in the sermon by portraying them as lame and outside of the presence of God and vindicate Peter through the healing. The sign also offers the implied audience the hope of healing as the lame man was restored. As an image, the sign crystallizes the scope of the message expressed in the sermon and provides the implied audience with the ability to characterize the lame man, Peter, and the people being addressed in the narrative.

CONCLUSION

The sign-sermon literary pattern was employed so often in early Greek and Hebrew literature that it was probably familiar to the actual/implied author of the Gospel of Mark as a means to arrange material and communicate in a visual and visceral way the content of the message being told to the implied audience. Its use in literature also provided the implied audience with an understanding of how the literary pattern was used in narrative so that they would know how to understand the organization of the discourse and create characterization through this method of discourse. The literary pattern of the sermon/sign will be specifically discussed in this study in the narrative dealing with the Syrophoenician woman in Mark 7:34–40.

---

19. O'Reilly writes, "What Luke is now proclaiming, through the lips of Peter, is not only that this particular realization of salvation (the miracle at the temple) has taken place by means of the name of Jesus, but that all salvation takes place by this means" (O'Reilly, *Word and Sign*, 156).

20. See Acts 4:9, 12; O'Reilly, *Word and Sign*, 444; Tannehill, "Functions of Peter's Mission Speeches," 33.

6

Four Roman Watches as Narrative Timestamps

INTRODUCTION

THE FIFTH ISSUE TO be discussed concerns the use of Roman time watches as structural markers in the passion and resurrection accounts of Mark to alert the implied audience to evaluate the characters in those narratives in light of the warnings issued in Jesus' parable of the Doorkeeper at the conclusion of the Olivet Discourse in Mark 13:34–36. The parable of the Doorkeeper warned those receiving the Gospel to act as those who are "alert" or on guard, and not as those who are "asleep." By using these time markers, the implied author will show, and the implied audience will look to see, whether the characters in the narrative are alert or asleep. These structural markers will appear in chapters 15 and 17 of this work. Even though they are the subject of a literary, critical analysis of Mark, they are structural markers employed by the actual/implied author in the development of the discourse to alert the implied audience that these are critical moments in the narrative to create, and especially evaluate, the character of the actors in the narrative.

Joanna Dewey openly objects to discrete, obvious divisions in the Gospel of Mark because of the work's use of oral/aural soundings, namely foreshadows and echoes, that she claims obfuscate structure.[1] Yet, even Dewey recognizes a central section to the Gospel.[2] Many recognize the tight flow of the narrative in the Passion account along a linear, chronological progression.[3] However, a linear analysis leads to linear outlines that do not seem to show what the implied author is doing with what he is saying. For instance, Williams outlines the Markan passion narrative as follows:

> III. Jesus' Death on the Cross and Resurrection (14:1—16:8)
>   A. Anointing at Bethany and Betrayal Plot (14:1-11)
>   B. The Last Supper (14:12-25)
>   C. Prayer and Arrest at Gethsemane (14:26-52)
>   D. Trial before Sanhedrin and Denials by Peter (14:52-72)
>   E. Trial before Pilate and Mocking by Soldiers (15:1-20)
>   F. Crucifixion and Burial (15:21-47)
>   G. Resurrection (16:1-8).[4]

Tolbert's outline emphasizes time markers in the Passion narrative, but is also linear:

> A. 14:1—16:8
>   1. 14:1-11—time reference; death plot, unnamed woman anoints Jesus for burial.
>   2. 14:12-26a—the supper
>   3. 14:26b-52—on the Mount of Olives
>   4. 14:53-72—Jesus affirms identity; Peter denies
>   5. 15:1-15—Jesus before Pilate
>   6. 15:16-39—crucifixion
>   7. 15:40—16:8 Epilogue[5]

---

1. Dewey, "Mark as Interwoven Tapestry," 221-36. However, this writer is not persuaded that the falling of the text back on itself through foreshadows and echoes obfuscates and precludes the geographical structure of the Wilderness, Galilee, the Way, Jerusalem, and the Tomb (which will be discussed more fully in chapter 7). The actual author may be doing more with these echoes than providing a mnemonic device for the presenter and reinforcing themes for the listener. These repetitions may actually be a means of communicating the implied author's theological themes and messages that will be used by the implied audience to create character.

2. Dewey, "Mark as Interwoven Tapestry," 229; "Mark as Aural Narrative," 53. Dewey's description of the central section sounds like structure to this writer. However, it does appear that units can function in multiple ways within a narrative. See Geddert, *Watchwords*, 78.

3. Williams, "Does Mark's Gospel Have an Outline?," 521-22.

4. Williams, "Does Mark's Gospel Have an Outline?," 525.

5. Tolbert, *Sowing the Gospel*, 314-15. However, Tolbert's more detailed outline shows the relationship of many of the units to one another, and her commentary on this section emphasizes much of what the implied author is doing with what he is saying.

THE FOUR ROMAN WATCHES IN THE PARABLE OF THE DOORKEEPER

Closer to what this author understands to be the implied author's emphasis, is introduced in the programmatic nature of the parable of the "Lord of the House" or "Doorkeeper" at the conclusion of the Olivet Discourse in Mark 13:34–36.[6]

Others have more fully developed the programmatic nature of the parable of the Lord of the House, or the Doorkeeper, focusing on the four Roman watches listed in Mark 13:35, "evening ... midnight ... cockcrow ... early morning" (ὀψὲ ... μεσονύκτιον ... ἀλεκτοροφωνίας ... πρωΐ).[7] The parallels between the four Roman Watches in Mark 13 and the narrative in Mark 14 may be laid out as follows:

Four (Roman) Watches of the Night	Jesus Keeps Watch during the Night
Evening (ὀψὲ) (13:35)	"Evening" (ὀψὲ) (Last supper 14:17)
Midnight (μεσονύκτιον) (13:35)	"Midnight" [μεσονύκτιον][8] (Judas's betrayal and the disciples' abandonment of Jesus, 14:37–41)

---

6. It appears that R. H. Lightfoot may have been the first to connect the watches in the parable of the Doorkeeper to the passion account in Mark 14–15: "It is very noticeable that in the Passion narrative of this gospel the last hours of the Lord's life are reckoned at three-hour intervals, which is also the method adopted in 13[35]—an exactness of temporal reckoning to which St. Mark is usually indeed a stranger" (Lightfoot, *Mark*, 53).

7. Geddert, *Watchwords*, 89–103; Stock, *Mark*, 346–57; Kuruvilla, *Mark*, 294–95; Shepherd, *Markan Sandwich Stories*, 270–71.

8. There is no explicit mention of "midnight" (μεσονύκτιον) in Mark 14:37–41. The timing is suggested from the following: (1) the evening watch is mentioned in 14:17 and ended at 9:00 P.M. ("When it was evening [ὀψίας] he came with the twelve"); (2) Jesus refers to "one hour" having passed in 14:37 ("Simon, are you asleep? Could you not keep watch for one hour?"); (3) Jesus comes back to the disciples three times (14:37, 40, 41), implying the passage of three hours; (4) this effectively depicts Jesus' arrest as occurring at midnight. See Kuruvilla, *Mark*, 308n4. Geert van Oyen suggests that the religious trial of Jesus takes place at midnight (Oyen, "Intercalation and Irony," 968). Geddert suggests that midnight is not specifically mentioned to manage eschatological expectations with the hour: "The fact that Mark is describing, not just any night, but a Passover night, adds eschatological colouring to the statement, for it was widely held that eschatological fulfillment was to be expected during the Passover night, perhaps even specifically at the midnight hour.... In the Synoptic tradition, 'midnight' had very strong eschatological overtones of its own, quite apart from being the name of one of the night watches (cf. Matt 25:6). Perhaps the reason 'midnight' is not specified as the time of the Gethsemane 'watch' is that Mark does not want to over-stress the eschatological significance of the Gethsemane scene itself. After all, it is the whole passion, not

Cockcrow (ἀλεκτοροφωνία) (13:35)	"Cockcrow" (ἀλεκτοροφωνία) (Peter's denial, 14:68, 72)
Early morning (πρωΐ) (13:35)	"Early morning" (πρωΐ) (Jesus handed over to the Romans, 15:1)

THE FOUR ROMAN WATCHES AT THE GARDEN OF GETHSEMANE

Verbal echoes to the parable of the Doorkeeper are also found in the narrative at the garden of Gethsemane where Jesus prays and urges the disciples to keep watch; but they sleep:

Threefold Command in the Parable	Threefold Command in the Garden
"He commanded the doorkeeper to stay on the alert (γρηγορῇ)" 13:34	"My soul is deeply grieved to the point of death; remain here and keep watch (γρηγορεῖτε)" 14:34
"Therefore, be on the alert (γρηγορεῖτε)" 13:35	"Simon, are you sleeping (καθεύδεις)? Are you not strong one hour to keep watch (γρηγορῆσαι)?" 14:37
"And what I say to you, I say to all, 'Be on the alert (γρηγορεῖτε).'" 13:37	"Keep watch (γρηγορεῖτε) and pray" 14:38

The dangers of sleep (καθεύδω) are underscored in both the parable and the garden (Mark 13:36; 14:37, 40, 41).

THE FOUR ROMAN WATCHES AT THE PASSION AND RESURRECTION

These time stamps do not cease with the trial of Jesus before Pilate. The outer parameters of the Roman watches, "evening" (ὀψέ) and "early morning" (πρωΐ), reoccur in the narrative following the crucifixion (Mark 15:42; 16:2).[9] These textual time stamps seem to provide the struc-

---

only the midnight arrest in the garden, which constitutes 'the hour' that has arrived and that fulfills, on one level, at least, eschatological expectations" (Geddert, *Watchwords*, 282–83n51; *Mark*, 324).

9. Perhaps only the outer watches, evening and early morning, are mentioned because there was not relevant activity during the Sabbath. Jesus is placed in the tomb on the *evening* of the Sabbath, and the next activity is the women coming forth in the *early morning* following the Sabbath. Even Jesus is not active during the Sabbath. He said that he will not rise until the third day (see Mark 8:31; 9:31; 10:33–34).

ture of 13:34—16:8 and show what the implied author is *doing* with what he is *saying* by not only demonstrating the positive example of "being alert" (through the faithfulness of Jesus) and the negative example of not being alert (through the failure of the disciples), but by providing the continuation of that theme following the crucifixion in 15:42—16:8. In particular, it was becoming evening (ὀψὲ) when Joseph of Arimathea obtained Jesus' body from Pilate and the two of the women saw where Jesus was placed (15:42–47). Then in 16:2 it was early morning (πρωΐ) when three women came to the tomb. In other words, the outworking of the parable of the doorkeeper continues for disciples beyond the initial cycle of the Passion. This broadened application is explicitly stated in the parable of the Doorkeeper when Jesus expands his exhortation from "you" (ὑμῖν), meaning the four disciples with him, to "all" (πᾶσιν) in Mark 13:37. As Geddert suggests:

> The broadening of the application . . . is then not simply *expanding an audience* from four disciples to the whole group (within the story line) or from Jesus' first apostles to Mark's audience. It is *universalizing a model*: Jesus will serve as model doorkeeper for all disciples until he returns as the glorious Son of Man.[10]

This continued application of the parable of the doorkeeper is unfolded in the final section of the Gospel with some characters who have hitherto not acted in the discourse (Joseph of Arimathea, Mary Magdalene, and Salome).[11] Through this extension of the watches following the crucifixion, the implied author is showing the implied audience that the exhortations of the parable of the Doorkeeper are still in effect, even after previous failures, and the characters in the narrative should be evaluated based on whether they act as those who are "alert" or "asleep." This will be explicitly discussed in the analysis of the woman at the crucifixion and the tomb in Mark 15:42—16:8.

---

10. Geddert, *Watchwords*, 93.

11. It is true that the three women were mentioned in 15:40, but they will be major actors in the development of the discourse around the tomb. Mary, the mother of Joses and James, may be the one who acted in 3:20–21, 31–35. Pilate and the Centurion were also actors in Jesus' passion, and the young man at the tomb, though not the same young man who fled in 14:53, will be connected through lexical links with that earlier young man for theological purposes. See Kuruvilla, "Naked Runaway and the Enrobed Reporter," 527–45; Lincoln, "Promise and the Failure," 293; Williams, *Other Followers*, 191.

7

The Geographical/Chiastic Structure of the Gospel of Mark

THE SIXTH INTERPRETIVE ISSUE concerns the narrative, chiastic structure of the Gospel of Mark around geographical markers, namely:

    Wilderness,
        Galilee,
             (the) Way,
        Jerusalem, and
    Tomb.

A unique feature of the Gospel of Mark is that there is only one journey to Jerusalem. That journey begins in Galilee where people generally respond positively to Jesus and ends in Jerusalem where Jesus is crucified. Therefore, Galilee and Jerusalem contrast with one another. However, the wilderness and the tomb have many common themes. It will be shown that this geographical outline relies on the implied author's structural clues in Mark and manages expectations and governs interpretation for the recipient of the Gospel (the implied audience) as a broader theological construct out of which particular narratives should be heard and understood. A full appreciation of this geographical structure may only be acquired through multiple exposures to the narrative.

OVERALL STRUCTURE

The overall structure of the Gospel of Mark is built around geographical locations where the activities take place. A proposed chiastic structure built around the geography of Mark is as follows:[1]

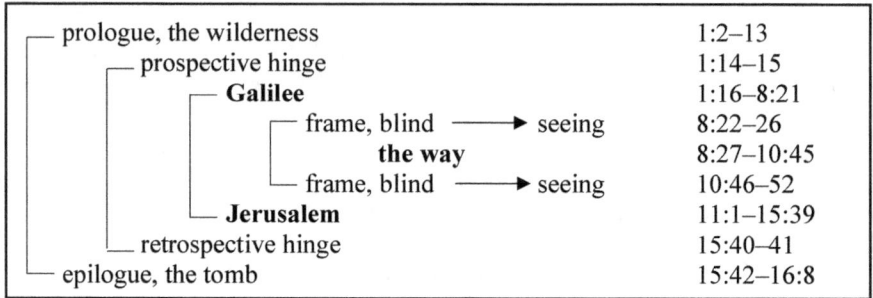

```
— prologue, the wilderness                          1:2–13
   — prospective hinge                              1:14–15
      — Galilee                                     1:16–8:21
         — frame, blind ——→ seeing                  8:22–26
            the way                                 8:27–10:45
         — frame, blind ——→ seeing                  10:46–52
      — Jerusalem                                   11:1–15:39
   — retrospective hinge                            15:40–41
— epilogue, the tomb                                15:42–16:8
```

The geographical locations are each central to the activity in the narrative. There is also a logic to the chiastic structure of the book as episodes move from the receptive geography in and around the sea of Galilee to the antagonistic religious capital of Jerusalem. In the Galilee section where people are generally receptive of the message of Jesus, it will be unusual to find the resistance of Jesus' mother and Herodias. Furthermore, the antagonism around Jerusalem may have an effect on women being portrayed as fallible, like the men, under pressure. The center of the chiasm which takes place on the way from Galilee to Jerusalem focuses on the "way" of suffering for Jesus and his followers. There is also a circular opening in the barren land of the wilderness and closing at the terminal land of the tomb that provides hope for the audience of renewal out of threatening chaos and death. Because women specifically appear in the area of the tomb at the end of the Gospel, the implied audience will look for significance from the parallel wilderness at the beginning of the Gospel.

---

1. See Iersel, *Mark*, 84. The chiastic structure of Mark around broad, geographical references is acknowledged by many. See also Kuruvilla, *Mark*, 5; Stock, *Mark*, 25–30; "Structure of Mark," 291–96; France, *Gospel of Mark*, 11–15; Voelz, *Mark*, 49. Many who do not identify an overall chiastic structure of the Gospel see a basic two-fold structure around Galilee and Jerusalem. Mann, *Mark*, 177–79; Tolbert, *Sowing the Gospel*, 113–21; Cranfield, *Mark*; Lane, *Mark*, 29–32; Williams, "Does Mark's Gospel Have an Outline?," 505–25.

The Galilee Section

Following the Gospel's title (Mark 1:1), a prologue takes place with John and Jesus in the wilderness (ἔρημος, cf. Mark 1:3, 4, 12, 13). The wilderness focus of the prologue transitions to Jesus' activity in Galilee (Mark 1:14). Each time Jesus calls disciples, he is reported to be near the sea of Galilee. There are then episodes at or near the sea of Galilee in Mark 1:16—8:21.[2] In Galilee, Jesus proclaims the gospel of the kingdom and manifests who he is to those who follow him through teachings and miraculous works. Except for the religious leaders, Jesus is generally well received by the crowds in the region of Galilee.

The Central Section

The central section contains Jesus' only journey to Jerusalem from the region of Galilee. This journey also unfolds his three-fold teaching on suffering as the "way" for a disciple to follow him to glory (Mark 8:31—9:29; 9:30—10:31; 10:32-45). The inner structure of the central section is as follows:

> The blind see; Who is Jesus? (Mark 8:22-30)
> 1. Prediction of Jesus' suffering—misunderstanding by Peter—instruction through Elijah (Mark 8:31—9:29)
> 2. Prediction of Jesus' suffering—misunderstanding by the Twelve—instruction through Moses (Mark 9:30—10:31)
> 3. Prediction of Jesus' suffering—misunderstanding by James and John—instruction through Jesus (Mark 10:32-45)
>
> The blind see; Who is Jesus? (Mark 10:46—11:10/11)[3]

The two miracles where Jesus heals the blind in Mark 8:22-26 and 10:46-52 surrounding Jesus' explanation "on the way" to Jerusalem (Mark 8:31—10:45) appear to be typologically integrated with the narrative they enclose. Like the first blind man, the disciples do not fully see (perceive) who Jesus is. The two-stage healing of the blind man in Mark 8:22-26 is not about Jesus' inability to heal but about an advance in perception which Jesus is going to bring "on the way" to Jerusalem. The disciples see that Jesus is Messiah (Mark 8:27-30), but they do not perceive that his

---

2. See Mann, *Mark*, 178-79.
3. See Mann, *Mark*, 183-84.

mission involves suffering; they are resistant to this message (Mark 8:31–33). The two-stage healing is a picture of what ought to have happened with the disciples during the central section of the narrative. However, they do not gain acuity of perception; they are recalcitrant. On the other hand, the healing of Bartimaeus is a picture of what a true disciple looks like. Bartimaeus is conscious of his own frailty (blindness), discerning of Jesus' person ("Son of David") and leaves all that he has (his cloak) to follow Jesus to Jerusalem (Mark 10:46–52). The healings that enclose the narrative "on the way" to Jerusalem are integral to the message of the narrative they surround.

The Jerusalem Section

Some clarification is needed to identify where the "Jerusalem" portion of the Gospel of Mark begins.[4] Many end the central section, "on the way" to Jerusalem, at Mark 10:52 with the healing of blind Bartimaeus.[5] Accordingly, the Jerusalem section begins at 11:1 with Jesus' triumphal entry into the city. There is no question that at the end of Mark's triumphal entry, Jesus enters the city of Jerusalem and the temple (Mark 11:11). However, much of the unit still anticipates Jesus' entrance into the city (see Mark 11:1, "and when they were near to Jerusalem"; 11:2 "Go into the village before you"). Furthermore, the term "road" or "way" (ὁδός) used to describe the journey to Jerusalem in the central section (Mark 8:27; 9:33; 10:17; 10:32, 46, 52; cf. 1:2–3), is repeated in Mark 11:8 when it states that "many spread their garments in the road." Therefore, the central section may extend into 11:1–11 or at least 11:1–10. The procession into Jerusalem and Mark 11:11, may function as a transitional section from the "way" to "Jerusalem."[6] Just as the first healing of the blind

---

4. Joanna Dewey argues that there is no clear dividing point because of "overlapping sequences and intertwined content" (Dewey, "Mark as Interwoven Tapestry," 231–32). Without denying these echoes and foreshadows, the following discussion will textually argue for a transitional division in the narrative.

5. Iersel, *Mark*, 270; Lane, *Mark*, 292–94; Stock, *Mark*, 230–87 (cf. 288); "Structure of Mark," 295; Cranfield, *Mark*, 266 (cf. 347); Williams, *Other Followers*, 167; "Does Mark's Gospel Have an Outline?," 524; Nineham, *Mark,* 221 (cf. 287); Tolbert, *Sowing the Gospel*, 178–79; France, *Mark*, 320–21 (cf. 426–27); Kuruvilla, *Mark*, 166; Voelz, *Mark*, 49.

6. See Mann, *Mark*, 179, 183–85. Similarly, Tolbert understands 11:1–11 to "overlap at the edges" with the central section and the Jerusalem section (Tolbert, *Sowing the Gospel*, 118–19).

man (Mark 8:22–26) is followed by a revelation of who Jesus is (Messiah) through Peter's confession that he is the Christ (Mark 8:27–30),[7] so too the last healing of the blind man, Bartimaeus (10:46–52), is followed by a public revelation of who Jesus is (Messiah) through his procession into Jerusalem (11:1–10).[8] However, Jesus' entry into Jerusalem is not triumphal, but anticlimactic by both Jewish[9] and Roman[10] standards. Jesus enters the temple as the Davidite (11:10), but instead of setting up his rule, he looks and leaves (11:11) foreshadowing difficulties with the temple to follow in the next portion of the narrative.[11]

Therefore, for the purposes of this study, the section "in and around Jerusalem" will begin with the transitional verse in Mark 11:11, and more properly, with the first intercalation beginning in Mark 11:12 regarding the cursing of the fig tree and the cleansing of the temple (Mark 11:12–14, 11:15–19, 11:20–28).

Discontinuity between Galilee and Jerusalem

There is discontinuity between Galilee (Mark 1:16—8:21) and Jerusalem (Mark 11:12—15:41).[12] In Galilee, Jesus calls and sends out his disciples (Mark 3:7–19; 6:7–13, 30–32). In Jerusalem there is no calling or sending of disciples. In Galilee there is miraculous ministry including exorcisms, but in Jerusalem there are no healings or exorcisms (only the cursing of the fig tree in Mark 11:12–14, 20–25, and the implicit resurrection in Mark 16:1–8). In Galilee, there is an imposition of silence about what Jesus has done (see Mark 1:40–45), but in Jerusalem there is an open proclamation of who Jesus is (Mark 14:66–72) which leads to his death. In Galilee a programmatic parable of the soils allows the audience to identify the different responses to Jesus and his message (Mark 4:1–20). In Jerusalem, a programmatic parable of the vineyard and tenants allows the audience to understand the final events in the narrative including the

---

7. Bateman, "Defining the Titles," 541–42.

8. Bateman, "Defining the Titles," 541–45.

9. See Zech 9:9; Gen 49:10–12. See also 1 Sam 8:10–11, 17; 2 Kgs 9:13; Ps 118:26.

10. Catchpole, "Triumphal Entry," 319–21, sets out parallel examples of entrances into Jerusalem including that of Alexander, Apollonius, Simon Maccabeus, Marcus Agrippa, Archelaus. See also Duff, "March of the Divine Warrior," 59–64; Kuruvilla, *Mark*, 244.

11. Kuruvilla, *Mark*, 245.

12. Eck, *Galilee and Jerusalem*.

rejection and suffering of Jesus that lies ahead at the hands of the religious leaders (Mark 12:1–12). In Galilee the narrative is fast paced with 31 occurrences of "immediately," but in Jerusalem, time slows down with only 6 occurrences of "immediately"; the last week forming one-third of the entire narrative, and the last 24 hours forming one-sixth of the narrative.

Continuity between the Wilderness and the Tomb

The wilderness and the tomb have numerous similarities. Both are uninhabited; both are the dwelling places of demons (Mark 1:13; 5:2); both have a movement in Mark's story from the outside to the inside (1:12; 15:46), and from the inside to the outside (1:13–14; 16:8); both contain a messenger (ἄγγελος/νεανίσκος) with narrative comments about the messenger's eschatological clothing, speaking concerning the advent of Jesus (1:3–4; 16:5–6); and both include a call to follow (1:17, 20; 16:7).[13] As will be explained below, these similarities provide a circularity to the narrative that gives the implied audience hope in the midst of loss, chaos, death, and fear.

The geographical structure of Mark will be discussed in the following analysis of the passages involving women as it contributes to an understanding of a passage within the architectural structure and logical flow of the narrative as a whole. Other gospel accounts indicate that Jesus had multiple journeys to Jerusalem, so Mark's account is unique in that it describes a single journey to Jerusalem. By this fact alone it becomes evident that the actual/implied author is doing something with what he is saying about Jesus' travels on the way to Jerusalem. This manner of laying out the discourse of the Gospel has an impact on the implied audience, even if it only becomes fully aware of the structure upon multiple exposures to the narrative. The implied audience will use the presentations of the discourse to evaluate characters and construct their understanding of who characters are—especially those characters who stand in stark relief with the general nature of those in each individual, geographical section, or surprisingly change from the portrayal of women in earlier parts of the narrative. Women are never left out of the geographical structure of the Gospel but are given a "presence" and "visibility" throughout the different parts.

13. See Stock, *Mark*, 26–28.

Part 2

Narrative Analysis of Passages Involving Women in the Gospel of Mark

THE SECOND MAJOR SECTION of this study contains the heart of the work in its narrative analysis of all of the passages in the Gospel of Mark involving women including: (1) The healing of Simon's mother-in-law (Mark 1:29–31); (2) Jesus' Relatives [Mother] and the Beelzebul controversy (3:20–35); (3) Jairus's daughter and the woman with a hemorrhage of blood (5:21–43); (4) Herodias, her daughter, and the beheading of John the Baptist (6:7–32); (5) the Syrophoenician woman (7:34–40); (6) the poor widow who gave at the temple (12:41–44); (6) the death plot of the religious leaders and the anointing of Jesus at Bethany (14:1–11); (7) the maidservant's trial of Peter (14:53–72); (8) the women at Jesus' crucifixion (15:40–41), and (9) the women at the tomb (15:42—16:8).

The analysis will focus on a narrative interpretation of the Markan passages considering the theoretical issues and literary structure discussed in Part One of this work. A narrative analysis of these Markan passages provides the recipient (implied audience/actual audience), whether hearing or reading the Gospel, with the actual/implied author's presentation of women that at times distinguishes them from other, male, fallible followers of Jesus, and at times shows them to be quite similar to fallible male followers and opponents of Jesus based upon their response to the revelation that has been given to them. Within this analytical framework, the focus will be on "how" the formation of women characters has taken place by the implied author, and how characterization is created by the implied audience.

8

The Healing of Simon's Mother-in-Law (Mark 1:29–31)

THE FIRST NARRATIVE PASSAGE involving women in the Gospel of Mark discusses the healing of Simon's mother-in-law from a fever. The significance of this short narrative, comprised of just three verses, will become evident from the placement of the narrative in its immediate context, and in the broader context of the Gospel of Mark.

INTRODUCTION

Performance criticism, or an oral-aural presentation of the text, focuses on the progressive nature of the narrative as presented from beginning to end for the first-time reader/listener, rather than on the final form of the narrative which is only discerned upon second, third, or multiple readings/listenings.[1] The argument is that texts were originally heard in their progressive development and not with an understanding of the whole. Certainly, a first reading, or hearing, differs from a subsequent reading or hearing; however, it does not seem necessary to limit the interpretation of a text to only one approach. Those who originally presented the Gospel may have memorized it, or at least read it multiple times before reading it aloud. Therefore, the presenters had a sense of the whole, and their presentations may have emphasized significant themes for the first-time

---

1. See Moore, *Literary Criticism*, 84–88. See also Bassler, "Parable of the Loaves," 157–72; Rhoads et al., *Mark as Story*; Tannehill, *Gospel According to Luke*, 1.

listener.² Furthermore, a text may have been read aloud more than once for an audience. Accordingly, a strict dichotomy between first and subsequent readings may be an overemphasis. Mark's account of the healing of Simon's mother-in-law occurs early in the narrative and benefits from both the perspective of a first-time reading and a subsequent reading.

A FIRST READING/HEARING OF THE NARRATIVE

The Gospel of Mark opens with a prologue that foreshadows many themes that will be developed in the book including: geographical themes (wilderness, Galilee, Jerusalem, the way); the centrality of Jesus through the multiple witnesses of Isaiah, John the Baptizer, the Father, and the Spirit; the identity of Jesus as the Son of God; and a story that is characterized by an authoritative revelation of Jesus in the midst of an ambiguous human response.³ Many of these themes are only fully discerned upon a subsequent reading/hearing of the gospel, but they still express themselves in the first exposure to the text. As the account continues, the audience will be able to identify the echoes of earlier voices.⁴

The wilderness focus of the prologue (cf. ἔρημος in 1:3, 4, 12), transitions to Jesus' activity in Galilee (1:14). Each time Jesus calls disciples, he is reported to be near the sea of Galilee.⁵ Four disciples are explicitly

---

2. Rhoads, Dewey, and Michie speculate that "ancient storytellers brought out the dynamics of the story in their telling, putting their stamp on the story, and shaping it to each particular audience. The performer used voice, volume, pace, gestures, facial expressions, and bodily movement to express an interpretation of the story and to engender certain impacts on different audiences. The performance would stimulate the audience's imagination and bring out the emotion, the humor, and the irony of the story" (Rhoads et al., *Mark as Story* loc. 178–92).

3. See Tolbert, *Sowing the Gospel*, 108–13.

4. In a more modern sense, one might liken these foreshadows in the prologue to the overture of a musical. The first time the audience hears an overture, all of the music is unfamiliar. However, it sets up themes that are revisited later in the show. Then, upon subsequent listening, the overture is filled with meaning from the fullness of the musical. Present-day audiences seem to more easily comprehend literary theory expressed through the mediums of auditory and visual expression. The foreshadows of the prologue will resonate with the audience upon an initial reading/listening, and then become more explicitly meaningful upon subsequent readings/listenings.

5. The call of Simon and Andrew, James, and John in 1:16–20 ("and going by the sea of Gailiee," Καὶ παράγων παρὰ τὴν θάλασσαν τῆς Γαλιλαίας); the call of Levi in 2:13–14 ("and he went out again by the sea," Καὶ ἐξῆλθεν πάλιν παρὰ τὴν θάλασσαν); the call of the Twelve in 3:7–19 ("And Jesus with his disciples withdrew to the sea," Καὶ ὁ Ἰησοῦς μετὰ τῶν μαθητῶν αὐτοῦ ἀνεχώρησεν πρὸς τὴν θάλασσαν).

The Healing of Simon's Mother-in-Law

named in 1:16–20: Simon, Andrew, James, and John. They will reappear by name in this brief narrative. Jesus then begins to demonstrate who he is through a sequence of cures, the last of which involves a conflict (1:21—2:12).[6] These cures have an alternating spiritual/physical pattern:

A (spiritual): casting out a demon (1:21–28)

    B (physical): healing Simon's mother-in law (1:29–31)

        B'/A' (physical/spiritual): healing many with diseases & casting out many demons (1:32–39)

    B'' (physical): healing man with leprosy (1:40–45)

A''/B''' (spiritual/physical): forgiveness of sins/healing the paralytic (2:1–12)

There is also an interchange between healing individuals (A, B, A'', B''), and healing the multitude (B'/A'). Simon's mother-in-law is the first individual physically healed in 1:29–31:

> And immediately after going out of the synagogue, they came into the house of Simon and Andrew with James and John. And Simon's mother-in-law was lying down with a fever, and immediately they spoke with him concerning her. And coming, he raised her up taking hold of her hand, and the fever left her, and she was serving them. (author's translation)

---

6. Mann, *Mark*, 180–81. The overall structure of this section is construed differently by others who group the controversies as a unit in 2:1—3:6. See Harrington, *New Testament Message*, 24–25; Beernaert, "Jésus Controversé," 129–49. Joanna Dewey groups the controversies as a unit (Dewey, *Markan Public Debate*, 110). However, it seems to this writer that some of Dewey's parallels are strained. For instance, Dewey combines the call of Levi with the pericope about Jesus eating with sinners in 2:13–17. This grouping enables her to see a pattern in 2:13–17 and 2:23–27 where the activity begins out of doors and then continues indoors (Dewey, *Markan Public Debate*, 113). However, this arrangement of the text appears to have overlooked the textual clues that structure the narrative around Jesus going by the sea to call the four disciples (1:16–20), Levi (2:13–14), and the Twelve (3:7–19). With these textual clues in view, it seems better to break the narrative into an alternating pattern:

A Call of four disciples (1:16–20)
B Jesus demonstrates who he is through a sequence of cures, the last involving a conflict (1:21—2:12)
A' Call of Levi (2:13–14)
B' Jesus demonstrates who he is through a sequence of conflicts, the last involving a cure (2:15—3:6)
A'' Choice of the Twelve (3:7–10)

This is not to say that correlations do not exist between 2:1–12 and 3:1–6, but these correlations do not seem to be significant enough to move 2:1–12 from the narrative logic of the units that precede it in 1:21–45.

Interestingly, the location of Simon's mother-in-law is in the house, the usual, first-century location of a woman in Israel. However, this typical location will be the place where a major theme of "service" is first shown to the implied audience. Many interpret the "serving" response of Simon's mother-in-law merely as a verification of her healing.[7] However, even in a first reading/hearing of the Gospel, the word describing her service (διακονέω) was already used in close proximity of angels who served, or ministered, to Jesus after his temptation in the wilderness (Mark 1:13).[8] Therefore, whatever Simon's mother-in-law is doing in response to Jesus' healing is similar to what angels did for Jesus after his temptation. In both cases, that ministry may have included table service, which appears to be what Simon's mother-in-law is providing in the house. This similarity would not be lost on the implied audience in Greek.

In addition, every miracle in this broader section of the narrative (1:21—2:12) includes a *response*, and the action of Simon's mother-in-law is the only *positive* response in the entire section:[9]

A (spiritual): casting out a demon (1:21–28)
    [An improper response of a demon (24–26)]
    B (physical): healing Simon's mother-in law (1:29–31)
        [A proper response of Simon's mother-in law (31)]
        B'/A' (physical/spiritual): healing many with diseases & casting out many demons (1:32–39)
            [An improper response of the disciples, corrected, (35–39)]
            B" (physical): healing man with leprosy (1:40–45)
                [An improper response of a healed man, magnified (44–45)]
                A"/B'" (spiritual/physical): forgiveness of sins/healing the paralytic (2:1–12)
                    [An improper response of scribes, controversy (2:7)]

---

7. Corley, *Private Women*, 88; Williams, *Other Followers*, 94; Nineham, *Mark*, 81; Lane, *Mark*, 78. Some others interpret the woman's activity as a proclamation that she is free from Sabbath restrictions. See Stock, *Mark*, 80; Iersel, *Mark*, 138–39.

8. "And the angels served, or ministered, to him" (καὶ οἱ ἄγγελοι διηκόνουν αὐτῷ). See also Tolbert, *Sowing the Gospel*, 137n20.

9. It may be argued that the onlookers appear to have a positive response to the healing of the lame man when the narrator states that "all were amazed and glorified God saying that we have never seen this." However, it is questionable whether the term for "amazed" (ἐξίστημι) is explicitly positive. It is used in the LXX for astonishment mingled with fear (Gen 43:33; Ruth 3:8; 1 Sam 14:15). The term in Mark is used elsewhere with the same sense (Mark 5:42; 6:51; see also Acts 2:7, 12). Nevertheless, the onlookers do glorify God (δοξάζειν τὸν θεόν). Therefore, one might say that this is a mixed response by the people, but the response of the religious leaders is clearly negative (Mark 2:6–7), and it is the focus of the unit—the reason for the healing.

The first-time reader/hearer would notice this responsive contrast in the progress of the narrative once again magnifying the *service* of Simon's mother-in-law.[10]

Characterization happens by means of association with other characters, and the implied audience would make these connections from the implied author's discourse. Moreover, the use of names in the response to Jesus' healing of the multitude highlights a contrast between Simon and his mother-in-law. As set forth above, the names of all four of the disciples called in 1:16–20 are repeated in 1:29: "And immediately after going out of the synagogue, they came into the house of Simon and Andrew with James and John." However, in the response to Jesus' healing of the multitude, Jesus goes away to a secluded place (ἔρημος τόπον) to pray.[11] Only Simon is specifically identified among those searching for him: "and Simon and those with him hunted for him" (1:36). The diffusion of those with Simon, and the highlighting of Simon once again reminds the reader of the anonymous woman earlier identified as "*Simon's* mother-in-law" in 1:29. This linking of names sets-up an implied comparison between the woman and Simon. In response to Jesus' personal healing, Simon's mother-in-law served them. However, in response to Jesus' healing of the multitude, Simon hunted, or tracked down, Jesus (κατεδίωξεν, third person singular). This term is used elsewhere to describe the pursuit of someone in a hostile sense.[12] Then Simon and his companions say: "All are seeking you" (1:37). These words appear to be a rebuke, or correction, of Jesus for secluding himself. Then Jesus redirects their attention away from the multitudes to his purpose of proclaiming his message in other rural towns ("κωμόπολις," 1:38). Jesus' correction of Simon's response may be the first indication in the Gospel that these eager followers may not be perfectly aligned with what Jesus is doing. It is a flag for the implied audience who has identified with the followers. Jesus' correction also places in stark relief the unique response of Simon's mother-in-law who alone offers to *serve* them.[13]

---

10. See Malbon, "Minor Characters," 59.

11. Because there is not a "wilderness" per se in Galilee, the use of the term ἔρημος may echo the spiritual testing of the temptation (cf. Mark 1:12–13).

12. See LXX of Psalms of Solomon 15:8, "For they will flee from the holy ones like those *pursued* in battle." See also BDAG s.v. "καταδιώκω."

13. Simon's mother-in-law is being shown to be an "exemplar" in her service while Simon is showing himself to be a "fallible follower" early in the narrative as he attempts to redirect Jesus' activity. See Malbon, "Minor Characters," 65.

The first-time reader/hearer of Mark is given many contextual clues through the repetition of terms and the contrasting responses to Jesus' healing to suspect that the serving response of Simon's mother-in-law was not only uniquely proper, but as significant as the service of angels after Jesus' temptation. After subsequent readings/hearings of the Gospel, these heuristic guesses will be fully validated.

SUBSEQUENT READINGS/HEARINGS OF THE NARRATIVE

Westerners are more adept at interpreting visual media than written media. Upon a first viewing of the movie *The Sixth Sense*, most audiences were stunned to realize at the end of the show that the child psychologist, Dr. Malcolm Crowe, was actually dead. And the reason the troubled boy, Cole Sear, was able to talk with Dr. Crowe was because he sees "dead people." Upon a re-viewing of the movie, the careful observer discovers clues throughout the show that point to Dr. Crowe being dead—his conversations with his wife and Cole's mother are one-sided; the color red prominently appears when the dead are near (red concrete, red clothes, a red door knob, red hats, red fingernails, a red balloon); Dr. Crowe mostly wears the same clothes he was wearing when he was shot; and rooms become cold whenever the dead are near—or are at least upset. Then when Dr. Crowe's wife drops his wedding ring, he suddenly realizes he has not been wearing it, and the past and the present merge in an awareness that he is in-fact dead. There are also parallels in the show—the former patient who shot Dr. Crowe also saw "dead people"; so by helping Cole, who now sees ghosts, Dr. Crowe is able to correct a fatal flaw in his care for an earlier patient. These subsequent viewings make the movie more fascinating for the viewer as the patterns, which were always there, become more evident. Similar insights, depths, and delights are present for subsequent readers and hearers of the Gospel of Mark. Since first-century audiences were more familiar with the written/oral presentation of story, they may have made connections sooner than modern readers.

As noted above, even though the four, male disciples who were explicitly called to follow Jesus in 1:16–20 are named (Simon, Andrew, James, and John) in the unit describing the healing of Simon's mother-in-law (1:29), she is anonymous. Often in Mark's Gospel, the unnamed are exemplary followers of Christ who express faith: the Gerasene demoniac

(Mark 5:1–20); the woman with the flow of blood (5:25–34); the Syrophoenician woman (7:24–30); the widow who gave at the temple (12:41–44); the woman who anointed Jesus for his death (14:3–9); and the many women who came up with Jesus from Galilee to Jerusalem (15:41). Therefore, in the overarching pattern of the Gospel, Simon's mother-in-law is the first of a group of faithful followers who are anonymous.

In addition, the service of Simon's mother-in-law adumbrates the major theme of "service" in Mark. In the central section of Mark, Jesus emphasizes the need for the disciples to serve:

> Calling them to Himself, Jesus said to them, "You know that those who are recognized as rulers of the Gentiles domineer over them; and their people in high position exercise authority over them. But it is not this way among you; rather, whoever wants to become prominent among you shall be your servant; and whoever wants to be first among you shall be slave of all. For even the Son of Man did not come to be served, but to serve, and to give His life as a ransom for many." (Mark 10:42–45, NASB 2020)

Some might object that the statement in Mark 1:31 only has the sense that Simon's mother-in-law was providing them "table service" and is not parallel to the service described in Mark 10:42–45.[14] However, a similar discussion of "service" in the central section of the Gospel clarifies that the service Jesus has in view includes "table service":

> And sitting down, He called the twelve and *said to them, "If anyone wants to be first, he shall be last of all and servant of all." And He took a child and placed him among them, and taking him in His arms, He said to them, "Whoever receives one child like this in My name receives Me; and whoever receives Me does not receive Me, but Him who sent Me."
>
> John said to Him, "Teacher, we saw someone casting out demons in Your name, and we tried to prevent him because he was not following us."
>
> But Jesus said, "Do not hinder him, for there is no one who will perform a miracle in My name, and be able soon afterward to speak evil of Me. For the one who is not against us is for us. *For whoever gives you a cup of water to drink because of your name as followers of Christ, truly I say to you, he shall by no means lose his reward.*" (Mark 9:35–41, NASB 2020) (emphasis added).

---

14. Corley, *Private Women*, 87.

In other words, serving children and serving water are the kind of activities for which disciples will be rewarded. The implied author's use of διακονέω infuses a character with positive value for the implied audience, first in the sense of "following," but second in elevating what could have been regarded as a mundane social activity (which was why it was relegated to womanhood) to an elevated social status.

Finally, the only other place in the Gospel of Mark where the verb for service (διακονέω) is used for people in the company of Jesus is in the description of the women who provided for Jesus' needs from Galilee to Jerusalem:

> Now there were also some women watching from a distance, among whom were Mary Magdalene, Mary the mother of James the Less and Joses, and Salome. When He was in Galilee, they used to follow Him and *serve* Him; and there were many other women who came up with Him to Jerusalem (Mark 15:40–41, NASB 2020, emphasis added).[15]

Here Mark describes women who have been a part of the story all along but have not been brought to the narrative's foreground. Even though three women are explicitly named in verse 40, they have functioned in the story as the ultimate expression of the anonymous in that their presence was active but unknown to the audience. And the essence of their activity was serving, or ministering (διακονέω) to Jesus—whatever that entailed. In their *service* they have multiplied and magnified the initial response of Simon's mother-in-law to her healing.

Service is the pattern of discipleship that Jesus is showing his followers, and the example he will give in Jerusalem—not by leading, *per se*, but by giving up his own life for them. The very first example of a person who follows in this pattern of service is Simon's mother-in-law, whose response to being healed was to *serve* them—even if what she provided was "table service."[16] To separate "table service" from the service of discipleship is to make a distinction without a difference—especially from the perspective of subsequent readings/listenings of the Gospel of Mark.

---

15. See Iersel, *Mark*, 117.

16. Others have correlated the response of Simon's mother-in-law to discipleship. See Lane, *Mark*, 78n128; Dewey, "Women in the Gospel of Mark," 22–23; Malbon, "Fallible Followers," 34–35; Iersel, *Mark*, 117, 138n33; Kuruvilla *Mark*, 38–39.

CONCLUSION

The implied author has employed a lexical description of Simon's mother-in-law that characterizes her for the implied audience as a faithful woman who responds properly to the healing she received from Jesus and foreshadows an essential message in the Gospel of Mark for followers of Jesus. Her act of service resonates with the prior act of angels and future acts by other women in the Gospel. The implied audience would view her response to healing as positive and be encouraged to similarly respond to revelation by serving.

This positive presentation of a woman in the Gospel of Mark will be followed by a more questionable presentation of another family member, the mother of Jesus, in Mark 3:20–35.

9

Jesus' Relatives (Mother) and the Beelzebul Controversy

(Mark 3:20–35)

(Outer Story 3:20–21; Inner Story 3:22–30; Outer Story 3:31–35)

THE SECOND PASSAGE DISCUSSING a woman in Mark's Gospel involves Jesus' mother in Mark 3:20–25. This passage is the first one in this analysis following the narrative technique of an intercalation. A full understanding of what the writer is doing with what he is saying is not evident until the outer and inner stories are read together leaving the audience with an ambivalent impression about Jesus' mother who is placed outside of the "house" throughout the narrative.

INTRODUCTION

In this passage, the outer story in Mark 3:20–21 is unique to the Gospel of Mark. The inner story in Mark 3:22–30 is told in different contexts in Matthew 9 and 12 and in Luke 11 and 12. Mark's resumption of the outer story in 3:31–35 is told on its own in Matthew 12:46–50 and Luke 8:19–21. Mark's intercalation adds material not found in the other synoptics and arranges the material in a way that is distinct from the synoptics.[1] This arrangement of the narratives not only enhances the audience's

1. For a more canonical approach to this narrative, see Malick, "Jesus' View of Women," 4–15.

understanding of the two narratives but also provides insight into the characterization of Jesus' family, including his mother. Jesus is the only character who appears in both stories:[2]

    A **Jesus** (3:20a)
        B Crowd (3:20b)
            C Relatives (3:21)
                D Scribes (3:22)
                      E **Jesus** (3:23–29)
                D' Scribes (3:30)
            C' Relatives (3:31)
        B' Crowd (3:32)
    A' **Jesus** (3:33–35)

Jesus is emphasized in the narratives by being at the beginning and ending of the outer story, and by being at the center of the inner story. Accordingly, what Jesus does and says is central to both of the stories.

Frank Kermode notes an audience's tendency not to give intercalations interpretive attention.[3] James Edwards is of the opinion that the middle story provides the key to the theological purpose of the stories.[4] However, Rhoads and Michie seem to be more correct in observing that the stories "illuminate and enrich each other."[5]

Telling stories through the use of intercalations invites the audience to compare and contrast the outer and inner stories[6] resulting in a new story outcome that includes, but also transcends, the component stories.[7] A key to interpreting an intercalation is to recognize the way in which the writer has brought the two stories together and yet holds them apart to produce an interpretation of the stories.[8] Robert Fowler explains that the technique invites the audience to hear/read "the framed episode in the light of the frame episode and vice versa" with the result that "neither episode has begun until both have begun, and neither is concluded until

---

2. Kuruvilla, *Mark*, 69.
3. Kermode, *Genesis of Secrecy*, 123.
4. Edwards, "Markan Sandwiches," 196.
5. Rhoads and Michie, *Mark as Story*, 189.
6. See Kermode, *Genesis of Secrecy*.
7. Shepherd, "Narrative Function of Markan Intercalation," 522–40.
8. Shepherd, "Narrative Function of Markan Intercalation," 523–25.

both are concluded."⁹ Shepherd describes the two stories as commenting on one another leading to a new outcome.¹⁰

NARRATIVE CONTEXT

As explained in Chapter 7 above, the overall structure of Mark is built around geographical locations:

> Title (1:1)
> Prologue, the Wilderness (1:2—15)
> > Galilee (1:16—8:21)
> > > Frame, blind →seeing (8:22—26)
> > > > The Way (8:27—10:45)
> > >
> > > Frame, blind →seeing (10:46—11:11)
> >
> > Jerusalem (11:12—15:41)
>
> Epilogue, the Tomb (15:42—16:8)¹¹

Following the Gospel's title (1:1) and prologue which takes place with John and Jesus in the wilderness (ἔρημος, cf. 1:3, 4, 12, 13) there are episodes at or near the sea of Galilee in Mark 1:16—8:21.¹² The unit immediately preceding this intercalation consists of Jesus' choice and selection of disciples (Mark 1:16—3:19). The structure of Mark 1:16—3:19 appears to be an interchange:¹³

---

9. Fowler, *Let the Reader Understand*, 143–44.

10. Shepherd, "Narrative Function of Markan Intercalation," 524. Picking up on dramatic irony in intercalations, F. Gerald Downing writes, "There is then a dramatic irony evoked, for the author and the hearer obviously understand more than the protagonists can, unable as the latter are to share in comparing and contrasting the stories which both link and separate them" (Downing, "Markan Intercalation," 120–21).

11. See Iersel, *Mark*, 84.

12. See Mann, *Mark*, 178–79.

13. The arrangement of this material is disputed. Joanna Dewey groups the controversies as a unit in a chiastic structure (Dewey, *Markan Public Debate*, 65–105):
A Healing of the paralytic (2:1–12)
B The call of Levi/eating with sinners (2:13–17)
C The sayings on fasting and on the old and new (2:18–22)
B' Plucking grain on the Sabbath (2:23–27)
A' The healing on the Sabbath (3:1–6)
See also Joel Williams, who follows Dewey (Williams, *Other Followers*, 98–102). Dewey's structure appears to overlook the repeated phrase "by the sea" (παρὰ τὴν θάλασσαν) with the calling of disciples (see Mark 1:16; 2:13; 3:7).

A Call of four disciples (1:16–20)
   B Jesus demonstrates who he is through a sequence of cures, the last involving a conflict (1:21—2:12)
A' Call of Levi (2:13–14)
   B' Jesus demonstrates who he is through a sequence of conflicts, the last involving a cure (2:15—3:6)
A" Choice of the Twelve (3:7–19)[14]

Significant to this study is the message communicated by the climactic choice of the Twelve. This choice includes many allusions to the exodus including "prepare the way," "forty" days (years) in the wilderness, and Israel coming to the "mountain." Now twelve are called on a mountain to be with Jesus, to preach, and to have authority over demons (Mark 3:13–14). What may be implied through the exodus allusions is the forming of a new Israel through the twelve disciples. In any case, these Twelve are to be close to Jesus and do many of the same things that he does. In listing and naming the twelve disciples, the narrator makes an anachronistic statement about Judas Iscariot "who also betrayed him" (Mark 3:19).[15] Clearly, this statement by the implied author/narrator is to inform the implied audience in advance of the development of the discourse so that they might anticipate what is coming in the narrative. This foreshadow about Judas may have significant meaning in the following intercalation where another group that is close to Jesus, his mother and brothers, are shown to be at odds with him.

The structure of the subunit in Mark 3:20—6:6 is concentric around the theme of Jesus' family:

A The true family of Jesus (3:20–35)
   B Teachings of Jesus (4:1–34)
   B' Miracles of Jesus (4:35—5:43)
A' The supposed family of Jesus (6:1–6)[16]

The entire subunit appears to revolve around how people respond to Jesus' revelation. In 3:20–35 the paradigm is set with examples of negative responses to Jesus' ministry by his family and the religious leaders. This sandwich of stories has been set up by the negative response of Judas at

---

14. Mann, *Mark*, 180. The structure of this unit is discussed more fully in chapter 8 under the Healing of Simon's Mother-in-Law in Mark 1:29–31.

15. Even though one could argue that this is a proleptic statement, this writer considers it anachronistic because it projects an event from the end of the narrative to its beginning. It does not properly fit within the present, historical, temporal setting.

16. See Mann, *Mark*, 181–82.

the edge of the previous unit. It is as if the character, Judas, and his act of betrayal, has been introduced for the implied audience in preparation for the characterization of Jesus' family, thereby alerting the implied audience to the introduction of characters that will be formed in the narrative incorporating what the implied audience might not yet understand.

THE OUTER STORY (MARK 3:20–21)

The outer story begins by providing the reader with a setting. Jesus entered a house (οἶκος). The term, "house," (οἶκος) will be played upon as a *Leitwort* throughout the intercalation with reference to the "house divided" (ἐὰν οἰκία ἐφ' ἑαυτὴν μερισθῇ) and the "house of the strong man" (τὴν οἰκίαν τοῦ ἰσχυροῦ) in the inner story (Mark 3:26–27), the physical "house" in the outer story, and Jesus' metaphorical "house" (his relatives) standing outside of the physical house (ἔξω στήκοντες).[17] An irony of the passage is that Jesus' mother is portrayed as being outside of the house— the usual domain of women—while Jesus is portrayed as being inside the house—the unusual domain for a man in the first century. The implied author is doing something which the implied audience will notice with this reversal of characters around the familiar context of the "house."

When Jesus entered a house, a crowd (ὄχλος) gathered with the result (ὥστε) that Jesus and his disciples were unable to eat bread (ἄρτον, probably a metonymy for a meal, Mark 3:20). When his "own people" (οἱ παρ' αὐτοῦ)[18] heard of this, they went out to seize or take custody[19] of him

---

17. See Shepherd, *Markan Sandwich Stories*, 114, 135.

18. The Western witnesses (D, W, *it*) move the focus away from Jesus' family to the scribes and others (περι αυτου οι γραμματεις και οι λοιποι). By expanding the cryptic reference to include the religious scholars, the Western witnesses show a correlation of Jesus' mother and brothers with the religious leaders in the intercalation. However, when the outer story resumes in 3:31, it is clear that this phrase referred to Jesus' mother and brothers (ἡ μήτηρ αὐτοῦ καὶ οἱ ἀδελφοὶ αὐτοῦ). Bruce Metzger observes: "The original reading οἱ παρ' αὐτοῦ ('his friends' or 'his relatives') apparently proved to be so embarrassing that D W *al* altered it to read, 'When *the scribes and the others* had heard about him, they went out to seize him, for they said, 'He is beside himself''' (Metzger, *Textual Commentary*, 70). See also Witherington, *Women in the Ministry of Jesus*, 86; Brown et al., *Mary in the New Testament*, 55–57. The difficulty of this passage may be a reason why it is omitted in the recent study by Jeffrey W. Aernie (see Aernie, *Narrative Discipleship* loc. 129n2).

19. This verb (κρατέω) has the sense of taking control of someone, seizing someone, or taking someone into custody. See BDAG s.v. "κρατέω." In Mark 6:17 the verb is used for the *arrest* of John the Baptizer. In Mark 12:12 and 14:1 it is used of the religious leaders' desire to *seize* Jesus. In Mark 14:44 Judas instructs those with him to *seize* the one

Jesus' Relatives (Mother) and the Beelzebul Controversy

saying that "he has lost his senses," or is out of his mind (ἐξέστη). The term, ἐξίστημι, can have the meaning of losing one's mind, or being out of one's senses.[20] This description directs the implied audience to a characterization of Jesus and his mother. Madness, insanity, evokes a complete loss of self-control. A loss of self-control is in itself non-masculine in the first century. To an extent, in an ironic manner, it portrays the character Jesus as approximating effeminacy, because of how women were often habituated as "normally" out of control. However, here the "mother" is associated with the brothers, "men," intensified by her being "out of the house" where she was habituated to belong. Then the extremely strong use of κρατέω, of which she is a participant, aligns her with an act belonging to the characters of men.

This section, unique to Mark, is clarified with the resumption of the outer story in Mark 3:31 where his "own people" are identified as his mother and his brothers.[21] The outer story has raised a tension in Jesus' household that will be suspended, but addressed indirectly, in the telling of a second story.

As Shepherd observes, discourse time continues between the two stories allowing for continuity in what otherwise might appear to be discontinuity in the narratives.[22]

THE INNER STORY (MARK 3:22–30)

The outer story breaks off prior to its completion, and an inner story commences describing a conflict between Jesus and the learned, Jerusalem scholars[23] who accuse him, not of being out of his mind or beside himself,

---

whom he kisses. In Mark 14:46 it is used of *seizing* Jesus in the garden. In Mark 14:51 it is used to describe the *seizing* of the young man who followed Jesus in the garden and then fled naked. See also Mann, *Mark*, 252.

20. See BDAG s.v. "ἐξίστημι." See also Johannes P. Louw, who states: "To think or reason in a completely irrational manner—'to not be in one's right mind, to be insane, to be mad, to be out of one's mind, insanity, madness'" (Louw et al., *Greek-English Lexicon*, 353). See also Mann, *Mark*, 252. The motive of Jesus' family is not given. It is possible that they are seeking to protect him from himself.

21. In Mark 3:32 "sisters" are included (καὶ αἱ ἀδελφαί σου) in A D Γ 700 *pm* it vg^mss sy^hmg, but this reading is disputed even though Jesus does add "sister" in 3:35. See Metzger, *Textual Commentary*, 70.

22. Shepherd, "Narrative Function of Markan Intercalation," 525–26; *Markan Sandwich Stories*, 130–33.

23. The term γραμματεύς refers to highly educated scholars, or experts, in the Mosaic law. See BDAG, 206; Louw et al., *Greek-English Lexicon*, 329.

118   Part 2: Narrative Analysis of Passages Involving Women in the Gospel of Mark

but of being possessed by Beelzebul (Βεελζεβοὺλ),²⁴ and of casting out demons by the power of the ruler of demons (Mark 3:22). These religious scholars are accusing Jesus of being polluted and empowered by evil. Summoning them, Jesus speaks to them in parables (ἐν παραβολαῖς) (3:23). These metaphorical stories expose the unreasonableness of the scholars' claims by analogy to undisputed scenarios.

Jesus confronts the scholars' accusation stating that Satan cannot cast out Satan because a divided kingdom cannot stand (3:23–24). Jesus then moves the metaphor from a "kingdom" to a "house" stating that a divided house cannot stand (3:25).²⁵

ἐὰν βασιλεία ἐφ' ἑαυτὴν μερισθῇ, οὐ δύναται σταθῆναι ἡ βασιλεία ἐκείνη

ἐὰν οἰκία ἐφ' ἑαυτὴν μερισθῇ, οὐ δυνήσεται ἡ οἰκία ἐκείνη σταθῆναι

This movement from "kingdom" to "house" provides the audience with an echo from the outer story where Jesus entered a "house" (3:20) and his family was standing outside of the house (3:21, 31, 32). As Andrew Le Peau observes:

> Perhaps two meanings of "house" are at work here—not only the physical dwelling of a family but *house* in the sense of all the extended members [of] a family, as in household or "the house of Windsor." So Jesus is using Hebrew parallelism equating "a kingdom is divided" and "a house is divided" (Mark 3:24–25) as two ways of saying the same thing in order to emphasize the point—it would be to fight your own dominion.²⁶

Through this parabolic statement by Jesus, an obvious question arises for the implied audience whether Jesus' house is divided. If so, how can his house stand? Will it come to an end just as Satan's house must come to an end if he rises against himself (Mark 3:26)? Furthermore, by this parabolic statement, the implied author/narrator simultaneously confronts

---

24. The term Βεελζεβοὺλ may be a play on the Philistine deity בַּעַל זְבוּב meaning *Baal* (lord) of flies or of the corrupted world (cf. 2 Kgs 1:2). See BDAG, 173; BDB, 261.

25. Even though Lane does not acknowledge the structure of an intercalation in this passage stating that this is a "self-contained unit," he cannot help but hear the echo of the outer story where Jesus states that a house divided cannot stand, writing in a footnote: "Is there a reference here to the division in Jesus' own household, which is illustrated by Ch 3:20f, 31–35?" (Lane, *Mark*, 143n90).

26. Le Peau, *Mark through Old Testament Eyes*, 79.

the implied audience with an exposure of the elites' attempt to vilify the character Jesus. It serves to show how that vilification originates from misunderstanding.

Jesus then warns the scholars of the dire consequences of their accusation that he is doing his work by an unclean spirit because they are slandering both him and the Spirit who works through him (Mark 3:28–30). Jesus has sternly warned those making false accusations against him. By reading the outer and inner stories together, the audience may wonder if this warning has any relevance to Jesus' family who is making an accusation that he has lost his mind.

David May argues that in the first-century social world, this conflict was an honor/shame dispute between the scholars and Jesus. Jesus is shown to win the dispute by the lack of any reply by the scholars.[27] While May's analysis appears to have validity in the contest between Jesus and the scholars in the inner story, his treatment of Jesus' family in the outer story may distract from the narrative effect of reading the stories on top of one another. May's honor/shame analysis of the family is that they have come to seize Jesus because his actions have a shaming effect on the family resulting in the loss of their social currency.[28] However, because a "person cannot enter into a shame/honor contest with one's own family," Jesus resolves the narrative tension "in the legitimating norm of 'doing God's will.' When he places the honor of God above his family, Jesus does not dishonor his family and is shown at the same time to be even more honorable."[29] Without denying that the honor/shame theme is present in the passage, the resolution of the tension with the family seems to lessen the effect of reading the passages together and seeing the alignment of Jesus' family with the scholars in their opposition to Jesus. Either story could be told separately so that the honor/shame themes would be seen by the audience, but something more, not less, seems to be occurring by reading the stories together.

THE OUTER STORY (MARK 3:31–35)

The outer story resumes in Mark 3:31 where the audience is explicitly told that those who came to seize Jesus were his mother and brothers.

---

27. May, "Mark 3:20–35," 86.
28. May, "Mark 3:20–35," 85.
29. May, "Mark 3:20–35," 86.

They are described as standing outside (ἔξω στήκοντες) and sending someone into the house to call Jesus (Mark 3:32). The crowd, referred to in Mark 3:20, is now seated around Jesus when he is told that his mother and brothers are seeking him from outside (ἔξω) (Mark 3:32). Jesus then describes, or perhaps better redefines, his household as those who do the will of God as opposed to those with whom he is biologically related (Mark 3:34–35).

When the outer and inner stories are read together, Jesus' parabolic proclamation in the inner story appears to be problematic to the outer story. If a house divided cannot stand, how can his house stand since his own family appears to be divided with his mother and brothers waiting to seize him? While the scribes in the inner story make a charge against his character that he is demon possessed (based upon his activity of casting out demons), Jesus' family makes a charge against his character that he is out of his mind (based upon his activity of ministering without eating). As Shepherd keenly observes:

> Interesting parallels exist between these two diverse groups, the relatives of Jesus (his "friends") and the scribes from Jerusalem (his enemies). Both groups bring charges against Jesus based upon some activity he has been doing. The judgment of each party makes some statement about Jesus' interior state. They contend that the activity he carries on reflects negatively on his character. Jesus, on the other hand, indicates the fallacy of each of these groups by means of authoritative statements. The two groups, who never meet, are nevertheless drawn together by the juxtaposition of the two stories and by the intertwining of the charges and rebuttals which link their individual stories. What is so interesting is that the two *opposite* groups, relatives (friends of Jesus) and scribes (enemies of Jesus), actually act in *similar* ways against Jesus and are countered by his authoritative word.[30]

Moreover, in the context leading up to this intercalation, Jesus' closest followers are identified in the call of the Twelve (Mark 3:13–19). In the last verse of the unit, just before the story dealing with Jesus' family, one of the Twelve is identified as "Judas Iscariot, who also betrayed him" (Mark 3:19). Every manifestation of Jesus' "house" appears to be divided—from the Twelve, to his family. The audience is left with the question presented by Jesus himself—how can Jesus' house stand?

---

30. Shepherd, "Narrative Function of Markan Intercalation," 529. See also Shepherd, *Markan Sandwich Stories*, 121–22.

Jesus' Relatives (Mother) and the Beelzebul Controversy

The answer is given when the outer story is resumed in Mark 3:31–35. So often Jesus' words are read outside of the control of this context and appear to be the musing of one in a daze:

> "Who are my mother and my brothers?" And looking about on those who were sitting around Him, he said, "Behold, my mother and my brothers. For whoever should do the will of God, this *is* my brother and sister and mother." (Mark 3:31–35, author's translation)

These words are not those spoken by someone in a spiritual trance but make explicit the truth that Jesus' family consist of those who obey his Father, even if one of the Twelve will betray him and his own mother and brothers think he has lost his mind. In other words, Jesus' house may appear to be divided, but it is not because his house does not consist of those who are called as part of the Twelve, or of those who are biologically related to him. Rather, his house consists of those who obey his Father—they comprise his true family.[31] Therefore, Jesus' house will stand.[32]

CONCLUSION

Unlike Homer's use of an inner story to explain the outer story, Mark's sandwiched stories are distinct from one another; the inner story provides more than background for the outer story. The only explicit relationship between the two stories is the passage of time during the inner story. Otherwise, the stories could have been told separately without any reference to one another. However, when the stories are combined as the implied author has arranged them, several correlations arise between the stories for the benefit of the implied audience.

One contribution of this Markan intercalation is that it characterizes Mary as a fallible person who profoundly misunderstands Jesus to the extent of casting him as insane, as out of control, and to be controlled. Jesus' ministry did not develop as she expected, and she appeared to find herself at odds with him even to the point of thinking he had lost his mind. Furthermore, her actions are so similar to the religious scholars in

---

31. Jesus transforms the social understanding of family into a moral understanding. This transformation is fitting as the social accusation that he has lost his mind in 3:21 shifted to a moral accusation in 3:22 that he had Beelzebul. See Shepherd, *Markan Sandwich Stories*, 113–14n1, 117.

32. See also Shepherd, "Narrative Function of Markan Intercalation," 539.

the inner story that she is aligned with them, outside the house in which Jesus sits with his true "family." The placement outside of the house is a narrative device meant to show that in this particular pursuit, she stands outside of the family pictured by Jesus and his followers in the house. This link between the misunderstanding of Mary and the religious leaders invokes tragedy for the implied audience. The implied audience then comes to understand that true discipleship cannot oppose the mission of Jesus even when the mission appears "crazy" from a human viewpoint. Mary's accusation does not appear to be as extreme as that made by the scholars in the inner story in that she is not accusing him of doing something by a demonic spirit, but she is resistant to what he is doing. Her motive may be maternal, or honor/shame based; the audience is not told, but by acting as she does, she is placed literally and metaphorically outside of the house, or household, where Jesus' "family" sits with him. Christologically speaking, Jesus is on the side of God; he has the Holy Spirit, and his true family will do the will of God.

This reading is further strengthened by Mary's unusual position of being outside of the "house." The house or home is where a first-century Israelite woman would commonly be associated. Jesus is in the house, but Mary is outside of the house. This spatial displacement of Jesus' mother aligns with the awkward narrative placement of her alongside of the religious leaders in the intercalation. At this moment, things are upside down: the woman is outside of the house and the man, Jesus, is inside of the house with his "family." Not only is Mary in an unusual place, but so is Jesus. It is almost as if he replaces his mother in the home with family. This displacement appears to have been done to emphasize for the implied audience how essential it is to respond positively to what Jesus is saying and doing. If Mary can be outside of the house, so might the implied audience with an improper response.

Mark will later record what appears to be a deriding statement against Jesus' mother by those in Nazareth who identify Jesus as "her son," rather than "Joseph's son": "Isn't this the son of Mary?" (Mark 6:3).[33]

---

33. "'Son of Mary' itself might be a slur: even if Joseph were deceased, it appears that the practice was to continue to use the patronymic designation (b. Yoma 38b, noting the case of a Doeg ben Joseph)" (Metzger, *Textual Commentary*, 73–74). See also Andrew Le Peau, who writes: "People were identified in this era by their father's name, not their mother's name—as seen in Mark 1:19 and 3:17 (James the son of Zebedee), 2:14 (Levi, the son of Alphaeus), 3:18 (James, the son of Alphaeus), 10:46 (Bartimaeus, the son of Timaeus) and 10:47 (Jesus, Son of David). This unusual usage—especially here, where the people are ridiculing Jesus—may be a reference to his possible illegitimate birth"

However, because this apparent slight is coming from those who are hostile toward Jesus, it does not, in-and-of-itself, characterize Mary for the audience who identify with Jesus in the narrative. What may be more telling, however, will be the narrator's mention of Mary at Jesus' crucifixion, burial, and tomb in Mark 15:40, 47, and 16:1. The details of analysis will be discussed thoroughly in those passages, but suffice it to say, Mary's fallible character in chapter three of Mark will be remembered by the implied audience when she is mentioned again in Mark 15 and 16.

This unique and unusual grouping of narratives in Mark 3:20–35 introduce the audience to a fallible Mary early in the Galilee portion of the narrative. During a time in Mark's story world when all, but the religious leaders, are responding well to Jesus, Mary is portrayed as being closer to the religious leaders than the multitudes in her response. While a positive message is communicated that Jesus' true family consists of those who do the will of his Father and not of those with whom he is related so that his house can be understood by the implied audience to be undivided and not about to collapse, the implied audience also leaves the narrative with a perspective of Jesus' mother as being outside of Jesus' inner circle and in conflict with what he is doing at the time. This characterization of Mary will place the audience on alert when she reappears as an actor at the end of the Gospel. The implied author's treatment of Mary will not be unique to his treatment of other followers, like the Twelve, who resist what Jesus is saying to them.

This narrative will be followed by another narrative involving a woman outside of the house with the healing of the woman with a hemorrhage of blood in Mark 5:21–43. However, unlike the ambivalence concerning Jesus' mother in this narrative, the woman in the following narrative will provide an exemplar of faith meant to instruct a man—even a leader of a synagogue.

(Le Peau, *Mark Through Old Testament Eyes*, 116). Contrary to this understanding is Lynn Cohick's hypothesis that Jesus alleged brothers and sisters were from a previous marriage by Joseph with the result that the people are referring to all of the children that Mary bore (Cohick, *Women in the World*, 154). But this would still be an unusual way to refer to children in the Gospel of Mark.

10

Jairus' Daughter and the Woman with a Hemorrhage

(Mark 5:21–43)

(Outer Story 5:21–24; Inner Story 5:25–34; Outer Story 5:35–43)

THIS THIRD NARRATIVE IN Mark's Gospel discussing women involves two women: a woman with an issue of blood, and the daughter of the synagogue official named Jairus. Once again, the narrative is told through the technique of interchanging stories. These stories must be heard on top of one another for the implied audience to fully understand what Mark is saying about the women in this passage.

INTRODUCTION

This material is set forth as an intercalation in all three synoptic gospels (cf. Matt 9:18–26 and Luke 8:40–56). However, this analysis will not be a synoptic reading of stories, but one focusing exclusively on Mark's presentation.

In the development of Mark's Gospel, this unit falls in the section geographically associated with episodes at or near the sea of Galilee (Mark 1:16—8:21):

Title (1:1)
The Wilderness (1:2–15)
   Galilee (1:16—8:21)
      Frame, blind →seeing (8:22–26)
         The Way (8:27—10:45)
      Frame, blind →seeing (10:46—11:11)
   Jerusalem (11:12—15:41)
The Tomb (15:42—16:8)[1]

After Jesus chose his disciples (1:16—3:19), he then identified obedient disciples with his true family (Mark 3:20—6:6). The structure of Mark 3:20—6:6 is concentric around the theme of Jesus' family:

A The true family of Jesus (3:20–35)
  B Teachings of Jesus (4:1–34)
  B' Miracles of Jesus (4:35—5:43)
A' The supposed family of Jesus (6:1–6)[2]

The entire subunit appears to revolve around how people respond to Jesus' revelation. In 3:20–35 the paradigm is set with examples of negative responses to Jesus' ministry. His family thinks he has lost his mind and seeks to seize him, and the religious leaders think that he casts out demons by the power of Satan. Jesus then clarifies the proper response to his ministry by stating that his true family consists of those who do the will of the Father.

In Mark 4:1–34 the implied author provides revelation of Jesus through a long teaching discourse wherein he clarifies proper and improper responses to his word through the parable of the soils (4:1–25)[3]

---

1. See Iersel, *Mark*, 84.

2. See Mann, *Mark*, 181–82.

3. Mann understands the parable of the Sower to foreshadow the intercalation in chapter 5, stating: "A 'teaching within a teaching' (parable of the seed, with its explanation interpreting the parable and the explanation that follows) can be seen to interact with the cure of a woman inserted within a cure" (Mann, *Mark*, 182). This correlation seems questionable on two levels: the structure in the parable of the soils is in two parts rather than a teaching within a teaching (parable 4:3–9; explanation 4:10–25). Even if one breaks the explanation into two parts, with a first interpretation in verse 10–23 and a second interpretation in verse 24–32, the pattern is not one of returning to the initial story/parable. See Tolbert, *Sowing the Gospel*, 148–49. Kuruvilla suggests a three-fold structure, with (1) the Seed Parable 4:3–9, (2) a private discussion 4:10–25, and (3) Seed Parables 4:26–34 (Kuruvilla, *Mark*, 77). Even so, a thematic link does not appear to exist between the teaching of the parable of the soils and Jairus' daughter or the cure of the woman with a flow of blood other than the possibility that the women are examples of the typology of the good soil.

and describes the nature of the coming kingdom through the additional parables (4:26–34). This discourse is followed by a grouping of miracles performed by Jesus that show his power over nature, demons, disease, and death. Proper and improper responses to Jesus' self-revelation is displayed by the characters in the narratives. In the storm at sea, Jesus is revealing himself to be powerful over the forces of chaos just as YHWH is powerful over chaos.[4] Demons may also be the source of the storm—perhaps even the demons they are about to encounter on the other side of the sea.[5] The disciples do not react to the storm well. They have forgotten all that they have seen, heard, and learned in chapters 1–4. Jesus himself asks them why they are afraid, and if they have no faith. A great storm has been turned into a great calm, but the disciples only have a great fear (φοβήθησαν φόβον μέγαν). They also have no idea who Jesus is (4:41). However, the demonized man calls Jesus, "Son of the Most High God" (5:7), and the demoniac worships Jesus. The man delivered from demons wants to be with Jesus (5:18; cf. 3:14), and Jesus' response to him is similar to his call of the Twelve: preach (5:20; cf. 3:14).

The miracles continue in the sandwich story in Mark 5:21–24 where like the demoniac, a woman will be delivered from a long illness, and like the disciples threatened by the storm, a young girl will be delivered from death. Again, the narrative will focus on the response of Jairus, the woman, and the disciples.

Finally, Jesus will appear before his own people in his hometown (Mark 6:1–6). As in chapter 3, these people grew up with Jesus. They are astonished/amazed/overwhelmed with fright (ἐξεπλήσσοντο). They have nothing to do with him—even after seeing his miracles and wisdom (6:2). They appear to speak derogatorily of him. They refer to him as "this one/This" (οὗτος) (2 times in Mark 6:2, and 1 time in Mark 6:3). They refer to him as the "son of Mary" (ὁ υἱὸς τῆς Μαρίας). As first stated in Mark 3:20–35, obedient disciples are part of the true family of Jesus. Mark shows those who are responding well to his word and revelation

---

4. Mark refers to this body of water as a "sea," θάλασσα (Mark 1:16; 2:13; 3:7; 4:1; 4:39; 4:41; 5:1; 5:13; 5:21; 6:47; 6:48; 6:49; 7:31). This so-called "sea" is really a "lake" (λίμνη) (cf. Luke 5:1–2). In crossing the sea, Jesus is crossing traditional limits. In the Hebrew Scriptures, the sea is associated with chaos, threat, and danger—but Jesus' power is stronger. The sea also pictures traveling to those far away, namely, the Gentiles. See Malbon, "Mark and the Sea of Galilee," 363–77.

5. See the explicit parallels set out by Kuruvilla between the exorcism in the Synagogue in Mark 1:21–28 and the "exorcism" on the sea in Mark 4:35–41 (Kuruvilla, *Mark*, 95). See also Lachs, *Rabbinic Commentary*, 160–61.

in the persons of the demoniac, Jairus, and the woman with the flow of blood. Jesus' family, home-town residents, and even the disciples are not responding to him in the way one might have expected those closest to him to respond.

THE OUTER STORY (MARK 5:21-24)

After the deliverance of the Gerasene demoniac, Jesus crosses the Sea of Galilee from east to west, from the Gentiles back to the land of Israel (Mark 5:21), and there meets a Jewish official, a ruler of the Synagogue (ἀρχισυνάγωγος) named Jairus (Ἰάϊρος) (5:22). There is a spatial movement in the outer story from broad to narrow, and in the inner story from narrow to broad. In the outer story, Jesus comes across the sea of Galilee (5:21), is on the seashore (5:21), is on the way to Jairus' house (5:24) and is within Jairus's house (5:38-39). In the inner story, the woman comes secretly from behind Jesus (5:27), Jesus exposes the woman (4:30), and she confesses all of the truth before Jesus and the crowd (4:33).[6] The outer story ends in a command by Jesus not to tell anyone (5:43) while the inner story required the woman to speak publicly (5:30-34).

Time seems to run as a continuous thread throughout the two stories and thus becomes a constant that highlights a contrast.[7] Other than Jesus, the only other main character named in these stories is Jairus,[8] and he is named only once (Mark 5:22); everywhere else he is identified as an important man, the ruler of the synagogue (ἀρχισυνάγωγος, see Mark 5:35, 36, 38).[9] He also comes with a matter of extreme urgency announcing that his dear daughter (θυγάτριον)[10] is near death and asking Jesus to come and lay hands on her so that she might be made well (σῴζω) and live (ζάω) (5:23).

---

6. See Shepherd, *Markan Sandwich Stories*, 141.

7. Shepherd, *Markan Sandwich Stories*, 140.

8. The name Jairus is absent from several Western witnesses (D it). See Metzger, *Textual Commentary*, 73-74. The name in Hebrew means "he who enlightens" (יָאִיר) BDAG, 103). Jairus himself is about to be "enlightened" by the faith of the woman in the inner story.

9. Peter, James, and John are also named as disciples whom Jesus allowed to follow him to Jairus's house (5:37).

10. The diminutive (θυγάτριον) is probably used as a term of affection or endearment. See Mark 7:25; BDAG s.v. "θυγάτριον"; Mann, *Mark*, 284.

THE INNER STORY (MARK 5:25–34)

As Jesus travels with Jairus, he is interrupted by a woman with a flow of blood who is in the crowd, an unusually public place for a woman in first-century Israel. Perhaps the desperateness of her situation has motivated her to move into a public setting. The implied audience would notice this anomaly in its creation of characterization. The woman touches Jesus' garment, and unintentionally stops the rescue mission as Jesus turns to ask the crowd: "Who touched my garments?" (Mark 5:25–30). Although Jairus says nothing, Jesus' disciples are indignant:[11] "You see the crowd pressing around you, and yet you say, 'Who touched me?'" (5:31–32). Their response to Jesus' question once again shows them as being without understanding. But Jesus continues his search to find the one who did this.

The woman is also outside of the usual, first-century setting of the house. Instead, she is in a public gathering. She is not there with her family, but on her own. To enter into this male-like activity of a crowd shows the audience the weight of her peril. Whether she was Jewish or Gentile, this would not be a socially acceptable setting for a first-century woman in Israel. However, Jesus never speaks to her possible breach of social custom. Instead, her male-like assertiveness will be met by Jesus' female-like response. As the woman has a flow of blood from her body, Jesus has a flow of power from his body (see Mark 5:30), perhaps showing himself to be the perfect, first-century, one-sex model of a human.[12] Another option is that Jesus is showing himself to be vulnerable as a man who is in some sense penetrated.[13]

It is at this crossroad, as the clock continues to click for Jairus and his daughter, that the tension in the two stories rises, contrasts multiply,

---

11. Shepherd sees a comedic identification with the disciples in this passage. Shepherd, *Markan Sandwich Stories*, 148n1. Even if one questions the strength of an analogy between Jesus and Jerry Lewis, there is dramatic irony taking place for the implied audience that magnifies the gap between the understanding of Jesus and the understanding of his disciples. See Lane, *Mark*, 193.

12. See Stewart, "Masculinity in the New Testament," 94.

13. See Walters, "Invading the Roman Body," 29–43. Although writing in a sexual context, Walters defines the Roman man as "impenetrable penetrators." See also Jonathan Jodamus, who describes the Graeco-Roman ideology of a penetrated body as an (un)masculine, feminine body (Jodamus, "Paul, the 'Real' Man," 80). However, ironically, when Jesus is *willingly* penetrated and dies for others, his death become a manly, hypermasculine act (Jodamus, "Paul, the 'Real' Man," 81). Whether one agrees with Jodamus's "hypermasculine" description of Jesus, one can say that Jesus encompassed the breadth of the experience of humanity rather than simply the masculine ideal.

and the implied audience is given a glimpse into Jesus' attitude towards women. Jairus is obviously male, and the woman with the hemorrhage is obviously female. Jairus is named, but the woman is anonymous. Jairus is a leader of a synagogue, but the woman, if she was Jewish, may not have gone to synagogue because her constant bleeding would have made her ritually impure according to Leviticus 15:25–27,[14] or for the first-century audience, a source of pollution.[15] Jairus is a father with an ailing daughter, but the woman has no family identified in the story.[16] Jairus has asked Jesus publicly to heal his daughter, but the woman sought Jesus secretly.[17] The looming question at this nexus is whether Jesus will arrive in time to heal Jairus' daughter. This delay for an unknown, unclean woman may cause the death of Jairus' daughter. Maybe that is one reason why the

---

14. Mark does not comment on this or on the ethnicity of the woman, but those aware of the purity laws in Leviticus, perhaps the implied audience, would have understood this implication. Regarding Leviticus 15:26–27, Baruch Levine notes: "This is the primary symptom: irregularity of blood discharges, which either persist beyond the regular menstrual period or are unconnected with it altogether. A woman who has discharges of blood not due to her menstruation bears the same impurity as a menstruating woman for as long as the discharges last" (Levine, *Leviticus*, 98). Accordingly, in discussing the earlier passage in Leviticus 15:19, Levine states: "Anyone who has contact with a woman during her menstrual period is impure until evening" and "whatever the woman sits on or lies on becomes impure, and whoever touches such objects becomes impure in turn" (Levine, *Leviticus*, 97). Leviticus 15:31 emphasizes that the uncleanness separated the person from God's sanctuary. As Allen Ross explains, concerning a woman with a chronic discharge of blood: "Such infections are very personal. Naturally, a woman did not make this kind of condition known outside the home. In all probability, some may have feigned purity for the sake of participation in worship services or in society. But devout believers who walked in faith and good conscience before God realized that they could not go to the sanctuary until this chronic disorder cleared up and they had gone through the prescribed ritual" (Ross, *Holiness to the Lord*, 309). Even though the synagogue was not the sanctuary, by attending or being a part of a crowd, she would at least risk spreading her impurity to others. If the woman was not Jewish, she still suffered from her flow of blood which would have marginalized her in a Jewish community for many of the same reasons, not to mention her ethnicity.

15. As Anne Carson explains: "Woman is subject not only to incursion from without but to leakage from within, and, for this reason, her very presence may pose a threat to the integrity of the *oikos* of which she is part and the *polis* that encompasses it" (Carson, "Dirt and Desire," 86).

16. Shepherd suggests, "If she had been married, she was probably divorced since she could not have had sexual intercourse with her husband. Cf. Lev 15:25–27" (Shepherd, "Narrative Function of Markan Intercalation," 529n1). More accurately, she could have sexual relations with her husband, but every encounter would have rendered him impure for seven days. See Lev 15:24. Of course, Mark does not speak to any of this.

17. Perhaps she comes secretly because of her ritual impurity. See Edwards, "Markan Sandwiches," 204.

disciples were so impatient with Jesus' question. Certainly, the implied author's/narrator's telling of the discourse in this way has also had an impact on the implied audience who is kept in tension by an unnamed, "polluted" woman while Jesus delays in responding to a named, high social class male's desperate plea.

Nothing in these stories disparages Jairus, but everything coalesces to focus on the obscure woman. Jesus will bring this vital rescue mission for a prominent, religious leader to a stand-still to exalt the woman's faith. The implied author/narrator has allowed the implied audience to know the woman's musings before she was publicly identified:[18] "If I touch even his garments, I shall be made well." And her thoughts are realized when she touches his garments and "immediately the hemorrhage ceased; and she felt in her body that she was healed from the suffering, or torment (ἀπὸ τῆς μάστιγος)."

Jesus does not allow her faith and healing to remain private. He asks, "Who touched my garments?" and looked around to see who had done it. The Greek text suggests that the implied author has Jesus already knowing who touched his garment by the use of the feminine form of the interrogative, τίς, twice in Mark 5:30–31, and the feminine article, τὴν, followed by the feminine singular accusative aorist participle, ποιήσασαν, in Mark 5:32 (τίς μου ἥψατο τῶν ἱματίων. ... καὶ λέγεις· τίς μου ἥψατο; ... καὶ περιεβλέπετο ἰδεῖν τὴν τοῦτο ποιήσασαν) (emphasis added).[19] She alone knows the answer to his question, and humbly comes to him in fear and trembling, telling all the truth. That truth probably included the information the narrator already shared with the audience about her long period of uncleanness, her suffering (παθοῦσα) at the hands of many physicians who only made her condition worse, and her poverty because she "had spent all that she had" for treatment. When Jesus stops an emergency run for the leader of a synagogue for this anonymous woman, he emphasizes just how important she is to him. And then he emphasizes

---

18. Shepherd correctly observes: "The introduction of the woman is an extended anachrony (in this case an analepsis the placement of an event from the story time past within the discourse of the present), but her 'present' is with Jesus in the crowd" (Shepherd, "Narrative Function of Markan Intercalation," 526).

19. As Shepherd observes, "When Jesus looked 'to see who it was that did this' do we have Jesus' inner knowledge, or a slight intrusion of the narrator who has already revealed to the reader who it was in 5:25–29?" (Shepherd, "Narrative Function of Markan Intercalation," 534n28). Failure to perceive that the text indicates that Jesus knows who touched him can lead to faulty theological and practical conclusions as set out in the article by Rambo, "Trauma and Faith," 233–57.

her faith: "Daughter, your faith (πίστις)[20] has made you well; go in peace and be healed of your suffering (ἀπὸ τῆς μάστιγός σου)."

THE OUTER STORY (MARK 5:35–43)

At this point in the narrative, the first story resumes with the hard announcement from those that came from the house of the ruler of the synagogue that his daughter is dead. In story time, the healing of the woman and the death of Jairus' daughter are simultaneous and show the impact of one story upon the other.[21] But the echo and example of the woman from the inner story becomes a lesson that Jesus gives to the ruler of the synagogue: "Stop being afraid, only believe" (μὴ φοβοῦ, μόνον πίστευε).[22] Perhaps there is a correlation between the fear of the woman (φοβηθεῖσα, Mark 5:33) and the fear of Jairus (φοβοῦ, Mark 5:36) in the two stories. The woman may have been fearful to publicly proclaim her previous unclean life when she told "all the truth," and now Jairus was fearful of his life without his daughter. It is almost as if the fear of the woman has transferred itself to Jairus, even though its content is distinct, so he must be told to stop being afraid, or said differently, stop acting like a woman![23] It is the faith of each in Jesus that delivers them from their suffering lives.[24] This unknown, unclean woman who suffered for twelve years believed that Jesus could save her and exercised a manly characteristic of courage. Jairus is told to emulate the woman's faith as he hears that his twelve-year-old daughter has died.[25] Not only did Jesus show his interest in the unknown woman by stopping to make public her faith, but it is her faith that is now used to instruct the ruler of the

---

20. Jesus saw the woman's faith, not her non-traditional location or ritual uncleanness. See Selvidge, "Mark 5:25–34 and Leviticus 15:19–20," 619–23. The implied audience who identifies with Jesus will also adopt his point of view in its characterization of the woman.

21. See Shepherd, *Markan Sandwich Stories*, 157–58.

22. The present imperative plus μή allows for the idea of cessation of activity in progress. See Wallace, *Greek Grammar*, 724.

23. As Johnathan Jodamus explains: "It was a common *topos* in the sex-gendered system of the Ancient Mediterranean for women to be regarded as weak. According to the sex-gendered logic of that epoch women were naturally seen as weak, fearful, emotional and uncontrolled (Philo, *Questions and Answers on Exodus 1:8*)" (Jodamus, "Paul, the 'Real' Man," 81n63).

24. See Edwards, "Markan Sandwiches," 204.

25. See Edwards, "Markan Sandwiches," 204.

synagogue. These narrative encounters of Jesus with women are not only stories about what happened, but of what happens; they are theological pictures displayed by an implied author to an implied audience of the exemplary character of women to instruct others in the narrative, even male leaders in the community. This would not be lost on the implied audience as it sees the development of characters who do not conform to their first-century stereotypes.

The narrative chords between Jairus's daughter and the woman who was healed sympathetically resonate for the benefit of Jairus and the implied audience.[26] Both Jairus's daughter and the woman are called "daughter" (θυγάτηρ in Mark 5:34, 35, and θυγάτριον in Mark 5:23).[27] These emotional titles enliven the narrative by enabling the implied audience to enter into the skin of Jesus who appears to feel the endearment of family toward the suffering woman, as Jairus feels for his daughter. The implied author/narrator uses these identical emotional titles to evoke an identification between Jesus and Jairus in their affection for the woman and the daughter. No doubt, when Jesus called the woman, "daughter," that word resonated within Jairus as he thought about his dear, sick girl. Just as Jairus's daughter needed to be healed, or saved (σῴζω, Mark 5:23), so too was the woman healed, or saved, from her illness (σῴζω, Mark 5:29, 34). Now that Jairus's daughter has died, the need for salvation is even greater, and it will result in a resurrection (ἀνίστημι, Mark 5:42). Furthermore, it is only at the end of the first story that the implied audience learn that Jairus's daughter was twelve years old (Mark 5:42).[28] Obviously, Jairus

26. See Shepherd "Narrative Function of Markan Intercalation," 529–30.

27. The term for Jairus's daughter is actually a diminutive. All but one of the words used for Jairus's daughter are diminutives: "little daughter," "daughter," "little child," "Talitha," (diminutive of "lamb" "טַלְיְתָא") and "little girl." See Shepherd, *Markan Sandwich Stories*, 150.

28. As Frank Kermode observes: "Yet in matters of this kind there is really no such thing as nonsignificant coincidence, and we are entitled to consider that this coincidence signifies a narrative relation of some kind between the woman and the girl" (Kermode, *Genesis of Secrecy*, 132). However, the significance of the correlation is not always obvious or agreed upon. Kermode argues for sexual innuendo (132–33). Michele Connolly agrees, stating: "The daughter threatens to provoke disorder in Jesus' career as a preacher of God's order, since his mode of healing her by touching as well as by word, symbolically awakens her sexually. The coherence of Jesus' image as the completely altruistic, disinterested agent of God is strained by this depiction of him taking a sleeping pubescent female by the hand, to waken her to the onset of her adult life" (Connolly, *Disorderly Women*, 127). This reading seems unlikely. At no other place in this narrative is any sexual innuendo made or is any implication of a sexual relationship developed. Moving in a different direction, Mary Ann Tolbert provocatively writes: "In the case of

knew his daughter's age all along, but now the audience is brought under the umbrella revealing that the length of the woman's suffering, and the age of the suffering daughter were the same (Mark 5:25, 42). The woman's faith after twelve years of suffering was directly applicable to Jairus whose twelve-year-old daughter had just died. And just as Jesus made an unclean woman who touched him instantly clean, he was able to make an unclean daughter who had died[29] instantly clean by touching her and telling her to rise.[30] The first healing happened in secret but was made public by having the woman confess in public, while the second healing occurred before others, Peter, James, John, and the girl's parents, but was then sworn to secrecy,[31] emphasizing that the point of the miracles may not have been the healings themselves, but the interaction between the faith of the woman and the needed faith of Jairus in Jesus.

CONCLUSION

The juxtaposition of the two stories invites the implied audience to compare the disparate characters of Jairus and the woman. Their stories are not only entwined in space and time as the woman's need arrests Jairus's deliverance but are enmeshed in essence as Jairus has a "daughter," and the woman is called "daughter" by Jesus; Jairus' daughter is twelve years old, and the woman has suffered her flow of blood for twelve years; and Jairus's daughter is in desperate physical need as is the woman. These distinct stories are carefully crafted into one interrelated account so that

---

the twelve-year-old child and the woman with a twelve-year illness, it is very tempting to note that the only use of twelve prior to their appearance is related to the disciples, the Twelve. That those twelve turn out to be rocky ground, while these two healed ones demonstrate the fruitfulness of faith raises the possibility of seeing this use of twelve as a subtle clue to the identity of Jesus' true family" (Tolbert, *Sowing the Gospel*, 168n58). This view is possible due to the emphasis on family relations in the intercalation. Edwards also suggests that "twelve, moreover, may signify Israel to Mark's readers, indeed, Israel coming to faith in Jesus" (Edwards, "Markan Sandwiches," 204–5n34). This view seems less likely since it requires a typology from the narrative that is not emphasized elsewhere in the narrative.

29. Setting forth arguments that Jairus's daughter actually died, Shepherd uncovers another parallel between the outer and inner stories: "The ironic character in which Jesus' remark in 5:39 ['Why make a commotion and weep? The child has not died but is asleep'] is parallel to the ironic question in the inner story 'Who touched me?' (5:30) suggests that Jesus' central statements in the inner and outer story carry a truth beyond their surface expression" (Shepherd, *Markan Sandwich Stories*, 156n6).

30. See Kermode, *Genesis of Secrecy*, 133.

31. See Shepherd, *Markan Sandwich Stories*, 141.

the implied audience will see more in their combination than in either account on its own.³²

One effect of the confluence of the stories is that Jesus is seen to be interested in the needs of an unclean women at the distress of a prominent, male, religious leader. However, even more significant is Jesus' admonition to Jairus to have "faith" right after he has extolled the woman's "faith" that delivered her from her agony. This unclean woman's faith became a lesson to the religious leader. This woman who could not even enter a synagogue becomes an example of faith to the leader of the synagogue. In a religious, patriarchal setting, the implied audience would have expected just the opposite to have been shown—Jairus's faith being a lesson for the woman—but these stories surprise. Jairus and the woman both begin their stories with a common need for Jesus' deliverance, but as the woman's story unfolds, it is the woman's great faith that becomes the guide for Jairus as his situation darkens with the death of his daughter.

It is not the Twelve who provide an example for Jairus. They are obtuse to what Jesus is doing and saying, much like the mourners at Jairus's house (cf. Mark 5:31, 40). The woman in her exercise of faith is a foil to the Twelve. When her healing occurs, only she and Jesus know it (Mark 5:29–30). The disciples are sarcastically critical of Jesus' inquiry about who touched his clothes. Just as the blood flowed from the woman's body, power flowed from Jesus' body (καὶ εὐθὺς ὁ Ἰησοῦς ἐπιγνοὺς ἐν ἑαυτῷ τὴν ἐξ αὐτοῦ δύναμιν ἐξελθοῦσαν, Mark 5:30).³³ These porous bodies understand what has occurred. In some measure, Jesus has made himself "female" for the woman by having power flow from his body just as the woman had blood flowing from her body. Now, hope for the little girl whose life has poured out from her body is somehow wrapped in the woman and Jesus. It is the woman who shines a light of faith in Jesus that Jairus must take up as he returns to his house of mourning. The implied audience will want to adopt her faith in their struggles.

The implied author has crafted this discourse for the implied audience to form character by showing a woman, who like the sea, is in chaos

---

32. Andrew Le Peau lists several other parallels between the woman and Jairus and his daughter, including: "Touch brings healing (5:28–29, 41), falling at Jesus' feet (5:32, 22), incredulous response to Jesus by those around him (5:31, 40), poor and rich (5:26, 5:22), and touching/being touched by Jesus for healing (4:28–29, 41)" (Le Peau, *Mark*, 107–8).

33. See Moss, "Man with the Flow of Power," 507–19.

and is polluted because she is leaking blood.³⁴ However, the woman's status is reversed as she comes to Jesus in faith. Consequently, instead of being a woman characterized by chaos, the implied audience sees a woman who is like a daughter to Jesus, and for whom, Jesus makes himself vulnerable, or porous.³⁵ Her character is transformed from someone who has been exploited and desperate to someone who is a teller of truth who like a dear daughter models faith for the male leader of the synagogue whose little daughter has died. The ignored mother in the narrative, Jairus' wife, who might have had social status in the house and through her husband, is only impliedly involved in the aftercare of her healed daughter. The implied author/narrator brings about these reversals in characterization for the implied audience through an intercalated discourse.

In this narrative, two incomplete women are made whole by Jesus who gives of himself allowing power to flow from him unto them. In the next chapter, two complete women, Herodias and her daughter, will refuse to respond to words from Jesus' forerunner, John the Baptizer. Their response will lead to death for John, and sorrow for Herod and John's followers.

---

34. The reference to the "sea" reaches back to the storm at sea in the prior context of Mark 4:37–40. Which may have been caused by the demons Jesus met on the other side of the sea (Mark 5:1–20). The woman with the flow of blood may provide a literary echo of the prior rough sea crossing when in 5:21 the narrator tells the audience that Jesus crossed over the sea again before he met Jairus and the woman in the following narrative. The implied author has contextually shown the chaos of waters to be implied audience as a potential foreshadow of the woman who, from a first-century perspective, was associated with chaos.

35. In Matthew Thiessen's recent work, he observes that with the woman's touch of Jesus' garment, not only does the woman's discharge of blood dry up, but Mark's Jesus experiences an uncontrolled discharge of power leaking from his body which, like contact with certain of the tabernacle furnishings, rendered the woman clean or holy: "Contact with Jesus, the holy one of God, causes a discharge of holiness to surge out of Jesus—a holiness that overpowers the source of impurity in the one touching Jesus" (Thiessen, *Jesus and the Forces of Death*, 9).

11

Herodias, Her Daughter, and the Beheading of John the Baptizer

(Mark 6:7–32)

IN THIS FOURTH MARKAN narrative addressing women, two women appear as main actors: Herodias and her daughter. As will be shown below, even though the narrative is built on an interchange of two stories (outer story 6:7–13; inner story 6:14–29; outer story 6:30–32), an analysis of the parallels and comparisons from the intercalation offers little insight about the women in the narrative. Therefore, another narrative approach will be adopted using the implied author's narrative typology as a means of characterization. Through this typology, the implied author/narrator vilifies Herodias and her daughter, as unstable, deceptive women, as a subtle means of vilifying Herod who's feminine, lack of self-control and inability to control those under him, including the women in his house, exposes him to the implied audience as depraved and unmanly.[1] Correla-

1. Jennifer Knust has written extensively on how Christians in the first century AD used virtues to praise or vices to expose the "elite" in Roman rulers (Knust, *Abandoned to Lust*). Although Knust's focus is often on the deviant sexual behavior (which was admittedly different for men than for women) that vilified those who were culturally considered to be virtuous, she emphasizes that virtues were broader than sexual behavior. For instance, elite Roman men included those who ruled well over themselves and others, and elite Roman women included those who remained loyal to their husbands and did not bring shame on themselves or their families. "Generations of Greek and, later, Roman schoolboys were trained in the repertoire of categories appropriate for praise or blame" (Knust, *Abandoned to Lust*, 47). Therefore, the implied audience of

Herodias, Her Daughter, and the Beheading of John the Baptizer 137

tions will also be made between Herod and Pilate to show how weak and unable to rule these Roman representatives were in the face of surrounding chaos. All of this comes to focus for the implied audience through the implied author's discourse of Herodias and her daughter.

INTRODUCTION

This narrative is being examined because of the two women who appear in the inner story of this intercalation, Herodias and her daughter.[2] Some

---

Mark would know that: "A man is virtuous when he is in control of himself and his household, when he is courageous in battle, and when he is wise in his dealings with his subordinates" (Knust, Abandoned to Lust, 48). When a man renounced his prerogatives of masculinity, that man was corrupt and worthy of blame. Similarly, "if a man cannot be trusted to keep his women in line, then he should not be trusted with the well-being of the state" (Knust, Abandoned to Lust, 49). Accordingly, capricious, lack of self-control by Herod when he offered up to half of his kingdom to Herodias' daughter in appreciation for her dance shows to the implied audience that Herod is not virtuous. Furthermore, the allowance of Herodias to trick Herod into killing John the Baptizer shows to the implied audience that Herod is not able to control the women in his household and thus not fit to be a ruler over his Galilean tetrarchy.

2. Because of textual variants in Mark 6:22, there is some question over the identity of the daughter who danced. Josephus identifies her as the daughter of Herodias and Herod Philip stating: "Their sister Herodias was married to Herod [Philip] the son of Herod the Great by Mariamme, daughter of Simon the high priest. They had a daughter Salome, after whose birth Herodias, taking it into her head to flout the way of our fathers, married Herod [Antipas], her husband's brother by the same father, who was tetrarch of Galilee" (Josephus, *Antiquities*, 92–93).

One reading of the textual variant containing αὐτοῦ could mean that the unnamed girl in Mark was Herod Antipas' daughter who name is Herodias (εἰσελθούσης τῆς θυγατρὸς αὐτοῦ Ἡρῳδιάδος); see ℵ B D L Δ 565. But in 6:24 the daughter is identified as Herodias' daughter (εἶπεν τῇ μητρὶ αὐτῆς). The committee for Nestle-Aland text "decided, somewhat reluctantly, that the reading with αὐτοῦ, despite the historical and contextual difficulties, must be adopted on the strength of its external attestation" (Metzger, *Textual Commentary*, 77). See also Burer et al., *NET Bible*, 821–22. However, even this difficult reading does not demand that the unnamed girl be the daughter of Herod Antipas. As Shepherd explained: "Other [syntactic] possibilities could be ablative of agency ('his daughter by Herodias'), or genitive of relationship ('his daughter through Herodias'). In the last case, the relationship would be something comparable to an adoptive daughter, cf. 6:24 in conjunction with 6:19" (Shepherd, *Markan Sandwich Stories*, 182n2).

The other readings of αυτης της (A C K N Γ Θ *f*13 28. 33. 579. 700. 892. 1241. 1424. 2542 𝔐), αυτης (W) and της·(*f*¹ [aur b c f]) in 6:22 all identify the daughter with Herodias. For a more thorough discussion of the external and internal evidence in support of Salome being the daughter of Herodias by Herod Philip see Herold Hoehner who states in support of the variant αυτης της: "(1) the Gospel narrative implies the illicit marriage was a recent one and so the child could not have been more than two years old. (2) The context of Mark indicates that the girl was Herodias' daughter. (3) The parallel verse works on Mark completely omit this passage;³ most works discuss the correlations between Jesus and Herod, Jesus and John the Baptizer, and the disciples and John the Baptizer; the women are only tangentially mentioned.⁴ Another approach has been to correlate Herod and Herodias with the typological characterization of the "tyrant" king and his queen, as in Ahab and Jezebel, and Ahasuerus and Esther.⁵ While there is much insight from these canonical, intertextual readings, this study will limit its scope to reading the passage within the narrative boundaries of Mark in order to see how the implied author/narrator is showing his implied audience who these women are.

This unit falls in the section geographically associated with episodes at or near the sea of Galilee (Mark 1:16—8:21) in the development of Mark's Gospel:

Title (1:1)
The Wilderness (1:2–15)
   Galilee (1:16—8:21)
      Frame, blind →seeing (8:22–26)
         The Way (8:27—10:45)
      Frame, blind →seeing (10:46—11:11)
   Jerusalem (11:12—15:41)
The Tomb (15:42—16:8)

---

in Matthew has ἡ θυγάτηρ τῆς Ἡρῳδιάδος. (4) It fits well with Josephus who states that Herodias by her first marriage had a daughter called Salome. (5) It is in agreement with Justin Martyr's της εξαδελφης αυτου του Ηρωδον and ἡ μητηρ της παιδος" (Hoehner, *Herod Antipas*, 151–52). See also Gundry, *Mark*, 320. Accordingly, it seems as though the daughter who dances should be identified as the daughter of Herodias and Herod Philip as stated by Josephus. Of interest is the new Greek text published by Tyndale House (2017) which does not note textual variants at Mark 6:22. Its Greek text also reads: "καὶ εἰσελθούσης τῆς θυγατρὸς αὐτῆς τῆς Ἡρῳδιάδος" (Jongkind, *Greek New Testament*, 20).

3. See Williams, *Other Followers*, 17; Grassi, *Hidden Heroes*, 17–22; Malbon, "Fallible Followers," 36. David Rhoads, Joanna Dewey, and Donald Michie state: "There are minor characters whom we will not treat: John the Baptist, Herodias and her daughter, the young man who flees naked, and the maid of the high priest" (Rhoads et al., *Mark as Story* loc. 4406). See also Glahn, *Vindicating the Vixens*; Aernie, *Narrative Discipleship* loc. 129.

4. See Shepherd, *Markan Sandwich Stories*, 172–209; "Narrative Function of Markan Intercalation," 530–31; Culpepper, "Mark 6:17–29 in Its Narrative Context," 145–63; Edwards, "Markan Sandwiches," 205–6.

5. Smith, "Tyranny Exposed," 259–93; Culpepper, "Mark 6:17–29 in Its Narrative Context," 146–53.

Herodias, Her Daughter, and the Beheading of John the Baptizer

After Jesus has chosen his disciples (Mark 1:16—3:19), he then identifies obedient disciples with his true family (Mark 3:20—6:6) and urges his disciples to open their minds to the revelation of who he is and what he is saying and to turn away from the critical threats and contamination of Herod Antipas and the Pharisees (Mark 6:7—8:21). Because of the parallel threats by Herod and the Pharisees, the overall unit can be structured around a two-fold interchange:

> A Herod / feeding of five thousand (6:7–44)
>   B Jesus on the sea / the disciples' hard hearts (6:45–52)
> A' Pharisees / feeding of four thousand (6:53—8:13)
>   B' Jesus on the sea / the disciples' hard hearts (8:14–21).

As Mann observes:

> The closing scene itself [8:14–21], with its warnings against the "yeast of the Pharisees and the yeast of Herod," provides a clue to the organization of the entire segment. Set within the mission of apostles and their return is an account of Herod's wickedness (6:14–28); following the walking upon the sea, a second section deals with the perversity of the Pharisees, itself bracketed by a reference to miracles (6:53–56) and two cures (7:24–30 and 31–37). Those latter cures involve Gentile regions, thus setting the conflict with Pharisees over "clean" and "unclean" into a real situation.
>
> Both sections, dealing with Herod and the Pharisees, are followed by multiplications of loaves. The idea of the first as a "Jewish feeding" is reinforced by the mission of the Twelve and mention of Herod; the concept of the second as a "Gentile feeding" is enhanced by the discussion concerning cleanliness and the cures that take place in Gentile areas.

He continues further on:

> With a series of questions, the blindness of the disciples is made apparent. With its mention of "yeasts" and references to the two feedings, this scene brings Segment Three [6:7 to 8:21] to an end.[6]

An example of the disciples being influenced by Herod is seen at the beginning of the central section of the Gospel where the disciples initially respond to Jesus' question about his identity in a way that is parallel to those around Herod (cf. Mark 6:14–15 with 8:28). An example of the disciples

---

6. Mann, *Mark*, 182–83.

being influenced by the Pharisees is seen in their inability to understand Jesus' words about clean and unclean (Mark 7:17) while the Syrophoenician woman (a Gentile) understands Jesus' parabolic words and builds upon them in her response to Jesus (Mark 7:27–28). Jesus addresses the inability of the disciples to open their minds to an understanding of his self-revelation by telling them that they are being influenced by the threats and teachings of Herod and the Pharisees (Mark 8:14–21). This unit of the Gospel focuses on the threat of Herod (Mark 6:7–32), and the implied author will demonstrate that threat through the characterization of Herod through those around him—Herodias and her daughter.

CORRELATIONS FROM THE INTERCALATION

This full intercalation is only found in Mark's Gospel. Matthew separates the mission of the Twelve (Matt 9:35; 10:1, 7–11, 14) from the beheading of John (Matt 14:1–12). Luke employs an abbreviated intercalation. He reports Jesus' commissioning of the Twelve (Luke 9:1–6) and Herod's opinion regarding Jesus (Luke 9:7–9) followed by the disciples' report to Jesus about their mission (Luke 9:10a). Luke does not record the death of John, only his imprisonment, and that is set out in an earlier section of the Gospel (Luke 3:19–20). The Gospel of John does not include any of this material.

The overall structure of this unit is in the form of an intercalation where the outer story recounts Jesus sending his disciples on mission (Mark 6:7–13) and then receiving them after the mission is completed (Mark 6:30–32); the inner story recounts the death of John the Baptizer at the command of Herod Antipas (Mark 6:14–29). A detailed analysis of the two stories alone will not provide significant insight about the women in the narrative. The intercalated stories emphasize common themes between Jesus, his disciples, and John the Baptizer, and contrasting themes between Jesus and Herod.

In the two stories, the ministry of Jesus' disciples, and thus Jesus, is confused by Herod for the ministry of John. This confusion allows for an explicit, though mistaken, correlation between Jesus and John (Mark 6:14–16). The Markan narrative made an implicit correlation between John and Jesus earlier in the narrative through the lead words for "preach" (κηρύσσω), "repent" (μετανοέω), and to be "handed over" (παραδίδωμι). In Mark 1:4 the narrator stated that John the Baptizer was in the desert preaching (κηρύσσων) a baptism of repentance (μετανοίας) for the forgiveness of sins. Then in Mark 1:14–15 the narrator explained that after John was handed over (παραδίδωμι), Jesus came into Galilee preaching (κηρύσσων) the gospel of God and saying repent (μετανοεῖτε) and believe in the gospel. Herod's words in Mark 6:14–16 specifically correlate Jesus with John in their ministries. John proclaimed the need for Herod and his wife, Herodias, to repent from their marriage because "it is not lawful for you to have your brother's wife" (Mark 6:18). Herodias responded by wanting John to be killed (Mark 6:19). John's death shows the effect of proclaiming repentance to those who will not repent. Since Jesus is preaching the same message (cf. Mark 1:14–15), it is probable that he will experience a similar fate to John (cf. Mark 9:11–16), which he in fact does experience as Judas "hands him over" (παραδίδωμι, Mark 3:19, 10:33; 14:10, 18, 21, 41) to the religious leaders who then "hand him over" (παραδίδωμι, Mark 9:31, 10:33; 15:1, 10, 15) to Pilate to be killed. Furthermore, the narrative suggests that the Twelve will follow the same path of John and Jesus. In the outer story, it is reported that the Twelve went out and preached (κηρύσσω) that people should repent (μετανοέω, Mark 6:12). Then in the later, eschatological discourse, Jesus warned the disciples that they will be "handed over" (παραδίδωμι) to local councils, governors, kings, and unto death (Mark 13:9, 11, 12).[7] Therefore, one effect of the intercalated stories is to foreshadow the suffering of Jesus and the disciples through the suffering of John the Baptizer because they are walking in John's footsteps. In the intercalation, Jesus and the disciples move freely, but the looming shadow of John will catch up with Jesus in the narrative, and with the disciples in the future as explained in Mark 13. John's experience casts a shadow on the ministry of the disciples and Jesus in the outer story. Similarly, Herod's mistaken statement that John has been raised (ἠγέρθη) from the dead (Mark 6:14–15) is an early foreshadow of the raising (ἠγέρθη) of Jesus from the dead (Mark 16:6).

The intercalation also raises contrasting themes between Herod and Jesus as "king." Herod is called king (βασιλεὺς, Mark 6:14, 22, 25, 26, 27) even though he was only a tetrarch over Galilee and Peraea.[8] The implied

---

7. Tom Shepherd also observes: "The disciples and Jesus end up in 6:32 in a 'desert place' (ἔρημον τόπον). Furthermore, John is killed on an 'opportune day' (ἡμέρας εὐκαίρου), 6:21, and the disciples go to the desert because they do not have opportunity to eat (φαγεῖν εὐκαίρουν), 6:31–32" (Shepherd, *Markan Sandwich Stories*, 183n1).

8. Josephus states: "Then because of the change of mind he [Herod the Great] had undergone, he once more altered his will and designated Antipas, to whom he had left his throne, to be tetrarch of Galilee and Peraea" (Josephus, *Antiquities*, 252–53). See also Matt 14:1; Luke 3:19; 9:7.

author's designation of Herod as "king" was probably for theological purposes. The implied author will sometimes use descriptors which are not precise to make a theological point. For instance, the implied author will call the lake of Gennesaret (τὴν λίμνην Γεννησαρὲτ, cf. Luke 5:1) the "Sea" of Galilee (τὴν θάλασσαν τῆς Γαλιλαίας) to emphasize the great gulf between those on one side (the Jews) and those on the other side (the Gentiles).[9] Likewise, by using the title of "king" for Herod Antipas, the author is asking the recipient to compare Herod with Jesus.[10] As Tom Shepherd observes, Jesus is in ironic contrast with Herod as king:

> Jesus is the "sender" of the Twelve on mission, Herod is the "sender" to imprison and kill John. Jesus is moral and godly, rugged and stern (rather like the Baptist), the king is immoral and wavering. Jesus commands the Twelve and they obey in mission, Herod commands his workers and they obey in killing John. This has the influence of setting forth Jesus as the righteous king, since Herod is obviously immoral, vacillating, and wicked. Interestingly, of the twelve occurrences of the word βασιλεύς in Mark, five occur in chapter 6 with reference to Herod, while six occur in chapter 15 with reference to Jesus. Indeed, the inscription over the cross reads: "The King of the Jews." The Christological significance of the title is plain, and hence the intercalation in chapter 6 addresses this theological theme in Mark.[11]

Furthermore, Herod provides a banquet for a three-fold group of men[12] described as: great ones (μεγιστᾶσιν); military commanders of a thousand (χιλιάρχοις); and the first ones (men) of Galilee (τοῖς πρώτοις τῆς Γαλιλαίας) (Mark 6:21). Jesus also provides a meal for a group of men who have a threefold description related to their seating arrangement: company by company (συμπόσια συμπόσια), group by group (πρασιαὶ πρασιαί), and according to a hundred and according to fifty (κατὰ ἑκατὸν

---

9. See Malbon, "Sea of Galilee," 363–77. Malbon states: "In crossing the sea, Jesus may also be said to cross traditional limits."

10. Robert Fowler states: "We suggest that the sharp emphasis on the kingship of Herod functions to make the comparison between Herod and Jesus in 6:14–44 an implicit comparison of kingly figures" (Fowler, *Loaves and Fishes*, 121).

11. Shepherd, *Markan Sandwich Stories*, 181–82.

12. Fowler states: "As befits an oriental banquet, Jesus' guests are all men (ἄνδρες; 6:44), as were the guests at Herod's banquet table" (Fowler, *Loaves and Fishes*, 86, 120). Women could be a part of a public banquet in the Greco-Roman world (Cohick, *Women in the World*, 86–91). Kathleen Corley suggests that Herodias was in a separate dining room for women (Corley, *Private Women*, 94n58).

Herodias, Her Daughter, and the Beheading of John the Baptizer 143

καὶ κατὰ πεντήκοντα) (Mark 6:39–40).[13] Both Herod and Jesus send (ἀποστέλλω) their representatives (Mark 6:7, 17, 27). Herod's meal ends with John's head served on a platter (6:28). Jesus' meal ends with the disciples collecting twelve baskets of leftover food (6:43).[14]

Speaking even more broadly in Mark, Alan Culpepper observes: "The death of John the Baptist in a context connected with a meal scene sets up a striking resonance with Jesus' last meal with his disciples, at which he serves them his body and blood as signs of a new covenant (14:22–25)."[15]

The correlations that arise through reading the two stories of the intercalation together are significant to the message and theology of Mark. However, together they do not reveal much about the women in the narrative. Nevertheless, the correlations provide a structure for a broader narrative theology in the book of Mark to understand the function of the women in Mark's typological characters. They play a specific role in the development of the inner story of the intercalation in that they are the ultimate cause of Herod's change of mind and John's death, but their characterization is more fully understood through the broader narrative world of the Gospel.

THE INITIAL CONTEXT OF THE NARRATIVE

The implied author provided the implied audience with a grid for understanding the upcoming characters in his gospel through the parable of the soils in chapter 4. The broad message of all of the parables in Mark 4:1–34 is that although many will not respond to the word, some will; therefore, Jesus proclaims the word knowing that it will bring about the kingdom which will start small but will expand under its own power for God to harvest. The first of the parables, which is subsequently interpreted by Jesus, concerns the four soils (Mark 4:3–9, 14–20). Jesus states that it is necessary to understand this parable to be able to understand any parable (Mark 4:13). A broad diagram of the parable is as follows:[16]

---

13. Fowler, *Loaves and Fishes*, 85–86.
14. Fowler, *Loaves and Fishes*, 86.
15. Culpepper, "Mark 6:17–29," 161.
16. Blomberg, *Interpreting the Parables*, 226.

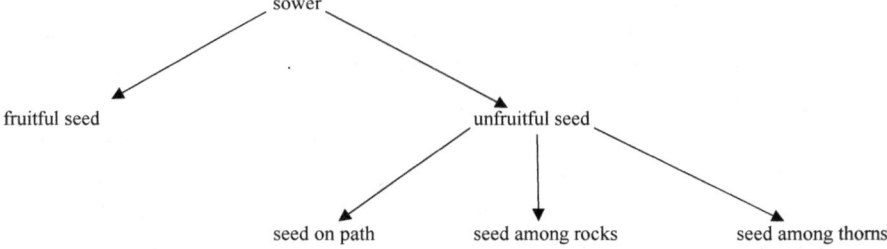

Commenting on this structure, Craig Blomberg states: "The parable itself describes in detail four kinds of soil. This detail is superfluous if each portion of the ground on which the seed falls does not stand for something fairly specific."[17] Mary Ann Tolbert has argued persuasively that the parable of the soils in Mark 4 provides a plot synopsis for the implied audience early in the Gospel in that it identifies the different, typological responses that people will have to the word.[18] Each of the main groups in the parable are instructive for the audience. There are not only fruitful and unfruitful responses, but different kinds of unfruitful responses. Tolbert has summarized the responses as follows:

	Parable of the Sower		*Interpretation*		*Gospel Group*
1.	seed sown along the way; eaten by birds	=	these in whom the word is immediately removed by Satan	=	scribes, Pharisees, Jerusalem Jewish leaders
2.	seed sown in rocky ground; comes up quickly but has no root; withers with the sun	=	these who accept the word immediately; endure for a time, but fall away when tribulation or persecution comes	=	disciples, especially Peter, James, and John

---

17. Blomberg, *Interpreting the Parables*, 226.

18. Tolbert, *Sowing the Gospel*, 148–64. Tolbert also observes: "Jesus teaches from a boat on the sea and the massive crowd is by the sea on the earth (ἐπὶ τῆς γῆς). It is typology, not geography or history, that stands behind this setting. In the parables that follow, those who hear the word that Jesus speaks may respond in one of the same four ways in which the four different types of earth (γῆ) respond to the seed sown in them. The huge crowds who listen to Jesus 'on the land' are types of the parabolic 'earths' about to be expounded" (Tolbert, *Sowing the Gospel*, 149).

3.	seed sown among thorns; thorns choke it and it produces no fruit	=	others in whom the word is choked by the cares of the world, delight in riches, and desire for other things	=	Herod; rich man of 10:17–22
4.	seed sown on the good earth; brings forth grain in triple abundance	=	those who hear the word, accept it, and bear fruit in triple abundance.	=	ones healed (or saved) by their faith.[19]

Each type of soil is identified as a group of people:

- These (οὗτοι) in 4:15;
- These (οὗτοι) in 4:16;
- Others (ἄλλοι) in 4:18; and
- Those (ἐκεῖνοί) in 4:20.

As Tolbert observes: "The contrast should suggest to the audience that 'these' are groups nearby, recently discussed; 'others' and 'those' are not yet fully explicated."[20]

The group in Mark that has opposed Jesus up to this point in the narrative are the religious leaders (scribes, Pharisees, Herodians, and Jerusalem Jews) (cf. Mark 2:6–7, 15, 24, 3:2, 6, 22). They hear but do not heed to what he says.

The other nearby group in the narrative (οὗτοι) is the disciples. There are several textual links to suggest the disciples are the rocky soil. The first link is that the name of the leader of the Twelve, Peter (Πέτρον), is a play on the word for "rocky" soil (πετρώδης) (cf. Mark 3:13; 4:5). The second link is that the rocky soil sprang up quickly (εὐθὺς) (Mark 4:5, 16). Following the call of Peter and Andrew, and of James and John, the narrator reported that they "quickly" (εὐθὺς) followed Jesus (Mark 1:18, 19). Finally, the rocky soil is said to fall away (σκανδαλίζω) when trouble or persecution comes because of the word (Mark 4:17). Before Jesus is arrested, he announces that all the disciples will fall away (σκανδαλίζω) (Mark 14:27).

The other group not yet fully disclosed in the narrative (ἄλλοι), appears to be first encountered in the person of Herod in Mark 6. Herod is described as someone who feared John the Baptizer as a righteous man, even though John spoke against Herod for taking his brother's wife

19. Tolbert, *Sowing the Gospel*, 171.
20. Tolbert, *Sowing the Gospel*, 153.

(Mark 6:18, 20). Herod was perplexed by what John said to him, but preserved John from his wife, Herodias, who had a grudge against him and wanted to kill him; despite pressure from Herodias, Herod gladly heard John (Mark 6:19–20). However, when Herodias' daughter danced for Herod and he swore to give her whatever she asked for, he found himself caught in a bind when she, in collusion with her mother, asked for the head of John the Baptist. Like the seed sown among thorns, Herod was pressured by his oath before his dinner guests who were prominent men in his world—nobles, commanders of thousands, and prominent ones of Galilee (Mark 6:21). His desire to protect the righteous man, John, was choked out by the cares of his world sitting around him in the banquet hall. So, he acquiesced and had John beheaded (6:26–27).[21]

Theological argument is being used to show the type of character produced in the person of Herodias. What is interesting at this intersection of the narrative is who Herodias shows herself to be in the typological characterization of the soils. The audience would recognize her similarity to the first soil that has been observed in the religious leaders. When John the Baptizer speaks against the divorce of her first husband and marriage to Herod, she cannot receive the prophet's revelation. Like the religious leaders with Jesus, she has a grudge against John for his exposing words and wants to kill him. It is also of interest that she is named in the narrative. Unlike the anonymous women of Peter's mother-in-law and the woman with the flow of blood, who are all positively portrayed in the narrative, Herodias is named and shows herself to be flawed, even ruthless.

Moreover, in her strength and resolve, Herodias weakens Herod. As Catharine Edwards explains:

> Male members of the Roman elite . . . were expected to display the greatest degree of control over themselves, just as they exercised the greatest degree of power over other people: over the non-Romans they ruled, the poorer Romans to whom they were patrons, their female relatives, and of course their slaves.[22]

Continuing, Edwards explains:

---

21. Tolbert states: "Herod values his position, his reputation, and his oath more highly than what he has been hearing gladly. Riches, worldly power, and concern about the regard of others are all noxious weeds that kill the word" (Tolbert, *Sowing the Gospel*, 158).

22. Edwards, "Suffering Body," 255.

> Martial bravery was symbolically central in Roman culture. Romans celebrated themselves as a nation that had conquered an empire through *virtus*. *Virtus* (a word cognate with *vir*, "man") denotes the physical courage felt to be the specific characteristic of the male and of the Roman male in particular.[23]

The endurance of pain was not limited to the physical; it included mental pain.[24] However, in the conflict between Herodias and Herod, it is Herodias who shows herself to have the greater self-control and Herod who cannot display self-control over his own feelings: "The king was greatly distressed (περίλυπος) but because of his oaths and his dinner guests, he did not want to refuse her" (Mark 6:26). In an ironic twist, Herod shows himself as feminine by not exercising self-control over Herodias and her daughter and over the pressure created by his words before his subjects. The strong, immoveable, self-controlled one was Herodias who wanted to kill John and then arranged to accomplish her will. This kind of reversal was spoken of by Seneca (ca. 4 BC to AD 65) who observed that even slaves may despise death (i.e., lack self-control), while a girl in childbirth may set an example for the endurance of pain.[25] This reversal of roles is further emphasized in the narrative by the actions of the executioner. Herod orders the executioner to bring John's head in Mark 6:27. After beheading John, the executioner brought back John's head on a platter and did not present it to Herod, but to the girl who then gave it to Herodias (Mark 6:28). As Michelle Connolly observes: "In a sense, Herod is bypassed in the chain of command and the women have taken over."[26]

Unlike the women previously portrayed in Mark's narrative, Herodias and her daughter come from a different/higher social class. As Connolly observes: "In a sense, their world represents the Roman Empire in Palestine."[27] This statement will gain greater importance in the broader narrative of Mark where a similar pattern occurs with the religious leaders, the crowd, and a Roman procurator named Pontius Pilate. For the implied audience versed within the value system of the Romans, this

---

23. Edwards, "Suffering Body," 262.

24. Edwards, "Suffering Body," 257.

25. Seneca the Younger states: "And thou, silence the groans, the cries, and the bitter shrieks ground out of the victim as he is torn on the rack! Forsooth thou are naught but Pain, scorned by yonder gout-ridden wretch, endured by yonder dyspeptic in the midst of his dainties, borne bravely by the girl in travail. Slight thou art, if I can bear thee; short thou art if I cannot bear thee!" (Seneca, *Epistles* 24.14).

26. Connolly, *Disorderly Women*, 139–40.

27. Connolly, *Disorderly Women*, 134.

emphasis on the Roman class in Israel will provide a subtle critique of these male Roman underlings.

THE BROADER CONTEXT OF THE NARRATIVE

In Mark 15 we encounter another Roman ruler, the procurator/governor in Judea, Pontius Pilate (AD 26–36).[28] Mark's portrayal of Pilate has many similarities to his portrayal of Herod:

Herod	Pilate
A feast (birthday party)	A feast (Passover)
Herod offers daughter anything she wishes;	Pilate offers the people the freedom of any prisoner they wish;
Moved by her mother, the girl asks not for a trinket, but John the Baptizer's head;	Moved by the priests, the people ask not for Jesus, but for Barabbas;
Herod is lukewarm-would spare the preacher (John) if he could;	Pilate is lukewarm-would spare the preacher (Jesus) if he could;
Herod is subject to pressure (party guests) which he fails to resist;	Pilate is subject to pressure (Jewish leaders) which he fails to resist;
Herod is trapped by his princely promise;	Pilate is trapped by his princely promise;
John is executed.	Jesus is executed.[29]

These parallels would resonate with those receiving the gospel of the parable of the soils in Mark 4. Like the seed sown among thorns, Pilate was pressured by his offer before the religious leaders and the crowds (Mark 15:6–15). His desire and attempts to protect Jesus (15:10) were choked out by the cares of his world as the priests and the crowds called for the release of Barabbas and the crucifixion of Jesus. Consequently, Pilate acquiesced (satisfied the crowd) and handed Jesus over to be flogged and crucified (15:15). This parallel with Pilate demonstrates how the associated character Herod also corresponds with another, subtle, vilified character, Pilate.

Not only are there parallels between Jesus and John and between Herod and Pilate, but there are parallels between Herodias and her

---

28. For a more detailed discussion of Pilate, see Brown, *Death of the Messiah*, 1:693–705; Schürer, *History of the Jewish People*, 2:81–89.

29. See Fowler, *Loaves and Fishes*, 123–24, quoting Farrer, *St Matthew and St Mark*, 14. See also Malbon, "Minor Characters," 70.

daughter and between the religious leaders and the crowd that become evident to the implied audience. We have already seen that Herodias was like the religious leaders in that they both could/would not receive the revelation from the preachers. What is enlightening when comparing Mark 6 and 15 are the parallels which arise between Herodias' daughter and the crowds. Just as the chief priests stirred up the crowd to have Pilate release Barabbas to them instead of Jesus (15:11), so was it that Herodias stirred up her daughter to ask Herod for John's head instead of anything else a young girl might desire (6:24–25). The daughter and the crowd are lethal instruments in the hands of the more powerful mother and religious leaders. Furthermore, both the crowd and the daughter go beyond what they are encouraged to do by the religious leaders and by Herodias. Not only do the crowds ask, as instructed, for the release of Barabbas, but they then call for the crucifixion of Jesus (15:11–14). Likewise, Herodias' daughter goes beyond the request of her mother. As Connolly observes:

> She does not merely repeat what her mother said, but makes it her own, insisting, "I want you to give me at once." She adds her own grotesque recognition of the birthday scene, asking that her request be presented "on a platter," as though it is to be yet another course of the banquet.

CONCLUSION

Writing from a feminist perspective, Connolly concludes that Mark has portrayed women badly in the Herod narrative because they are shown to combine to disrupt male power and dominance:

> The misogynist message of this rich narrative is never to let women collaborate together on what is otherwise an entirely civilized relationship of agreement to differ, between two powerful men. Women, when they get power, are frighteningly violent and vindictive in a way that men cannot imagine. Female bonding, when women consult together, is particularly prone to grave disorder. Male bonding does not protect men but will be turned against them, to destroy them. The obvious solution is not to allow women to collect together.

Although a fascinating theory and possible if Mark 6 is considered in isolation, Connolly's conclusion is not founded on the full narrative of the Gospel of Mark. Obviously, the parallels between the proximate causes of John's and Jesus' deaths explicitly show that the collusion is not one of women against men since Mark 15 has men in a parallel role with Herodias and the crowd in a parallel role with Herodias' daughter. These disruptive, disorderly, deadly consequences do not arise as the result of a clash between the sexes. They arise because of how people respond to the revelation they are given as foretold in the parable of the soils in Mark 4. Herodias is shown to act like the religious leaders, and her daughter becomes a pawn like the crowd to force the hand of a Roman official. Yes, Herodias and her daughter are portrayed negatively in the narrative—sly, seductive, deceitful, not to be trusted, not given to repentance, and characterized by uncontrolled revenge—but only because they do not respond well to the message of the prophet and use their power to bring about the prophet's death. As women, they are powerful—even more powerful, strategically, than their male, Roman ruler. But they are not unique in this struggle. They are like the other characters, including male religious leaders and the crowd in the broader narrative who back the Roman governor into a corner to do their will and crucify Jesus. The subtle message for the implied audience is that these Roman representatives are not "manly" but womanlier than the women in Mark 6 because these Roman pawns are weak, irresponsible, out of control, and without knowledge about how to rule. Connolly's conclusion is not founded on a thorough reading of Mark and unfortunately points to a problem that is less weighty than the one asked of those who receive the stories. The rhetorical concern is not to beware of the disruption that can arise from females who bond together, but to beware of those who will not receive the word of God, whether male, female, or even a crowd, because they can be treacherous—even deadly.

This narrative of a mother and daughter who respond negatively to divine revelation with deadly consequences to John the Baptizer stands in stark contrast to the next Markan narrative where a mother uniquely understands Jesus' parabolic statement, receives it, and extends Jesus' metaphor in a way that brings blessing to her and life to her daughter.

12

The Syrophoenician Woman
(Mark 7:24–30)

THE FIFTH MARKAN NARRATIVE involving women concerns an unnamed, Gentile woman from the non-Jewish area of the Syrian, coastal plain, called Phoenicia, who asks Jesus to heal her demonized daughter. In addition to being a woman, she symbolizes a request from the Gentile world to share in the blessings of Israel's Messiah. She is shown to be more astute than Jesus' Jewish followers, and pictures, in narrative form, a broader extension of Messiah's ministry to all who respond well to his words. Through the discourse of a sermon-sign, the implied author/narrator will enable the implied audience to develop its characterization of the Syrophoenician woman as a virtuous woman, distinct from Israel's religious leaders and Jesus' own disciples, as she hears Jesus' metaphoric words to her, understands their meaning, and applies the metaphor to the specific condition of her life.

INTRODUCTION

The narrative involving the Syrophoenician Woman in Mark 7:24–30 falls within the larger section of Mark 6:7—8:21. For the placement of Mark 6 in the overall structure of the book, see the discussion regarding "Herodias, Her Daughter, and the Beheading of John the Baptist" in Mark 6:7–32. This discussion will focus on the placement of Mark 7:24–30 within the structure of Mark 6:7—8:21. In broad strokes, the narrative unit has a two-fold interchanging structure emphasizing parallel threats to Jesus and the disciples by Herod and the Pharisees, with hard-hearted responses by the disciples:

> A Herod / feeding of five thousand (6:7–44)
>   B Jesus on the sea / the disciples' hard hearts (6:45–52)
> A' Pharisees / feeding of four thousand (6:53—8:13)
>   B' Jesus on the sea / the disciples' hard hearts (8:14–21)

The structure of 6:7—8:21 can be further developed through the following detailed layout:

> A Controversy with Herod (6:1–34)
>   B Feeding of the five thousand (6:35–44)
>   C Boat trip; Walking on water; disciples' hearts are hard (6:45–52)
>   D General healing; immediately recognized (6:53–56)
> A' Controversy with the Pharisees over outer tradition v. inner heart (7:1–23)
>   D' Healing of Syrophoenician woman's daughter (7:24–30)
>   D" Healing of deaf mute (7:31–37)
>   B' Feeding of four thousand (8:1–9)
> A" Controversy with the Pharisees over a sign (8:10–12)
>   C' Boat trip; disciples' hearts are hard (8:13–21)

What immediately stands out in the above structure is the irregularity in the second half of the interchange in that the healing section designated by the letter "D" precedes sections B' and C', and a second controversy with the Pharisees is introduced in section A" before the boat trip in section C'. Charles Talbert surveyed the break of perfect symmetry, or "symmetrophobia," in classical Greek literature and in Near-Eastern writings and art and concluded:

> Given the aversion to perfect symmetry in both classical and Near Eastern Cultures, it is no surprise to find imperfections in the patterns of the early Christian writings of our survey and of Luke-Acts. They are to be expected in the midst of the most perfect symmetry.

Furthermore, the rearrangement of the units allows for a three-fold emphasis in the second half of the interchange, namely (1) a repetition of the controversy with the Pharisees (Mark 7:1–23; 8:10–12) as a means of

The Syrophoenician Woman 153

emphasizing that this controversy is even greater, or of more importance, than the controversy with Herod; (2) an emphasis on the hard-hearted response of the disciples by making it the closing section (Mark 8:13–21) of the larger unit (Mark 6:1—8:21); and (3) an emphasis on Jesus' ministry to the Gentiles by the content of his message in Mark 7:1–23, and by repeated miracles among the Gentiles in Mark 7:34—8:9 with the healing of the Syrophoenician woman's daughter (Mark 7:24–30), the healing of the deaf mute in the Gentile region of the Decapolis (Mark 7:31–37), and the provision of food for what appear to be Gentiles in the feeding of the four thousand (Mark 8:1–9). Even though the feeding of the four thousand has a parallel in the feeding of the five thousand in Mark 6:35–44, there may be a reformulating of the feeding narrative's function by making it part of three *signs* following Jesus' *sermon* about clean and unclean in 7:1–23. If so, the rearrangement of the units would be as follows:

A Controversy with Herod (6:1–34)
  B Feeding of the five thousand (6:35–44)
    C Walking on water; disciples' hearts are hard (6:45–52)
      D General healing; immediately recognized (6:53–56)
A' Controversy with the Pharisees over outer tradition v. inner heart (7:1–23)
Sermon
Signs
      D' Healing of Syrophoenician woman's daughter (7:24–30)
      D" healing of deaf mute (7:31–37)
      D'" Feeding of four thousand (8:1–9)
A" Controversy with the Pharisees over a sign (8:10–12)
    C' boat trip; disciples' hearts are hard (8:13–21)

As discussed above in Chapter 5, the sign-sermon literary pattern was employed so often in early Greek and Hebrew literature that it was probably familiar to the actual author and implied audience of the Gospel of Mark and used in the work to clarify and emphasize the emotive significance of the message in chapter 7. The structure of the narrative in 7:1—8:9 is as follows:

A' Controversy with the Pharisees over outer tradition v. inner heart (7:1–23)
Sermon
Signs
      D' Healing of Syrophoenician woman's daughter (7:24–30)
      D" healing of deaf mute (7:31–37)
      D'" Feeding of four thousand (8:1–9)

Each of the signs in 7:24—8:9 emphasize in a crystallized fashion Jesus' message in the controversy set out in Mark 7:1–23.

THE SERMON—CONTROVERSY WITH THE PHARISEES IN MARK 7:1–23

The Sermon's Context (Mark 7:1–5)

The last, specific, geographical indicator prior to this narrative places Jesus on the northwest coast of the Sea of Galilee, south of Capernaum, in the plain of Gennesaret (Mark 6:53) and in the surrounding villages, towns, and countryside (6:56). In other words, Jesus was located in Jewish Galilee when the Jewish Pharisees and teachers of the law came to him from Jerusalem (7:1).

For a moment, the narrative is told from the point of view of the religious leaders stating that they saw some of Jesus' disciples eating bread[1] with common, or profane hands (κοιναῖς χερσίν) in that they were unwashed (ἄνιπτος) (7:2).[2] The narrator then provides an aside to the audience explaining the Pharisaic practice of ceremonial washing wherein he describes this activity as holding to the "tradition of the elders" (7:3–4).

Jesus then explains that the "tradition of the elders" consists of "the teachings of men" which are distinct from the written Law of Moses and which nullify the written Law (7:10–13). As Moisés Silva explained: "The Pharisees made the Torah easier to obey.... The divine standard had been relaxed. The Torah had been accommodated to meet the weaknesses of

---

1. The term "bread" (ἄρτος) is a lead word running as a unifying string through the subsections of the overall unit (Mark 6:7—8:21). The disciples were not to bring bread with them when they were sent out (Mark 6:8). Bread was used to feed the five thousand (Mark 6:37, 38, 41). The disciples did not understand about the bread because their hearts were hardened (Mark 6:52). The disciples were eating bread with "unclean hands" (Mark 7:2, 5). Jesus tells the Syrophoenician woman that it is not right to take the children's bread and toss it to dogs (Mark 7:27). Bread is used to feed the four thousand (Mark 8:4, 5, 6). Finally, the disciples forgot to bring bread except for one loaf (Mark 8:14, 17) whereupon Jesus chides the disciples for not understanding the significance of the bread (Mark 8:17) in the feeding of the five thousand and the four thousand (Mark 8:19). "Bread" will feature in how the characterization of the Syrophoenician woman takes place.

2. As Emil Schürer explained, "It was needful that the hands should always have water poured on them before eating" (Schürer, *History of the Jewish People*, 4:111).

The Syrophoenician Woman

the people."[3] Discussing the controversy between Jesus and the Pharisees in Mark 7, Silva further explained:

> The controversy described in this passage centers on the law that ceremonial washing was required before eating. In fact, this is not an Old Testament law; it is not part of the *Written* Torah. But it was part of the *Oral* Torah, that is, the traditions of the elders. . . . The Oral Law was viewed as on par with the Written Law—indeed, in some respects, as more important, for a ruling that a part of the Oral Law may in effect set aside the Written Law, as in the case of the *prozbul*.[4]

In other words, in this incident Jesus argues that through their oral traditions, the Pharisees had relaxed the standards of the written Law making it easier to obey, or okay to disobey.

The Sermon's Content (Mark 7:14–15)

In the context of Jesus' exposure of the Pharisees' erroneous traditions that break the written Law, Jesus calls the crowd and urges them to hear (ἀκούσατέ) and understand (σύνετε) what he is saying to them. This charge is similar to the charge made in chapter 4 prior to the telling of the parable of the soils (Ἀκούετε. ἰδοὺ, 4:3). Then Jesus states the essence of his sermon in a maxim of antithetical parallelism: "Nothing outside a person can defile a person by entering into a person, but the things coming from a person defile a person." The lead word "defile" (κοινόω) ties Jesus' message to the context of the Pharisees' charge (cf. κοινός in Mark 7:2, 5). Contextually, the relevance of the maxim is that the breach of the Pharisees external requirements of ceremonial washing do not defile, make unclean, or make common the food the disciples are eating, but the inner motivation of the Pharisees to use their traditions to relax and actually breach the requirements of the written Law defiles them. The characterization that will take place in the pericope involving the Syrophoenician woman incorporates what the narrative conveys at this stage concerning purity and impurity. This theme becomes even more prominent when this public scene is departed from to enter a "house" once again.

---

3. Silva, "Historical Reconstruction," 120.
4. Silva, "Historical Reconstruction," 120–21.

The Sermon's Explanation (Mark 7:17–23)

The scene now changes; Jesus leaves the crowd and enters a house, and his disciples ask him to explain what he has said, identifying his message as a parable (παραβολή) (Mark 7:17).[5] The placement of the disciples alone with Jesus where they asked about the meaning of a parable is an echo of chapter 4 where the disciples previously asked Jesus to explain the parable of the soils (Mark 4:10). Jesus' response to the disciples is also a foreshadow of chapter 8 where Jesus will rebuke the disciples for being hard-hearted using language from Isaiah 6 which was used in chapter 4 to describe those who are "outside" without insight (cf. Mark 4:11–12 with Mark 8:17–21). Jesus asks the disciples: "Are you without understanding (ἀσύνετοί)?" The question uses the a-privative prefix with the same word used in Mark 7:14 when Jesus urged the crowd to understand (σύνετε) his saying. The disciples show themselves to lack understanding (cf. Mark 4:12; 6:52; 8:17, 21). This lack of understanding on the part of the disciples functions implicitly in the thorough understanding that forms one of the constituents of the Syrophoenician's character.

Jesus then expands upon his maxim by explaining that that which enters a person (presumably food from unwashed hands) does not defile a person because it enters into the stomach and then enters into the latrine; it does not enter the person's heart (Mark 7:18–19). At this point, it appears that the narrator inserts a side-bar comment for the audience that by these words Jesus was "cleansing all foods."[6] But the focus of the explanation is not about the nature of foods, but the nature of the heart. Food does not enter the heart. Continuing, Jesus explains that it is that which journeys out from a person that defiles a person (7:20). Then, so there can be no confusion over what comes out of a person (because Jesus just said that food comes out of a person in verse 19), the implied

---

5. Verse 16 is omitted as a scribal gloss. It exists in the majority of witnesses (A D K W Γ Δ^c Θ $f^{1.13}$ 33. 565. 579. 700. 892. 1241. 1424. 2542 𝔐 latt sy sa^{mss} bo^{pt}) but is absent from the Alexandrian witnesses (ℵ B L Δ* 0274. 28 sa^{mss} bo^{pt}). See Metzger, *Textual Commentary*, 81.

6. καθαρίζων πάντα τὰ βρώματα. As Bruce Metzger observes: "The overwhelming weight of manuscript evidence supports the reading καθαρίζων. The difficulty of construing this word in the sentence prompted copyists to attempt various corrections and ameliorations" (Metzger, *Textual Commentary*, 81). In a footnote, Metzger also states: "Many modern scholars, following the interpretation suggested by Origen and Chrysostom, regard καθαρίζων as connected grammatically with λέγει in v. 18, and take it as the evangelist's comment on the implications of Jesus' words concerning Jewish dietary laws" (81n14). See also Guelich, *Mark 1–8:26*, 378.

author/narrator makes Jesus explain that it is that which comes out of the heart—the seat of volition—that defiles a person, namely bad reasonings (διαλογισμοὶ οἱ κακοί), immoralities (πορνεῖαι), thefts (κλοπαί), murders (φόνοι), adulteries (μοιχεῖαι), covetings (πλεονεξίαι), wickedness (πονηρίαι), deceit (δόλος), self-abandonment (ἀσέλγεια), the evil eye, or envy (ὀφθαλμὸς πονηρός,), slander (βλασφημία), pride (ὑπερηφανία) and foolishness (ἀφροσύνη) (7:21–22).[7] Then Jesus sums up his statement that all these evil things just given in the vice list journey forth from within a person, and they are what defile a person (7:23).

Jesus' explanation aligns perfectly with the context of his message. It was not that which the disciples ate with unwashed hands that defiled them, but that which the Pharisees plotted in their heart to "legally" nullify the Law of God with their "traditions" that defiled them. The message may be clear, but the implications of the sermon are yet to be shown to those in the narrative and those receiving the narrative (the implied audience). This *showing* will be accomplished through the following signs where Jesus heals the Syrophoenician Woman's daughter (Mark 7:24–30), heals a deaf mute (7:31–37), and feeds the four thousand Gentiles in the Decapolis (8:1–9). These three signs will crystallize the meaning and scope of the message in the sermon for and in interaction with the implied audience. The focus of this study will be on the first sign following the sermon, the healing of the Gentile woman's daughter in Mark 7:24–30.

---

7. Robert Guelich seems to correctly observe: "The list includes thirteen vices summarized by the first, 'evil thoughts' (διαλογισμοὶ οἱ κακοί). The following twelve fall into two groups of six each with the first group in the plural and the second in the singular" (Guelich, *Mark 1–8*, 379). Praise lists and vice lists were common in early Christian communities as tools to substantiate or vilify characters, so the implied audience would understand this vice list and be able to use it to vilify the religious leaders and later praise the Syrophoenician woman when she shows herself to be distinct. See Knust, *Abandoned to Lust*, 19–22. Unlike the Pharisees and disciples who do not understand (Mark 7:7, 14, 18), the Syrophoenician woman's character will be built showing "understanding."

THE FIRST SIGN—THE HEALING OF THE SYROPHOENICIAN WOMAN'S DAUGHTER IN MARK 7:24–30

Setting the Scene (Mark 7:24–26)

The geographical location of this narrative switched from Jewish Gennesaret and its surrounding locations to the Hellenized region of Tyre on the coast of the Mediterranean Sea among the city states of the Syrian coastal plain called Phoenicia (Mark 7:24).[8] It is in this foreign land that Jesus will encounter a Syrophoenician woman with a request.

Once again, Jesus seeks a respite from public ministry (cf. Mark 1:35; 6:31–32; 7:24) but is unable to escape those with need (cf. Mark 1:36–37; 6:33–34; 7:25). In this case, it is a woman whose daughter (θυγάτριον) has an unclean (ἀκάθαρτος) spirit, who hears (ἀκούσασα) about Jesus and comes to the house (οἰκία) where he is staying and falls at his feet (προσέπεσεν πρὸς τοὺς πόδας αὐτοῦ). All of the Greek words identified in the previous sentence are significant to the development of the contextual narrative and in the construction of character. In the immediate context, the issue concerned *defilement*, and the woman's daughter has an *unclean* spirit. Furthermore, Jesus prefaced his sermon in Mark 7:14 with the exhortation to "hear" him (ἀκούσατέ); in this unit the woman comes to Jesus because she heard (ἀκούσασα) about him. The other words reach into a broader context of the narrative.

In terms of characterization, we will now analyze how the implied author, by means of association, works toward the construction of the Syrophoenician's character. The audience would remember that Jairus also fell at Jesus' feet (πίπτει πρὸς τοὺς πόδας αὐτοῦ) when he first sought Jesus to heal his daughter (θυγάτριον) (Mark 5:22–23). And by association, it reminds an implied audience of a similarity between someone who was well-accepted (that is, someone completely aligned with the *habitus*, the in-group) and someone who might be rejected. The diminutive form for the word "daughter" (θυγάτριον) is only used in Mark 5 and 7. The similarities between the two passages, where parents make a plea for the healing of their "little daughter," could not be more similar lexically, and yet at first glance, more different in the identity of the parents petitioning Jesus. In Mark 5:22 it is a Jewish man, identified repeatedly as one of the

---

8. Josephus describes those from Tyre as bitter enemies of the Jews. See Josephus, *Life*, 190–91 (1.70).

rulers of the synagogue (εἷς τῶν ἀρχισυναγώγων) who humbly beseeches Jesus' help. In Mark 7:24–26 it is a Greek woman (ἡ δὲ γυνὴ ἦν Ἑλληνίς) born in Syrian Phoenicia (Συροφοινίκισσα τῷ γένει) who humbly seeks Jesus' help. Jairus' daughter is deathly ill; the woman's daughter has an unclean spirit.

The double description of the woman as Greek and Syrophoenician may be a double entendre in that it can be understood in two different ways. It is possible that the term "Greek" distinguishes the woman socially. As Jennifer Glancy observes:

> To single out an individual as "Greek" suggests the location of that person in a thoroughly Hellenized and therefore privileged household. "Greek" functions as a marker of cultivated and privileged ethnicity that is consistent with an identity as Syrophoenician by descent.[9]

If so, she was prominent in her community as Jairus was in his community. However, Robert Guelich thinks the term "Greek" may be better understood as a religious contrast to "Jewish."[10] One problem with Guelich's analysis is that all of his examples come from Pauline epistles and not the Gospel of Mark or any other Gospel narrative. If "Greek" is meant to distinguish the woman from Jairus by emphasizing her Gentile nature as being alien to a Jewish person's life (from the perspective of a Jewish person), this fits the design of the sermon-sign as Jesus interacts with someone who would have been considered unclean. Certainly the "unclean" (ἀκάθαρτος) spirit inhabiting the woman's daughter aligns with the earlier theme of defilement. Together they would make a strong contrast to Jairus. On the other hand, if "Greek" is meant to emphasize the prominent position of the woman in her culture, the audience has one more parallel with Jairus who was prominent in his culture. Both of these prominent parents humbly petition Jesus for their little daughters.[11] These parallels suggest that those receiving the Gospel narrative

---

9. Glancy, "Jesus, the Syrophoenician Woman," 352. See also Connolly, *Disorderly Women*, 142. In support of this view, it is also noted that the woman's daughter is found on a "bed" (κλίνη) rather than a mattress (Mark 7:30). See Perkinson, "Canaanitic Word," 67.

10. Guelich, *Mark 1–8*, 385.

11. This bodily act of lowering expresses deference to perceived power and authority which the implied audience would understand. See Glancy, "Jesus, the Syrophoenician Woman," 352–55; *Corporal Knowledge*, 17–18; Mark 1:7; 5:22; 10:17; 15:19.

should compare Jesus' response to each parent. As a double entendre, both meanings could be operative.

There is another contrast that is appropriate in the narratives of Mark 5 and Mark 7. When the ruler of the synagogue approaches Jesus, he comes in a public setting where a crowd is gathered (Mark 5:22–25). However, when the Gentile woman approaches Jesus, she comes in the privacy of a house (οἰκία). As Bourdieu has demonstrated, as well as other Greek and Israelite studies, the house would fall within the *habitus* of a first-century woman.[12] The implied author used the setting of the household in the characterization of the Syrophoenician woman to portray her favorably as an insider in terms of the socio-political expectations of the implied audience with a value system that identifies with the broader context of an ancient Mediterranean society. So even though she may be a foreigner to Israel, she is functioning within acceptable social customs by coming to Jesus in a house. Of course, this is distinct from the woman in Mark 5 who joins the public crowd and touches Jesus' garment in public (5:26). Jesus makes nothing of the propriety of either woman's actions. All three characters fall to the ground before Jesus (5:22, 33; 7:25). Jairus and the Greek woman in supplication and the woman with the flow of blood in fear. As Jennifer Glancy explains: "In these Markan scenes deference and authority are negotiated through posture and gesture as well as through words. Such negotiations of the hierarchies of power and social status would have been familiar to Mark's readers and indeed throughout the Roman Empire."[13]

Glancy understands Jesus' response to Jairus to be positive and to the Greek woman to be negative (recoiling),[14] but there may be more similarities than differences in Jesus' response to these two parents. Both

---

12. Connelly argues that the woman brought shame upon herself and potentially upon Jesus by coming to him without a male chaperone (Connolly, *Disorderly Women*, 142–43). Without denying the social expectation identified by Connolly, it appears to be an argument from silence, and nothing is made of this supposed breach of social custom in the narrative. We do not know whether the woman was accompanied by a male chaperone. We do not know the woman's marital status. We do not even know the woman's name. This is not to say that this information was not available or present in the encounter. It is to say that the implied author has chosen not to discuss any of this information because it does not contribute to *how* s/he wants to tell the story. For instance, the implied author never tells us whether the disciples are with Jesus in the story. That does not mean that they were not present, only that they do not contribute to what the author is doing with what s/he is saying.

13. Glancy, "Syrophoenician Woman," 354; *Corporal Knowledge*, 14–19.

14. Glancy, "Syrophoenician Woman," 358–59, 363; *Corporal Knowledge*, 17–18.

parents experienced a delayed response to their requests; both parents were instructed by Jesus; and both parents were granted their petitions, although for Jairus, his daughter's condition worsened before it improved. The implied author is doing something with what s/he is saying in these two accounts for the benefit of his implied audience, and that something does not appear to be showing disdain for the Greek woman who acts appropriately in the socio-political setting. The narratives have different theological purposes in Mark 5 and 7. The implied author is using discourse to communicate his theological message in each passage so that the implied audience can create characterization.

The Interaction of Jesus and the Woman (Mark 7:27–29)

The implied author/narrator tells the implied audience that the woman kept asking Jesus to cast the demon from her daughter. The verb "to ask" is in the imperfect tense, ἠρώτα, emphasizing repeated action (7:26).[15] This is similar to Jairus who implored Jesus much (πολύς) (5:23).[16] We are not told about any conversation that transpired between Jairus and Jesus in Mark 5, but the conversation between Jesus and the Greek woman is given because it serves the implied author's purpose in this sermon-sign narrative of crystallizing his narrative and developing the characterization of the woman for his implied audience.

Jesus' initial words to the woman are obviously figurative. She has asked him for the deliverance of her daughter (Mark 7:26), and he speaks to her about giving the bread of children to dogs (7:27). The disciples have repeatedly not been able to understand Jesus' figurative language (see Mark 4:12; 7:17–18; 8:17, 21). When they are alone with him, they repeatedly ask him to interpret the parabolic saying, as they did in Mark 7:17 when they entered the house (οἰκία). But now in the house (οἰκία, Mark 7:24), Jesus does not interpret a parabolic saying to the woman, but begins a new parabolic saying (7:27), and unlike the disciples, the woman immediately understands the parable and expands its scope in a way that is consistent with the metaphoric world of the parable and provides for her needs:[17]

15. See Wallace, *Greek Grammar*, 546.

16. As Glancy observes: "Perhaps hinting that Jesus is initially resistant to Jairus, Mark states that the synagogue leader begs Jesus repeatedly" (Glancy, "Syrophoenician Woman," 358).

17. Michele Connolly posits that the Syrophoenician woman responds to Jesus as

And he said to her, "First, let the children be fed. For it is not good to take the bread of the children and throw it to the little dogs."

And she answered and said to him: "Lord, even the little dogs under the table eat from the crumbs of the children."

And he said to her: "On account of this word, go, the demon has gone out of your daughter." (Mark 7:27–29, author's translation)

The parable is never explicitly interpreted for the disciples (if they are present) or for the audience. Everything is figurative. Does the implied audience understand? Clues to meaning of the parable have been providing in the larger narrative.

From the beginning of the Gospel, Jesus has been identified as a Jewish Messiah fulfilling Old Testament Scriptures and ministering to the Jewish people primarily in the area of Galilee (Mark 1:1–3, 9, 11, 14–15, 16, 21, 28, 38–39; 2:1, 13). Jesus' family members have been identified in Mark 3:34–35 when he says to those in the house (οἰκία, 3:20), that those who do the will of God are his family—brother, sister, and mother. In chapter 7 he talks about bread (ἄρτος) for family members, children. Bread was symbolic of Jesus' provision for Israel as the new Moses in Mark 6 where the five thousand men were fed in the wilderness and *twelve* baskets of leftovers were gathered.[18] Should the provisions for Israel now be given to those who are not part of the family, namely to Gentiles who are described as little doggies, or household dogs, or lap-dogs (κυνάριον)?[19]

---

a Cynic providing a "witty one-line rejoinder" in a competition with Jesus in a "game of wit" (Connolly, *Disorderly Women*, 144–45). However, none of this philosophical positioning is necessary to the interpretation of the narrative—especially in view of Jesus' earlier parabolic teaching.

18. Another verbal echo from the feeding of the five thousand that is also found in the dialogue between Jesus and the Syrophoenician woman is the verb "to be filled" (χορτάζω) (Mark 6:42; 7:27).

19. BDAG s.v. "κυνάριον." This is one of several diminutive words used in the passage: θυγάτριον, κυνάριον, ψιχίον, παιδίον. Guelich thinks the diminutives are "without significant force" (Guelich, *Mark 1–8*, 386). France agrees (France, *Mark*, 298n43). However, as has been shown above, the diminutive of "little daughter" raises a parallel between the woman and Jairus. Furthermore, in a passage that is criticized so often for Jesus' harsh tone toward the woman, the diminutives show a softened, more attenuated tone. A. T. Robertson states that diminutives can have an endearing sense. See Robertson, *Grammar of the Greek New Testament*, 155. As Voelz observes: "The unusual concentration of such forms [diminutives] in this relatively short pericope ... may indicate a more friendly and informal scene than is usually supposed" (Voelz, *Mark*, 480–81). Therefore, the argument that Jesus' use of the term "dogs" could only be understood as pejorative, completely misses the force of the diminutive. See Harrocks, "Body in Biblical, Christian and Jewish Texts," 91. Harrocks relies on Old Testament

The woman replies by not asking that the bread itself be given to the little dogs but by requesting that the overflow of that provision be given to them, and thus her, by analogy. In metaphoric language, she demonstrates an understanding that she is not a part of Israel but requests that some of the overflowing benefits to Israel be shared with her—a Gentile. The implied audience knows that there are overflowing benefits to Israel by virtue of the twelve baskets that were gathered after the feeding of the five thousand (Mark 6:43).[20]

Unlike the disciples who did not understand the loaves (τοῖς ἄρτοις, 6:52),[21] the Syrophoenician woman understands the abundance of Jesus' provisions. Out of her heart comes forth understanding, superior to that of the male disciples. Even though she is externally a Gentile, she is clean because her heart is clean (cf. Mark 7:15, 18–23). She may have appeared to be unclean as a genetic, Syrophoenician Gentile, but out of her heart comes forth understanding. She *hears* about Jesus' presence, understands

---

LXX passages (Exod 22:31; 1 Sam 17:43; 2 Sam 16:9; Ps 22:16; Isa 56:10–11) and New Testament passages (Matt 7:6; Phil 3:2; 2 Pet 2:22; Rev 22:15) using the term κύων, rather than the diminutive κυνάριον.

20. The number of baskets and the kind of baskets containing leftovers in each of the feeding narratives may be significant. In Mark 6:43 the narrator reports that there were twelve baskets (δώδεκα κοφίνων) and in Mark 8:8 there were seven baskets (ἑπτὰ σπυρίδας). In Mark 6:43 the term for basket described a smaller basket used for carrying food by the Jews, and in Mark 8:8 the term for basket described a larger basket used by the Gentiles as in the basket used to lower the Apostle Paul from an opening in the wall in Damascus (Acts 9:25). See Louw, *Greek-English Lexicon*, 2:71 (6.149–50). As Juvenal states: "Iudaeis, quorum cophinus fenumque supellex" (Juvenal, *Juvenal and Persius*, 198 [3.14]). The number of baskets in each case may also be significant. Twelve baskets may represent enough for the twelve tribes of Israel. Seven may represent the number of completeness for all peoples (the Gentiles). In support of this view, see Guelich, *Mark 1–8*, 343–44; Stock, *Mark*, 196; Voelz, *Mark*, 429. Against this view, see Fowler, *Loaves and Fishes*, 88–89n117.

21. The implied author/narrator's indictment of the disciples follows Jesus' appearance to them walking on the water after the feeding of the five thousand (Mark 6:46–52). The narrator tells the listener that Jesus was about to *pass by the disciples* (Mark 6:48), when the disciples thought he was a ghost. This water scene is still playing off the New Moses theme. In Exodus, God had Moses lift up his staff so that the sea would divide, and the sons of Israel could pass through it on dry land (Exod 14:16–22). Through Moses, God also fed the sons of Israel bread in the wilderness during their wandering (Exod 16:4–7). In Mark 6, Jesus, like the New Moses, feeds the multitude in the wilderness. Then Jesus does a greater miracle than Moses by walking *on* the water, rather than through it. By doing this, Jesus was showing the disciples that he was not only the New Moses, but greater than the New Moses; he was Yahweh who *passed by* Moses in Exodus 33:19–22. However, the disciples did not understand the second, greater revelation of who Jesus was because they did not understand the first revelation about the loaves of bread. The narrator explains that their hearts were hardened.

his power to cast out demons, and pursues him to cast the *unclean* demon from her daughter. She calls him "Lord" (κύριε) which may have been more than a polite address but an acknowledgment of Jesus' authoritative status (see the previous uses of κύριος in Mark 1:3; 2:28; and 5:19).[22] Even though she is a Gentile, she is an example *par excellence* of a disciple, and Jesus grants her request because of the word she spoke to him (διὰ τοῦτον τὸν λόγον, 7:29). Moreover, she is in stark contrast with the Jewish religious leaders in chapter 7 who by implication are defiled because out of their heart comes forth provisions to break the Law of God (Mark 7:6–15). Even though this Gentile woman would be considered impure by the hypocritical Pharisees and scribes so much that they would have washed their hands and utensils to ensure purity from the likes of her, the implied author/narrator constitutes her character as of such a purity that her "word" performs as the reason for the exorcism of the unclean spirit.

The Deliverance of the Daughter (Mark 7:30)

The implied author/narrator then summarizes the deliverance of the woman's daughter: "And going into her house, she found the child lying on the bed and the demon having gone out" (Mark 7:30). Again, the woman and her child are located in a socially-proper place, her house (οἶκον). We are also told that the demon had come out of her daughter using the perfect participle ἐξεληλυθός to emphasize an activity that occurred prior to the woman's arrival and continued into the present.[23] The implication is that the woman's daughter was delivered when Jesus told the woman in Mark 7:29 that the demon has gone out of your daughter (also a perfect tense of the same verb, ἐξελήλυθεν). Jesus instantaneously delivered the woman's daughter from a distance.

CONCLUSION

Some argue that by not following the woman to her home, as he did with Jairus, Jesus was not showing the respect for the woman that he showed

---

22. See also Guelich, *Mark 1–8*, 388.

23. As Dan Wallace states: "The force of the perfect tense is simply that it describes an event that, completed in the past (we are speaking of the perfect indicative here), has results existing in the present time (i.e., in relation to the time of the speaker)" (Wallace, *Greek Grammar*, 573).

to Jairus.[24] Others argue that by not touching the woman or her daughter, Jesus was avoiding contact with ritual impurity.[25] Both of these objections seem to require that Jesus always act in the same way, or that the implied author always communicate similar acts in identical ways. Said differently, external expectations are placed on the text rather than allowing the implied author to tell the story as s/he chooses to tell it for the purposes s/he may have. One could just as easily ask whether Jairus would have rather had Jesus heal his daughter from a distance than wait to follow him to the house and have him raise her from the dead. Also, the Markan narrative has no difficulty showing Jesus touching a Gentile as he does in the next "sign" when he heals a deaf, presumably Gentile man (from the Decapolis), by putting his fingers in the man's ears and touching the man's tongue (Mark 7:31–35). What the implied author has done in the passage with the Syrophoenician woman is add a dialogue that does not exist in the other units to demonstrate to the implied audience just how astute the woman is in her ability to hear a parable and expand upon it in a meaningful way theologically and personally.

Through the parable and the healing of the woman's daughter, the implied author has confirmed Jesus' sermon through a first sign by showing that it is what comes out of a person's heart that makes a person clean or unclean, and not something external to the person such as ethnicity. He has crystallized the scope of Jesus' sermon to include more than food, but people (Gentiles) through the first sign.[26] Unclean Gentiles may share in the benefits to Israel when what comes out of their heart is good and not defiling. And a Gentile woman demonstrates much greater understanding than Jesus' male disciples when Jesus speaks in parables. Unlike Herodias, the Syrophoenician mother has heard and received God's word and is blessed for it also bringing healing to her tormented daughter. All stories do not need to be told in the same way and are in fact not told in the same way by the implied author to communicate an intended message to the implied audience.

The implied author/narrator subverts gender expectations in the process of characterization by making an unnamed woman visible, interesting, pure, and an example of a true disciple by her understanding of

24. See Glancy, "Syrophoenician Woman," 357.
25. Harrocks, "Gentile Healings," 93–94.
26. This is exactly how the implied author develops the vision to Peter in Acts 10. The vision is about unclean food coming down from heaven, and Peter interprets the vision to refer to Gentiles when he appears before Cornelius.

Jesus' parabolic words in the religious/male context of misunderstanding. The implied audience would see the subversion of habituated constraints on this woman through the discourse of the sign-sermon and create a positive characterization of her.

In the next Markan unit involving a women, a contrast will be made between this woman who speaks and directly engages with Jesus' teaching, and a poor widow who says nothing and appears to be unaware of Jesus' presence, but is pointed out by the narrator's Jesus as an example for the benefit of his disciples.

13

The Poor Widow Who Gave at the Temple

(Mark 12:41–44)

THIS SIXTH MARKAN NARRATIVE discussing women takes place outside of the private home but inside of the house of God—the Temple. Through a series of rhetorical comparisons, the implied author characterizes a poor widow as honorable by portraying her as giving a whole-hearted response to God by giving him her whole life. Her sacrificial giving becomes an example of Jesus' earlier instruction about sacrificially following him. This characterization is done by demonstrating the protagonist, Jesus', evaluation of her act. Acts constitute characterization in the narrative.

INTRODUCTION

A simple word like "trunk" can have several meanings depending on its context: the back of a car, the "nose" of an elephant, the stem of a tree, a storage unit, the core of a person. What is true for individual words is also true for units of material. On a macro level, Jesus' proclamation in John 1:51 to Nathaniel that "you will see the heaven open and the angels of God ascending and descending upon the Son of Man" only has clarity when it is read within the context of Jacob's encounter with God at "Bethel" in Genesis 28:10–19. The canonical context of Genesis allows the audience to understand that Jesus is proclaiming himself to be the new "Bethel" or house of God where God mediates blessing to humankind in John 1:51. Likewise, in a narrative context, the account of the poor widow who gave at the temple (the "Widow") in Mark 12:41–44 is clarified and delivered from disparate interpretations through narrative readings/hearings of the macro and micro contexts of Mark.

On a macro level within the broad, geographical structure of Mark's Gospel, the account of the Widow falls "in and around Jerusalem":

    A The Wilderness (1:1–15)
      B Galilee (1:16—8:21)
        C The Way (8:22—11:11)
      B' *Jerusalem* (11:12—15:41)
    A' The Tomb (15:42—16:8)

The wilderness and the tomb have many similarities including being uninhabited places, places of the dead, places that Jesus enters and exits, and places where a herald's voice pronounces good news. Galilee and Jerusalem are contrasting lands. In Galilee Jesus calls and sends disciples, performs many miracles, and is received by many. In Jerusalem, there are less miracles, no calling or sending of disciples, and the religious leaders reject and kill Jesus. The central section not only marks the physical "way" to Jerusalem from Galilee but unfolds suffering as the "way" to follow Jesus to glory.

The more particular, literary, "contextual" setting of the account of the Widow is disputed leading to numerous, and at times disparate, understandings of the significance of this minor character in the Markan narrative. Many interpret the Widow positively.[1] However, Addison Wright argues that Jesus' discussion of the Widow should be read negatively as a lament of her actions and not as an approbation because she illustrates "the ills of official devotion" to the religious system of the day.[2] In other words, "Her religious thinking has accomplished the

---

1. Smith, "Closer Look," 27–36; DiCicco, "What Can One Give?," 41–49; Malbon, "Poor Widow," 589–604; "Minor Characters," 77–78; Kozar, "Owl and the Pussycat," 41–53; Iersel, *Mark*, 385–86; Lane, *Mark*, 441–43; Stock, *Mark*, 318–21; Cranfield, *Mark*, 385–87; Williams, *Other Followers*, 176–78; Nineham, *Mark*, 334–35; France, *Mark*, 492–93; Tolbert, *Sowing the Gospel*, 256; Kuruvilla, *Mark*, 277–81.

2. Wright, "Widow's Mites," 256–65. See also Sugirtharajah, "Widow's Mites," 42–43; Mpolo, "L'offrande de La Veuve," 259–86; Kerr, "Enigmatic Gospel," 629–30; Mann, *Mark*, 44). Timothy Geddert attempts to bridge the gap by arguing: "The solution is that Jesus commended the woman for her piety and self-giving, but simultaneously condemned the religious leaders for interposing themselves between this woman and her God, grasping for themselves what was intended to be for God's glory" (Geddert,

very thing that the scribes were accused of doing," namely, devouring her house.³ For Wright, the broader, controlling context of this unit is Mark 7:10–13 regarding Jesus' instruction on "corban," where those who withdraw the support of their parents by dedicating their goods to God are "wrongheaded."⁴ Likewise, a widow who gives all that she has to the temple is "wrongheaded" because "human needs take precedence over religious values when they conflict."⁵ Wright also argues that Jesus' words do not correspond with the larger context of Mark's portrayal of Jesus as a religious reformer rather than a philosopher opining about the value of giving.⁶ Wright then argues that the immediate context of scribes who devour widows' houses (Mark 12:40) and the following discussion about the future destruction of the temple (Mark 13:1–2), require that the audience understand Jesus' evaluation of the Widow negatively:

> It is hard to see how anyone at that point [referring to Jesus' prediction of the temple's destruction in Mark 13:1–2] could feel happy about the widow. Her contribution was totally misguided, thanks to the encouragement of official religion, but the final irony of it all was that it was also a waste.⁷

One response, in opposition to Wright's reading of this passage, is made by Elizabeth Malbon who argues that the Widow's account should be read "in six Marcan narrative contexts."⁸ Those contexts include: (1) the scribes who "devour widows' houses" (12:40);⁹ (2) the closing of Jesus' activity with the temple in Mark 12–15;¹⁰ (3) the woman who anoints Jesus for his burial in Mark 14 making a frame around chapter 13;¹¹ (4) all of the women characters in Mark's Gospel—especially the

---

Watchwords, 136). However, Geddert's interpretation seems strained in that it attempts to connect themes but does not show explicit contextual and textual support for reading the account of the Widow negatively beyond the prediction of the temple's destruction in 13:2. See Geddert, *Watchwords*, 38; *Mark*, 293–94; Lane, *Mark*, 494–95. For a detailed response in opposition to Wright's position, see Kubiś, "Poor Widow's Mites," 360–62.

3. Wright, "Widow's Mites," 262.
4. Wright, "Widow's Mites," 261.
5. Wright, "Widow's Mites," 261.
6. Wright, "Widow's Mites," 260.
7. Wright, "Widow's Mites," 263.
8. Malbon, "Poor Widow," 589. See also Williams, *Other Followers*, 177n1.
9. Malbon, "Poor Widow," 595–96.
10. Malbon, "Poor Widow," 596–98.
11. Malbon, "Poor Widow," 598–99.

hemorrhaging woman, the Syrophoenician woman, and the anointing woman;[12] (5) Jesus as teacher making solemn proclamations about the kingdom;[13] and (6) Markan characterization on what it means to be a follower of Jesus.[14] While Malbon's article has provided a brief, biblical theology on women in Mark's Gospel with insightful correlations between other characters and the Widow, one wonders if she has actually identified an interpretative "context" for the pericope on the Widow. To that point, Malbon argues against a single, interpretive context for this unit, or any other unit for that matter.[15] She supports this position, in part, by an analogy from the field of law:

> Perhaps we interpreters are like attorneys defending our clients (our contextual readings), always dedicated to our own clients' best interests. One obvious advantage of this metaphor is that it makes room for areas of expertise; if one wanted to argue an interpretive case concerning the relative value of *lepta*, one would surely retain Swete as a consultant. Another useful application of the metaphor is this: just as attorneys have limited free choice of their clients (specialty, location, financial needs or desires dictate accepting some clients; others may be assigned by the court system), so many interpreters select the context or contexts on which they focus neither at random nor with perfect freedom and fully conscious deliberation (I doubt that the feeling of being "drawn" by one's approach—or one's text—is rare). In addition, the image of advocacy suggests the strength of the bond between an interpreter and his or her contextual reading.[16]

As an attorney, this writer takes issue with Malbon's analogy. Whether one is counsel for plaintiff or defendant, the law is, or at least is expected to be, the same for both parties. What varies is the application of the law to the facts. When there are differences in statutory construction, for instance, the meaning is clarified on the appellate level (at least in common law jurisdictions like the United States). In other words, advocacy does not change the meaning of a text, which is analogous to the Gospel of Mark in this case. There are rules for statutory construction, and common-law interpretation of statues is binding on the parties. It is

---

12. Malbon, "Poor Widow," 599–600.
13. Malbon, "Poor Widow," 600–601.
14. Malbon, "Poor Widow," 601–2.
15. Malbon, "Poor Widow," 602.
16. Malbon, "Poor Widow," 603. See also Kubiś, "Poor Widow's Mites," 341.

in the realm of application, or significance, that differences lie, not in the meaning of the text, *per se*. Context is an element of construction, and not analogous to clients for whom attorneys advocate. Malbon appears to have made a category mistake through her analogy with advocacy. If anything, the scholar is more analogous to an appellate judge who carefully reads the law and applies its meaning to the facts, than to an attorney who advocates for a client.[17]

Malbon herself concedes: "Not that all readings are equal. Some are richer, some are poorer."[18] Her "complications" through multiple "contexts" provide some more-probable and some less-probable readings of the Widow. In the realm of biblical theology, there is value to Malbon's correlations. However, to call all of them "contexts" for the meaning of the passage involving the Widow, without specific, textual correlations, may not be feasible nor helpful hermeneutically.

Accordingly, the following discussion will identify the macro and micro context of the Jerusalem passages leading up to, and following, the unit involving the Widow to show Mark's positive portrayal of the Widow in the architecture of his narrative logic.

THE MACRO AND MICRO CONTEXT TO THE PASSAGE

The Larger, Macro, Context to the Passage (Mark 11:12—13:37)

Many arrange the material in the Jerusalem section of the Gospel in chiastic/concentric structures around the Olivet Discourse in Chapter 13;

---

17. Antonin Scalia, former Associate Justice of the Supreme Court of the United States (1986–2016), commented on the confusion that arises from reading the text as an advocate: "Distortion of text to suit the reader's fancy is by no means limited to the law. T. S. Eliot warned about literary critics who forget that they are dealing with a text and instead find in a work such as *Hamlet* 'a vicarious existence for their own artistic realization.' They substitute 'their own Hamlet for Shakespeare's. . . . It was about early nontextual expositors that John Locke wrote when he asked: '[Does] it not often happen that a man of an ordinary capacity very well understands a text or a law that he reads, till he consults an expositor, or goes to counsel; who, by the time he [has] explain[ed] them, makes the words signify either nothing at all, or what he pleases?'" (Scalia, *Cosmic Constitutional Theory*, 116). Furthermore, Judge J. Harvie Wilkinson III of the United States Court of Appeals for the Fourth Circuit insightfully summarized: "It is altogether conventional to note that liberty is best preserved under law and that law is something above and apart from the personal preferences of men and women on the bench" (Wilkinson quoted in Scalia, *Cosmic Constitutional Theory*, 116).

18. Malbon, "Poor Widow," 604.

however, these macro arrangements appear to suffer from lack of true parallels and/or questionable narrative logic. The distinct pericopies in this section are as follows:

- The cursing of the fig tree / cleansing of the temple (Mark 11:12–25)[19]
- Controversy on authority to cleanse the temple (in the temple with the chief priests, scribes, and elders) (Mark 11:27–33)
- Parable of the vineyard and the tenants (an indirect answer to the question about authority) (Mark 12:1–11)
- Controversy concerning payment of taxes (Mark 12:13–17)
- Controversy concerning the resurrection (Mark 12:18–27)
- Controversy concerning the "greatest commandment" (Mark 12:28–34)
- Teaching concerning David's Lord (Mark 12:35–37)
- Teaching concerning hypocrisy of the scribes (Mark 12:38–40)
- Teaching concerning the Widow's offering (Mark 12:41–44)
- The Olivet discourse (Mark 13:1–37)

Iersel understands the Olivet Discourse to be the central section between 11:1—12:44 and 14:1—16:1.[20] In 11:1—12:44 he sees a chiastic structure that places the passage with the Widow in parallel with an inspection of the temple.[21] However, his parallel summaries appear to be too broad to capture the narrative logic of the passage and do not always show parallels.[22]

Kuruvilla also understands the Olivet Discourse to be the center of the Jerusalem narrative between the controversies in 11–12 and the passion narrative in 14–16.[23] He observes that Mark 11–12 is framed by references to the Mount of Olives in 11:1 and 13:3 and Jesus' entering and leaving the temple in 11:11 and 13:1.[24] Kuruvilla limits his chiastic struc-

---

19. Verse 26 is not in the earliest manuscripts, making it "highly probable that the words were inserted by copyists in imitation of Matt 6:15" (Metzger, *Textual Commentary*, 93). See also Burer *et al.*, *NET Bible*, 128n5.
20. Iersel, *Mark*, 346–50.
21. Iersel, *Mark*, 346–47.
22. Iersel, *Mark*, 346–47.
23. Kuruvilla, *Mark*, 242.
24. Kuruvilla, *Mark*, 242.

ture to chapter 12, and although his structure does have textual parallels, the narrative logic of the chapter is not evident, and one wonders if the question from the Sadducees in 12:18–27 is actually the logical center of the chapter.[25] He offers an interesting, conceptual structure for chapter 12 that positions the Widow as a positive counterpart to the demand for fruit bearing in the parable of the vineyard and the tenants, however, one wonders if the unifying theme of "God's ownership" is not too broad, or high up the ladder of theological abstraction, for the content of the passage.[26]

Mary Ann Tolbert offers a more linear, logical, rhetorical layout of the units in chapters 11–16 placing the Olivet Discourse with chapters 11–12.[27] Tolbert's structure recognizes the intercalation in 11:12–25 as introducing the larger discussions in and around the temple, geographically and conceptually.[28] She understands the parable of the Vineyard and the Tenants to be a "parabolic plot synopsis to aid the audience's understanding and assimilation of the upcoming final events."[29] She also places the unit involving the Widow at the end of the tests-and-teachings section of the narrative and in parallel with the positive response in the last test regarding the great commandment (Mark 12:28–34), suggesting that the Widow may be a positive, individual response at the end of the teachings section.[30] It appears that Tolbert's rhetorical layout provides a helpful contextual structure of the overall unit showing the narrative logic leading up to the unit involving the Widow.

---

25. Kuruvilla, *Mark*, 255. See also Dowd, *Reading Mark*, 128.

26. Kuruvilla, *Mark*, 256.

27. Tolbert, *Sowing the Gospel*, 231–32.

28. Tolbert, *Sowing the Gospel*, 193.

29. Tolbert, *Sowing the Gospel*, 193. Tolbert understands the parable of the Tenants to function similarly to the parable of the Sower—as a plot synopsis for the major sections of the gospels (Tolbert, *Sowing the Gospel*, 122).

30. As Tolbert explains: "Indeed, the Gospel often seems to describe good actions or good responses as **individual** actions, whereas groups are portrayed neutrally or negatively. Those healed are single individuals emerging from the crowds; the true offering of the *one* poor widow is contrasted to the abundance of the *many* rich people (12:41–42); the one wise scribe stands apart from the typical beliefs and actions of scribes in general" (Tolbert, *Sowing the Gospel*, 256). See also Williams, "Does Mark's Gospel Have an Outline?," 520, 524–25.

The Immediate, Micro Context to the Passage

The more immediate context to the passage involving the Widow has a parallel structure of three controversies to test Jesus followed by three teachings by Jesus.[31] Within the parallel structure there is also a duality and balance of two negative, or corrective, controversies/teachings followed by a positive controversy/teaching. The relationship of these units might be shown as follows:

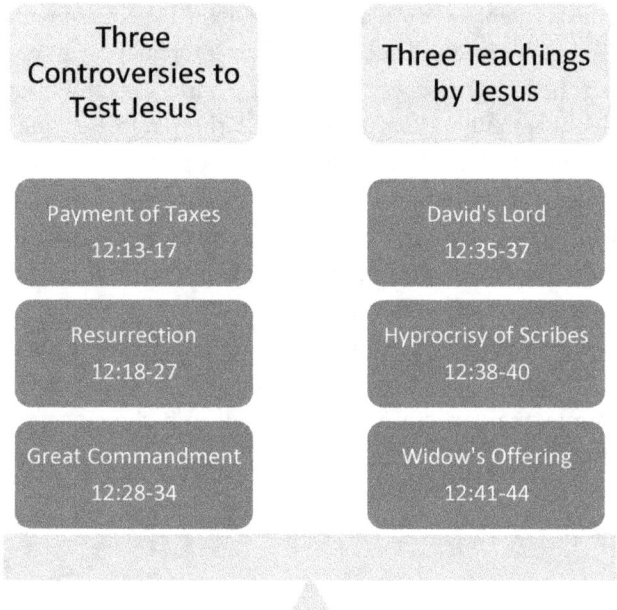

The controversies arise from those (Pharisees, Herodians, Sadducees) intending to trap Jesus in a statement (ἵνα αὐτὸν ἀγρεύσωσιν λόγῳ) (Mark 12:13, 18). Using abbreviated syllogisms, known as enthymemes, Jesus turns the first two controversies on his interlocutors (12:13–17, 18–27).[32] The tone of the third controversy, initiated by *one* of the scribes, is much more positive (12:28–34).[33] First, the scribe heard the religious

---

31. Williams, "Does Mark's Gospel Have an Outline?," 524–25.

32. Tolbert, *Sowing the Gospel*, 250–54.

33. Iersel is more reserved in arriving at this conclusion (Iersel, *Mark*, 377–81). See France, *Mark*, 476; Kozar, "Owl and the Pussycat," 45–46; Williams, *Other Followers*, 49–50; Smith, "Closer Look," 30n12.

leaders and Jesus arguing and recognized that Jesus answered them well (12:28). The scribe then asked Jesus a sincere, or positive, question about which commandment was the first, or most important, of all the commandments.[34] This question was not unique to the time.[35] After Jesus answered the scribe by identifying the first commandment as loving God, and the second commandment as loving your neighbor (12:29–31), the scribe once again approved of Jesus' answer with the word "well" (καλῶς) (12:32, cf. 12:28). The scribe also agreed that loving God and one's neighbor are greater than religious, ritual activities, whole-burnt offerings, and sacrifices (12:33). Whereupon Jesus proclaimed that the scribe was not far from the kingdom of God (12:34).

The *leitwort*, "whole" (ὅλος), connects the passage involving the scribe and the passage involving the Widow.[36] Jesus pressed upon the scribe the necessity of loving God with one's whole (ὅλης) heart, whole (ὅλης) soul, whole (ὅλης) mind and whole (ὅλης) strength (12:30). The scribe agrees with Jesus on the importance of loving God with one's whole (ὅλης) heart, whole (ὅλης) understanding, and whole (ὅλης) strength (12:33). In the account with the Widow, Jesus proclaimed that the Widow gave her whole (ὅλον) life (12:44). In other words, the Widow exemplified the whole-hearted response that people are to give to God by giving her whole life (ὅλον τὸν βίον αὐτῆς) in the temple.

The scribe and the Widow are both singular people in contrast to larger groups.[37] The friendly scribe and the Widow are an unlikely pair. Viewing the friendly scribe as a singular enables the implied audience to see the singular action of the Widow. With the scribe, Jesus proposes a new standard that goes beyond Temple norms, and the scribe embraces the standard and explicates the new norm—"You are right teacher, God

---

34. Williams, *Other Followers*, 174. France, *Mark*, 476.

35. As Kuruvilla notes: "The attempt to locate the foremost commandment of the 613 in the Torah was not unique to the dialogue: Rabbi Hillel's 'silver' rule, the negative of Jesus' 'golden' rule (Matt 7:12), stated: 'What is hateful to you, do not do to your neighbor: that is the whole Torah, while the rest is commentary thereof' (b. Sabb 31a; also Tob 4:15); b. Mak. 24a reduced the law to the eleven principles of Ps 15, the six of Isa 33:15–16, the three of Mic 6:8, the two of Isa 56:1; and the one in Amos 5:4 (and Hab 2:4); b. Ber. 63a asserted that the basis for all the essential principles of the Torah was found in Prov 3:6, etc." (Kuruvilla, *Mark*, 274n12). See also Stein, *Mark*, 560; France, *Mark*, 477n62.

36. See Williams, *Other Followers*, 176–77.

37. See Kozar, "Owl and the Pussycat," 49; Tolbert, *Sowing the Gospel*, 256.

is one and to love him with all heart and understanding and strength is more than sacrifices" (Mark 12:32–33). Likewise, the Widow's

> complete offering acts out the *Shema* which is the basis of Jesus' singular creed. . . . The positive attentiveness of the scribe and the positive action of the Widow surrounds the negative rapacious actions of the scribal class.[38]

Therefore, the units involving the scribe and the Widow are not only connected in their placement within the narrative structure of Mark 12:13–44 as third, positive narratives that contrast corrective controversies/teachings, but are also connected by sympathetically resonating the common theme of whole-hearted love for God.

The unit immediately preceding the passage involving the Widow contains Jesus' denunciation of the scribes (τῶν γραμματέων) (Mark 12:38–40). Again, a *leitwort*, "widow" (χήρα), connects the two passages (cf. Mark 12:40 with 12:42, 43). Derrett has argued persuasively that when Jesus addresses the scribes, he is specifically commenting on their activity as lawyers appointed to be guardians or administrators (ἐπίτροπος, from אפיטרופוס) of a decedent's estate and, thus, the estate of a widow.[39] A guardian was either appointed by the owner of an estate, by a parent prior to death, or by the courts.[40] They were remunerated by either the former owner or the Court giving the administrator a percentage of the income of the estate. The administrator would sometimes exploit the estate. This was commonly described as "eating or drinking" or "clothing or covering" himself:

---

38. Kozar, "Owl and the Pussycat," 49.

39. Derrett, "Eating up the Houses," 1–9.

40. "Orphans who boarded with a householder, or for whom their *father appointed a guardian*—he [who provides for their keep] is liable to separate tithe from the produce. *A guardian whom a father of orphans has appointed* is to be subjected to an oath. [*If*] *a court appointed him*, he is not subjected to an oath. Abba Saul says, 'Matters are reversed'" (m. Git. 5:4A–F in Neusner, *Mishnah*, 474–75 [emphasis added]).

1.9 A. Amram the dyer was guardian [*apoteropos*] for some orphans. The relatives came before R. Nahman. They said to him, "He's *clothing himself* out of the property of the orphans."
B. He said to them, "That is so that he will be listened to with respect."
C. "*He's eating and drinking* out of the proceeds of the estate, since he's not particularly well-to-do."
D. "I might say he found something of value [to support his new life-style]."
E. "He's causing them loss to their property."
F. He said to them, "Bring proof that he's causing them loss and I'll remove him. For said R. Huna our colleague in the name of Rab, 'As to a guardian who causes a loss—we remove him.'"
G. For it has been stated:
H. As to a guardian [*apoteropos*] who causes a loss—
I. R. Huna said Rab [said], "We remove him."
J. Members of the household of R. Shila say, "We do not remove him."
K. And the decided law is, we remove him.[41]

In the Markan passage, the scribes are figuratively described as "eating up" (κατεσθίοντες) widows' houses (Mark 12:40).[42]

No one would appoint an administrator unless he had a reputation for piety and fearing God. Therefore, the administrator would show himself worthy of appointment (advertise) by publicly promoting himself, i.e., "walking in robes," receiving "greetings in the marketplace," having "seats of honor in the synagogues," having "places of honor at feasts," and "making long prayers" (Mark 12:38–41).[43] Then once the administrator was appointed and in charge of the decedent's estate, he would consume, or eat away, the estate through exorbitant fees and costs (κατεσθίοντες τὰς οἰκίας τῶν χηρῶν) (Mark 12:40). To these corrupt lawyers, Jesus says that there will be greater judgment than having themselves removed as an administrator (οὗτοι λήμψονται περισσότερον κρίμα) (Mark 12:40).

---

41. b. Git. 52B 1.9 A–K in Neusner, *Babylonian Talmud*, 222–23 (emphasis added).

42. BDAG, 532. In a literal sense the word is used to describe devouring something completely as in the birds eating up the seed that is sown in Matt 13:4; here it is a figurative extension of "eating" or "consuming" so as to take over by dishonest means the property of someone else (Louw, *Greek-English Lexicon*, 585).

43. Derrett, "Eating up the Houses," 4–5.

The Widow in Mark 12:41–44 may, or may not, have been taken advantage of by the scribes in the immediate context. Smith concludes that "even if she were not an actual, literal victim, she is representative of victims of scribal exploitation by virtue of her severe poverty as well as of Mark's placement of this account in this context."[44] One thing is certain, if the above-explanation of Jesus' denunciation of the scribes is correct, there is no correlation of the Widow's giving in the temple with the practices of the corrupt scribes spoiling the assets of estates. Wright assumes that the Widow is being subjected to scribal abuses of religion in the temple,[45] but that scenario is not present in the immediate context. If anything, the connection of the Widow with the previous passage may be as a foil to the scribes. In other words, as Jesus and his disciples are passing through the temple, Jesus instructs them not to be like the scribes who devour widows' houses, but to be like the Widow who gives all that she has. Once again, the implied author develops characterization for the implied audience by means of an example, and once again, the example is made from the very low within the social hierarchy.

THE PASSAGE INVOLVING THE WIDOW

The scene with the Widow opens with Jesus still in the Temple sitting opposite the treasury (γαζοφυλάκιον).[46] While the term for treasury may be used for rooms or places for storing valuables (Esth 3:8 [king's treasuries]; Neh 12:44; 13:5; 2 Macc 3:6 [temple treasuries]),[47] it was also used for contribution boxes or receptacles:

> Thirteen *shofar*[48] chests were in the sanctuary. And written on them were the following [in Aramaic]: (1) "New *sheqels*"[49] and (2) "old *sheqels*," (3) "bird offerings," and (4) "young birds for a burnt offering"; (5) "wood" and (6) "frankincense"; (7) "gold for the Mercy seat," and on six, "for freewill offerings." *New*

---

44. Smith, "Closer Look," 30n12.

45. Wright, "Widow's Mites," 256–65.

46. This location appears to be in the Court of the Women. Josephus, *Wars of the Jews*, 5:190–200.

47. Josephus, *Wars of the Jews*, 6:282.

48. The term *shofar* ("שׁוֹפָר") refers to a "ram's horn blown on set occasions in Temple and synagogue worship" (Neusner, *Mishnah*, 1143; HALOT s.v. "שׁוֹפָר").

49. A *šeqel* (שקל) was "the chief silver coin of the Israelites, weighing between a quarter and a half of an ounce" (Neusner, *Mishnah*, 1142; HALOT, 1642).

sheqel—those for each year [that is, for the present year]. *Old sheqels*—He who did not pay his *sheqel* last year pays his *sheqel* in the coming year. *Bird offerings*—these are for turtledoves. *Young birds for a burnt offering*—these are for pigeons. "And all of them are burnt offerings," the words of R. Judah.[50]

Evidently, these were treasury chests, each with a receptacle in the shape of a ram's horn, or trumpet, where the offerings were placed.[51] The implied author will develop his discourse that enables the implied audience to characterize the Widow by money that is being thrown into these chests. The narrator explains that as Jesus was sitting across from these treasury chests, he observed a large number of people (ὄχλος) placing or casting (βάλλω)[52] metal money (χαλκός) into the treasury chests (12:41). He then focused on two distinct groups comparing the rich (πλούσιοι) and the poor (πτωχή); the many (πολλοί) and the one (μία); the much (πολλά), and the little (λεπτός); the act from those with abundance, surplus, or overflow (ἐκ τοῦ περισσεύοντος αὐτοῖς) and the act of one from her lack, want, or poverty (ἐκ τῆς ὑστερήσεως αὐτῆς).

The many rich were throwing much money into the treasury chests, possibly making a loud noise as the metal coins touched the horned-shaped receptacles. Then the implied author/narrator describes an individual, poor Widow who came (ἐλθοῦσα) and cast (ἔβαλεν) two of the smallest coins (two *lepta*, the smallest Palestinian coins, which amount to a *kodrantēs*, the smallest Roman coin)[53] into the treasury chest (12:42). Jesus' words are introduced with somber phrases. First the narrator states that Jesus called his disciples (Mark 12:43). The term for calling (προσκαλέω) has the sense of summoning, inviting, or calling in a legal or official sense.[54] This is the same term that is used to describe Jesus summoning the Twelve (Mark 3:13), summoning the religious leaders to

---

50. M. Sheqalim 6:5; Neusner, *Mishnah*, 261; BDAG, 186. See also m. Seqal. 2:1 "Just as there were *shofar* chests [for receiving the *sheqel* tax] in the Temple, so there were *shofar* chests in the provinces" (Neusner, *Mishnah*, 253).

51. Thayer, *Greek-English Lexicon*, 108; Louw, *Greek-English Lexicon*, 71.

52. The imperfect, ἔβαλλον, is used in Mark 12:41 to show the scene in progress: "the rich were casting much" (Wallace, *Greek Grammar*, 502–3; Porter, *Idioms*, 29).

53. The λεπτός was the Greek term for "the smallest coin" in the Palestinian (pruta-shamin) system. The κοδράντης was the smallest unit of currency (coin) in the Roman monetary system. See Sperber, "Mark 12:42," 178–90; BDAG, s.v. "κοδράντης." A δηνάριον was a Roman silver coin, a "worker's average daily wage" (BDAG, s.v. "δηνάριον"; Louw, *Greek-English Lexicon*, 63).

54. BDAG, s.v. "προσκαλέω." See also Acts 5:40; Matt 18:32.

instruct them through a parable (Mark 3:23), summoning the Twelve to send them out on mission (Mark 6:7), summoning the multitude to teach a parable (Mark 7:14), and Pilate summoning the Centurion to determine if Jesus was dead from the crucifixion (Mark 15:44). Therefore, in Mark's narrative world, the term describes an official gathering of someone or a group for instruction or information. Second, Jesus prefaces his words with a solemn statement that is only used by Jesus in Mark before a significant, surprising, and sometimes difficult teaching: "Truly I say to you" (ἀμὴν λέγω ὑμῖν) (Mark 12:43).[55] This manner of introducing Jesus' comment alerts the audience that the disciples have been summoned for an important, significant, and perhaps surprising or difficult teaching by Jesus (Mark 12:43).

The content of Jesus' statement uses much of the same language that the narrator used in introducing the passage, but Jesus turns the language around: "This poor Widow cast more than all who cast into the treasury" (ἡ χήρα αὕτη ἡ πτωχὴ πλεῖον πάντων ἔβαλεν τῶν βαλλόντων εἰς τὸ γαζοφυλάκιον) (Mark 14:44). The Widow was introduced as an individual (μία χήρα), but now Jesus emphasizes her individuality: "The Widow, this *one*, the poor *one*" (ἡ χήρα αὕτη ἡ πτωχὴ). Furthermore, the contrasting group was described as "many rich ones were casting much," (πολλοὶ πλούσιοι ἔβαλλον πολλά) but here, it is not the many, but this poor Widow who casts more than all who were casting into the treasury (πλεῖον πάντων ἔβαλεν τῶν βαλλόντων εἰς τὸ γαζοφυλάκιον). They cast much, but she cast more, even though technically, she cast a very small amount of money into the treasury chests. Jesus then provides the reason for (γὰρ) this paradoxical reversal with another contrast: "For all, out of the surplus to them cast, but she, out of her lack, as much as she had, she cast—her whole life" (Mark 12:44). The subjects on each side of this compound sentence are emphasized by specific pronouns that are placed at the beginning of each sentence with a post-positive conjunction: "for all" (πάντες γὰρ), "but she" (αὕτη δὲ). Then each pronoun is modified by a prepositional phrase beginning with ἐκ followed by the genitive: "For all, out of the surplus to them (ἐκ τοῦ περισσεύοντος[56] αὐτοῖς)"; "but she, out of her lack (ἐκ τῆς

---

55. BDAG, s.v. "ἀμὴν."

56. The verb περισσεύω, here is a present, active, substantive participle. It could be translated as "abundance" but also has the sense of "overflow" as in 2 Cor 9:12. It is to "exceed a fixed number or measure; to be over and above a certain number or measure" (Thayer, *Greek-English Lexicon*, s.v. "περισσεύω"). The noun describes what is left over in Mark 8:8, "They ate and they were satisfied, and they took up the leftover (περισσεύματα) fragments, seven baskets." Likewise, the parallel word describing the

ὑστερήσεως αὐτῆς).⁵⁷ They both cast (ἔβαλον, ἔβαλεν) their offering. However, the symmetry is broken when Jesus makes a double reference to what the Widow gave—all as much as she had (πάντα ὅσα εἶχεν), her whole life (ὅλον τὸν βίον αὐτῆς).⁵⁸ The piling up of descriptors for the content of the Widow's gift weights the comparison in her favor:

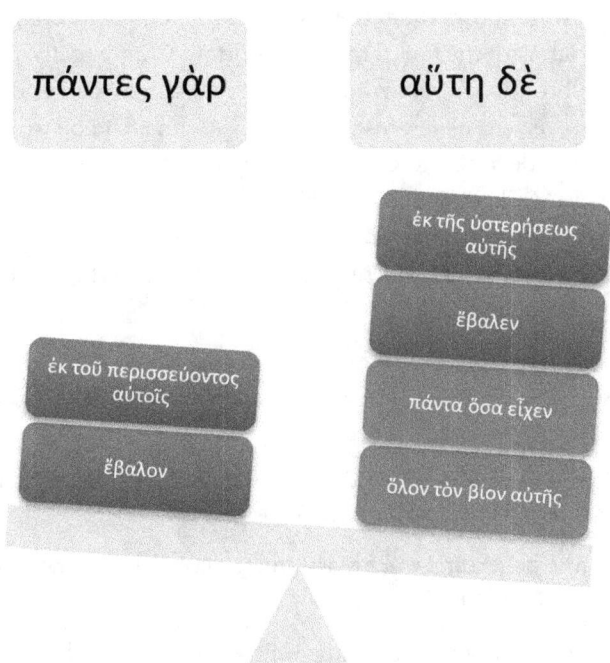

The significant, surprising, and difficult teaching that Jesus summoned his disciples to hear was that it was not the rich who gave out of their excess that God sees, but this poor Widow who gave out of her

source of the widow's gift, ὑστέρησις, could have the sense of poverty, but also describes the source of poverty, i.e., her lack, or need of what is essential. See Phil 4:11, "Not that I speak from want (καθ᾽ ὑστέρησιν); Thayer, *Greek-English Lexicon*, 646; Louw, *Greek-English Lexicon*, 562. Accordingly, the many gave out of their excess, but the poor widow gave out of her want.

57. The preposition "ἐκ is more restricted, perhaps best translated in its basic sense as 'out of', as opposed to ἀπό meaning 'from' or 'away from' in a more general sense" (Porter, *Idioms*, 154; Wallace, *Greek Grammar*, 371).

58. The phrase, "her whole life" "ὅλον τὸν βίον αὐτῆς" may have the sense of all her wealth, riches, or living. See textual variant in Luke 8:43, "And spending with physicians her whole life (ὅλον τὸν βίον)"; Song of Solomon 8:7, "If a man were to give all his life (ὅλον τὸν βίον) for love, it would be utterly despised."

need. In accordance with Deuteronomy 27 and 28, the disciples may have assumed that riches were an indication of God's pleasure, but Jesus instructs them on the more significant gift of the poor Widow who gave out of her need in contrast to the rich who gave out of their surplus. When Jesus discussed the role of riches "on the way" with his disciples in Mark 10:23, they were "amazed at his words" (ἐθαμβοῦντο ἐπὶ τοῖς λόγοις αὐτοῦ) in 10:24. Now he shows them the lesson in the temple by comparing the gifts of the rich with the gift of the poor Widow. Contextually, the Widow may be a foil to the lawyers who gain their wealth by eating up widows' estates. However, she also foreshadows those who are to be willing to risk their life out of devotion to God as Jesus will instruct the disciples in the next chapter (Mark 13:9–13, 9–20).[59]

Once again, Mark has portrayed a woman as an example of faithfulness. She *shows* what Jesus required of disciples in the central section of Mark:

> "For whoever wishes to save his life will lose it, but whoever loses his life for My sake and the gospel's will save it" (Mark 8:35);

> "Go sell all you possess and give to the poor, and you will have treasure in heaven; and come, follow Me" (Mark 10:21);

> "Many who are first will be last, and the last, first" (Mark 10:31, author's translation).

She may also adumbrate Jesus' upcoming crucifixion. The Widow *gave her whole life* (ἔβαλεν ὅλον τὸν βίον αὐτῆς) (Mark 12:44); likewise, Jesus will give *his life* as a sacrifice for humankind: "The son of man came to give his life a ransom for many" (δοῦναι τὴν ψυχὴν αὐτοῦ λύτρον ἀντὶ πολλῶν) (8:35).

CONCLUSION

Contrary to Wright's negative reading of the Widow in Mark 12:41–44, the broad structure of the narrative, the parallelism of the individual scribe and the individual Widow, the use of the *Leitwort*, "whole," and the weighing of descriptors between the "many" and the "one" favor a

---

59. The correlation of the Widow in Mark 12 with the woman who anoints Jesus for his burial in Mark 14 is discussed in detail in chapter 14 below in the narrative context to "The Death Plot of the leaders and the Anointing at Bethany (Mark 14:1–11)."

macro and micro contextual reading/hearing of the Widow's narrative as positive.

Once again, the implied author has developed the discourse of the narrative to show the implied audience that a lowly woman of extreme poverty on the periphery of society and vulnerable to exploitation, as opposed to the religious leaders, is a true follower of God through her wholehearted living. Moreover, the woman willingly foreshadows the suffering ahead for Messiah and the disciples by giving her "whole life" to God. The widow has been shown by the implied author to be similar to many other vulnerable women like Simon's mother-in-law, the woman with the flow of blood, and the Syrophoenician woman. The implied audience will be using these tellings of the narrative to subvert their preunderstandings about women and characterize them as true followers of God.

In the next Markan passage another woman will give a gift of great, monetary value to Jesus. Like the Widow, Jesus will defend her gift because it is given in response to Jesus' impending death. Through these two narratives involving gifts, the implied author is showing his implied audience the preeminence of the giver's motivation over the amount of the gift.

14

The Death Plot of the Leaders and the Anointing at Bethany

(Mark 14:1–11)

(Outer Story 14:1–2; Inner Story 14:3–9; Outer Story 14:10–11)

THIS IS THE SEVENTH Markan narrative involving a woman. In the discourse of this narrative the implied author employs the architectural force of an intercalation to create a heightened contrast between a woman in the inner story and the men in the outer story. The anonymous female protagonist steps forward to do all that she can to provide for Jesus' impending death which the male religious leaders, including a disciple, named Judas, plot to arrange. This contrast will highlight for the implied audience the difference between those who are metaphorically awake and responsive to Jesus in the peril of impending suffering, and those who are asleep and callously cause that suffering.

INTRODUCTION

This Markan intercalation is also employed by Matthew (Matt 26:1–16). Luke only includes the outer story (Luke 22:1–6). The inner story appears to stand on its own in the Gospel of John (John 12:1–8).

The broader structure of chapters 11 through 13 has been discussed in Chapter 13 in the analysis of the Poor Widow who gave at the temple

The Death Plot of the Leaders and the Anointing at Bethany 185

in Mark 12:41–44. This discussion will focus on the place of 14:1–11 in that larger context of the Gospel.

Some argue for continuity between the Widow who gave at the temple (Mark 12:41–44) and the woman who anointed Jesus for his burial (Mark 14:3–9). Joanna Dewey appears to be the first to make a detailed correlation between the two women.[1] Many similarities exist between the story of the Widow and the woman who anoints Jesus, but it is more difficult to explain how the stories function as a frame around the eschatological discourse in chapter 13. Malbon boldly states: "Even though the frame and middle of this large-scale intercalation are to be interpreted together, one can skip from 12:14 to 14:1 with no noticeable gap in the story line. Chapter 13, the eschatological discourse, is intrusive."[2] Dewey offers a cryptic correlation of the bookends to the inner discourse when she states, "in the two stories about women, there is a progression from the giving up of life to burial after death," but an explicit tie to the eschatological discourse is wanting. Dean Deppe offers the most extensive explanation of how the two narratives of the Widow and the woman who anoints Jesus frame, and thus relate to, the central eschatological discourse in chapter 13.[3] Deppe argues that the central part of the eschatological discourse is found in 13:9–11 where Jesus discusses persecution.[4] Jesus predicts that the post-resurrection handing over of the disciples follows the pattern of John the Baptist's and Jesus' pre-resurrection handing over (παραδίδωμι).[5] Thus Deppe correlates the bookends to the eschatological discourse around the topic of suffering.[6]

Deppe's explanation is plausible, thematically, but it may over generalize some areas in the narrative to make the theory work. For instance, it is true that the Widow in chapter 12 gives sacrificially, but we do not know that the gift of the woman in Mark 14 is sacrificial. Her activity may

---

1. Dewey, *Markan Public Debate*, 154; Malbon, "Fallible Followers," 38; "Poor Widow," 597–98; Grassi, *Hidden Heroes*, 35–36; Kuruvilla, *Mark*, 299; Deppe, *Theological Intentions*, 184.

2. Malbon, "Fallible Followers," 39. See also Malbon, "Poor Widow," 598.

3. Deppe, *Theological Intentions*, 190–91.

4. In Deppe's discussion of possible structures of Mark 13, he appears to hold to a chiastic structure (Deppe, *Theological Intentions*, 188). Deppe's presentation of optional interpretations of Mark 13 does not clearly identify his view, but his constant reference to 13:9–13 leads this writer to conclude that a chiastic structure represents Deppe's position.

5. Deppe, *Theological Intentions*, 190.

6. Deppe, *Theological Intentions*, 190–91. See also Grassi, *Hidden Heroes*, 39.

be better described as "generous" than "sacrificial." She could be wealthy, so the personal cost of her gift may not be comparable to the Widow in Mark 12. The narrative in Mark 14 discusses the value of the gift but not its economic effect on the woman. The implied author/narrator's later statement that many of the women who followed Jesus up to Jerusalem ministered to him (καὶ διηκόνουν αὐτῷ) (Mark 15:41) may suggest that they provided for him financially making them women of means. Although not explicit, if so, the cost of the perfume may not have been prohibitive to some of these women as the offering was to the Widow. Accordingly, it is less obvious how the woman who anoints Jesus for his burial is an example of sacrificing all one has for Jesus. It appears that the theme of suffering was borrowed from the Widow in Mark 12 and imposed upon the generous woman in Mark 14.

Deppe also compares the frame of chapter 13 with the frame of chapters 8–10 to support his theory.[7] However, the two miracles where Jesus heals the blind in Mark 8:22–26 and 10:46–52 surrounding Jesus' explanation "on the way" to Jerusalem (Mark 8:31—10:45) appear to be typologically integrated with the narrative they enclose. Like the first blind man, the disciples do not fully see (perceive) who Jesus is. The two-stage healing of the blind man in Mark 8:22–26 is not about Jesus' inability to heal but about an advance in perception which Jesus is going to bring "on the way" to Jerusalem. The disciples see that he is Messiah (Mark 8:27–30), but they do not perceive that his mission involves suffering; they are resistant to this message (Mark 8:31–33).[8] In the central section of the Gospel "on the way" to Jerusalem, Jesus gives three predictions of his passion each of which is followed by misunderstanding and Jesus' clarifying instruction:

1. Prediction—misunderstanding by Peter—Instruction through Elijah (Mark 8:31—9:29);
2. Prediction—misunderstanding by the Twelve—Instruction through Moses (Mark 9:30—10:31); and
3. Prediction—misunderstanding by James and John—Instruction through Jesus (Mark 10:32–45).

The two-stage healing is a picture of what ought to have happened with the disciples during the central section of the narrative. However, they

---

7. Deppe, *Theological Intentions*, 185.
8. See Geddert, *Watchwords*, 77.

do not gain acuity in their perception; they are recalcitrant. On the other hand, the healing of Bartimaeus is a picture of what a true disciple looks like. Bartimaeus is conscious of his own frailty (blindness), discerning of Jesus' person ("Son of David") and leaves all that he has (his cloak) to follow Jesus to Jerusalem (Mark 10:46–52). The healings that enclose the narrative "on the way" to Jerusalem are integral to the message of the narrative they surround. This integration is not present in Deppe's correlation of the narratives involving the women and the eschatological discourse in chapter 13. The correlations between the Widow who gives her whole life and Jesus who gives his life do not follow through with the woman in Mark 14. Yes, she anoints Jesus for his burial, but her act may not be sacrificial or even an antitype of the Widow in chapter 12 as Bartimaeus is an antitype of two-stage healing and the disciples in the inner section of chapters 8 through 10. There are similar themes between the women in chapter 12 and 14, but one wonders if the acts of these women are integrated enough into chapter 13 to argue that the Widow in 12 and the woman in 14 are bookends to the eschatological discourse.

Moreover, it does not appear that those who emphasize the similarity of the acts by the women in Mark 12 and 14 give appropriate consideration to the fact that the narrative in Mark 14 is itself an intercalation other than to generally state the contrast between the woman and the religious leaders. Verses 1–2 of Mark 14 are not discussed in the development of the narrative by those who propose correlations between the two women. It is almost as though the verses do not exist in order to emphasize the parallels between the Widow and the woman who anoints Jesus in Mark 14. However, the most immediate juxtaposition of verses to the discourse in chapter 13 is the plot by the religious leaders in the outer story to kill Jesus and not the woman's anointing of Jesus for his burial.

Accordingly, even though similarities exist between the Widow in chapter 12 and the woman who anoints Jesus in Mark 14, these parallels may be due to something other than the narrative structure surrounding the eschatological discourse in chapter 13. The similarities may be due to the actual author's and implied author's general portrayal of women in the narrative as the good soil referred to in Mark 4.⁹ Furthermore,

---

9. As Tolbert states: "The contrast between the generosity of the anonymous woman and the deal of Judas ('who was one of the twelve') with the chief priests to exchange Jesus for money (14:19–11) dramatizes starkly the different production of good earth and rocky ground" (Tolbert, *Sowing the Gospel*, 274). Deppe observes: "Woman characters in Mark are regularly connected with discipleship, including the service of Peter's mother-in-law (1:31), the faith of the bleeding woman (5:34), the insight of the

the implied author's portrayal of these women communicates to the implied audience the value of these women as subversive characters who provide a critique on the existing social order. The Widow in Mark 12 is presented in her social role as being poor—yet her actions perform a critique on those who have an abundance. The woman in Mark 14 is criticized by others in the narrative as being prone to excess, wasting her resources, and lacking self-control, yet her act signifies an appreciation of value that will exceed her lifespan. The implied author's subversive characterization of these women would affect an implied audience steeped in Graeco-Roman engendered values by drawing them into a new order portrayed in the Gospel.

Mark 14 appears to mark the beginning of Jesus' journey to the cross. It provides the first of several time stamps that become more and more particular in the rest of the narrative.[10] As discussed extensively above in Chapter 6, the parable of the Lord of the House, or the Doorkeeper, in Mark 13, provides a programmatic reference point for viewing the acts of characters in the following narrative—whether they are awake and on guard, or asleep—with respect to their relationship with Jesus. This intercalation beginning in Mark 14 is the first of many narratives to follow the parable of the Doorkeeper whereby the followers of Jesus are evaluated for their watchfulness. Unlike Judas in the following narrative who shows himself to be metaphorically asleep or inattentive to Jesus, the woman who anoints Jesus is on-guard and very attentive to his words. The acts of the woman stand out in bold relief against the dark background of the outer, hostile story.

THE OUTER STORY (MARK 14:1–2)

The outer story begins two days before the Passover and the Feast of Unleavened Bread with a plot by the Jewish, religious leaders (the chief priests and the scribes) to secretly apprehend Jesus and kill him (Mark 14:1–2). This timestamp tells the implied audience upon a subsequent exposure to the full gospel story that this account occurred two days

---

Syrophoenician woman (7:28–29), the sacrifice of the anointing woman (14:8–9), and the presence of women at the cross (15:40–41)" (Deppe, *Theological Intentions*, 184).

10. See Mark 14:1, 12, 17, 72; 15:1, 33, 34, 42; 16:1, 2.

before Jesus' crucifixion. In view of Jesus' popularity with the people, the dilemma before the leaders was how to secretly[11] arrest him:

> The chief priests and the scribes were seeking[12] how to seize Him by stealth and kill Him; for they were saying, "Not during the festival, otherwise there might be a riot of the people."

The Jewish leaders did not wish to seize Jesus publicly. They were fearful that the people would interfere with their actions; so, they wanted to seize him away from the crowds.

The outer story is broken off mid-stream, and a new inner story appears. However, the theme of Jesus' impending death crosses over into the inner story where Jesus is anointed for his burial. The unspoken question arises: How is the death of Jesus going to happen? Further, the inner story appears to take place at a different location—not in the holy city but in Bethany at the house of Simon the leper (Mark 14:3). The irony is apparent—in the setting of the holy feast of Passover and Unleavened Bread, the religious leaders are plotting Jesus' murder, while Jesus is just outside of the holy city in the home of an unclean leper. The implied audience may wonder: Who are the upright? Appearances may be deceptive. This irony will only increase as the stories unfold and this macabre background of a home with a leper gives even more prominence to the act of the woman in the inner story.

THE INNER STORY (MARK 14:3–9)

In the inner story, everything is told in a pattern of three around three people: (1) the woman; (2) some; (3) Jesus:[13]

---

11. A question arises as to whether "in secret" and "not in the feast" are temporal or spatial descriptions. The obvious problem with the temporal interpretation is that Jesus was apprehended during the time of the feast. Shepherd argues convincingly for a spatial description with an emphasis occurring in the narrative away from many people (Shepherd, "Markan Sandwich Stories," 244–45).

12. Mann correctly observes: "The Greek verb translated *were looking* (ezêtoun) [ἐζήτουν] is an imperfect tense and implies a scheme which had been in train for some time" (Mann, *Mark*, 553).

13. Shepherd, *Markan Sandwich Stories*, 250.

- *The woman*
  - comes,
  - breaks the flask, and
  - anoints.
- *"Some"* are
  - indignant,
  - complain, and
  - censure her.
- *Jesus*
  - defends the woman,
  - contrasts Himself with the poor, and
  - teaches on the woman's memorial.

Furthermore, each part of Jesus' speech expands into three parts:

- *Jesus defends the woman:*
  - "Leave her alone!"
  - "Why are you troubling her?"
  - "She has done a good work for me."
- *Jesus contrasts himself with the poor:*
  - "You always have the poor with you."
  - "You can do good to them any time."
  - "You will not always have me."
- *Jesus teaches on the woman's memorial:*
  - "She has done what she could."
  - "She has anointed my body for burial."
  - "Wherever the Gospel is preached throughout the world, also what she has done will be told for a memorial."

The series of threes telescopes in the inner story to a climax with Jesus' threefold statements showing the implied audience the most important part of the narrative.

The inner story develops as an anonymous woman breaks an alabaster jar of nard and pours it down (κατέχεεν) upon Jesus' head (Mark 14:3). The value of the oil is amplified by the piling up of adjectives: an alabaster vase of ointment, pure nard, expensive (ἀλάβαστρον μύρου νάρδου πιστικῆς πολυτελοῦς). The value of her gift marks the turning point in the story as certain, unidentified ones (τινες),[14] are reported as being inwardly aroused with disapproval (ἀγανακτοῦντες πρὸς ἑαυτούς) and asking why this ointment has been ruined (τί ἡ ἀπώλεια αὕτη τοῦ μύρου γέγονεν), since it could have been sold for nearly a year's wages (more than three hundred denarii) and given to people who are poor (τοῖς πτωχοῖς). So they were reproaching, or scolding, her (ἐνεβριμῶντο αὐτῇ) (Mark 14:4-5).

These "certain ones" are using their "moral" perspective to censor the woman and take for granted their "right" to criticize a "woman" who appears to be unable to restrain her excess. The implied author/narrator does not record any speech by the woman. She only acts. But her acts speak. She will not need to defend herself because she has an advocate who will speak on her behalf. The implied author will use characterization by association to infuse particular, positive significance to the woman's actions for the implied audience by integrating her into the suffering of Jesus and at the same time censor her critics.

At this point in the narrative, negative questions about Jesus may be rising in the audience's mind: the religious leaders are seeking to capture and kill him; he is in the house of an unclean leper; and some woman is pouring over him very expensive oil that could have been used to help the poor.

Jesus concludes the second story and changes the direction of the narrative as he pushes back with his understanding of the woman's actions:

> Let her alone! Why do you trouble her? She has worked a good work for me. For you always have the poor with you, and whenever you wish, you are able to do good for them, but you do not always have me. What she is capable of, she did; she anticipated to anoint my body unto burial. And truly, I say

---

14. In the textual witnesses of W and f^{13} these nameless people are identified as the disciples (των μαθητων), as well as in D and Θ (οι δε μαθηται αυτου). This may well reflect an understanding borrowed from Matthew 26:8. More particularly, John 12:8 identifies Judas as the one who rebuked the woman, who is also identified as Mary (John 12:3). However, the exclusion of Judas from the inner story and the woman from the outer story is one way in which the narrator holds the two stories apart. See Shepherd, "Narrative Function," 527. Nevertheless, when the outer story resumes, there is a hint that Judas was with Jesus in the inner story when it states that Judas "went off" or "went away" (ἀπῆλθεν) to the chief priests (Mark 14:10). See Shepherd, "Narrative Function," 527.

to you, wherever the good news[15] is proclaimed in the whole world, what she did will be told in memory of her.[16] (Mark 14:6–9, author's translation).

Did the woman know that she was anointing Jesus' body for burial? The audience is not told. But the implied audience is given an interpretation by the narrator deploying the character of Jesus who interprets her act in this way. This will later shed light on the act of the woman at the tomb in Mark 16:1–3. They come to do something that has already been done. Through dramatic irony in chapter 16, the implied audience will know that Jesus was already anointed for his death by this woman in Mark 14.

The death of Jesus seeps from the outer story into the inner story. The religious leaders are plotting to seize Jesus in an isolated place and then kill him. The woman in the inner story has anointed Jesus for his death. The implied author has developed the characterization of the woman so that the implied audience participates in the suffering and death of Jesus and recognizes the immense value of his death. Nevertheless, the question remains: "How is this death going to happen?" The outer story provides an answer as it resumes in the next two verses.

THE OUTER STORY (MARK 14:10–11)

Although the woman was anonymous in the inner story, the outer story resumes by specifically identifying "Judas Iscariot who was one of the Twelve" (Mark 14:10). The juxtaposition of the woman and Judas is the implied author's way of asking the implied audience to compare them, and accordingly, to say more through an intercalation than could have been said in either story on its own.

15. Shepherd insightfully observes: "These gaps [concerning the death of Jesus] interconnect the stories so that there is a modification of the plot. Whereas the leaders' and Judas's story portends a tragic end to the ministry of Jesus, the inner story pulls aside the curtain and illustrates that the death of Jesus will be Good News. Even the plot to betray and kill Jesus is used in the service of the Gospel" (Shepherd, "Narrative Function of Markan Intercalation," 537).

16. Jesus sets forth three prolepses: (1) "You will not always have me" (14:7); (2) "She has anointed my body beforehand for burial" (14:8), and (3) "Wherever the Gospel is preached in all the world what she has done will also be told as a memorial to her" (14:9). Shepherd comments: "Each of these prolepses is spoken by Jesus and each succeeding one has a further reach than the previous one.... All of the anachronies together have the influence of laying tremendous stress upon the significance of the woman's action. This repetitive reinterpretation of her act of devotion is what makes possible the dramatic comparison with the outer story" (Shepherd, *Markan Sandwich Stories*, 258–59).

The Death Plot of the Leaders and the Anointing at Bethany

The gap first raised in the outer story concerning *how* the religious leaders are going to arrange for Jesus' secret arrest to kill him is now answered in the resumption of the outer story as we are told that Judas, one of the Twelve,[17] is going[18] to betray Jesus. In other words, it is Judas who is going to provide a way for the religious leaders to secretly[19] apprehend Jesus and then kill him (cf. 14:1-2):

> Then Judas Iscariot, one of the twelve, went to the chief priests in order to hand him over to them. And those hearing rejoiced and promised to give him silver. And he sought[20] how he should conveniently[21] hand him over. (Mark 14:10-11, author's translation)

Unlike the woman who shows her devotion to Jesus by anointing his head with expensive oil, Judas betrays his master. Unlike the woman

---

17. The Greek text includes the definite article, "the one of *the* twelve" (ὁ εἷς τῶν δώδεκα) (Mark 14:10). Wallace identifies the article as fitting within the "well-known" category (Wallace, *Greek Grammar*, 233). Mann suggests that this use of the article emphasizes Judas among the Twelve: "Mark may be using the definite article here for emphasis: 'That one, the only one, of the Twelve' who proved treacherous" (Mann, *Mark*, 560).

18. The verb in 14:10 is a clue that this portion of the outer story is subsequent to the inner story: "It is stated that Judas 'went away' to the high priests. This implies subsequent time to the previous event where Judas was present. Although Jesus is the only character to appear in both stories, nevertheless, in 14:10 we are told that Judas 'went away,' obviously from the previous meeting place, which is Bethany. The reference in 14:10, in fact, goes out of the way to designate Judas as one of the Twelve. Hence, we can conclude that 14:10 occurs after the events of 14:3-9" (Shepherd, *Markan Sandwich Stories*, 242-43).

19. Shepherd rightly states: "Thus Judas is not an agent who shifts the plan of the rulers temporally. He does not somehow lead them to carry out their plot during the feast when they did not actually plan to do so. Rather, he is the conduit through which they accomplish their goal in a secretive way" (Shepherd, *Markan Sandwich Stories*, 245n1).

20. The outer story contains an *inclusio*: Just as the religious leaders sought (ἐζήτουν) how they could seize Jesus (Mark 14:1), now Judas seeks (ἐζήτει) how he should hand him over (Mark 14:11).

21. Shepherd observes: "In previous intercalations we have a noted return of the outer story to the inner story's point at the close of the outer story. But in the present story, the ending is about Judas the betrayer, and nothing 'good' can be said of his deed. However, an ironic twist is present, for Judas seeks to betray Jesus *conveniently* (εὐκαίρως 14:11). In the outer story alone this just adds to his perfidy, as though he enjoys or *plots well* how to hand over the Messiah. But the ironic twist is the way in which the εὐ-word stands in such close relation with so many 'good' words in the inner story, words which convey high ideals and holy concepts in the inner story (καλός, 14:6; εὖ, 14:7, and εὐαγγέλιον, 14:9). Thus the well-laid perfidious plot against Jesus becomes forever part of the *Good News*. The evil is turned back to good, even though the betrayer never shares in its goodness. Thus, in a way, there is a return to the point of the inner story" (Shepherd, *Markan Sandwich Stories*, 156-57).

who pours out perfume worth nearly three hundred denarii, Judas receives a promise of an unspecified sum of money[22] to hand Jesus over.[23] The implied author has shown the implied audience that a woman who culturally would have been considered to be of less value than a man is capable of giving great value to Jesus while Judas decreases the value of Jesus. Unlike those in Bethany who scorn the woman for the good work she has done, the chief priests rejoice over Judas' treachery. Unlike the woman who is praised by Jesus for taking what she had to perform a good work in preparation for his burial, Judas takes the knowledge he has and does a work of disloyalty.[24]

These contrasts between the nameless woman and the named member of the Twelve uniquely call out to the implied audience from the piling of the two stories, leading to the inevitable conclusion that Judas is an example, *par excellence*, of a failed disciple, while the woman is an example of a true, faithful disciple.[25]

---

22. The theme of money contributes toward dramatized irony between the two stories. "Jesus is highly valued in the inner story, but not even worthy of the specification of a betrayal price in the outer story. This irony centers on the Christological question and is closely connected with the discipleship theme. What value will the disciple place upon Jesus?" (Shepherd, *Markan Sandwich Stories*, 263).

23. Shepherd notes: "Whereas Judas places a low valuation upon Jesus (he is not worth even a *set sum* of money), the woman, representative of true discipleship, pours out upon her Lord the costly nard, worth more than 300 denarii. . . . The contrast between the actions of the two characters could hardly be greater" (Shepherd, "Narrative Function," 537). Likewise, after discussing the concurrent responsibility to the poor and to those who are loved, Tolbert states: "But whatever the moral choices involved in using money for various loving ends, giving money to purchase betrayal and accepting money to deliver up your teacher to his enemies is clearly evil. The contrast between the generosity of the anonymous woman and the deal of Judas ('who was one of the twelve') with the chief priests to exchange Jesus for money (14:10–11) dramatizes starkly the different production of good earth and rocky ground" (Tolbert, *Sowing the Gospel*, 274). Finally, Shepherd comments: "The plots of the two stories are interlinked. The two stories, although apparently of contrasting types, are actually similar. They are both stories of valuation. Money is mentioned in both stories and Jesus is the center of the 'money actions.' In the inner story, it is a case of giving (δίδωμι, 14:5), while in the outer story, it is a case of betrayal (παραδίδωμι, 14:10–11)" (Shepherd, *Markan Sandwich Stories*, 255).

24. Shepherd identifies the dramatic irony in this intercalation as follows: "The nefarious plot becomes Good News. The disciple, one of the Twelve, does not value his Master aright, but a nameless woman prepares his body for burial by an expensive gift of love" (Shepherd, "Narrative Function," 540). Ironically, just as what the woman did will be remembered, so too, what Judas did will be a lasting remembrance.

25. Similarly, Edwards states: "Is not Mark saying that in Jesus' 'hour' (14:35) there can be only one of two responses to him, that of the woman or that of Judas? Mark places the woman in the middle as the ideal" (Edwards, "Markan Sandwiches," 209).

CONCLUSION

The full measure of the beauty of the woman's act is only seen against the stark relief of Judas's betrayal. In the inner story, Jesus' elevation of the anonymous woman exemplifies the implied author's theology where often, the nameless are the true followers of Jesus as they come out of anonymity and fade back into it. Their wealth is gladly given in devotion to God, and they do not allow conventional practices to stand in the way of their faith and love. What she has done for her Lord will be remembered even if she will not. It's the named one in the narrative, Judas, who is part of the Twelve, who will be remembered as Jesus' enemy.

Unlike Judas, the woman is shown to be attentive or watching (γρηγορέω, cf. Mark 13:33–37). Her actions are interpreted by Jesus to be in continuity with the passion that necessarily lies ahead for him. Unlike the others in the room, and as a foil to their protestations, she aligns herself with the direction that Jesus is going by anointing him for his death. She is shown to be a true disciple. This characterization is only heightened by Judas's nefarious act of alignment with the religious leaders who have consistently been in opposition to Jesus in Mark's story world. One might argue that he, like the woman, is only aligning himself with what Jesus has predicted to occur, but there is significant difference between being supportive of Jesus as he faces his prophesied death at the hands of his enemies and plotting with Jesus' enemies to bring about his death. It is against the black canvas of the Judas's treachery—a betrayal by one who was to be with Jesus (cf. Mark 3:14)—that the radiance of the woman's character shines more brightly as a true disciple. In the inevitable world of suffering, she shows the way to walk by aligning herself with her Lord and doing what she can on his behalf. Judas chooses the nihilistic path of plotting Jesus' death. Once more, the actual author's/implied author's narrative structure brings a woman to the forefront for the implied audience—even over one of the Twelve.

The affirmation of a woman over one of the Twelve in this narrative is further shown in the following narrative where a maidservant exposes the head of the Twelve, Peter, in his self-preserving lies to disassociate himself from Jesus at his arrest. Unlike the woman in Mark 14 who only acts out of devotion to Jesus, but never speaks, the maidservant will speak out of devotion to the truth exposing the failure of Peter to be on alert at the third watch of the night.

15

The Maidservant's Trial of Peter
(Mark 14:53–72)

THIS IS THE EIGHTH Markan narrative involving a woman. In Mark's narrative world this account is concurrent with the trial of Jesus before the religious leaders. As Jesus prevails in his trial in the house of the High Priest, Peter devastatingly fails his trial in the courtyard of the High Priest. Peter's inquisitor is not a religious leader but a female maidservant—showing an expected imbalance of power between a servant girl and the head of the Twelve. Unlike most other women in the Markan narratives, this maidservant has no affinity with Jesus. The implied author forms her character from her relationship to a high-ranking male—the High Priest—who is an antagonist of Jesus. As such, she could be characterized as dangerous and threatening. However, unlike the religious leaders, she pummels Peter with questions of truth, while the religious leaders pummel Jesus with lies. By the time the cockcrow announces the third Roman watch, the light of her inquiry definitively shows Peter to be "asleep"—just as Jesus predicted. By the implied author's portrayal of this anonymous woman as a person who gives expression to Jesus' evaluation of Peter's disloyalty through her truth telling, the implied audience will be sympathetic with her virtuous character.

INTRODUCTION

As with the narrative involving Herodias and her daughter in Mark 6:7–32, this larger narrative is being examined because of the active role of the unnamed maidservant of the High Priest who questions Peter in and around the courtyard of the High Priest while Jesus is being questioned by the chief priests and the Sanhedrin in the house of the High Priest. The religious trial of Jesus is parallel with the questioning of Peter; therefore, it may be appropriate to characterize the two parallel narratives as trials—the trial of Jesus and the trial of Peter.

The broader, narrative context to this unit is discussed in detail in Chapter 6 above. However, in summary, it is believed that Mark structures the end of his narrative around the categories set out in the parable of the Doorkeeper at the conclusion of the Olivet Discourse in Mark 13:34–36 focusing on the four Roman watches listed in Mark 13:35, 'evening . . . midnight . . . cockcrow . . . early morning' (ὀψὲ . . . μεσονύκτιον . . . ἀλεκτοροφωνίας . . . πρωΐ). As Tannehill explained: "Our surest guide to the implied author's evaluation of the disciples is to follow the shifting relationship between Jesus and the disciples, noting where they are in concord and where they are not."[1] This measure of concord will be highlighted in the section under discussion during the third watch of the night.

Tom Shepherd categorizes the broader unit of 14:53–72 as an intercalation.[2] He identifies the inner and outer stories as follows:

> Outer Story: 14:54, 66–72 (Jesus' Trial)
> Inner Story: 14:53, 55–65 (Peter's Denial)

A difficulty with categorizing the units as an intercalation is that, unlike all the other intercalations in Mark, the verses running through the two stories are not in sequential order. The inner story actually begins in verse 53 before the outer story begins in verse 54, then the inner story resumes in verses 55–65, and the outer story resumes in verses 66–72. Shepherd is aware of the irregularity and suggests:

> The explanation for this break from the usual pattern may be that it would be difficult to tell the story in any other way and still intercalate it; since Peter follows Jesus into the high priest's

---

1. Tannehill, "Disciples in Mark," 33.
2. Shepherd, *Markan Sandwich Stories*, 267–310. See also Evans, *Mark 8:27—16:20*, 440–41; Connolly, *Disorderly Women*, 164; Tolbert, *Sowing the Gospel*, 217; Kuruvilla, *Mark*, 321; Malbon, "Major Importance," 71; Deppe, *Theological Intentions*, 77–84.

courtyard and the narration of Peter's denial must necessarily follow 14:65 in order for the dramatized irony to be apparent.³

However, it seems that the structure of intercalation is artificial and unnecessary to identify what the implied author is doing with the passages.⁴ Those receiving the Gospel are already familiar with the structure of an interchange that was used in 6:7—8:21:

> A Herod / feeding of five thousand (6:7–44)
>   B Jesus on the sea / the disciples' hard hearts (6:45–52)
> A' Pharisees / feeding of four thousand (6:53—8:13)
>   B' Jesus on the sea / the disciples' hard hearts (8:14–21)⁵

It appears that a similar structure is being employed by the implied author in this unit:

> A Jesus is taken from the garden to the high priest's home (14:53)
>   B Peter follows Jesus to the courtyard of the high priest (14:54)
> A' Jesus is tried by the Sanhedrin (14:55–65)
>   B' Peter is tried by the maidservant and bystanders (14:66–72)

The net effect of an interchange is the same as an intercalation in that the parallel units will be compared to one another displaying similarities, differences, and dramatic irony.⁶ However, the structure of an interchange is not so strained as to require the mental gymnastics necessary to untangle a modified, intercalated structure. Accordingly, for the purpose of this analysis, the structure of these units will be considered an interchange rather than an intercalation.

---

3. Shepherd, *Markan Sandwich Stories*, 280.

4. See Brown, *Death of the Messiah*, 1:427.

5. See also Mark 1:21—2:12, discussed above, with respect to the overall narrative including the healing of Simon's mother-in-law.

6. As Iersel states: "The question ... about whether this is a case of intercalation or of two simultaneous actions does not seem of much interest to the reader. In either case the reader connects them with one another" (Iersel, *Mark*, 443n65).

STORY TIME IN MARK 14:53–72

Shepherd argues extensively that story time runs continuously through 14:53—15:1.[7] This reading of the narrative is possible, but not necessary[8] and may detract from a more dramatic reading of the stories simultaneously.[9] Even story time in the first interchange need not be read as occurring sequentially. Jesus is taken from the garden to the high priest's house and at the same time, Peter follows Jesus at a distance to the courtyard of the high priest. Yes, Jesus may have arrived first, but as Jesus was being led, Peter was following at a distance. From an observer's point of view, these two descriptions can be seen as occurring simultaneously. It is not possible to provide the audience with a split screen to view the simultaneous activities, so they are told in an interchanging structure. Part of the implied author's technique of bringing the audience back to the start of story time to run Peter's denial simultaneously with Jesus' confession, is the repetition of the term for courtyard (αὐλή) in Mark 14:54 and 14:66 and the participle at the end of 14:54 (Peter "was warming himself" θερμαινόμενος) and in Mark 14:67 (seeing Peter "warming himself" θερμαινόμενον). The narrator picks up on Peter's story exactly where Peter was left, warming himself in the courtyard by the fire. This technique allows the audience to imagine story time to run simultaneously through the two examinations of Jesus and Peter and enhances opportunities for the audience to make comparisons.

SELECTED ANALYSIS

This unit contains a great deal of significant narrative, theological material that focuses primarily on the persons of Jesus and Peter who are in contrast to one another. While some of these parallels and contrast will necessarily be addressed, the focus will be upon the maidservant who questions Peter. She is usually discussed tangentially to the focus on Peter

---

7. Shepherd, *Markan Sandwich Stories*, 267–74.

8. Shepherd states: "If, after these arguments, one still argues for a pause of the outer story, it is interesting to note that this contention leads to seeing the inner and outer stories proceeding simultaneously in the pattern of the other intercalations in which the two stories have contrasting actions occurring at the same time" (Shepherd, *Markan Sandwich Stories*, 274–75n1).

9. See Tolbert, *Sowing the Gospel*, 218; Brown, *Death of the Messiah*, 1:417–20; France, *Mark*, 619; Iersel, *Mark*, 443.

and Jesus. In this analysis, the emphasis will be on her interactions with Peter and her counterparts in the trial of Peter. This analysis is most fully accomplished by reading the narrative with its interchanging parallels in which the implied author will exalt Jesus as a direct truth teller before a highly regarded male, religious leadership and whittle away Peter as a liar through a lowly regarded, unnamed maidservant in the eyes of the implied audience.

The Location of Jesus and Peter (Mark 14:53–54)

Immediately prior to this narrative, Jesus participated in the Passover meal with his disciples (Mark 14:12–25). Jesus then went to the Mount of Olives with his disciples where he prophesized the that he would be struck and the disciples would be scattered, but that he would go ahead of them into Galilee after he had risen (14:26–28). Peter protested that he would never fall away (14:29), but Jesus predicted, against Peter's continued resistance, that before the rooster crowed twice that very night, Peter would deny him three times (14:30–31). Jesus and his disciples then went to a place called Gethsemane to pray (14:32–41). At the end of that period, Judas came with a crowd bearing swords and clubs from the religious leaders—the chief priests, the teachers of the law, and the elders—and handed Jesus over into their custody (14:42–49). As Jesus had predicted, everyone deserted him (14:50–51), and the present narrative ensues.

In Mark 14:53, Jesus was led from Gethsemane to a new venue, the High Priest's house, where all the religious leaders came together—the high priests, the elders, and the scribes (the Sanhedrin, cf. Mark 14:55). This is an *ad hoc* assembly of a religious court, in the middle of the night, in the great hall of the High Priest's house in Jerusalem.[10]

In verse 54, Peter is described as following Jesus *from a distance*. The phrase "from a distance" (ἀπὸ μακρόθεν) is curious in Mark, because when Jesus called his disciples, he called them to be *with him* (μετ' αὐτοῦ) (cf. Mark 3:14). Peter is following (ἀκολουθέω) as a disciple should follow Jesus (cf. Mark 1:18, 2:14, 15; 5:24; 6:1, 8:34; 10:21, 28; 11:9; 15:41), but he is not *with* him but following at a *distance*. This may foreshadow an incongruity in his following of Jesus. The divergence between Jesus and Peter continues as Peter entered into the courtyard of the High Priest and was sitting with the servants and warming himself at the fire or light (φῶς). Already

---

10. See France, *Mark*, 598.

contrasts exist. Jesus is in the house of the High Priest while Peter is in the courtyard of the High Priest. Jesus is before the powerful religious counsel of Israel, and Peter is with the subordinate guards of the high priest. Peter is supposed to be with Jesus (μετ' αὐτοῦ, Mark 3:14), but he is with the attendants (μετὰ τῶν ὑπηρετῶν). This same word for "attendants" will be used to describe those who beat Jesus in Mark 14:65.

The location of Jesus and Peter has not only set the stage for what is to follow in the next interchange but has set the tone for Peter's upcoming test. He is not spatially where he should be; this special shift may portend a greater shift ahead when he meets his female inquisitor in the courtyard, and the implied audience would be taking note of this.

The Trial of Jesus and Peter (Mark 14:55-72)

Within the contrasts between Jesus and Peter are significant parallels. Jesus is accused by numerous false witnesses whose testimony does not agree (Mark 14:57-59). Peter is accused by numerous witnesses whose testimony does agree. Both Jesus and Peter are questioned. Jesus boldly answers with a threefold affirmation ("I am" the Messiah, the Son of the Blessed one, the Son of Man who will come sitting at the right of the one with power) (Mark 14:62), and Peter boldly answers with a threefold denial of Jesus and any relationship with him (Mark 14:68, 70, 71).

Twice, the inquisitor of Peter is described as a female slave or maidservant using the diminutive term παιδίσκη.[11] First, she is described as one of the maidservants of the High Priest (μία τῶν παιδισκῶν τοῦ ἀρχιερέως)[12] (Mark 14:66); then she is simply described as "the maidservant" (ἡ παιδίσκη) (Mark 14:69). Because of the definite article used in

---

11. Bernadette Kiley argues that the diminutive form of παιδίσκη in Classical Greek could suggest that the girl was a prostitute of the high priest's household or of the high priest himself (Kiley, "Servant Girl," 52-53). Even if the high priest or his household had authority sexually over the servant girl, the Markan narrative makes nothing of her sexual relationships. Perhaps the implied author used the term παιδίσκη to characterize her for the implied audience as someone of low esteem. Louw further explains that παιδίσκη probably refers to someone younger than would be the cause for a δούλη (Louw et al., Greek-English Lexicon, s.v. "παιδίσκη"). Again, the servant girl's youth diminishes her apparent status for the implied audience. However, because she is identified with the prestigious house of the high priest, she may have had a measure of prestige for a Jewish audience (Cohick, Women in the World, 265).

12. There is a textual variant in 14:66 where ℵ C[vid] sa[ms] bo[ms] substitute the singular "servant girl" (παιδίσκη) for the plural servant girls (τῶν παιδισκῶν). With either reading, the sense is the same for our purposes.

Mark 14:69, it seems likely that this woman was the same maidservant who was mentioned in 14:66, rather than a second maidservant. The implied audience only knew she was a woman by the feminine gender of the term παιδίσκη.

Elizabeth Malbon correlates the maidservant with Herodias whose actions result in the death of John the Baptizer who used "a person of lower status and authority than herself, her daughter, to influence a person of higher status and authority than herself, her husband, King Herod." Malbon concludes: "The high priest and the chief priests are the archenemies of the Markan Jesus, and two women characters [Herodias and the maidservant] function in comparable roles in relation to John the Baptist who comes before Jesus and Peter who follows after him."[13] From a feminist perspective, Connelly arrives at a similar conclusion stating:

> My interest lies in the fact that a female character here facilitates a form of recognition scene focused on Peter in Mark 14:66–72. What is recognized about Peter is his cowardice and the degree to which fear has overcome his faith, his relationship with Jesus. It is possible to see that Mark has created a lively female character here, who is powerful enough to have this effect. Indeed, she brings about a reversal in Peter's fate, the complete destruction of Peter's relationship with Jesus, indicated by Peter's abject weeping (14:72). Thus we see in this story, as we witnessed in the story of Herodias and her daughter, that when a woman intervenes in the context of male relationships, especially by speech, she actively catalyzes the collapse of male relationships.[14]

The proposed parallels between Herodias and the maidservant seem to be misplaced—especially by the way the implied author presents the actions of the maidservant. There is truth to the observation that Peter appears to act less manly out of fear, and the servant girl acts more like a man in her confrontation of Peter.

The counterpart to those giving false testimony against Jesus (Mark 14:56–59), appears to be the servant girl who only says what is true about Peter.[15] Those who gave the false testimony against Jesus are spoken of generically with terms like "many" (πολλοί), and "certain ones" (τινες),

---

13. Malbon, "Fallible Followers," 46.
14. Connolly, *Disorderly Women*, 333.
15. Aernie suggests that "the servant girl plays a contrarian role in the narrative in her interrogation of Peter" (Aernie, *Narrative Discipleship* loc. 896–913). This writer will show that this maidservant stands on the side of truth. The fallible one is Peter.

"we" (ἡμεῖς) and "their" (αὐτῶν) (Mark 14:56–59). In contrast, a specific reference is given to the woman who questions Peter; she is described as "one of the servant girls of the high priest" (μία τῶν παιδισκῶν τοῦ ἀρχιερέως). She is anonymous, the significance of which will be discussed below, but she is a specific person as opposed to the vague plurality of witnesses against Jesus. She is connected with the high priest as a servant, but not in any other official capacity. So, her questioning of Peter has no real authority; but the implied author shows her to wield power that causes Peter to distance himself in stages from her and her accusations. She is a woman; she is a servant. Peter is a man, and a free man at that. There is a power differential in Peter's favor in this interchange except for the fact that Peter probably feels threatened because of the high priest's actions against Jesus. If the religious leaders want to condemn Jesus to death, they may also seek out his followers. It appears that it is the potential threat of the high priest that drives Peter's response. However, the servant girl exercises a power of her own in speaking the truth to Peter. The servant girl's power seems to widen as bystanders join in with her truth telling. Peter's lies may be driven by his fear of being guilty by association with Jesus, but the maidservant is the powerful presence that exposes Peter's unwillingness to be with Jesus at this time.

In the resumption of the Peter narrative, he is described as being "below" (κάτω) in the courtyard (Mark 14:66). The adverb apparently distinguishes Peter's location from Jesus' location in the high priest's house. The servant girl is described by three verbs as coming, seeing Peter warming himself, and looking at him (Mark 14:66–67). The verbs progressively show the woman moving and coming to a stop to look at Peter. She is probably able to distinguish Peter because he was warming himself by the light (φῶς) of the fire (see Mark 14:54). She then makes her first statement to Peter: "You also were with the Nazarene, Jesus" (καὶ σὺ μετὰ τοῦ Ναζαρηνοῦ ἦσθα τοῦ Ἰησοῦ) (Mark 14:67). This direct, true statement associates Peter with Jesus of Nazareth. In response, the narrator tells us that Peter denied (ἠρνήσατο)[16] her statement and then quotes Peter's de-

---

16. As Paul Danove observers: "Deny (ἀπαρνέομαι) initially appears in Jesus' statement that anyone wishing to be his disciple must deny himself (8:34). It subsequently appears in Jesus' prediction that Peter will deny him three times (14:30), Peter's responnse that he will not deny Jesus (14:31), and in Peter's remembrance of Jesus' statement after he has denied Jesus three times (14:72). Peter's denial of Jesus and not himself places Peter in an indirect negative relationship with Jesus. Deny (ἀρνέομαι), the root of ἀπαρνέομαι, occurs in Mark only with Peter as subject and only in Peter's denials of Jesus (14:68, 70) and places Peter in an indirect negative relationship with Jesus" (Danove, "Narrative Rhetoric," 160).

nial: "Neither do I know nor understand what you are saying" (οὔτε οἶδα οὔτε ἐπίσταμαι σὺ τί λέγεις) (Mark 14:68). By adding the second person singular pronoun "you" (σὺ) with the inflected verb "saying" (λέγεις), Peter is emphasizing that his response is particularly pointed to the slave girl. It may well be that the servant girl's use of "you" (σὺ) in her statement to Peter in 14:67 resulted in Peter using the pronoun in response. But the use of the pronoun may also be a means to silence her by intimidation. The narrator then tells the audience that Peter went out of the courtyard to the forecourt, or gateway to the court, (προαύλιον). The narrator also tells his implied audience that the rooster crowed. If this is part of the original text,[17] it is clearly an allusion to Jesus' prediction in Mark 14:30 that "before the cock crows twice, thrice you will deny me" which Peter vehemently denied, but the implied audience remembers. In the implied author's story world, Peter's denial of Jesus is not because of the slave girl, but because of Jesus' prediction and Peter's fear. The slave girl is merely one of the means through whom the prophecy is realized. The implied author's determinism is emphasized by dramatic irony at the end of Jesus' interrogation where it is reported that certain ones struck Jesus with their fists and said, "Prophesy!" (Mark 14:65). The irony is that the characters who struck Jesus did not think that he could prophecy even though Jesus boldly stated that he was Messiah, but the implied audience knows that Jesus can prophesy, and Peter's simultaneous denial of Jesus is proof *par excellence*.

The slave girl did not appear to be intimidated by Peter's first response to her because when she saw him by the gateway to the court, she spoke to the bystanders and said: "This one is from them" (οὗτος ἐξ αὐτῶν ἐστιν) (Mark 14:69). The maidservant is not directly addressing Peter but a generic group called "bystanders" or "those who were present" (παρεστῶσιν) in the forecourt. Even if she was hesitant to speak directly to Peter, she makes a similar affirmation to those who are present at the

---

17. The words "and the rooster crowed" (καὶ ἀλέκτωρ ἐφώνησεν) are in later manuscripts: A C D K N Γ Δ Θ Ψ^c 067 $f^{1.13}$ 28. 33. 565. 700. 1241. (+ ευθεως α. αλεκτωρ 1424)§§. 2542s 𝔐 lat sy$^{p.h}$ (sa^{mss} bo^{ms}); Eus. The words are omitted in good and early Alexandrian witnesses: ℵ B L W Ψ* 579. 892 c sys samss bo. The editors of the NA^{28} decided to include the words in the text in brackets because of the difficulty of the external evidence for each reading. See Metzger, *Textual Commentary*, 97. Internally, the evidence can go in either direction. The words may have been inserted to fulfill Jesus' prophecy in Mark 14:30 or excluded to align with other gospel accounts that only mention a rooster crowing once (Matt 26:75; Luke 22:60; John 18:27). However, in view of the statement in Mark 14:71 that the cock crowed a second time, it may be best to understand these words as part of the original text. The decision is difficult.

gateway to the court that Peter was with the group who were with Jesus. Perhaps this is a reference to those who were present with Jesus at his arrest (cf. Mark 14:42-52). If so, some of these "bystanders" may also have been present when Jesus was arrested. In any case, the implied audience knows that the words the servant girl has spoken are true, but Peter lies. The narrator tells the audience, without a quotation, that Peter again denied (ἠρνεῖτο) the claim (Mark 14:70). This denial certainly includes the claim that Peter was with Jesus, but also includes the claim that Peter was with those who were with Jesus. Peter is denying the community he has been a part of since he was called to be with Jesus (Mark 3:14-16).

The maidservant's words first moved Peter, and then moved the bystanders so that they adopted her words and said: "Truly, you are from them, for you are also Galilean" (Mark 14:70). The generic word for bystanders (οἱ παρεστῶτες) does not tell the audience the gender of the group that is speaking to Peter. Masculine terms in Greek can be used to describe men and women.[18] Therefore, it is conceivable that other maidservants would be among the group of bystanders. It would be unusual for a woman to be by herself in this more-public setting unless perhaps her work required her presence. We are not told, but the Greek text allows for the possibility that other women joined in with men in making the third statement to Peter. Perhaps it was a composite statement made by several of those present. In some ways, the final statement is a composite of the maidservant's previous two statements. Like her second statement, the bystanders say "Truly, you are from them" (ἀληθῶς ἐξ αὐτῶν εἶ). This language is very similar to the maidservant's second statement in Mark 14:69 except she spoke about Peter to them (οὗτος ἐξ αὐτῶν ἐστιν) whereas they speak directly to Peter (ἐξ αὐτῶν εἶ). This heightened, direct address may in part explain Peter's heightened response. In addition, the second statement made by the bystanders "for you are also Galilean" (καὶ γὰρ Γαλιλαῖος εἶ) is similar to the maidservant's first statement that "You also were with the Nazarene,

---

18. "One rule in many languages, including Koine Greek, is that grammatically masculine expressions regularly describe groups that include both men and women. An example is Matthew 19:4, 'he who created . . . made them male and female . . .' (ESV). The word 'them' here is a masculine plural pronoun, though it obviously refers to a man and a woman" (Miller, "Gender-Accurate Bible Translation," 9). See also Mark 10:21; Luke 1:6; Rom 16:7, 15-16; 1 Cor 16:22; 2 Cor 13:12; 1 Thess 5:26; 1 Pet 5:14. The gender of ancient-Greek terms does not always correlate with sexual gender. It is often simply a category of inflection, or "grammatical gender." See Porter, *Idioms*, 100-101; Dana and Mantey, *Grammar*, 34-35; Blass and Debrunner, *Greek Grammar*, 76; Robertson, *Grammar*, 252-70.

Jesus" (Mark 14:67) since Nazareth was in the region of Galilee. Accordingly, the double, third statement that echoes the maidservant's two earlier statements is a climax to the claims identifying Peter with Jesus. Furthermore, in Mark, Galilee has been a major geographical focus of Jesus' activity where miracles were performed, and many followed after Jesus. Therefore, to say that Peter is a Galilean is to identify him with all that has occurred in chapters 1 through 8 of Mark's Gospel.

The climactic statement by the bystanders results in a climactic denial by Peter when the narrator reports that Peter started to curse (ἀναθεματίζειν) and swear (or take an oath with an implied invitation of punishment if he is untruthful) (ὀμνύναι):[19] "I do not know this man of whom you speak" (Mark 14:71). Peter's lies place him under his own curse. Furthermore, Peter's denial uses the most generic word available (τὸν ἄνθρωπον) so that he does not have to say the name of Jesus. Through nothing but truthful statements made by the servant girl and the bystanders, Peter exposes himself as a liar. Jesus has courage to speak the truth before his false accusers knowing that it will cost him his life, but Peter refuses to speak the truth before truthful accusers so that he can preserve his life.

As Paul Danove explained:

> Repetition may cultivate the beliefs of the narrative audience either by developing or by undercutting particular aspects of pre-existing belief. When the resulting beliefs of the narrative audience do not challenge those of the authorial audience, repetition serves as a sophisticating rhetorical strategy. However, when the resulting beliefs of the narrative audience are contrary to those of the authorial audience, repetition serves as a deconstructive rhetorical strategy.[20]

In this case, Peter's repeated denials place him in a negative relationship with Jesus, and the implied audience disassociates itself from him. On the contrary, the repeated statements by the slave girl associate her with the truth about Peter and Jesus, and the audience identifies with her.

In order for the implied audience to know that Peter's undoing was not the result of the woman or the bystanders who testified truthfully, the narrator reports that "immediately, for the second time,[21] the cock

---

19. BDAG, s.v. "ὀμνύω."
20. Danove, "Narrative Rhetoric," 154.
21. As Metzger states: "Several witnesses omit ἐκ δευτέρου (ℵ C*vid L itc Diatessaroni, s), probably in order to harmonize Mark with the account in the other Gospels

crowed, and Peter remembered the words Jesus spoke to him that "before the cock crowed twice, thrice you will deny me" (Mark 17:72). Jesus has openly identified himself as Messiah and is willing to suffer in that role, but Peter is unwilling to take up his cross and suffer, so he denies Jesus when all of the witnesses, including the maidservant, truthfully state that he was with Jesus.

CONCLUSION

The maidservant of the high priest who identifies Peter as being with Jesus stands in a long line of anonymous women in the Gospel of Mark. Connolly believes that the maidservant's anonymity is the author's way of disrespecting and subjecting her in a patriarchal world.[22] However, it may be better to look at what the implied author of Mark is *doing* with what s/he is *saying*. Said differently, there may be a theology that is being communicated and a rhetorical effect that the implied author hopes to accomplish by bringing anonymous women into the narrative as foils that subvert the named disciples. As Mary Ann Tolbert observes, many, but not all, of the named characters in Mark (the disciples, especially Peter, James, and John; Herod; Herodias; Pilate) "want to be great (9:34), to be first (9:35), to rule over others (9:38; 10:13); to be rich (10:26–28); glory (10:37); concrete honors (9:5; 13:1), their physical needs to be satisfied before considering the needs of their hearts, minds, or spirits (2:23; 8:14–17; 14:37–41), and their words and views to supplant those of Messiah (8:31–33; 14:29–31)."[23]

(Matt 26:74; Luke 22:60; John 18:27)" (Metzger, *Textual Commentary*, 97). Those witness that include ἐκ δευτέρου are ℵ B C* D L W Θ ƒ13 565. 579. 700. 2542s latt syp sams boms; Eus |□ p) ℵ C*vid L 579 c vgms.

22. "Like all female characters in this gospel to date, she has no individual name, but she is identified by her relationship with a male figure" (Connolly, *Disorderly Women*, 164). Of course, Connolly errs. All female characters in Mark are not anonymous. Connolly reads Mark from a contemporary perspective focusing on the subjugation of women that was part of a Graeco-Roman *ethos*. However, to have expected otherwise from a first-century author is unfair owing to the habituation of early Christian male authors. Instead of placing contemporary values on an ancient narrative, it may be better to acknowledge the first-century social hierarchies, to warn against identifying with those value systems, and to acknowledge, identify, and make explicit where an author has gone beyond only aligning with the *habitus* of his day, as appears to be the case in the Gospel of Mark.

23. Tolbert, *Sowing the Gospel*, 225.

However, the anonymous ones "come out of anonymity and fade back into it."[24] Their money is freely given in devotion to God or Jesus (Mark 12:41–44; 14:3–9). They gladly serve the needs of others (Mark 1:31; 2:3–5; 5:18; 14:8–9). They do not allow conventional practices of rules to stand in the way of their faith or love (Mark 2:4; 5:27–34; 7:25–30; 10:48; 14:3–5). They do not seek fame, wealth, personal glory, reputation, or honor. They hear the word and emerge to respond in faith, are saved, and then go.[25] They are similar to Jesus who actively strives to suppress his reputation, keep his name from becoming known, and stay hidden from crowds (Mark 1:34; 3:12; 5:43; 7:24). Jesus becomes known, but it was not his desire, but his fate. As he becomes known, he suffers, is crucified, and dies. As with Peter in this passage, what the disciples most wanted—greatness, repute, renown, power—runs the risk of bringing them what they most want to avoid—suffering and possible death.[26]

Anonymity appears to be the way of Jesus, and the anonymous women who reflect that value become foils to the named disciples who subvert their appearances of strength and move towards the realities of Jesus. The anonymous women demonstrate a proper response to Jesus and do not seek their own glory. They are unnamed as a rhetorical means of contrast between them and the named actors. And it is not only women who are anonymous, for instance, the demoniac in Mark 5 remains unnamed, and he too is a foil to the disciples in his response to Jesus.[27] This is part of the effect the implied author wants to have upon the implied audience. They want to be like the good soil and not like the rocky soil shown in the disciples, or the thorny soil shown in Herod and Pilate, or the first soil shown in the religious leaders. It is the anonymous who are most like Jesus and who point the way to how a disciple should follow him. The anonymous women at the end of the Gospel show a proper response to Jesus by serving him, but the named women raise a flag for the

24. Tolbert, *Sowing the Gospel*, 225.
25. Tolbert, *Sowing the Gospel*, 226.
26. Tolbert, *Sowing the Gospel*, 226–30.

27. In the storm, the disciples call Jesus "teacher" and ask "who then is this?" (Mark 4:38, 41). The demon addresses Jesus as "Son of the Most High God" (Mark 5:7). In the storm, the disciples do not worship Jesus, but the demoniac worships Jesus (Mark 5:6). In the storm, the disciples are "fearful with a great fear" (φοβήθησαν φόβον μέγαν) (Mark 4:41), showing themselves to be like the town's people who are afraid of Jesus (ἐφοβήθησαν) (Mark 5:15). The disciples are no better than the demons or town's people. In their deficient address of Jesus, they are worse than the demons. In the greatness of their fear, they are worse than the town's people.

implied audience and prove to be fallible when faced with the message from the anonymous young man at the tomb.

Rather than reading a political disdain for patriarchy back into the narrative world of Mark, it seems more helpful to look at what the implied author is doing with how the story is being told; to ask what the implied author hopes the implied audience will adopt from the presentation of characters in the narrative. There are some named characters who show themselves faithful including Jesus, John the Baptizer, Jairus, and Bartimaeus, but they are the exceptions. A named character usually alerts the audience to a potential flaw in what they will do, and a potential lesson about what not to do. This is not the case with the anonymous—especially the anonymous women in Mark.

Therefore, it seems best to understand the anonymous servant girl to be a truth teller. Her truth gives Peter an opportunity to publicly follow Jesus during the time between midnight and the cockcrow watch, but as predicted, he fails; he lies to protect himself; he is not watching and alert when the cock crows. The maidservant has not undone Peter but provided the perfect opportunity for him to follow Jesus in the light of the truth she proclaims. As with other anonymous women in the Gospel, she is a foil that subverts the first follower of Jesus and the first of the Twelve. Accordingly, the implied audience is more drawn to the maidservant than to Peter and reminded that discipleship is no easy task.[28]

Unlike the maidservant in this passage who is male-like in her steadfast interrogation of Peter, are the women looking on at Jesus' crucifixion. In the upcoming transitional narrative, the audience learns more about a group of women disciples who followed Jesus from Galilee and hears narrative echoes which suggest that some of these women may be fallible like Peter.

28. Vorster, "Characterization of Peter," 69.

16

The Women at Jesus' Crucifixion
(Mark 15:40–41)

This ninth Markan narrative is in the form of a transitional, retrospective hinge that provides a seamless transition from the Jerusalem panel to the panel associated with the tomb. It summarizes earlier themes in the Gospel including Galilee, "on the way," and Jerusalem, and introduces women who will play a strategic part in the last panel of the book at the tomb where Jesus has been buried. However, the introduction of these women has negative echoes from the earlier narrative that suggest that some of these women may be fallible.

A TRANSITIONAL HINGE

Mark provides a literary/structural transition to this final panel of his narrative. According to Lucian, transitions should be easy, natural, and smooth:

> For, though all parts must be independently perfected, when the first is complete the second will be brought into essential connection with it and attached like one link of a chain to another; there must be no possibility of separating them; no mere bundle of parallel threads; the first is not simply to be next to the second, but part of it, their extremities intermingling.[1]

---

1. Lucian, *Works of Lucian*, 55.

The Women at Jesus' Crucifixion

Mark provides what Iersel and others have described as a retrospective hinge to transition from the geographical section of "Jerusalem" to the final panel of the book at the "Tomb":

> Title (1:1)
> prologue, the wilderness (1:2–13)
>   *prospective hinge (1:14–15)*
>   Galilee (1:16—8:21)
>   frame, blind →seeing (8:22–26)
>   the way (8:27—10:45)
>   frame, blind →seeing (10:46–52)
>   Jerusalem (11:1—15:39)
>   *retrospective hinge (15:40–41)*
> epilogue, the tomb (15:42—16:8)[2]

Parunak explains the nature of a "hinge" used to provide a transition from one panel to another within a narrative:

> The hinge is a transitional unit of text, independent to some degree from the larger units on either side, which has affinities with each of them and does not add significant information to that presented by its neighbors. The two larger units are joined together, not directly, but because each is joined by the hinge. Two patterns are common. In the direct hinge, *A /ab/ B*,[3] the affinity between the hinge and each of the larger units follows the pattern already described in the link.[4] The inverted hinge, on the other hand, offers the pattern *A /ba/ B* and reverses the order of the joining elements from that of the larger blocks of text.[5]

Parunak also observes that: "[a]t higher levels of synthesis, a paragraph that serves as a hinge with regard to its neighbors may also contain material of its own, material not treated in the sections it unites. In this case, it serves not only to unify its context but also to advance the argument by adding material."[6] The prospective and retrospective hinges in Mark

---

2. Iersel, *Mark*, 84.

3. Capital letters "A" and "B" refer to the major panels. Lowercase "a" and "b" refer to themes from the respective, major panels.

4. Parunak explains the pattern of the "link" to be where a word at the end of a unit is taken up again at the beginning of the following unit. "We call a feature that joins two sections together in this way a 'link'" (Parunak, "Transitional Techniques," 531).

5. Parunak, "Transitional Techniques," 540–41.

6. Parunak, "Transitional Techniques," 541–42.

both appear to be inverted hinges that provide higher levels of synthesis containing unique material.

As Stock explains, the inverted hinge was an effective tool in "helping the listener follow the speaker's shift in thought" by "hesitating at the point where the topic changes and hinting at the change before actually making it."[7] Discussing the same functional purpose of the transition, Parunak explains:

> The one-dimensional nature of spoken language imposes restrictions that produce these structures. In particular, when a speaker moves from one topic to another, a moment's lapse on the part of a hearer can be disastrous. A speaker can help an audience follow a transition by hesitating at the point where the topic changes and hinting at the change before actually making it. A move directly from topic A to topic B presents only one point of shift. A hearer who misses that point is lost. On the other hand, in a transition with the pattern *AbaB*, the topic shifts three times: once from A to b, once from b to a, and finally from a to B. The effect is to slow down the transition and give listeners more opportunity to note that a change is taking place.[8]

These structural cues can profit both the listener and the reader:

> Our world is graphically oriented. Comparatively speaking, that of the ancients is oriented more toward the spoken word. Where we use signals specially tailored to the printed page, they employ a system of indicators that can function in either oral or written presentations.[9]

Both the "prospective" and "retrospective" hinges in Mark slowdown the narrative by looking backward and forward.[10] Furthermore, by looking backward and forward, the hinges integrate parts of each panel to link them together and add additional information that enriches the narrative. The prospective hinge in Mark 1:14–15 is as follows:

> [14] Now after John was handed over, Jesus came into Galilee, preaching the gospel of God,
> [15] and saying that, "The time is fulfilled, and the kingdom of God is near; repent and believe in the gospel."

---

7. Stock, "Hinge Transitions," 27–31.
8. Parunak, "Transitional Techniques," 546.
9. Parunak, "Oral Typesetting," 154.
10. Stock, "Hinge Transitions," 28.

The Women at Jesus' Crucifixion

These verses create an inverted hinge. Verse 14 looks forward into the Galilee panel, and verse 15 looks backward into the Prologue, or Wilderness, panel. Stock observes how the prospective hinge swings forward and backward:

> Verse 14 points to the following main section (Galilee) and all the rest of the book, while verse 15 refers back to the prologue (Wilderness). The former points ahead to Jesus' words and actions in Galilee, while the latter proclaims the fulfillment of what is anticipated by the presentation of John as *Elijah Returned* and by John's proclamation that the time is fulfilled, and that with Jesus the Kingdom of God has arrived.[11]

However, a new element is added in this inverted hinge.[12] In verse 14, we are told that John the Baptizer was handed over (Μετὰ δὲ τὸ παραδοθῆναι τὸν Ἰωάννην). The word for "handed over" (παραδίδωμι) foreshadows Jesus' fate in the following narrative (Mark 3:19; 9:31; 10:33; 14:10–11, 18, 21, 41–42, 44; 15:1, 10, 15). As part of this foreshadow, Jesus now stands in John's shoes. Therefore, it is reported that he comes heralding the good news of God saying: "the time has been fulfilled, the kingdom of God is near, repent and believe in the good news" (Mark 1:14–15; cf. 1:4).

Similarly, verses 15:40–41 form a "retrospective hinge" transitioning the audience from the earlier panels of the book to its Epilogue, at the Tomb. The verses are as follows:

> [40] There were also women looking on from a distance, among whom *were* also Mary Magdalene, and Mary the mother of James the younger and Joses, and Salome.
> [41] When He was in Galilee, they were following Him and ministering to Him; and *there were* many other women who came up with Him to Jerusalem. (Mark 15:40–41)[13]

---

11. Stock, "Hinge Transitions," 28.

12. Parunak, "Transitional Techniques," 541.

13. Verse 40 has also been translated to identify four women and not just three: "Mary Magdalene, and Mary the [*daughter/mother/wife*] of James the less, and the [*nameless/Mary*] mother of Joses, and Salome." The textual variants B and Ψ allow for this reading placing a definite article before Joses [η Ιωσητος or the variant Ιωση]. However, the textual evidence for the variant is late and without versional support. See Pesch, *Das Markusevangelium*, 504–7; France, *Mark*, 664n83. See also Brown, *Death of the Messiah*, 2:1016, 1152–54, 1276–77; Gundry, *Mark*, 976–79. It seems best to understand the "ἡ" before "Ἰακώβου" to be a kataphoric, definite article for μήτηρ thereby bracketing and thus grouping together, or pointing to, all of the terms between the article and "mother": "ἡ Ἰακώβου τοῦ μικροῦ καὶ Ἰωσῆτος μήτηρ" (emphasis added). See Wallace, *Greek Grammar*, 220–21.

Once again, the structure is that of an inverted hinge slowing down the narrative to give the audience a cue that a transition is occurring and adding new materials to the narrative. Verse 40 looks forward to the Tomb where the same, three women (Mary Magdalene, Mary *mother* of James, and Salome) will once again be named as characters who saw where Jesus was laid (Mark 15:47), purchased spices, and came to the Tomb (Mark 16:1). Verse 41 looks backward: first to Galilee where we are explicitly told for the first time that women were following Jesus and ministering to him. The central panel, "On the Way," and the "Jerusalem" panel are also mentioned as the narrator explains that "many other women went up with him to Jerusalem."[14] Therefore, this retrospective hinge provides a seamless transition summarizing earlier themes in the book and introducing the women who will play a strategic part at the tomb.

CHARACTERIZATION OF THE WOMEN

The implied author of Mark has been criticized for waiting so long to introduce these women into the narrative.[15] However, rather than ascribing negative, philosophical motives that the implied author is androcentric or paternalistic, it might be better to consider what the implied author is *doing* with what is being said.[16] What effect did the implied author want to have upon his implied audience by telling the narrative in this way.[17] This is a question concerning the *discourse* of the narrative rather than its *story*. This is connected with how the implied author develops the characterization of women in the telling of the narrative.

The informed implied audience knows this is not the first time that women have appeared in the narrative. Women have been active characters from the beginning of the narrative and, except for Jesus' mother (Mark 3:20–35) and Herodias and her daughter (Mark 6:7–32), the

---

14. Stock states: "This [verse 41] refers back to everything that has gone before, and in particular it makes mention of the three central topographical divisions: Galilee, Jerusalem, and the Way to Jerusalem" (Stock, "Hinge Transitions," 29). See also Iersel, *Mark*, 83.

15. Fowler, *Let the Reader Understand*, 111; Dewey, "Women in the Gospel of Mark," 28.

16. Kuruvilla, "'What Is the Author Doing,'" 565. How does *what* was said *affect* the hearer? See also Kuruvilla, *Privilege the Text!*, 48–54.

17. Robert Fowler, *Let the Reader Understand*, 23.

women have been characterized positively.[18] In Mark 15:40-41, the implied author skillfully employs several, lexical links to unite the women just mentioned with some of the earlier women in his narrative. Some of these links are positive characterizations exposing the inconsistencies of the *status quo* and some may be negative characterizations where contemporary *habitus* remains in place, or the women are portrayed as unresponsive to the message of God. These intentional echoes also function within the design of the retrospective hinge as verse 41 looks backward to the earlier narrative and verse 40 looks forward to the next panel at the Tomb.

The women in Mark 15:40 are first described as watching Christ's crucifixion "from a distance" (ἀπὸ μακρόθεν). While some interpret this distance as understandable due to their fear of arrest,[19] in the narrator's story world, this prepositional phrase appears to have an immediate, negative echo and reference. When Jesus was arrested and led away from Gethsemane to the religious leaders, Peter was not with him (μετ' αὐτοῦ, cf. Mark 3:14),[20] but was following him from a distance (ἀπὸ μακρόθεν) into the courtyard of the high priest where he then denied knowing Jesus three times (Mark 14:54, 66-72).[21] Furthermore, if "Mary, the mother of James the younger and Joses" is in fact the mother of Jesus,[22] the im-

---

18. See Simon's mother-in-law (1:29-31), the woman with the flow of blood/Jairus's daughter (5:21-43), the Syrophoenician woman (7:1-30), the poor widow who gave at the temple (12:41-44), the woman who anointed Jesus (14:1-11), and the maidservant who confronted Peter (14:53-72).

19. Schüssler Fiorenza, *Memory of Her*, 319-22; Dewey, "Women in the Gospel of Mark," 28; Miller, "Women Characters," 190; *Women in Mark's Gospel*, 189.

20. See Tannehill's discussion of the positive characterization of the disciples in the early chapters of Mark by Jesus' call for the disciples to be "with him" and by the description of the disciples who were "around him" (Tannehill, "Disciples in Mark," 396-97).

21. Other writers who also interpret "from a distance" to be a negative foreshadow of the women include: Malbon, "Fallible Followers," 43; Munro, "Women Disciples in Mark," 235; "Women Disciples," 50; Williams, *Other Followers*, 188; Stock, *Mark*, 415; Brown, *Death of the Messiah*, 2:1158. But see France, *Mark*, 663n79. Iersel states: "The Greek ἀπὸ μακρόθεν refers, as a rule, to physical distance in Mark (5:6; 8:3; 11:19; 14:54). The connotation of fear, cowardice, and beginning disloyalty, caused by 14:54, need not be present in 15:40 at all" (Iersel, *Mark*, 488n11). It may also be that women would not be present at a public, Roman gathering like a crucifixion. However, Mark's implied correlations between the female and male disciples in verses 40-41 suggest that the geographical description of Peter in Mark 14:54 may be foreboding when it is so quickly applied to the women.

22. Support for "Mary" being the mother of Jesus is that the two children mentioned in Mark 15:40, "James" and "Joses," are identified, in the same order, earlier in

plied author has introduced a second suggestion of fallibility (cf. Mark 3:20–35)—not in the women as a group, but in a specific woman in the midst of the three particularly identified. In addition, the three women in 15:40 are named. While not all named people in the Gospel of Mark are portrayed negatively (see Bartimaeus, Son of Timeaus in Mark 10:46–52; Simon of Cyrene, the father of Alexander and Rufus in Mark 15:21; and Joseph of Arimathea in Mark 15:43–46), among the women in Mark, all of those portrayed positively are anonymous.[23] Like the Twelve, these three women are named, which may suggest fallibility in Mark.[24] All three of these negative echoes fall in the first verse of the inverted hinge which looks forward to the narrative at the tomb where these same three women will be major characters (cf. Mark 16:1). Even though the first verse of the inverted hinge looks forward, lexical echoes arise from the prior narrative raising concern for the implied audience.

The second verse of the inverted hinge looks backward and uses positive, lexical links from earlier in the narrative. The first lexical link is the word "Galilee." The implied audience knows that Galilee was a place of significant ministry where Jesus revealed who he was and called people to follow him. The significance of associating the three named women[25]

---

the narrative as children of Jesus' mother, Mary. When Jesus ministered in his hometown, the people responded: "Is not this the carpenter, the son of *Mary*, and *brother of James and Joses* and Judas and Simon?" (Mark 6:3) (emphasis added). Kuruvilla suggests that Mary is not overtly identified as the mother of Jesus so that she might be a generic character with whom the audience will identify: "The Evangelist's intention must be to portray her as 'everywoman' without affording her any pride of place; any woman (or man, for that matter) could be in her shoes/sandals, or in those of the other Mary or Salome" (Kuruvilla, *Mark*, 354n5). Gundry suggests that this Mary may not be identified as the mother of Jesus to avoid confusion with the proclamation of the centurion who just proclaimed Jesus to be the Son of God (Gundry, *Mark*, 977). While these interpretations are possible, it may be that by the implied author identifying Jesus' brothers with Mary, the negative echo of Mark 3:20–35 is that much stronger for the implied audience. While she is identified as a follower of Jesus in this narrative, the earlier narrative casts a shadow. For those who do not construe Mary to be Jesus' mother, see Brown, *Death of the Messiah*, 2:1017; France, *Mark*, 664–65.

23. See Simon's mother-in-law (Mark 1:29–31), the woman with the hemorrhage/Jairus's daughter (Mark 5:21–43), the Syrophoenician woman (Mark 7:1–30), the poor widow who gave at the temple (Mark 12:41–44), the woman who anointed Jesus (Mark 14:1–11), and the maidservant who confronted Peter (Mark 14:53–72).

24. Tolbert concurs, stating: "Also, naming three of them casts a possible shadow on their natures, for throughout the Gospel naming has often been associated with the human desire for fame, glory, status, and authority all longings that harden the heart and encourage fear rather than faith" (Tolbert, *Sowing the Gospel*, 33, 293).

25. It is not clear who the pronoun is referring to at the beginning of verse 41: "*Who* when he was in Galilee they were following him and serving him" (αἳ ὅτε ἦν ἐν τῇ

with Galilee might be seen by contrasting the Galilee panel with the Jerusalem panel:[26]

Galilee Panel	Jerusalem Panel
Calling and sending of disciples	No calling or sending of disciples
Miraculous ministry	Non-miraculous ministry
Jesus imposes silence, but proclamation continues	Jesus makes open proclamation and is silenced
Fast paced (31 occurrences of "immediately")	Time slows down (only 6 occurrences of "immediately"). The last week forms 1/3 of Mark; the last 24 hours form 1/6 of Mark.
A remote corner of the country	The center of the country
A province	The capital
Many synagogues	One Temple
Inhabited by fishermen, farmers, tax-collectors, many of whom do not know the law	Seat of Temple authorities and scribes who know the law
The home of Jesus and his followers	The home of temple authorities
There is proclamation of the gospel	There is no proclamation of the gospel
There are many healings	There are no healings
There are many exorcisms	There are no exorcisms
The public responds positively	The public responds negatively
Jesus' authority is acknowledged	Jesus authority is rejected
The beginning of the kingdom	The end of the Temple
Jesus is the subject of the action	Jesus is the object of the passion
Jesus helps people	Jesus falls into the hands of people
The atmosphere was one of euphoria	The atmosphere was one of dysphoria

The Galilee period was a time of significant ministry where many were responsive to Jesus, while the Jerusalem period was a time of curtailed

---

Γαλιλαίᾳ ἠκολούθουν αὐτῷ καὶ διηκόνουν αὐτῷ) (emphasis added). It is possible that the pronoun (αἵ) refers to everyone mentioned in verse 40. However, the nearest referent of the feminine plural pronoun "who" (αἵ) is to the three women specifically identified and not the women (γυναῖκες) in the first part of verse 40. This is further supported by the second half of verse 41 that once again broadens the reference to a larger group of women: "And many other *women* who came up with him to Jerusalem" (καὶ ἄλλαι πολλαὶ αἱ συναναβᾶσαι αὐτῷ εἰς Ἱεροσόλυμα). See Brown, *Death of the Messiah*, 2:1153; Gundry, *Mark*, 978.

26. Many of these parallels may be found in Kuruvilla, *Mark*, 7; Iersel, *Mark*, 76–77; Stock, *Mark*, 288–90.

ministry and negative responses to Jesus. Furthermore, Mark 15:41 aligns the women with the journey from Galilee to Jerusalem: "And many other [women] went up with him to Jerusalem." This description shows that women were active in the central part of the Gospel "on the way" to Jerusalem. Iersel provides the following table comparing the Galilee panel, the Way panel, and the Jerusalem panel:[27]

Galilee	On the way	Jerusalem
home and place of action	itinerary	place of action
Jesus travels to and fro	goes in one direction	enters and leaves
appoints the twelve	goes ahead of them	they abandon him
he speaks to whoever cares to listen	private instruction of the twelve	no instruction, but disputes
he speaks in parables	speaks frankly	tells one more parable
continual healings	only occasional healings	no healings at all
opponents attack Jesus	opponents are absent	Jesus attacked
Jesus is successful with the crowd	hardly any contact with the crowd	the crowd turns against him
two mass meals	no meal	a meal with the twelve
opponents plot Jesus' death	Jesus announces his death	opponents kill Jesus

As in Galilee, so the journey "on the way" to Jerusalem was a time of significant ministry to Jesus' followers where he explained the role of suffering in his ministry and in the lives of his followers. Furthermore, in Jerusalem, Galilee is declared as the place where Jesus will go ahead of his disciples after he has been raised from the dead (Mark 14:28). Even when Peter is confronted before his last denial of Jesus, he is identified as being a follower of Jesus because he is a Galilean: "And after a little while the bystanders were again saying to Peter, 'Surely you are *one* of them, for you are a *Galilean*'" (Mark 14:70, emphasis added). Accordingly, by saying that the three women were following Jesus in "Galilee," and that the larger group of women came up with him to Jerusalem, the audience not only connects the women with Jesus but with the positive teaching, preaching, and healing aspects of his ministry.[28]

---

27. Iersel, *Mark*, 78.

28. Even though the implied author did not previously tell the implied audience that women were following Jesus in Galilee and on the way to Jerusalem, there are indications in the overall narrative of Mark that those following Jesus were larger than

In addition, the narrator states that when Jesus was in Galilee these three women had been following him (ἠκολούθουν αὐτῷ) and ministering to him (διηκόνουν αὐτῷ). By repeating the word "him" (αὐτῷ) after each verb, the writer identifies Jesus as the specific object of the women's actions. They were not just following a crowd, they were following him, and they were not ministering to a group in general but were ministering to him. The audience knows well that when Jesus called the first disciples (Simon and Andrew), they left their nets and "followed him" (ἠκολούθησαν αὐτῷ) (Mark 1:18).[29] When Jesus calls Levi he says, "Follow me" (ἀκολούθει μοι) and Levi got up and "followed him" (ἠκολούθησεν αὐτῷ) (Mark 2:14). In Levi's house many tax collectors and sinners are said to be "following him" (ἠκολούθουν αὐτῷ). When Jesus is by the sea of Galilee a great number from Galilee and Judea followed (ἠκολούθησεν) him (Mark 3:7; see also 5:24; 6:1). On the way to Jerusalem, Jesus told the crowds and his disciples: "If anyone wishes to follow after me (ὀπίσω μου ἀκολουθεῖν), he must deny himself, and take up his cross and follow me (ἀκολουθείτω μοι)" (Mark 8:34). To the man who asked Jesus what he must do to inherit eternal life, Jesus said: "One thing you lack: go and sell all you possess and give to the poor, and you will have treasure in heaven; and come, follow me (δεῦρο ἀκολούθει μοι)" (Mark 10:32). When Bartimaeus was healed of his blindness by Jesus, the audience is told that, unlike the rich man, Bartimaeus "began following him on the way" (ἠκολούθει αὐτῷ ἐν τῇ ὁδῷ) (Mark 10:52). Finally, those crying out praise at Jesus' entry into Jerusalem are described as "those going ahead and following" (οἱ προάγοντες καὶ οἱ ἀκολουθοῦντες) (Mark 11:9). Accordingly, the implied audience has heard the verb "follow" (ἀκολουθέω) numerous times in the Markan narrative to conclude that those "following him" (ἠκολούθουν αὐτῷ) are disciples. Moreover, the verb "to follow" is in the imperfect tense (ἠκολούθουν) describing an ongoing progressive aspect.[30] They did not follow him once

---

just the Twelve, as in Mark 4:10 where it states: "When he was alone, *those around him with the Twelve* asked him about the parables" (Mark 4:10) (emphasis added). It now appears that the women were among "those around him" (cf. Mark 4:33–34). See Tannehill, "Disciples in Mark," 388n8.

29. A different phrase with the same sense is used for James and John: "ἀπῆλθον ὀπίσω αὐτοῦ."

30. Wallace explains: "Like the present tense, the imperfect displays an *internal aspect*. That is, it portrays the action from within the event, without regard for beginning or end. This contrasts with the aorist, which portrays the action in summary fashion. For the most part, the aorist takes a *snapshot* of the action while the imperfect (like the present) takes a *motion picture*, portraying the action as it unfolds. As such, the imperfect is often incomplete and focuses on the *process* of the action" (Wallace, *Greek*

but were continually following him. The Galilee section functions as a constituent of character building—specifically in terms of "service" and of being associated with the circle of Jesus followers.

Likewise, these three women had been serving Jesus (διηκόνουν αὐτῷ).³¹ The word διακονέω is first used in Mark to describe the activity of the angels after Jesus' temptation in the wilderness: "καὶ οἱ ἄγγελοι διηκόνουν αὐτῷ" (Mark 1:13). This verb and indirect object are identical to that used for the three women in Mark 15:41. Interestingly, most English translations gloss the word διακονέω in 1:13 with the verb "minister" to describe what the angles did: "And the angels were *ministering to him*" (emphasis added).³² However, when the word is next used in Mark 1:34 for the action of Simeon's mother-in-law, it is often translated as "waited" or "served" and not as "ministered."³³ Because Simeon's mother-in-law is a woman, this "service" is usually described as waiting on tables.³⁴ Then when the word is used again of the women in Mark 15:41, this construction reappears stating that the women were only providing table service.³⁵

Grammar, 541). Brown notes that "these verbs in the imperfect have pluperfect force" and translates them "used to follow him and serve him" (Brown, *Death of the Messiah*, 2:1156). But as Wallace states, "The difference between this [pluperfective imperfect] and a pluperfect is that the imperfect's *internal* portrayal is still intact" (Wallace, *Greek Grammar*, 549 [emphasis added]). Another Markan example may be found in Mark 6:18: "For John *had been telling* (ἔλεγεν) Herod, 'It is not lawful for you to have your brother's wife.'" Therefore, as a pluperfective imperfect, the verb may be translated "they had been following him." The progressive aspect continues.

31. This sentence "and they had been serving him" (καὶ διηκόνουν αὐτῷ) is omitted in C D Δ 579 and n. These fifth- (C, D, n), ninth- (Δ), and thirteenth- (579) century texts do not provide a strong basis to omit this reading. Of the earlier texts, both C and D have problematic variants. Codex Δ is a Koine or Byzantine type, but the Gospel of Mark in Δ belongs to the Alexandrian type. Metzger and Ehrman, *Text of the New Testament*, 82–83. Moreover, Codex D has been shown to omit or change texts that show women in a positive light in the book of Acts. See Malick, "Contribution of Codex Bezae Cantabrigiensis," 158–83.

32. See Mark 1:13 in NASB (1995, 1997); ASV; ESV; KJV; NKJV; NET; Duay-Rheims; but see NIV (2011) "and angels attended him."

33. See Mark 1:31 in NASB (1995, 1997) "and she *waited* on them"; NIV (2011) "and she began to *wait* on them"; ESV, NET "and she began to *serve* them"; NKJ "And she *served* them." But see ASV; KJV, D-R, "and she *ministered* unto them" (emphasis added).

34. Corley, *Private Women*, 87; France, *Mark*, 108; Iersel, *Mark*, 138; Gundry, *Mark*, 91; Lane, *Mark*, 78.

35. Gundry, *Mark*, 979. Brown muses: "We need to recognize that we may be asking something Mark never asked of himself, and that two questions may be in order to cover that situation. Would Mark consider these women disciples, where he asked? (I suspect so.) Did Mark think of them when in describing the ministry he wrote the word 'disciples'? (Perhaps not)" (Brown, *Death of the Messiah*, 2:1156).

The only other use of διακονέω (outside of Mark 1:13 for the activity of angels, 1:31 for the activity of Simon's mother-in-law, and 15:41 for the activity of the three women who followed Jesus in Galilee) is in Mark 10:45 where on the way to Jerusalem Jesus explains: "For even the Son of Man did not come to be served (διακονηθῆναι), but to serve (διακονῆσαι), and to give His life a ransom for many." In Mark 10:45, the word διακονέω is most often glossed as "serve" in English translations.[36] However, Jesus clarifies his "service" at the end of 10:45 as giving his life on behalf of many. Moreover, serving is described in Mark 10:42–44 as being the opposite of lording it over people:

> You know that those who are recognized as rulers of the Gentiles lord it over them; and their great men exercise authority over them. "But it is not so among you, but whoever wishes to become great among you shall be your servant (διάκονος); and whoever wishes to be first among you shall be slave (δοῦλος) of all." (Mark 10:42–44 NASB 1977).

The references to "service" in Mark 10:42–45 are the closest references to the use of the verb διακονέω in 15:41, and these references are broader than "table service." While the women in Mark 15:41 are not able to perform the salvific service of redemption that Jesus will do in 10:45, they can serve Jesus as a follower beyond providing a meal. Gundry astutely opines: "διακονέω suits very well whatever disciples may do on behalf of their teachers."[37] This service may include the provision of food, but it need not be limited to table service, it can include self-denying service. The angels may have ministered to Jesus by providing him with food and drink after his temptation, but they may have cared for him in other costly ways too. Simeon's mother-in-law may have provided them with a meal after she was healed, but she may have cared for them in other self-denying ways too. As Iersel observes: "One sometimes overlooks, however, that the verb [in 1:31] is not in the aorist but in the imperfect, which brings to expression that she looks after them repeatedly, not just once."[38] Therefore, even though the word for "service" may not be specifically described, it is a mark of discipleship just as "following" Jesus was a mark of discipleship. Accordingly, the three, named women in Mark 15:41 are

---

36. See Mark 10:45 in NASB (1995, 1997); ESV; NKJV; NET; NIV. But see ASV, KJV, D-R, "For the Son of man also came not to be *ministered* unto, but to *minister*, and to give his life a ransom for many" (emphasis added).

37. Gundry, *Mark*, 979.

38. Iersel, *Mark*, 138.

being positively characterized as disciples by what they do—following and serving Jesus.

Discussing the significance of Bourdieu's observations about the Kabyle to the Gospel narratives, F. Gerald Downing opines:

> Let us, accordingly, make a very tentative application of just a few elements of the highly structured Kabyle analogy. If Jesus takes men away from home (Mark 10:28; Q/Luke 9:57–60; Luke 9:61–62), he may not be opposing patriarchy, as some would have it; he could be exacerbating masculine domination, for males are "naturally" centrifugal, women centripetal. Only if he brings women out, too, would he be clearly disrupting patriarchy.[39]

In Mark 15:41, the implied author appears to be "disrupting patriarchy" by describing women as ministers in Jesus' itinerate ministry as they traveled with him outside of the home from Galilee, on the way to Jerusalem, and in Jerusalem. The enormous implications of the implied author's description of women as part of Jesus' itinerate ministry is evident in Downing's statement: "If Jesus is disrupting the home, or even just disturbing it, he could be disturbing the whole interwoven system, the whole cosmos that the home represents."[40]

Many suggest, and even affirm, that Mark's naming of the three women (Mary Magdalene, Mary the mother of James and Joses, and Salome) is meant to parallel and replace the three named, male leaders of the Twelve who failed as followers of Jesus (Peter, James, and John).[41] However, in view of the negative foreshadows of being fallible (watching from afar, the mother of Jesus, and being named), it seems unlikely that the implied author is presenting these women as the faithful replacement of the male followers who have all fled—especially since they too will be portrayed as fleeing at the end of the narrative. Rather, in view of the function of the retrospective, inverted hinge in 15:40–41, it appears that these named women are introduced at this juncture in the narrative because of the role they will play in the upcoming panel at the tomb.[42] They are not introduced as flawless followers, but as genuine followers who

---

39. Downing, "First-Century Galilee," 91.

40. Downing, "First-Century Galilee," 91.

41. Dewey, *Disciples of the Way*, 132–33; "Women in the Gospel of Mark," 28; France, *Mark*, 665; Schüssler Fiorenza, *Memory of Her*, 320; Tolbert, *Sowing the Gospel*, 291–92; Williams, *Other Followers*, 188; Lincoln, "Promise and the Failure," 288.

42. See Williams, *Other Followers*, 187; Nineham, *Mark*, 431.

have foreshadowed weaknesses which will play themselves out in the following narrative.

Continuity connects the women at Jesus' crucifixion with the women at the tomb in the next and final panel of Mark. The portents of echoes will unfold in the following narrative as the three women identified by name become major actors in the narrative leading up to and including the empty tomb at the end of the narrative.

CONCLUSION

The implied author employs the literary technique of a retrospective inverted hinge to slow down the narrative and provide the implied audience with a gradual transition from the Jerusalem panel to the Tomb panel in the narrative. But the implied author uses this literary technique as a means to introduce women who will play a strategic part in the last panel of the book at the tomb. Through this method of discourse, the implied author has connected some of these women with prior people and circumstances in the narrative to suggest to the implied audience that these women—especially the named women—may have flaws in their character. They watch the crucifixion of Jesus "from afar" as Peter followed Jesus "from afar." Echoes from Mark 3 cast a shadow over Mary, who may be Jesus' mother. They are also named, unlike the other women who have been portrayed positively so far in the Gospel. However, the implied author also shows the implied audience that all these women are true disciples of Jesus who have followed and served him since the Galilee days and on the way to Jerusalem where Jesus engaged in significant ministry and called his disciples to be servants. In Mark 15:41, the implied author appears to be "disrupting patriarchy" by describing women as ministers in Jesus' itinerate ministry as they traveled with him outside of the home from Galilee, on the way to Jerusalem, and in Jerusalem. Nevertheless, these women are portrayed as having potentially mixed character—followers with suggestions of weaknesses. The implied audience will be on the lookout for how these women behave at the upcoming evening and morning watches. Will they act like those awake or alert at the upcoming events, or will they show themselves to be metaphorically asleep when their response to Jesus matters.

17

The Women at the Tomb
(Mark 15:42—16:8)

IN THIS TENTH AND final Markan narrative involving women, the Gospel reaches its climax, and the women introduced in the transitional section at Jesus' crucifixion play major parts in the narrative. The timestamps introduced in the parable of the Doorkeeper in Mark 13 reappear as events unfold at the first Roman watch, evening, and the last Roman watch, early morning as discussed in Chapter 6 above. The implied audience with full knowledge of all that has proceeded will be watching to see whether these women, along with other characters who appear in the narrative, are awake or sleeping in their vigilant watch. The women will show themselves to be complex disciples as they attempt to be responsive to Jesus in his death and proclaimed resurrection. The continued application of the parable of the Doorkeeper is now unfolded in the final panel of the Gospel with some characters who have not previously appeared in the discourse (Joseph of Arimathea, Mary Magdalene, and Salome) and some who reappear.[1] Through this extension of the Roman watches, the

---

1. It is true that the three women were mentioned in 15:40, but they will be major actors in the development of the discourse around the tomb. Mary, the mother of Joses and James, may be the one who acted in 3:20–21, 31–35. Pilate and the Centurion were also actors in Jesus' passion, and the young man at the tomb, though not the same the young man who fled in 14:53, will be connected through lexical links with that earlier young man for theological purposes. See Kuruvilla, "Naked Runaway"; Lincoln, "Promise," 293. As Williams observes: "In this passage on Joseph of Arimathea Mark refers again to certain minor characters that he has introduced previously in the

implied author is showing his implied audience that the exhortations of the parable of the Doorkeeper are still in effect, even after previous failures. Like the other disciples in the narrative their response will be mixed showing the audience how hard it is to be a follower of Jesus—even after his resurrection.

THE EVENTS AT EVENING (ΟΨΙΑΣ) (MARK 15:42–47)

The first narrative expression of the expanded application of the parable of the Doorkeeper occurs immediately following the transitional, inverted hinge of Mark 15:40–41, with a time stamp introducing the epilogue of the Gospel: "And now, becoming evening (ὀψίας) since it was the preparation which is before the Sabbath" (Mark 15:42). The question for the implied audience is whether at this hour of the Roman watch, the characters will be alert (γρηγορέω) for their master.

Joseph of Arimathea

The first new character to appear is Joseph of Arimathea, a prominent person of the Counsel (Ἰωσὴφ ὁ ἀπὸ Ἁριμαθαίας εὐσχήμων βουλευτής). The Counsel may well be the Sanhedrin, the only Counsel identified in Mark's Gospel (cf. Mark 14:55; 15:1).[2] The audience has not encountered Joseph in the narrative; however, the audience has previously encountered the Jewish religious leaders who accused Jesus of blasphemy and condemned him to death (cf. Mark 14:53, 55, 64). Joseph is described by the implied author/narrator as someone who was looking for the kingdom of God (προσδεχόμενος τὴν βασιλείαν τοῦ θεοῦ). The "kingdom of God" is an echo of Jesus' message in the prospective hinge of Mark 1:15 where he states: "The time is fulfilled, and the kingdom of God is near. Repent and believe in the good news." Jesus also proclaimed the nature of the "kingdom of God" through his parables in Mark 4 (cf. 4:11, 26, 30). The audience and four of the disciples were shown the "kingdom of God" through Jesus' transfiguration (cf. Mark 9:1), and Jesus talked about

---

narrative. This is an unusual feature, since until this point minor characters have never appeared again once they have left the scene" (Williams, *Other Followers*, 191).

2. Josephus also uses the term βουλευτής to refer to the Sanhedrin (Josephus, *Wars of the Jews* 2.17.1). See also Williams, *Other Followers*, 189; France, *Mark*, 665–66; Brown, *Death of the Messiah*, 2:1213–14; Gundry, *Mark*, 984–85.

the attitude needed for people to enter the "kingdom of God" (cf. Mark 10:15, 23, 24–25). Therefore, Joseph's pursuit of the "kingdom of God" appears to align him with Jesus' message of the "kingdom of God" in Mark. Gundry does not identify Joseph of Arimathea with the Christian hope of the "Kingdom of God" because Joseph was among those who condemned Jesus to death in 14:64.[3] Williams's solution to the issue of Joseph being part of the Sanhedrin who condemned Jesus to death is to make Joseph an exception to the Sanhedrin just as the Centurion was an exception to the cohort of soldiers who were hostile to Jesus in 15:16.[4] However, in Mark's narrative, people make shifts in their positions. For instance, the Centurion was associated with Jesus' crucifixion, and yet at Jesus' death he proclaimed that Jesus was the Son of God (Mark 15:39). Joseph of Arimathea could have also had a change of mind following Jesus' crucifixion. The additional description of Joseph as waiting for the Kingdom of God may, in and of itself, be a vague Jewish description, but within the narrative world of Mark, it is explicitly associated with the message of Jesus. What Joseph does as a religious leader surprises the implied audience, and this surprise moves him into the realm of a round character. As Forster states: "The test of a round character is whether it is capable of surprising in a convincing way. If it never surprises, it is flat. If it does not convince it is flat pretending to be round."[5] Joseph of Arimathea surprises in a convincing way by what he does for Jesus.

During the evening watch (ὀψίας), Joseph acts on Jesus' behalf by obtaining and placing Jesus' body in a tomb.[6] This activity shows him as someone alert during the evening watch. Jesus' closest followers are nowhere to be found, unlike John the Baptizer's disciples who came and took his body and laid it in a tomb after Herod's execution of John (6:29).[7]

---

3. Gundry, *Mark*, 985. See also Brown, *Death of the Messiah*, 2:1213–19.

4. Williams, *Other Followers*, 190n1. See Kingsbury, *Conflict in Mark*, 123n46.

5. Forster, *Aspects of the Novel*, 78.

6. If the parable of the soils in Mark 4:3–20 is programmatic in that it identifies characters the implied audience has or will encounter in the narrative, and the first soil where the seed is sown "along the way" is equivalent to the scribes, Pharisees, and Jerusalem Jewish leaders, see Tolbert, *Sowing the Gospel*, 148–64, this portion of the narrative involving Joseph of Arimathea shows that the people identified with particular soils are not frozen in those characterizations. Joseph, a prominent, Jewish, religious leader, now responds favorably to Jesus displaying the virtues of courage, justice, loyalty, and wisdom. Perhaps Joseph foreshadows hope for the disciples associated with the rocky soil (τὸ πετρῶδες) that fell away (σκανδαλίζονται) under persecution (Mark 4:17, cf. 14:27) to also transition into being good soil.

7. The lexical parallels are striking for the burials of John and Jesus. John's disciples

Accordingly, Joseph of Arimathea acts as a stand-in disciple doing what Jesus' followers failed to do.[8] The theme of stand-in disciples is prevalent in Christ's passion: Simeon of Cyrene "takes up" (αἴρω) Jesus' cross (Mark 15:21, cf. 8:34);[9] two robbers are crucified with Jesus, one on his right, and one on his left (positions in the kingdom that James and John requested, Mark 15:27, cf. 10:37); the Centurion makes a confession about the identity of Jesus whom Peter denies (Mark 15:39; cf. 14:66–72); and now Joseph of Arimathea takes Jesus' body and lays it in a tomb (Mark 15:42–46; cf. 6:29).[10]

Two Women

Then, the narrator tells the audience that two of the women introduced in Mark 15:40, Mary Magdalene and Mary of Joses, were watching where Jesus was placed (Mark 15:47).[11] As two witnesses, the women appear to meet the requirements of Deuteronomy 19:15, even though women were probably not considered to be valid witnesses in first-century Judaism.[12] The verb "to see" (θεωρέω) is the same verb that was used in Mark

---

came, took his corpse and placed it in a tomb (ἦλθον καὶ ἦραν τὸ πτῶμα αὐτοῦ καὶ ἔθηκαν αὐτὸ ἐν μνημείῳ) (emphasis added). Likewise, Pilate gave Jesus' corpse (τὸ πτῶμα) to Joseph (15:45), and Joseph placed it in a tomb (ἔθηκεν αὐτὸν ἐν μνημείῳ) (15:46) (emphasis added). The word for corpse (τὸ πτῶμα) is only used in these two passages in Mark strengthening the comparison. See Williams, *Other Followers*, 191n1.

8. See Williams, *Other Followers*, 190; Kingsbury, *Conflict in Mark*, 27; Rhoads et al., *Mark as Story*, 133; Kuruvilla, *Mark*, 342, 355. Tannehill observes: "If certain minor characters in the narrative do what the disciples should but do not do, the contrast increases our sense of the disciples' failure" (Tannehill, "Disciples in Mark," 391).

9. Jesus' call to discipleship in 8:34 includes the same verb: "Whoever wishes to follow after me, let him deny himself and *take-up his cross*, and follow after me" (emphasis added). Therefore, the narrator is showing Simon of Cyrene as a stand-in disciple as he takes up Jesus' cross and follows him.

10. See Tannehill, "Disciples in Mark," 404–5.

11. It appears that "Mary of Joses" (Μαρία ἡ Ἰωσῆτος) is the same Mary identified in Mark 15:40 as Mary the mother of James the less and Joses (Μαρία ἡ Ἰακώβου τοῦ μικροῦ καὶ Ἰωσῆτος μήτηρ). Certainly, the textual variants for Ιωσῆτος in Mark 15:47 are connecting the Mary of 15:47 with the Mary of 15:40 (see Ιακωβου D it vgms sys ¦ Ιακωβου και Ιωσητος Θ ƒ13 565. 2542s [c] ¦ ᵀ μητηρ W ƒ13 2542s). It appears that after the implied author has more fully identified this Mary as the mother of James and Joses in Mark 15:40, he now uses an abbreviated form in 15:47 (Mary of Joses) and in 16:1 (Mary of James). However, when the abbreviated references are combined, one arrives at the earlier full reference of 15:40 (excluding the description of James as being "the less" [τοῦ μικροῦ]). See also France, *Mark*, 669.

12. Josephus writes: "But let not a single witness be credited; but three, or two at the

15:40 to describe the three women watching Jesus' crucifixion from a distance. However, here, the prepositional phrase, "from a distance" (ἀπὸ μακρόθεν), is not repeated. Instead, the verb appears to be a progressive imperfect (ἐθεώρουν)—they were watching where he was placed.[13] The narrator is providing a vivid image of these two women watching Joseph place Jesus in the tomb. Like Joseph, these women are shown to be present and alert during the evening watch (ὀψίας).

Actually, during this evening watch, everyone appears to be acting appropriately towards the character Jesus' death. The Centurion, presumably the same one who stood at the cross and said, "Surely this man was the Son of God" (15:39), now tells Pilate the truth that Jesus has died (Mark 15:44–45). Pilate, who had every right not to give Jesus' body to someone other than family—especially since Jesus had been crucified for sedition (being King of the Jews)—granted Joseph of Arimathea's bold request and gave him Jesus' body (cf. Mark 15:2, 9, 12, 17, 16–20 with 15:45).[14] Joseph of Arimathea acts as a stand-in disciple by taking responsibility for Jesus' burial. He takes Jesus' body down from the cross, wraps it in a cloth which he purchased, and places him in a tomb (15:46). And the women watch as witnesses to where Jesus has been placed (15:47). This is the second time that the women have been identified as witnesses. They were witnesses to Jesus' crucifixion (15:40), and now to his burial (15:47). In both cases, they were not alone as witnesses; others, including men like the Centurion and Joseph, were present. At this point, the women offer continuity having been witnesses of both Jesus' death and the location of the tomb where he was placed. Their role as witnesses will be heightened at the tomb.[15] Although the implied audience of Mark

---

least, and those such whose testimony is confirmed by their good lives. But let not the testimony of women be admitted, on account of the levity and boldness of their sex" (Josephus, *Antiquities of the Jews*, 4:219). Furthermore, m. Rosh Hashanah 1:8 states: "These are the ones who are invalid [to testify about the appearance of the new moon]: ... Any evidence which a woman is not valid [to offer], also they are not valid [to offer]" (Neusner, *Mishnah*, 300–301). Likewise, m. Shabout 4:1 states: "[The law governing] an oath of testimony (Lev 5:1) applies (1) to men and not to women" (Neusner, *Mishnah*, 626).

13. "This imperfect is often used to describe an action or state that is in progress in past time from the viewpoint (or more accurately, portrayal) of the speaker.... It speaks either of *vividness* or *simultaneity* with another action" (Wallace, *Greek Grammar*, 543).

14. See Brown, *Death of the Messiah*, 2:1208–9.

15. France seems to correctly observe that "these women, the only human witnesses of the fact of Jesus' resurrection in Mark's gospel, have been closely involved in the whole sequence of events, so that any possibility of a mistake, for instance, over the

might have expected other characters to act on Jesus' behalf, Joseph, the Centurion, Pilate, and now the women are all portrayed as being alert and acting well during the evening watch.

EVENTS AT EARLY MORNING (ΠΡΩΪ) (MARK 16:1-8)

The final unit of Mark is set out in 16:1-8.[16] As with the previous section, this unit begins with time stamps: "and when the sabbath was past" (διαγενομένου τοῦ σαββάτου) (Mark 16:1), "and very *early* on the first of sevens [Sunday]" (καὶ λίαν πρωΐ τῇ μιᾷ τῶν σαββάτων) (Mark 16:2, emphasis added).[17] The term for "early," or "dawn" (πρωΐ), once again marks the time of the Roman watch when disciples are to be on the lookout for

---

location of the tomb is ruled out. They saw him die, they saw him buried, and they saw that same tomb empty" (France, *Mark*, 661).

16. Very significant textual variants occur at this point in the text. The Gospel of Mark ends with verse 8 in some witnesses including two of the oldest and most respected Greek manuscripts (ℵ B). The following shorter ending (as part of verse 8) [*"They reported briefly to those around Peter all that they had been commanded. After these things Jesus himself sent out through them, from the east to the west, the holy and imperishable preaching of eternal salvation. Amen"*]) is found in some manuscripts (L Ψ 083. 099. 274[mg]. 579. *l* 1602 k sy[hmg] sa[mss] bo[mss] aeth[mss]), and is usually included with the longer ending (L Ψ 083. 099. 274[mg]. 579. *l* 1602 k sy[hmg] sa[mss] bo[mss] aeth[mss]). Most manuscripts include the longer ending (vv. 9-20) immediately after verse 8 (A B C D W Θ *f*[13] 33 2427 m lat sy sa[c.p.h.] bo). However, Jerome and Eusebius knew of almost no Greek manuscripts that had this ending. Several manuscripts have marginal comments noting that earlier Greek manuscripts lacked the verses, while others mark the text with asterisks or obeli (symbols that scribes used to indicate that the portion of text being copied was spurious). Internal evidence suggests the secondary nature of both the short and the long endings. Their vocabulary and style are non-Markan. All of the evidence suggests that as time went on, scribes added the longer ending, either for the richness of the material or because of the abruptness of the ending at verse 8. Because of such problems regarding the authenticity of these alternative endings, 16:8 is usually regarded as the last verse of the Gospel of Mark. See Burer *et al.*, *NET Bible*, 148; Metzger, *Textual Commentary*, 102-7; Magness, *Marking the End*. In support of the longer ending see Farmer, *Last Twelve Verses*. In response see book review by Fee, "Last Twelve Verses," 461-64; Wallace, "Mark 16:8," 1-39; Kelhoffer, *Miracle and Mission*.

17. Again, the midnight (μεσονύκτιον) and cockcrow (ἀλεκτοροφωνίας) watches are passed over in the discourse during the narrative gap of the Sabbath when apparently nothing relevant to Mark's narrative occurred. After Jesus was placed in the tomb at the evening watch (ὀψὲ), the next time period the narrator provides is the early morning watch (πρωΐ) on the first of the week following the Sabbath (Sunday). The double time stamp is typical of Mark who first provides a general temporal expression followed by one that is more precise. See Johnson, "Identity and Significance," 123-39. Nineham observes: "It is quite in St. Mark's manner to qualify a vague note of time with a more precise one" (Nineham, *Mark*, 444).

their Lord (cf. Mark 13:35). The three women first introduced by name in Mark 15:40 now reappear: "Mary Magdalene, Mary the *mother* of James, and Salome" (16:1).[18] For the audience, the question arises whether these women will act on their Lord's behalf at this morning watch (πρωΐ), as two of them appeared to do at the evening watch (ὀψίας) (Mark 15:42–47). Perhaps the women are named in Mark 15:40 and renamed in 15:46 and 16:1 so that the implied audience will know that they (or at least two of them), and not a larger group of other women (cf. Mark 15:40–41), were the ones who witnessed Jesus' death, burial, and empty tomb. In other words, the witness is not scattered among numerous, different people but consolidated in these women providing the implied audience stability in characterization.

Spices to Anoint

The narrator first tells the implied audience that the three women purchased spices in order that they might anoint Jesus (Mark 16:1).[19] The implied audience knows that in Mark 14:8 Jesus explained that the woman who poured perfume on his head had done it in preparation of his body for his burial. There is no indication in Mark that the three women in Mark 16:1 know about what occurred in the home of Simon the Leper. Even if they did know, it is possible that Jesus' words could have been understood to be symbolic since they were spoken days before his death (see Mark 14:1). The fact that Jesus' words about the significance of the anonymous woman's anointing (μυρίσαι) of him turn out for the implied audience to be true may not diminish, on the story level, the value of the three women's act in purchasing spices (ἀρώματα) with the purpose of coming to anoint (ἀλείψωσιν) Jesus' body as it lies in the tomb. The terms in the two accounts for pouring (κατέχεεν) / anointing (ἀλείψωσιν) and

---

18. It appears that the second Mary in the list is the same person introduced in 15:40 and mentioned again in 15:47. She is identified in a shortened form for ease of reference with only one of her two sons identified in Mark 15:47 and Mark 16:1. When Mark 15:47 and 16:1 are read together, the second Mary appears to be the mother of Joses and James, as she was introduced in Mark 15:40.

19. Tolbert suggests that the purpose of the anointing may be ambiguous: "Their very act of buying spices and going to the tomb to anoint Jesus raises troubling questions. If they had followed Jesus in Galilee and heard his predictions, they, like the authorial audience, should expect that he will be raised in three days. Are they going, then, to perform the ritual offices on a dead corpse or to anoint a risen Messiah-King?" (Tolbert, *Sowing the Gospel*, 294). The following verses suggest that it is the former.

perfume (νάρδου) / spices (ἀρώματα) are distinct and may provide additional support for an understanding that the two activities—at least in their intention—were distinct. On the story level, it may appear that the women are acting well at the early morning watch as they purchase spices to anoint Jesus' body in the tomb.[20] The women are doing what they are supposed to do as first-century women by fulfilling mourning rites. They are fitting into social order.

However, on the discourse level, dramatic irony occurs for the implied audience who has information that the characters within the narrative may not have about Jesus' prior anointing for his burial.[21] While the act of the women purchasing spices to anoint Jesus' body for burial may be positive, on its face, in the story world of Mark, the implied audience knows that this activity is unnecessary because it has already been done. The dramatic irony provides another clue for the implied audience that

---

20. Focusing on the narrator's inside view of the women, Boomershine argues for a positive, empathetic response by the audience to the women: "The resurrection narrative itself begins with the names of the three women who were witnesses at Jesus' death (15:40-41). The repetition of their names and the report of their purchasing spices in order to anoint Jesus' body sustain the atmosphere of mourning.... Thus, in this series of inside views, Mark gives a degree of insight into the sympathetic perceptions and feelings of the women" (Boomershine, "Mark 16:8," 232). Likewise, Malbon affirms: "Some interpreters fault the three women characters for this move; the women should have known, they argue, that Jesus would be resurrected, that Jesus' anointing for burial had already taken place at the hands of the unnamed woman in the house of Simon the leper. But the Markan narrative makes no mention of the presence of the women followers at Simon the leper's house and explicitly states that the predictions of Jesus' passion and resurrection are presented to the disciples, the twelve (Mark 8:31; 9:31; 10:33-34; cf. 9:9 contrast Luke 24:5-8). Those at Simon the leper's house do not understand the implications of the anointing (Mark 14:4-5; τινες at 14:4 is ambiguous), and the twelve do not understand the reference to the resurrection (Mark 9:32; cf. 9:10). It seems unlikely, then, that the Markan narrator and implied audience would expect the women followers to anticipate or understand the resurrection with no forewarning" (Malbon, "Fallible Followers," 43-44). However, Malbon is looking at the "facts" on the story level rather than on the discourse level.

21. Tolbert identifies three degrees of narrative:

these women may be fallible as they come to the tomb.[22] They do not appear to come expecting a resurrected Jesus, even though Jesus proclaimed that he would rise on the third day at least three times "on the way" to Jerusalem (see Mark 8:31; 9:31; 10:33–34), and these women were among those who came up with Jesus to Jerusalem (Mark 15:41).[23] Instead they

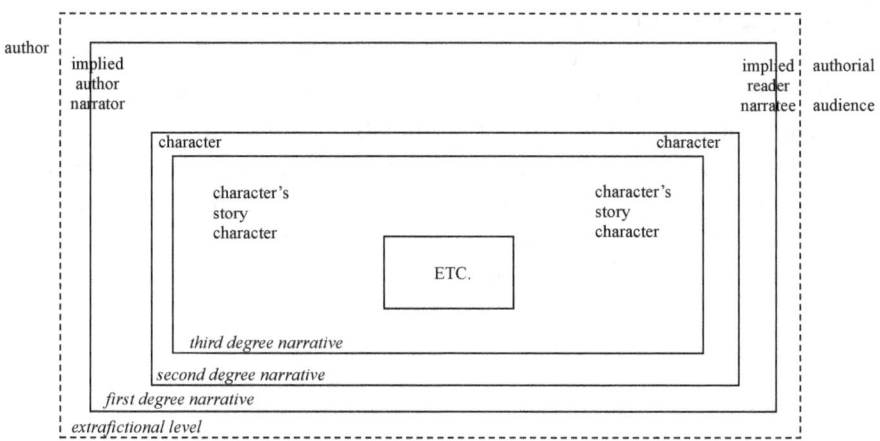

Tolbert, *Sowing the Gospel*, 93. In this Markan passage, the implied reader/implied narratee (audience) are in the first-degree narrative and the characters in the story are in the second-degree narrative. The implied reader/narratee can see what occurs in the second-degree narrative even though not all of the characters in the second-degree narrative (except for perhaps Jesus) know what all of the other characters are doing and saying. This leads to dramatic irony as the implied reader/narratee (audience) understands what the characters may not themselves understand. Tolbert, *Sowing the Gospel*, 90–106.

22. As Tolbert explains: "The rhetorical effect of irony, then is twofold: it builds and strengthens community among those with superior knowledge, and it excludes and denigrates those with inferior knowledge" (Tolbert, *Sowing the Gospel*, 103).

23. The intention of the women to anoint Jesus' dead body rather than see if he has risen creates additional, dramatized irony for the implied audience who knows what Jesus repeatedly predicted, and now sees the women acting as if nothing had been said. As early as the fifth century AD, Peter Chyrsologus, Bishop of Ravenna, preached: "In this text the women hasten with feminine devotion; they bring to the tomb not faith in One who is alive, but ointments for one who is dead; and they prepare for the duties of mourning for one who is buried instead of preparing for the joys of divine triumphs for One who is risen" (Chrysologus, *Selected Sermons*, 44). Commenting on Chrysologus's statement, Christine E. Joynes discusses the dramatic irony in play even though she does not identify it as such: "Chrysologus's interpretation emphasizes the resurrection as the fulfillment of prophecy, a point made clear in the Markan text by the phrase, 'there you will see him, just as he told you' (16:7), which refers back to Jesus' promise in 14:28 ('But after I am raised up, I will go before you to Galilee'). On this basis, according to Chrysologus, the women ought not to have gone to anoint Jesus" (Joynes, "Sound of Silence," 20).

come to do something already done—anoint Jesus for burial. This lack of understanding is reminiscent of the male disciples earlier in the narrative who did not understand who Jesus was and what he was doing in their midst.[24] For the implied audience, this failure to understand may portend an upcoming failure similar to that of the male disciples.

Interior Point of View

The implied author uses a psychological or interior point of view to provide the implied audience with an individual's subjective perspective. As the women approach the tomb, the implied author/narrator provides the implied audience with the subjective inner concerns of the women who are saying to themselves (ἔλεγον πρὸς ἑαυτάς) "who will roll away the stone from the door of the tomb" (Mark 16:3). Then looking, they saw that the stone was rolled away. The implied author/narrator then explains the reason for their concern by stating: "for the stone was very great" (Mark 16:4).[25] Perhaps the implied author is also characterizing the women as weak—a socially engendered characterization that the implied audience would expect. However, the inner concern of the women about removing the stone assumes that nothing has changed since Jesus was placed in the tomb by Joseph of Arimathea.[26] In other words, no raising of Jesus is expected. This is an extension of the dramatic irony discussed above regarding the women's lack of comprehension of Jesus' earlier predictions of rising from the dead. As they are coming to the tomb, they

---

24. See the response of the disciples when Jesus calmed the storm (Mark 4:41); the response of the disciples when Jesus came to them walking on the water after the first feeding of the multitude (Mark 6:47–51); the response of the disciples prior to the second feeding of the multitude (Mark 8:4); the disciples being concerned that they did not have enough bread in the boat after the second feeding of the multitude (Mark 8:13–21); and the disciples inability to understand what it meant for Jesus to die and rise from the dead (Mark 9:32).

25. Bryan A. Nash accurately argues that the implied author/narrator has used a "spatial point of view" to place the implied audience "amidst the action as opposed to far away" so as to identify the women as the "point of view character." Then the narrator uses the "psychological point of view" by telling the audience what the women saw "thus aligning the reader's experience with that of the women-the point-of-view characters" (Nash, "Point of View," 28–29).

26. Although Tolbert reads many of the markers of fallibility in the women as ambivalent, she does concede: "Still, having the only words the women are ever given to speak concern who will roll the stone away from the door for them (Mark 16:3) does appear to hint at a more mundane level of their expectations for the trip" (Tolbert, *Sowing the Gospel*, 294).

assume that nothing has changed since Jesus was placed in the tomb. Yet, when they arrive, the great stone is rolled away. The implied audience is probably less surprised by this situation than the women. The rolling away of the stone functions like a boundary in the narrative, opening the implied audience, and the women, to the world of a risen Jesus. Both the women and the audience wonder what might be next.

A Young Man

The first thing seen by the women as they entered the tomb was a "young man" (νεανίσκον) sitting to the right (αθήμενον ἐν τοῖς δεξιοῖς) wearing a white robe (περιβεβλημένον στολὴν λευκήν) (Mark 16:5). This initial image is saying something to the implied audience, if not to the characters, about life after Jesus has risen from the dead. It is not an image of Jesus *per se*, but of the effect of Jesus being raised from the dead. It is not showing the implied audience who Jesus is, but a consequence of his resurrection. Whatever the women understood by this image, the implied audience is fully aware that many of the descriptors of the man arose earlier in the narrative, and by these lexical links, the implied author was *doing* something with what was being said.[27]

It is not an angel (ἄγγελος) who is seen in the tomb, but a "young man" (νεανίσκος).[28] The implied author has not hesitated to refer to

---

27. Nash categorizes the narrative technique being used by the implied author as an "informational point of view" dealing with the convergence and/or divergence between what the audience and a given character knows. He employs this point of view to explain the difference between Jesus' prediction that he will rise, and the women's expectation when coming to the tomb, and to explain the difference between the "young man" that the women see and the connections the audience will make between the two "young men" in Mark's gospel (Nash, "Point of View," 229–31). It appears to this writer that what Nash is describing is not another "point of view" used by the implied author but the narrative technique of "dramatic irony." However one categorizes the narrative technique, the rhetorical effect is to distance the implied audience from the characters.

28. It may be concluded from the other, canonical gospels that this "young man" was an angel (Matt 28:2, 5; John 20:12). See also Nineham, who states: "Undoubtedly an angelic being is meant; for *young man* as a designation of an angel see 2 Macc 3[26] and [33] and Josephus, *Antiquities*, v, 8, 2, and cf. Rev 7[9] and [13f"] (Nineham, *Mark*, 444). However, rather than reading Mark through the lens of parallels in Hellenistic Jewish literature or the other evangelists, the implied audience must ask why the implied author/narrator in Mark gives the appellation of "young man" to the person seen in the tomb. "Indeed it may be asked whether, if we did not know the other gospels, there would be any question of assuming the young man to be an angel" (Jenkins, "Young Man or Angel?," 238).

angels earlier in the narrative (see Mark 1:13; 8:38; 12:25; 13:37, 32). Therefore, it is reasonable to consider why the implied author would identify this messenger as a "young man."[29] The term, νεανίσκος, is only used one other time by Mark. At Jesus' arrest in Gethsemane, a certain young man (νεανίσκος τις) was following (συνηκολούθει) Jesus wearing a linen cloth (περιβεβλημένος σινδόνα); he was seized, left the linen cloth (σινδόνα) and fled naked (γυμνὸς ἔφυγεν) (Mark 14:51–52). The implied audience does not know for certain who this young man was; he was anonymous (νεανίσκος τις). However, unlike the anonymous women earlier in the gospel who were positive foils to the named disciples, this anonymous young man following Jesus was just like the male disciples in that he fled (ἔφυγεν; cf. Mark 14:50 "Καὶ ἀφέντες αὐτὸν ἔφυγον πάντες"). In the implied author's stylistic way of employing repetition and duality, the narrator makes a double statement about the male disciples fleeing from Jesus at his arrest.[30] First is the general statement: "And leaving him, all fled." Then the narrator provides an image of the summary statement—a kind of emblematic parallelism—through the description of the young man. He not only flees (φεύγω) as all reportedly did in Mark 14:50, but he flees in shame as one who is naked (Mark 15:42).[31] Earlier in Mark, blind Bartimaeus left his cloak to follow Jesus (10:10–52); here the young man leaves his cloak to flee from Jesus and his captors (14:52).[32]

29. See Johnson, "Identity and Significance," 123–39; Jenkins, "Young Man or Angel?," 237–40; de Villiers, "Powerful Transformation," 1–7; Gardner, "Imperfect and Faithful Followers," 33–43; Kuruvilla, "Naked Runaway," 538–45; *Mark*, 355–56; "What Is the Author Doing," 565. For a contrary evaluation of this "symbolic" or typological approach to the narrative, France states: "Attempts such as those noted above to find a meaningful link between the two young men not only disagree with one another but also by their artificiality serve rather to reinforce the conclusion that the common vocabulary between the two passages is a matter of coincidence rather than of literary connection" (France, *Mark*, 679–80). France had only read Johnson's article at the time of writing and not the more recent articles—especially that of Kuruvilla. More importantly, France's dismissal of the parallels seems to arise out of a synoptic reading of the scene at the tomb rather than one focused on what the implied author is communicating to the implied audience in the discourse of Mark.

30. See Neirynck, *Duality in Mark*, 97.

31. For a discussion of the historical understanding of σινδόνα and the shame associated with this passage, see Jackson, "Why the Youth Shed His Cloak," 273–89.

32. As Jenkins observes: "The unknown young man alone sets out to accompany him. In the account of the arrest (1444–50) the seizing of Jesus is strongly highlighted by the repetition of the verb (*krateō*), and this forms a link with 1451ff. Just as Jesus is seized, so is the young man. Subsequently it is this unknown disciple who is the first to know of the resurrection" (Jenkins, "Young Man or Angel?," 239).

Part 2: Narrative Analysis of Passages Involving Women in the Gospel of Mark

The Young Man's Clothing

In addition, the implied author/narrator only uses the word for "wearing" or "clothed" (περιβάλλω) to describe the two young men (cf. Mark 14:51 with 16:5). In Mark 14:51, the young man is wearing a linen cloth; in Mark 16:5 the young man is wearing a white robe. The narrator's previous description of clothing has not been superfluous in Mark. At the beginning of Mark, the narrator told the implied audience that John was dressed like Elijah, wearing (ἐνδύω) the hair of a camel and a leather belt around his waist (Mark 1:6; cf. 2 Kgs 1:8). Here, the comparison of the young men is even more emphatic in that περιβάλλω is only used in Mark 14:51 and 16:5. Through these verbal echoes, the narrator is inviting the implied audience to compare the two young men—and especially their clothing.

Linen Clothing

The word used to describe linen clothing (σινδών) is only used four times in Mark—twice to describe the clothing of the young man who fled in Mark 14:50–51 and twice to describe the linen cloth that Joseph of Arimathea purchased and wrapped around Jesus before he placed him in the tomb (Mark 15:46). Through this parallel use of σινδών, it is as though, literarily, the shame associated with the young man, whose garment was taken when he fled (Mark 14:51) is placed upon Jesus at his death. Of course, the linen cloths are not the same, but the parallel use of the word allows the implied audience to make thematic and theological connections by way of analogy. Though this activity, the implied author/narrator appears to be *showing* the implied audience his theology of substitution. Literarily, Jesus takes upon himself the shame of the young man by being wrapped in the linen cloth.

Honor and Glory

Similarly, the "young man" in Mark 14:50–51 is not the same young man in the tomb in 16:5. However, the lexical links allow the implied audience to connect the figures literarily. Whereas the first young man is associated with the shame of fleeing naked, the second young man is associated with honor and glory. Honor is seen by the young man being seated on the right (καθήμενον ἐν τοῖς δεξιοῖς) (Mark 16:5). The positional term for "right" (δεξιός) is only used seven times in Mark (see Mark 10:37, 40; 12:36; 14:62; 15:27; and 16:5). It first appears when the sons of Zebedee ask Jesus for seats of honor (on his right and on his left) when Jesus comes in his glory (Mark 10:37). Jesus replies, in part, that the seats of honor (on his right and his left) are not for him to grant but are for those for whom they have been prepared (Mark 10:40). In Mark 12, Jesus quotes Psalm 110:1 where the Lord said to David's lord (εἶπεν κύριος τῷ κυρίῳ μου; cf. נְאֻם יְהוָה לַאדֹנִי) to sit at his right (κάθου ἐκ δεξιῶν μου). Clearly, being seated at the right hand of Yahweh is a position of honor. At the Jewish trial, Jesus is asked if he is the Christ, the son of the Blessed One (Mark 14:61). In response, Jesus states: "I am. And you will see the Son of Man sitting at the right of power (ἐκ δεξιῶν καθήμενον τῆς δυνάμεως) and coming with the clouds of heaven" (Mark 14:62). Again, the right-hand side is the side of honor.[33] The next time the term "right" is used is at the crucifixion of Jesus when the narrator tells the audience that two robbers are crucified with him, one on the right (δεξιῶν) and one on his left. This might be read as a simple designation of location without any allusion to honor. However, the implied audience knows that seats to the right and the left of Jesus were requested by James and John in Mark 10:37. Since they fled from being with Jesus in his suffering, these two robbers are presented as stand-in disciples, suffering with Jesus on his right and on his left. The positions of honor, next to Jesus, in suffering are maintained. Accordingly, when the young man is described as sitting to the right (καθήμενον ἐν τοῖς δεξιοῖς),[34] all of the previous, Markan allusions of Jesus, James, and John resonate with the implied audience suggesting that the young man too is in a position of honor.

Finally, the young man is described as being clothed in a white robe (περιβεβλημένον στολὴν λευκήν) (Mark 16:5). The term white (λευκός) only occurs in one other passage in Mark—on the Mount of Transfiguration, where Jesus' garment became radiantly, intensely white (τὰ ἱμάτια

---

33. Another seminal place where honor is associated with the "right" is with the birth of the *Ben-oni* (בֶּן־אוֹנִי) (son of sorrows) at the death of Rachel in Genesis. His name commemorated the sorrow associated with Rachel's death. However, Jacob renames the child *Benjamin* (בִנְיָמִין) (son of my *right hand*) so that the child's name does not commemorate sorrow, but honor—being to the right of his father Jacob (Gen 35:18–19).

34. Admittedly, whose "right" the man is seated at is not explicit in the narrative (the right of the women, or the right of where Jesus was lain). However, in view of the other usages of δεξιός in Mark, it may be best to conclude that the "right" is that of Jesus. See also Kuruvilla, "Naked Runaway," 544.

αὐτοῦ ἐγένετο στίλβοντα λευκὰ λίαν) (Mark 9:3). The young man's stole is now white, as Jesus' garment was white at the Transfiguration.[35] In other words, literally speaking, the young man's garment of shame is now replaced with the white garment of Christ.

Again, these are narrative pictures of substitution. The "linen cloth" the young man wore, that was stripped from him rendering him naked (Mark 14:51–52), covered Jesus' naked body in the tomb (Mark 15:46). In exchange, the brilliant, "white" garment Jesus wore at his Transfiguration (Mark 9:3) now covers the "young man" in the tomb (Mark 16:5).[36] So, the first thing the women see as they enter the tomb is a young man, in a place of honor, dressed in the glory of Jesus. The message of the risen Jesus for the implied audience, if not for these three women, is that there is hope for disciples who have failed to discern, accept, and be faithful to the suffering call of Jesus. There is hope for all who follow Jesus on the journey of discipleship, albeit stumbling and failing, clumsy, and hesitant. Failure is not a dead end. There is restoration—just look at the "young man."[37]

Internal Responses

The initial, internal response of the women was that they were moved to an intense emotional state of being overwhelmed (ἐξεθαμβήθησαν).[38] This term is only used in Mark (see 9:15; 14:33; 16:5, 6). The closest use of ἐκθαμβέω was of Jesus in Gethsemane when he took Peter, James, and John with him to pray; the narrator states: "he started to be *distressed* and troubled" (ἤρξατο ἐκθαμβεῖσθαι καὶ ἀδημονεῖν) (emphasis added). The women's sense of astonishment was probably more negative than positive because the young man's first words to the women is that they should "stop being distressed" (μὴ ἐκθαμβεῖσθε) (16:6).[39] If the response

---

35. Jenkins argues that "the white robe could have suggested to Mark's readers the dress of a Christian martyr, and so pointed to the outcome of discipleship of the sort ventured upon by the young man of 1451ff" (Jenkins, "Young Man or Angel?," 239).

36. See Kuruvilla, "Naked Runaway," 542–43.

37. See Iersel, *Mark*, 495–96, 505.

38. See BDAG, s.v. "ἐκθαμβέω": "To be moved to a relatively intense emotional state because of something causing great surprise or perplexity." This can be positive (cf. Mark 9:15) or negative (Mark 14:33).

39. The present imperative plus μή allows for the idea of cessation of activity in progress. As Dan Wallace states, "Here the idea is frequently progressive, and the prohibition is of the 'cessation of some act that is already in progress.' It has the idea, *Stop continuing*" (Wallace, *Greek Grammar*, 724).

of the women was positive, there would be no reason to tell them to stop. The implied audience might consider this to be a typical female response—being out of control. On the other hand, the response of the women, in-and-of-itself, is not categorically wrong because Jesus himself was "distressed" on the night before his crucifixion (Mark 14:33). What these women do with their distress will be important, not that they are emotionally distraught at seeing the man in the tomb.

The Words of the Young Man

The narrative now reports the words of the young man to the women (Mark 16:6-7). They are given without conjunctions, in a series of asyndeta: "Stop being distressed. You seek Jesus, the Nazarene, the crucified one; he has been raised; he is not here; behold the place where they placed him."[40]

As discussed above, first the messenger tells the women to "stop being distressed" (Mark 16:6). Then the young man demonstrates through his words to them that he knows what the women are doing: "You are seeking Jesus, the Nazarene, who was crucified." These words emphasize that the women are seeking a dead Jesus—"who was crucified." This has been the emphasis in verses 16:1-3. The women have purchased spices to anoint Jesus' body; they are concerned that the stone will block the entrance to the tomb where Jesus has been placed. They are coming to care for the dead body of Jesus. However, the term Ναζαρηνός may be a slight foreshadow of a transition to come.[41] This appellation to Jesus (Jesus *of Nazareth*) is used in Mark to describe the location from which Jesus came (see Mark 1:24, 10:47; 14:64). By using the appellation here, the young man could be simply identifying the human Jesus, but because Nazareth is a town in Galilee, the young man could be providing a foreshadow of his coming message about Galilee ("You are seeking Jesus the Nazarene ... he has been raised ... he goes before you into Galilee"). In any case, the young man moves from describing what the women were doing, or whom they were seeking—him who was crucified—to describing Jesus'

---

40. See Tolbert, *Sowing the Gospel*, 294.

41. The two sources that omit Ναζαρηνὸν, ℵ* and D, are both significant, late (fourth/fifth century) codices of the Alexandrian and Western text types. See Metzger and Ehrman, *Text of the New Testament*, 62-67, 70-73. However, without other supporting witnesses, it is doubtful that Ναζαρηνὸν should be omitted.

present condition: "He was raised (ἠγέρθη).⁴² He is not here. Look, the place where they placed him." These first words of the young man explicitly express the change that has occurred—Jesus who was crucified has now been raised. Read together with verse 5, the implied author has provided another example of emblematic parallelism for the implied audience. First the picture was given of the changed "young man" and then a statement is given about the change that has occurred from the women's expectation of a dead Jesus in the tomb to a risen Jesus absent from the tomb. What is of additional interest is the weaving of the women's expectation with the change that has occurred. This change may have an effect on them just as it did upon the young man, but they do not yet know how or why. The young man's instruction to the women will bring matters into focus for them and the audience.

In Mark 16:7 the young man instructs the women to do something with the knowledge they have just received. Instead of being distressed (Mark 16:6), the young man makes a contrastive statement (ἀλλ') explaining what the women must do with their distress: "But go, tell his disciples and Peter, that he goes before you into Galilee; there you will see him, just as he told you."

How one punctuates verse 16:7 makes a difference as to whether the message the women are told to relate includes them or only the male disciples, the Twelve.⁴³ As will be shown, the text is most probably inclusive of the women and the implied audience and not just the Twelve. The NIV translates the verse as a direct quote, using direct discourse:

> Go, tell his disciples and Peter, "He is going ahead of you into Galilee. There you will see him, just as he told you."⁴⁴

However, the NRSV translates the statement as an indirect quote, using indirect discourse:

> Go, tell his disciples and Peter that he is going ahead of you to Galilee; there you will see him, just as he told you.⁴⁵

---

42. The passive voice implies that God was the one who raised him.

43. See Geddert, "Beginning Again," 155; *Mark*, 396–97. The Greek text is as follows: ἀλλ' ὑπάγετε εἴπατε τοῖς μαθηταῖς αὐτοῦ καὶ τῷ Πέτρῳ ὅτι προάγει ὑμᾶς εἰς τὴν Γαλιλαίαν· ἐκεῖ αὐτὸν ὄψεσθε, καθὼς εἶπεν ὑμῖν.

44. See also NASV.

45. See also NET; ESV; NKJV; ASV; and D-R.

While either translation of the Greek text is possible, it may be more probable that the ὅτι clause should be understood as signaling indirect discourse rather than direct discourse. Wallace explains the grammar of indirect discourse using the declarative ὅτι clause:

> This is a specialized use of the direct object clause after a verb of perception. The ὅτι clause contains *reported speech* or *thought*. The contrasts with ὅτι *recitativum* [direct discourse], which involves direct speech. It is a very common use of the ὅτι clause. When the ὅτι introduces indirect discourse, it should be translated *that*....
>
> Like its recitative counterpart, the declarative ὅτι comes after a verb of perception (e.g., verbs of saying, thinking, believing, knowing, seeing, hearing). One could think of it as a recasting of an original saying or thought into a reported form.[46]

In Mark 16:7, the ὅτι clause follows a verb of perception, namely "say" the second person plural aorist active imperative of λέγω (εἴπατε). Furthermore, the indirect object of the speech is not the Twelve (δώδεκα, cf. Mark 3:16; 4:10; 6:7; 9:35; 10:32; 11:11; 14:10, 17, 20, 43), but the more generic term "disciples" (τοῖς μαθηταῖς αὐτοῦ) and also Peter. The audience knows from other passages in Mark that there are disciples other than the Twelve who followed Jesus (cf. Mark 4:10). Furthermore, the audience has just been told that women were with Jesus in Galilee and on the way to Jerusalem (Mark 15:40–41). Therefore, Jesus' statement in Mark 14:28 from the Mount of Olives following the meal that Jesus would go before them into Galilee may not have only been heard by the Twelve. For instance, the audience knows in Mark 14:51–52 that an anonymous young man (νεανίσκος) was also with Jesus and the Twelve when Judas came to arrest Jesus in the Gethsemane. Therefore, it is not impossible that the women were also with Jesus, even though they are not identified until now in the narrative.

Geddert explains the significance of understanding the verse as indirect discourse rather than direct discourse:

> The difference seems small, until we ask who the word *"you"* refers to. According to the NIV it refers to the male disciples. The women are to go tell *them*, "Jesus is going ahead of you into Galilee." In the NRSV version *"you"* includes the women. They are to join the male disciples and tell them, "Jesus is going ahead of *us* to Galilee."

---

46. Wallace, *Greek Grammar*, 456.

According to the NIV, the women's role is only to be a communication link to the male disciples, telling them what they already know. According to the NRSV, they are to join (actually *rejoin*, see below) the male disciples and as a (*re*)united group travel back to Galilee, meet Jesus, and "start over" once again.[47]

If the young man's statement should be translated as indirect discourse, the significance is greater for the women and the implied audience. The exhortation moves from a message to a small, male subgroup in the story world of Mark to a message for a larger group of men and women in Mark's world. The women are being elevated even though disappointment may be lurking in the narrative. If the pronoun "you" (ὑμῖν) in Mark 16:7 includes the women, this would also suggest that they were present in Mark 14:28 when Jesus said he would go before them into Galilee.[48] Furthermore, the message also reaches to the implied audience outside of the story world of Mark since they too heard Jesus' prediction that after he had risen, he would go ahead to meet the scattered sheep in Galilee (Mark 14:28). The inclusion of the women in the young man's injunction also provides added weight to why the women responded the way that they did in verse 8. If they only had to tell the male disciples about the young man's message, it would not be as difficult as realizing that the message was also for them to meet Jesus in Galilee.[49] The women's fallibility has been hinted at since they were introduced in Mark 15:40–41. The women have been *named* in Mark. If Mary, the mother of James and Joses, was also the mother of Jesus, she was shown to be resistant as someone who misunderstood Jesus in Mark 3. The women watched Jesus' crucifixion

---

47. Geddert, "Beginning Again," 155.

48. The implied presence of the women in Mark 14:28 may be a reason some translate the verse in 16:7 as direct discourse. The thought is that Jesus was only with his male disciples at the Passover meal and in Gethsemane, and thus, only spoke to his male disciples in Mark 14:28. Clearly, the Twelve were present at the Passover supper before Jesus was arrested (see Mark 14:17, 20). However, this does not necessarily preclude the women from also being present. The more generic word for disciples (μαθητής) is also used during this time (see Mark 14:12, 13, 14, 16). Furthermore, the plural verbs and pronouns may refer only to the Twelve but may also refer to others who were present with the Twelve. One thing is certain from Mark 15:40–41, women were with the male disciples in Galilee and on the way to Jerusalem even though they were not described as being present in the narratives. Some of the same women were also present during the crucifixion, at Jesus' burial, and now at the tomb. It is not impossible that women were also present after the meal when Jesus went to Gethsemane and heard what was said in Mark 14:28.

49. It seems unlikely, based upon the discourse of Mark's narrative, that "Galilee" should refer to the "Gentile world." For such a view, see Evans, "I Will Go Before You," 5.

from afar rather than with him. The three women came to anoint Jesus for his burial when he was already anointed in advance and did not appear to comprehend that Jesus would rise after his crucifixion even though he announced it three times on the way to Jerusalem. Now these women are told that they are to meet Jesus in Galilee. All of these foreshadows of fallibility may explain their response in Mark 16:8: "And going out, they fled from the tomb, for they had trembling and astonishment, and they told no one anything, for they were afraid." This response is probably not a surprise for the implied audience—it was foreshadowed.[50]

The Women's Response

When the narrator uses the aorist active participle, ἐξελθοῦσαι, to describe the women "going out," he appears to be referring to the women going out of the tomb that they entered in Mark 16:5. The narrator then uses two finite verbs to describe the activity of the women, and a reason (γὰρ) following each verb to explain their activity. The two finite statements are that "they fled from the tomb" (ἔφυγον ἀπὸ τοῦ μνημείου), and "they told no one anything" (καὶ οὐδενὶ οὐδὲν εἶπαν). Both of these statements appear to be negative descriptions of the women's actions,[51] even though

---

50. This understanding is contrary to many who state that the response of the women was a complete surprise for the implied audience. Boomershine states: "The shocking and unexpected character of the women's actions is, therefore, what Mark seeks to explain in his narrative comments" (Boomershine, "Mark 16," 229). Lincoln writes: "Yet, as has now become clear, the narrator's telling of the story has carefully created such an expectation only to shatter it immediately" (Lincoln, "Promise and the Failure," 290–91). Williams states: "Mark initially characterizes the women as committed to Jesus and to his values. However, after the young man's announcement of the resurrection and his command to report a message to the disciples, the women make a dramatic turn for the worse" (Williams, *Other Followers*, 198–99). Even Tolbert, who identifies many of the foreshadows of fallibility in the women, understands the foreshadows to be ambivalent and thus concludes: "For Mark, the women's denouement must wait until the very last words of the Gospel in order to build up the highest hopes possible in the audience before thoroughly disappointing them" (Tolbert, *Sowing the Gospel*, 294). If the implied audience identifies many of the same fallibilities in the women that were seen earlier in the men, one must question whether they would be "disappointed" by the women in the last verse.

51. Lincoln, "Promise and the Failure," 285–86. Iersel stated: "In the end the women fail no less than the twelve, for they too take flight" (Iersel, *Mark*, 500). See also Geddert, *Mark*, 398; Nash, "Point of View," 225. Malbon holds a mediating view: "Thus the women's fear and silence are as much signs of the limits of humanity in the presence of divinity as signs of fallibility as followers in the usual sense" (Malbon, "Fallible Followers," 44–45).

some have tried to rehabilitate them.⁵² The verb "to flee" (φεύγω) was last used in Mark 14:50 and 14:52. In 14:50 it described all of the male disciples fleeing from Jesus at his arrest in Gethsemane (Καὶ ἀφέντες αὐτὸν ἔφυγον πάντες). In 14:52 it described the young man leaving his garment behind and fleeing naked from Jesus' captors (ὁ δὲ καταλιπὼν τὴν σινδόνα γυμνὸς ἔφυγεν). As discussed above, Mark 14:50–52 are a case of emblematic parallelism with the statement given in verse 50, and the image given in verses 51–52. Now the word φεύγω is used again by the narrator at the early morning watch to describe the women who fled from the tomb. Like the male disciples at the midnight watch, the women too are shown to be fallible at the early morning watch.

The women's flight (φεύγω) is not merely descriptive, as in Mark 13:14,⁵³ but negative, as is shown by the second finite statement made by the narrator: "And they said nothing to anyone."⁵⁴ This might be considered to be a typical female response by the implied audience. This silence is exactly the opposite of what the young man in the tomb told them

---

52. Lightfoot, *Mark*, 87–97. Cranfield stated: "It is not surprising that the women were afraid and rendered speechless for a while. Mark's account . . . underlines the mystery and awe-fulness of the Resurrection" (Cranfield, *Mark*, 470). David R. Catchpole, stated: "The fear and silence of the women belong to the structure of epiphany" (Catchpole, "Fearful Silence," 9). Lane stated: "The response of the women to the evidence of God's decisive intervention in raising Jesus from the dead is described in the categories of terror. They fled from the tomb, unable to control the dread which overwhelmed them and reduced them to silence. For a time they kept their experience to themselves because 'they were afraid'" (Lane, *Mark*, 590–91). Magness stated: "The silence of the women is not necessarily absolute. . . . They kept silence in the midst of inappropriate audiences but gave a full report to the appropriate audience, the disciples, . . . silence either voluntary or commanded is a positive response to the heightened knowledge and understanding of Jesus' person and power on the basis of the observation of a demonstration of that supernatural power" (Magness, *Marking the End*, 100). Stock stated: "Eventually (it is clear) the women did tell the disciples about the resurrection. . . . The women were silent because they had been overcome by trembling and astonishment. All these things that belong to the structure of epiphany or theophany" (Stock, *Mark*, 431–32). Aernie describes "Mark's portrayal of the women as faithful witnesses" to the disciples (Aernie, *Narrative Discipleship* loc. 2546–2842). Gundry stated: "Mark is not criticizing the women for their trembling, astonishment, and fear. Rather, he is using these reactions to highlight the supernaturalness of Jesus' resurrection" (Gundry, *Mark*, 1015). However, as Iersel states: "The opinion borrowed by Catchpole that terror and silence are a common feature of epiphany stories meets with two difficulties. First, the story is not an epiphany story because neither God nor a risen Jesus manifests himself in the episode. Secondly, the manifestations in Mark are followed by terror but not by silence" (Iersel, *Mark*, 500n35).

53. "Then let those who are in Judea flee [φευγέτωσαν] to the mountains."

54. The Greek text has a double negative for emphasis: "and they said nothing to no one" (καὶ οὐδενὶ οὐδὲν εἶπαν).

to do: "But go, tell his disciples and Peter" (Mark 16:7). Some conclude that this was only a temporary silence, and that the women eventually told the disciples.[55] However, the implied author never gives any indication that the women ever told anyone. Instead, the narrator freezes the women's activity in a posture of silent flight, and only offers the implied audience explanatory descriptors for each finite verb. They fled from the tomb because they were having (or were seized by) trembling and astonishment (εἶχεν γὰρ αὐτὰς τρόμος καὶ ἔκστασις).[56] The word for trembling, τρόμος, is only used here in Mark. The sense is that the women were trembling, or quivering, from fear.[57] The only other place where "astonishment" (ἔκστασις) is used in Mark is in 5:42 for the healing of Jairus' daughter when the narrator states: "And immediately the little girl stood and walked (for she was twelve years *old*), and they were overcome with great astonishment." This term emphasizes a profound emotional experience to the point of being beside oneself.[58] Therefore, it appears that the women fled out of the tomb in a great emotional state—quivering because they were beside themselves. Again, this would have been an expected behavior by the implied audience from their culture, and perhaps

---

55. Catchpole states: "The cumulative effect of the preceding argument makes it difficult to believe that the message entrusted to the women did not, in Mark's view, get through" (Catchpole, "Fearful Silence" 6). Lane writes: "For a time they kept their experience to themselves because 'they were afraid'" (Lane, *Mark*, 590–91). Magness decides that: "The silence of the women is not necessarily absolute.... They kept silence in the midst of inappropriate audiences but gave a full report to the appropriate audience, the disciples" (Magness, *Marking the End*, 100). Aernie's argument is similar to Magness (Aernie, *Narrative Discipleship* loc. 2681–93). Stock opines: "Eventually (it is clear) the women did tell the disciples about the resurrection" (Stock, *Mark*, 431–32). France concludes: "We know, of course, and Mark's readers knew, that the message of the resurrection did somehow get out, whether through the three women or despite them" (France, *Mark*, 683). As Christine E. Joynes observes: "The impact of reading Mark 16 in light of the other Gospels illustrates a typical approach to Mark's concluding emphasis on silence, namely the assumption that the women did not really remain silent" (Joynes, "Sound of Silence," 19). Continuing, Joynes opines: "The frequency with which the Gospels are harmonized in such images again raises important questions about the extent to which Mark's note of silence was ever heard. More often than not, the Markan conclusion is subverted by reading his narrative through the lens of other biblical texts" (Joynes, "Sound of Silence," 27).

56. The term for "trembling," τρόμος, is replaced by the word "fear," φοβος, in D W it sa^ms. The external witnesses are late and few. This change may be explained by a scribe importing the noun form of the word "fear" from the second part of verse 8. Also "fear and trembling" are often combined elsewhere in the New Testament (see 1 Cor 2:3; 2 Cor 7:15; Eph 6:5; Phil 2:12).

57. BDAG, s.v. "τρόμος."

58. BADG, s.v. "ἔκστασις."

an expectation from the foreshadows identified in Mark 15:40–41. The cause of this emotional response must have been the young man, or what he told them, or both. It does not seem sufficient to suggest that this was the response to a theophany, since neither God nor Jesus appeared to the women. However, the appearance of the young man and his announcement that Jesus has risen appears to have caused just as great of an emotional reaction in the women as the raising of the young girl caused to her parents and the disciples in Mark 5. While this reaction, in-and-of itself, may appear to be ethically neutral, for the implied audience who knows that Jesus predicted that he would rise at least three times earlier in the narrative, the response of the women suggests that they did not apprehend and/or believe what Jesus had predicted. They saw that he was crucified (Mark 14:50). How could he be anything but dead?

Parallels with Mark 5

In Mark's use of duality, he provides a parallel, explanatory clause following the second finite statement that the women said nothing to no one—"for they were afraid" (ἐφοβοῦντο γάρ). Of what were the women afraid? The verb for being afraid, φοβέω, is used often in Mark (4:41; 5:15, 33, 36; 6:20; 6:50; 9:32; 10:32; 11:18, 32; 12:12; 16:8). Particularly instructive may be the use of this term in the passage concerning the deliverance of the demonized man in Mark 5. Unlike the passages where people were fearful in response to what they saw Jesus do (Mark 4:41; 5:33; 6:50) or heard Jesus say (Mark 9:32), this passage shows the fear of those who saw the *effect* of what Jesus did.[59] In both Mark 5:2–3, 5 and 15:46; 16:2, 3, 5, the setting is a tomb (μνημεῖον). Furthermore, before the transformation of the man in Mark 5:15 and the young man in Mark 14:52, both are naked (implied in 5:15 and stated in 14:52, γυμνός). After the demonized man is delivered, the audience is told that he is clothed (ἱματισμένον) (Mark 15:15), and of course the audience is told that young man in the tomb in 16:5 is wearing a white robe (εριβεβλημένον στολὴν λευκήν). More specificity is used to describe the young man at the end of the Gospel. In Mark 5, those who expressed "fear" were not present when the demons were cast out of the man into the pigs. They did not see Jesus do anything. Instead, they saw the effect of what Jesus did. The narrator tells the implied audience that those who witnessed the event reported

---

59. For the seeds of this discussion, see Villiers, "Powerful Transformation," 4–5.

it to those in the town and countryside, and the people went out to see what had happened (Mark 5:14). Verse 15 then states: "And they came to Jesus, and they saw the demonized one, who had the legion, sitting, clothed, and sound-minded; and they were afraid." The people who came to Jesus are then told by the eye witnesses about how the man who was demonized was delivered and about the pigs (15:16). The result was that the people began to beg Jesus to depart from their region (15:17). This account is not unlike that which occurs in Mark 16:8. Like the people in chapter 5, the women came to see the *effect* of what Jesus did through the transformed young man in the tomb. Then, like the people in chapter 5, the women have explained to them what occurred and became fearful. The women cannot ask Jesus to depart because he is not present at the tomb, so they themselves depart (flee) telling no one anything. Again, the fear appears to be over seeing the transformative *effect* of what Jesus has done, not over witnessing an epiphany. Furthermore, the effect on the young man is similar to the deliverance of the man from demons in Chapter 5. In Mark 5:19 Jesus tells the man to go to his house and to his people and announce to them how much the Lord has done for him and that he had mercy on him. Just as Jesus brought about the transformation of a demonized man into a witness for him, so did Jesus bring about the transformation of a failed young man into a witness for him to the women (Mark 16:6–7).

The parallels in Mark 5 and 16 suggest that the fear of the women was not simply reverent awe at the appearance and message of the young man they encountered at the tomb. As the fear of the people in Mark 5 led to a resistance of Jesus by asking him to depart from them, so it may be that the fear of the women is also a resistance to the appearance and message of the young man in the tomb. As with the man in Mark 5, the young man's appearance spoke of restoration—being seated at the right and wearing a white stole. Furthermore, the message of the young man is one of restoration—"Go tell his disciples and Peter that he goes ahead of you into Galilee; there you will see him" (Mark 16:7). By mentioning the "disciples" and "Peter," the implied author appears once again to be using a dualism for the purpose of clarification. Jesus is not just meeting disciples in Galilee, but *failed* disciples in Galilee, even Peter whose failure was magnified in Mark. As discussed above, the women who came to the tomb had many foreshadows of fallibility. Now they see one who was flawed like them, and then restored in appearance with a message of hope for failed disciples. It appears to be too much for them, so they flee, just as the young man previously did, and say nothing to anyone. The Gospel ends at the morning watch showing the fallibility of the female followers; they have failed to stay alert. However, this failure is in the context of a visual and verbal message of restoration from the young man in the tomb. The path of renewed discipleship awaits these fallible women in Galilee—if they will follow.

THE RHETORICAL EFFECT OF MARK'S ENDING

Many understand the rhetorical effect of the Gospel of Mark's ending to be that the implied audience should now take up the commands given to the failed followers in the story.[60] But how is this possible? How is the implied audience to tell the disciples and Peter what was said in the tomb? Is the implied audience actually to go to Galilee to meet Jesus?[61] It appears that placing the burden on the implied audience to do what the fallible women failed to do is less than satisfying as an intended rhetorical effect of the ending of Mark.

The rhetorical significance of the ending may be found through Marianna Torgovnick's observation that "endings invite the retrospective analysis of a text and create the illusion of life halted and poised for analysis."[62] Torgovnick further explains the concept of closure in relationship to the narrative as a whole: "The test is the appropriateness of the ending's relationship to beginning and middle, not the degree of finality or resolution achieved."[63] Obviously, the ending of Mark does not bring about finality or resolution, but it does provide the audience with an opportunity to analyze the women, frozen in their fallible states, and to consider the significance of a reunion with Jesus in Galilee as announced by the young man at the tomb. The fallibility of the women shows the

---

60. Tolbert, *Sowing the Gospel*, 288–99; Boomershine, "Mark 16," 239; Rhoads and Michie, *Mark as Story*, 61–62.

61. As Williams observes, having the audience go and tell in place of the women does not work, "because technically the women are not told to announce openly the gospel or the resurrection, but to report to the disciples a coming post-resurrection meeting" (Williams, *Other Followers*, 202n1). Tolbert reads "Galilee" in a metaphorical sense: "Literal geography is not the point, for Galilee represents the time of sowing" (Tolbert, *Sowing the Gospel*, 298). Nevertheless, she still has the audience announcing the gospel.

62. Torgovnick, *Closure*, loc. 3154. For a discussion of suspended endings in the Old and New Testaments see Magness, *Marking the End*, 49–85.

63. Torgovnick, *Closure*, loc. 93–94.

audience that no one, however hopeful he or she may be, is immune from falling off the way as a follower of Christ. The male disciples fled, and then the female disciples fled—even though they were present at the passion after the male disciples fled. Knowledge of the resurrection does not preclude the women, or the implied audience, from falling off the way.[64] Fallibility seems to be an endemic, character quality of followers in Mark. Accordingly, the portrayal of the women as fallible reaches back to the author's earlier portrayal of the men as fallible providing continuity with the end and the middle of the Gospel.

However, in the midst of that difficult reality, there is a picture and a message of hope.[65] The young man pictures the restoration available to fallible followers, and his message about meeting Jesus in Galilee shows the way to restoration, and thus, hope. Moreover, the "tomb" at the end of the Gospel functions, narratively, as the "wilderness" at the beginning of the Gospel positioning the audience for a new beginning.[66]

Everything occurs in the final panel in-and-around the tomb (μνημεῖον). This term is used four times in Mark 16:2–8 and six times in Mark 15:46—16:8 (15:46 x 2, 16:2, 3, 5, 8). The term is only used two other times in Mark. In 6:29 the tomb is the place where the body of John the Baptizer was placed by his disciples after he was beheaded, and in 5:2, the tomb was the place from which the man with an unclean spirit came out to meet Jesus. The tomb is clearly a place of the dead, and a place

---

64. Williams observes: "In moving away from an identification with the women, the reader must acknowledge that failure, fear and disobedience are all still possible in the period between the resurrection and the parousia" (Williams, *Other Followers*, 202–3).

65. Norman Petersen correctly argues that chapter 13 of Mark (13:9–11) goes beyond the discourse time of Mark's text, and this has an effect on how the ending is understood by the implied audience: "In this light the effect of 13 is to minimize the significance of the disciples' abandonment of Jesus and to emphasize the expectation that they will soon abandon their mistaken point of view and return to Jesus" (Petersen, "When Is the End Not the End," 166; see also 163–66).

66. Torgovnick identifies this technique as "circularity": "When the ending of a novel clearly recalls the beginning in language, in situation, in the grouping of characters, or in several of these ways, circularity may be said to control the ending. One of the most common of closural patterns, circularity may be obvious or subtle, immediately perceived or perceivable only upon retrospective analysis. A familiar and obvious kind of circularity is the 'frame' technique common in narratives. When language, situation, or the grouping of characters refers not just to the beginning of the work but to a series of points in the text, we may speak of *parallelism* as the novel's closural pattern. Often less obvious than circularity, parallelism sometimes becomes clear only upon retrospective analysis" (Torgovnick, *Closure*, loc. 191).

where demons reside. These are thematic echoes from the prologue of the Gospel.

In Mark 1:1–14, everything occurs in-and-around the wilderness (ἔρημος). This term is used four times in the Prologue (Mark 1:3, 4, 12, 13). The wilderness is the place from which the words of Isaiah are to be proclaimed crying out to the nation to prepare the way of the Lord and make straight his paths (Mark 1:3; cf. Isa 40:3–4).[67] John is described as being the one in the wilderness proclaiming the way—repentance unto the forgiveness of sins (1:4).[68] After Jesus' baptism, the Spirit casts Jesus

---

67. Much of the language in Isaiah 40:1–11 is figurative for the nation to prepare itself morally for the coming of the Lord. Isaiah most probably had the captive nation of Israel in view, but he also had more than what was historically experienced in her return to the land. All flesh (describing all people) never actually saw the glory of the Lord revealed (Isa 40:5). The message of the second major unit of Isaiah speaks beyond the historical experience of Judah's return from Babylon. She was still under the rule of the Gentiles as she entered the land. God had not brought about his eternal, earthly kingdom (Isa 40:10–11; 56:8–66). Therefore, the message of Isaiah 40:1–11 must refer to more than the return of the captives, even from Isaiah's vantage point. While it may be true that Isaiah may have expected the kingdom to be ushered in with the return of the captives to the land, this is not what transpired. The meaning of Isaiah 40:3–4 does not change from a literal sense in Isaiah to a spiritual-allegorical sense in Mark. If it were literal in its first expression, it might be asked, "How could captive Israel do this? How could she be released from Babylon to 'clear the way for the Lord in the wilderness?' How could she be released to 'make smooth in the desert a highway for our God?' And even if she would be allowed, could she physically accomplish the emblematic commands of 40:4 to lift up valleys, make low mountains, and in general, change the terrain of the land? In view of the historic condition of the nation as a people held captive, it is best to understand the exhortations of Isaiah 40:3–4 to be figurative describing the drastic spiritual changes which the nation must make to be ready for the Lord of Glory's wondrous return to set up his kingdom. This figurative sense is consistent with the sense employed by Mark. In other words, Mark 1:2–5 is alluding to a new exodus—a calling of Israel out of captivity; a regeneration of salvation history. Once Israel went to the Jordan to gain the inheritance, now they are returning to the same river for a fresh start, but with John the Baptizer heralding another "Joshua" (יהושע or Jesus).

68. Tolbert has argued that the one in the wilderness proclaiming forgiveness is not John so much in Mark as it is Jesus himself. She argues that Jesus is sent out by God on a mission (1:38; 9:37; 12:6), is the messenger, the sower of the word (1:14–15; 4:14, 33; 8:38), is the one on the way (8:3, 37; 9:33, 34; 10:32, 52), and makes proclamation in the wilderness (1:12–13, 35, 45; 6:31, 32, 25; 8:4). To follow Jesus, one must do as he does and teaches (8:34; 10:21, 28–31, 38–39). Furthermore, the term "Lord" (κύριος) is a reference to God in distinction to Jesus in Mark (5:19; 11:9; 12:9, 11, 29, 30, 36, 27; 13:20, 35); κύριος is only used of Jesus as a title of respect (7:28; 11:3). See Tolbert, *Sowing the Gospel*, 239–48; Fowler, *Loaves and Fishes*, 121–24. However, the parallels between John in the prologue and the young man in the tomb (see above) suggest that Mark is identifying John as the herald prophesied by Isaiah. Obviously, John and Jesus have many parallels in Mark. See Fowler, *Loaves and Fishes*, 121–26 (emphasizing the overlapping relationship of John and Jesus in Mark).

into the wilderness (Mark 1:12), and it is in the wilderness that Jesus is tempted by Satan for forty days (1:13).[69]

The wilderness and the tomb have numerous similarities: Both are uninhabited; both are the dwelling places of demons (Mark 1:13; 5:2); both have a movement in Mark's story from the outside to the inside (Mark 1:12; 15:46), and from the inside to the outside (Mark 1:13-14; 16:16); both contain a messenger (ἄγγελος/νεανίσκος) with narrative comments about the messenger's eschatological clothing, speaking concerning the advent of Jesus (Mark 1:3-4; 16:5-6); and both include a call to follow (1:17, 20; 16:7).[70]

The significance of these similarities is in how the parallels function for the implied audience. The interpreter must ponder what the author is *doing* with what is being said. By echoing themes of the wilderness

---

69. Mark is showing Jesus to be the New Adam:

ADAM	JESUS
In paradise	In the wilderness
Rules over animals	[a gap?]
Satan tempts	Satan tempts
Succumbs to temptation	Overcomes temptation
An angel guards against him	Angels come and minister to him
	Is among wild animals

As Leonhard Goppelt observes: "This connection seems to indicate that 'as Adam was once honored by beasts in Paradise . . ., so Christ is with the wild beasts after overcoming temptation. He thus ushers in the paradisiacal state of the last days when there will be peace between man and beast (Isa 11:6-8; 65:25)." Goppelt, *Typos*, 98. Goppelt's suggestion goes beyond the contrasting comparisons of Paul in Romans 5 to a true similarity between the two Adams in that Jesus, after the fall, regains the harmony with creation that the original Adam once had. Therefore, Jesus can bring with him this harmony for all to enjoy as he sets up his kingdom. "Jesus opens paradise closed to the first man." Furthermore, Jesus is being shown to be the true "Son of God" just as David and Israel's kings were sons of God (cf. 2 Sam 7:14-16):

DAVID	JESUS
Anointed by Samuel	Anointed by John/Spirit
Faced Goliath for forty days	Faced Satan for forty days
Was victorious	Was victorious

In other words, the implied author is showing Jesus to be worthy of following for both Jews and Gentiles as the new and greater David and the new and greater Adam.

70. See Stock, *Mark*, 26-28.

at the tomb, the implied author is suggesting a new beginning to his Gospel. This new beginning is quite similar to the original beginning. It is as though the call to prepare the way is once again being made. This preparation will involve: the risk of death but the hope of new life (tomb/wilderness); a messenger calling recalcitrant followers to prepare themselves spiritually for the Lord's coming; and spiritual attacks from demons and Satan himself. The epilogue at the tomb functions like the prologue in the wilderness by preparing the implied audience to metaphorically join Jesus in Galilee (Mark 16:7; cf. 1:14) where repentance and belief must occur to bring about the Kingdom of God foretold by John in the clothing of Elijah, and the young man in the white clothing of the transfiguration. The young man has told the women that Jesus has gone ahead of them into Galilee. Even after prior and subsequent failure, the way of discipleship remains open. A new start from the threatening terrain of death awaits.

CONCLUSION

At the Roman watches of evening and early morning, the named women in this narrative show themselves to be mixed, complex disciples. The implied author's characterization of them shows the implied audience both how to be a follower of Jesus and how hard it is to be a follower of Jesus—even after his resurrection. At the evening watch, the named women, Mary Magdalene and Mary of Joses (who is probably the mother of Jesus) show themselves to be alert, faithful witnesses to where Jesus has been buried. However, at the early morning watch, Mary Magdalene, Mary the *mother* of James, and Salome begin to show the implied audience signs of being fallible. The women do not come to the tomb with an expectation of a risen Jesus, but with spices to anoint Jesus' dead body. The implied audience sees the dramatic irony of the women's actions because they know from the implied author's discourse that Jesus was already anointed for his burial by the unnamed woman in Mark 14. The implied author further uses discourse to extend the dramatic irony by revealing the women's inner thoughts about their concern over who would roll away the great stone from the tomb. The implied author is showing the implied audience that the women lack comprehension of Jesus' earlier predictions of rising from the dead. This use of dramatic irony causes the implied audience to distance itself from these women.

Then at the tomb, these women meet a young man who pictures, in the narrative world of Mark, the effect the resurrection has on failed disciples. The implied audience would be able to connect the glowing young man with the failed young man earlier in Mark and see the transformation. However, the women at the tomb show first-century characteristics of women in their out-of-control response to the young man and his message to them, as well as their fearful response like other Markan characters when they do not understand who Jesus is and what he is doing. The implied author has the young man give a message to the women that elevates them to participate with the men—even Peter—in travel back to Galilee and to reunite with Jesus where discipleship can be reformed and restored. However, the women are described by the implied author as fleeing from the tomb in a great emotional state and telling no one anything—acts that the implied audience would view as typically female and might have anticipated by the foreshadows identified in Mark 15:40–41 and Mark 16.

However, by ending the narrative with this frozen scene, the implied audience is able to evaluate the significance of the message from the young man at the tomb and consider the hope available for followers who have fallen off the way of restoration by meeting Jesus in the land of Galilee where discipleship was first forged. Furthermore, by placing this narrative at the tomb, which has similarities to the "wilderness" at the beginning of the Gospel of Mark, the implied author positions the implied audience for an expectation of new beginnings.

Finally, even though the women have been portrayed with first-century characteristics of being out of control, perplexed, astonished, and fearful at the tomb, it is significant that the implied author has given the final word, albeit one that has not been said or articulated, to these women. The implied audience may be unsettled by the implied author's portrayed response of the women in this last portion of the narrative as those aligned with the *habitus* of their social contexts, but the implied author has also given these women presence in the discourse as final characters in the Gospel, and they are associated with the positive aspects of Galilee. They are given a message for themselves and other failed followers that the protagonist, Jesus, has already gone ahead of them to Galilee. These women have been given a mandate to convey a message to those whose fallible status would have been recognized by the implied audience. The women's stability of character at this stage seems to falter when the narrative ends with their flight and fear. So, there is a particular tension in their characterization, and it is with this that the Gospel concludes. Nevertheless, the implied author has depicted these women as having the capacity to recognize the restrictions and limitations of their response to the young man and to embrace a new social order that arises out of falling off the path, even if they do not act on this ability within the confines of the narrative.

18

Conclusion

CONTRIBUTION TO RESOLUTION OF THE PROBLEM

THE PROBLEM PRESENTED IN the Introduction of this study is that in the evangelical community, the difficult Pauline and Petrine passages on women dominate gender-oriented studies. While this integrated literary study of women in the Gospel of Mark has not solved that problem, it has argued and demonstrated that there is an alternative to a gendered view that insists that a woman know and keep her subordinate place in a male social hierarchy.

If characterization is, or can be, a mechanism for the valorization of personhood, that is, if characterization is the manner in which an author infuses bodies with value, then this study has shown that the actual/implied author of the Gospel of Mark has quite deliberately established a personhood for women enhanced with significant potential. This study has argued and demonstrated that the women characters in the Gospel of Mark are not merely subordinate to men in their world. On the contrary, even though no outright or direct critique has been made on the repressive social hierarchies of the Graeco-Roman/Graeco-Judaic world in which non-elite, "normal" women have occupied the lowest level of the social hierarchy—quite often similar to slaves and even animals—the actual and implied author of Mark has used narrative characterization to create women characters who perform so decisively that their presence as a gender can no longer be denied and shifted into the shadows of the early Christian community.

Using narrative to show, rather than tell, theology, the implied author of Mark has shown through discourse Peter's mother-in-law to be a person who has greater understanding than the disciples by immediately responding to her healing in a manner that echoes angels and foreshadows the essential characteristic of service found in Jesus and later women in the developing Gospel. The woman with a hemorrhage has been shown to have such a significant faith that Jesus uses her as an example for the ruler of the synagogue to adopt as he faces similar, life-threatening fears regarding the life of his daughter. A Syrophoenician woman shows understanding that is superior to the religious leaders and the Twelve as she comprehends and engages with Jesus' parable and expands its applicability to the larger Gentile world of which she is a member. A lowly woman of extreme poverty on the periphery of society and vulnerable to exploitation is shown to be a true follower of God, above the rapacious religious leaders, through her wholehearted living that foreshadows the suffering ahead for Messiah and the disciples. A woman who anoints Jesus for his burial is shown to be an example of true, faithful discipleship over and against Judas, one of the Twelve, who is shown to be an example of failed discipleship. Even a woman like Herodias is valorized in her deceptiveness as being more manly than her husband, Herod, who is vilified by her actions as being depraved, unable to control himself or his household, and thus unable to rule. And although the women at the tomb show fallibility, the implied author portrays them to be like the male disciples in the Gospel—including the leader of the Twelve—who are also fallible. Nevertheless, the actual author of Mark has exalted these fallible women by ending this ancient work without a man in sight except for the young man left at the tomb, and with these women as characters entrusted with a message of hope for the future for all those who fall off the way of discipleship. The ending of Mark performs in a socially critical manner, elevating women to a position of status within early Christianity.

A tension has arisen in this study concerning the formation of woman characters in Mark. Even though women characters are given a narrative presence by being featured throughout the Gospel, it might be argued that the engendered Graeco-Roman *habitus* which maintains "man" as the standard to be aspired to continues through the protagonist, Jesus. However, this is not a unique tension between "women and men," since even the men in the narrative aspire to be like Jesus. That said, the habituation of women is still featured prominently in many instances where no name, and therefore no real identity, has been given. Also, the household may still be the dominant setting for women in Mark, but it is not the only space for women, and the stereotypical acts that belong to the domain of women in the household are not emphasized in Mark. So, there is an alignment with Graeco-Roman *habitus,* but the narrative is not tied to that *habitus* in its characterization of women. Furthermore, the inquiry into the "how" of characterization has disclosed a subversive element—a constant pushing against the boundaries of engendered social hierarchies—to such an extent that the alignment with Graeco-Roman *habitus* can be seen as compromised, or at least problematized. "Man" as the perfect ideal is no longer so perfect. There is a new social order advocated where institutional domains such as the household, prime areas of women subjugation, will be questioned.

Accordingly, this integrated literary study of women in the Gospel of Mark has demonstrated that there is an alternative to a gendered view of women emphasized in the Pauline and Petrine passages that insists that a woman remain subordinate in a first-century, male social hierarchy. The characterization of women in the Gospel of Mark shows an intentional pressing, and at times reversal, of the prescribed, expected, social, hierarchical boundaries between men and women contributing to a different perspective on women.

SYSTEMIZATION OF STUDY'S RESULTS

Based upon the previous, narrative analysis of the implied author's discourse in the Gospel of Mark and the creation of character by the implied audience as it received the implied author's discourses involving women in the Gospel of Mark, conclusions may be made in four areas: (1) women as women; (2) women and men; (3) women and Jesus; and (4) women and the implied audience. These conclusions will confirm, systematize, and demonstrate how Mark's characterization of women has taken place within the interaction between implied author/narrator and implied audience. It will be indicated that the women characters he has constructed turned out to be both strong, virtuous, exemplary, and fallible, and at times corrupt. This writer will indicate how the characterizations of women displayed a particular tension. On the one hand, Mark has not departed from the given social and engendered hierarchies of the

Graeco-Roman world; on the other hand, his characterizations of women have displayed remarkable strides towards subverting those hierarchies and preempted the dawn of a different and alternative social and theological order.

Women as Women in Mark

Women, including Simon's mother-in-law, Jairus' daughter, the Syrophoenician woman, and the woman who anointed Jesus for his burial, often act within the socially acceptable confines of the house/household in Mark. However, the implied author deviates from this location by showing those who act outside of the confines of the house in their need, like the woman with the hemorrhage, and in their commitment to Jesus, like those who followed Jesus in his itinerate ministry from Galilee to Jerusalem. In the implied author's discourse, women are shown in traditional and non-traditional roles. What unifies these differences is a woman's desire to engage with Jesus and serve him. The implied author does not show Jesus to require women to be traditional or non-traditional, but to favorably respond to them wherever he encounters them.

The implied author characterizes women as significant participants in the ministry of Jesus. They serve; they model faith and giving; they understand and expand Jesus' teaching; they participate in his preparation for burial; they fulfill prophecy by reproving a disciple; they join in Jesus' itinerate ministry; they witness Jesus' crucifixion and burial; and they witness the empty tomb.

The implied author also shows women to be like men. A woman can be "manly" by being steadfast in her position—refusing to waiver, as Herodias was in her resistance to the message of John the Baptizer, or the maidservant was in her adherence to the truth in the trial of Peter. If women refuse to respond to the revelation they are given, they, like men, can use their position to bring about death, as Herodias did with John the Baptizer. Herodias shows herself to be powerful and influential as she accomplishes her will against John the Baptizer over Herod's will to protect him. Herodias also provides a subtle vilification of Herod who is shown to be unable to control himself or his own household, and thus as unfit to rule. Women can also be fallible like men when they are controlled by their fear rather than their trust in what they have been told about Jesus. It appears that for the implied author, the difference in every case, for men and women, boils down to how well they respond to Jesus, or more generally truth about God, as was the case with Herodias who rejected John the Baptizer's critique of her marriage to Herod based on God's law.

Women and Men in Mark

The implied author often distinguishes women from fallible men by showing their faithful responses to Jesus. Unlike Simon and the other men in the surrounding narrative of Mark 1, Simon's mother-in-law uniquely responds appropriately to Jesus' healing by serving—a theme shared by angels after Jesus' temptation, Jesus' description of true disciples, and other women in the progress of the Gospel. Even though the implied author has men severely criticize the woman who anointed Jesus for his death, the implied author shows that it is the woman, and not the critical men, who shows an understanding of Jesus and the times and acts appropriately. Even though Peter, one of the Twelve, vehemently denies the truthful inquiries of the maidservant in the courtyard of the High Priest, the implied audience knows the truth, and Peter stands exposed by his fear. The implied author has the men absent at Jesus' crucifixion, but has the women look on at a distance. The implied author has the men repeatedly censored because they do not understand the significance of what is being said or done, but the implied author has the Syrophoenician woman show the implied audience what it looks like for a follower to understand and engage with what Jesus is saying. The implied author shows her to be virtuous—full of understanding—while the religious leaders are vilified through a vice list from Jesus.

Concomitant with Jesus' definition of humble service is the implied author's choice to present many of the women who distinguish themselves as nameless, while the fallible men in juxtaposition with them are named: Simon/his mother-in-law; Jairus/woman with the hemorrhage of blood; the disciples/the Syrophoenician woman; Judas/the woman who anointed Jesus for his burial; Simon/the maidservant who interrogated him in the garden of the High Priest. While identifying a woman in terms of her relationship with another male may be considered a means of eroding her identity as a person, the implied author has shown that despite the namelessness of some women, despite those women being without identity except in terms of a man, empowerment of those women takes place in their closeness or association with the character Jesus.

The implied author also shows the women in Mark to function as role models to the men around them through characterizations of gratefulness of Simon's mother-in-law to the disciples, faith of the woman with the hemorrhage to Jairus, the wisdom of the Syrophoenician woman to the disciples, and the abundant generosity of the poor widow and the woman who anoints Jesus for his death to the disciples. The implied author will have Jesus repeatedly commend the work of the anointing woman against her criticism. Not only does the implied author characterize women as role models, but he characterizes them as those who expose the hardened hearts of men as the woman who anoints Jesus for his burial exposes Judas by means of contrast in the narrative, and as the maidservant exposes Peter's fear and cowardice. This latter contrast is strengthened by the fact that the maidservant is described as a young woman and Peter is described as first among the Twelve.

The implied author tells episodes that show that women may at times be just as fallible as the men. Like the men, women, like Herodias and her daughter, can be just as non-responsive to the revelation they received through the forerunner, John the Baptizer, and act in deadly ways as the political/religious leaders (Herod and Pilate) and the crowds who crucified Jesus. Like the men, women can show a lack of understanding about what Jesus has said and done as they come to the tomb with spices to prepare his body for burial. Like the men, women can also be overcome by fear and show that it is just as difficult to follow Jesus after the resurrection as it was before the resurrection. Therefore, like the men, women need restoration in their discipleship by going to meet Jesus in Galilee. The portrait painted by the implied author is not black and white in its portrayal of men and women, but abundant with multi-colored, shaded variants for both for the implied audience to create its characterizations.

Women and Jesus in Mark

The implied author often describes Women as having a favorable relationship with Jesus. Simon's mother-in-law is voluntarily healed by Jesus and naturally responds by serving him. Jesus seeks out the woman with the hemorrhage who sought to touch the edge of his robe for healing. He is willing to be porous as power flows out of him to fill the porous nature of her body. And even though this woman is in the non-typical setting of a public crowd, Jesus is never portrayed as mentioning the expected social constraints on the woman but focuses on her faith in her crisis. The implied author portrays Jesus as responding positively to the Syrophoenician woman who hears his parable about feeding dogs and steps up to extend its meaning to her situation by explaining that the dogs eat the food that falls from the children's table. Unlike his disciples whom the implied author repeatedly portrays as dull and slow to understand Jesus' parables, this unnamed, Greek woman demonstrates insight. The implied author does not portray Jesus as someone put-off by her contribution, but as someone who responds favorably to her by granting her request that her daughter be healed. The implied author shows Jesus to be receptive of a woman who understands—even a gentile woman—and immediately commends her as a person of faith. The maidservant does not encounter Jesus but is nevertheless aligned with him by the implied author by becoming the means by which Jesus' prophecy about Peter's threefold denial is realized as she adheres to the truth.

However, the implied author does not present all women as those who respond favorably to Jesus. Even if Jesus' mother's intentions were good in trying to seize him, the implied author portrays her in the intercalated narrative as being aligned with the religious leaders who misunderstand Jesus and are against him. This portrayal is reinforced by the implied author's placement of her outside of the house while Jesus is in the house with his true family members—those who hear and do the will of God.

Women and the Implied Audience in Mark

The implied author's discourse involving Simon's mother-in-law encourages the implied audience to serve Jesus exactly where they are with the means before them—even if that is within the home and involves table service. The implied audience is reminded that it is not their social position that is of primary importance to God but their proper, grateful response to the benefits they receive through Jesus. This theme of service is further emphasized through the poor widow who gave at the temple. The implied author's commendation of her by Jesus to his disciples also informs the implied audience that they are highly valued if they give to God from what they have, in a whole-hearted way, even if what they have is miniscule. Likewise, the woman who anoints Jesus for his burial is so well received and defended by Jesus that her narrative encourages the implied audience to do what they can for Jesus even if it is a private action in a home and is misunderstood by others. The implied author is showing the implied audience that outward appearances and social standing mean nothing compared to the response of a person to God. The effect of these women would be uplifting to those who may see themselves as socially marginalized or insignificant. The narratives would also encourage the implied audience to faithfully follow their inner response even if others around them are critical of them. In response to these narratives involving women, the implied audience will want to follow Jesus and sacrificially serve him even if they are unknown in their actions like the anonymous women in the Gospel.

The implied author's discourse involving Jesus' mother in Mark 3 encourages the implied audience in Mark to do what is in their power to be part of the true family of Jesus—obey the word of God. It is not necessary to be part of Jesus' bloodline to be part of his true family. However, it is necessary for those who are part of Jesus' biological family and inner circle to respond properly to the word of God for them to be in a familial relationship with him.

The implied author's discourse involving the Syrophoenician woman would encourage women to actively engage in the arena of thought. Like her, they too may understand the mysterious sayings of Jesus and be able to uniquely apply them to their times and situations, even if the men around them have veiled perception. Through the characterization of the Syrophoenician woman, the implied audience understands that those who are outside of socially acceptable circles of inclusion, including women and Gentiles, are welcome and invited to take an active part in Jesus' community as those who can hear what he is saying and understand what he is doing.

The implied author's discourse involving the woman with the hemorrhage encourages the implied audience to have courageous faith in Jesus even during a life of personal hardship. The implied audience sees that her faith enabled her to break the boundaries of social restriction by joining a public crowd following Jesus. Her faith took her beyond the fear of a potential pollution of others by her flow of blood. Her manly expression of courageous faith was used by the implied author and Jesus to address Jairus' womanly weakness of fear. Just as Jairus was bolstered to follow Jesus during great suffering, so too the implied audience would be encouraged to trust in Jesus in their own suffering.

Because the implied author shows both men and woman to be fallible followers of Jesus, the implied audience will be encouraged to examine what they personally understand to be true and is required of them and to not rely on their social, insider, or gender status as a basis for infallibility. No one, however hopeful he or she may be, is immune from falling from the way as a follower of Christ. Following Jesus is hard for men and women both before and following the resurrection. Knowledge of the resurrection does not preclude the women, or the implied audience, from falling off the way. Fallibility is an endemic quality of followers. Renewal is required for all. There is hope for disciples who have failed to discern, accept, and be faithful to the suffering call of Jesus. The implied author has the women at the tomb show the way to restoration through the promise of a new beginning. Repentance and belief must occur to bring about the kingdom of God. The implied author's discourse through the young man at the tomb shows that the way of discipleship remains open; a new start from the threatening terrain of death is available for all. The implied author's discourse of the maidservant who interrogated Peter would encourage the implied audience to align themselves with the truth, even if they are resisted by more powerful people in their world. Through the narrative at the tomb, the implied audience would be made aware that the exhortation to be alert in their watch for Jesus is still in effect for them.

The implied author's Herodias discourse shows the implied audience that an improper response to what God has said and done can prove to be deadly for themselves and others. Fear must not be allowed to dull their hearing and paralyze their actions. If they are responding favorably to what God is saying, they will be able to overcome their natural tendency toward fear and resulting fallibility.

In summary, the implied author and the implied audience characterize women in Mark as valuable, effective, modeling, discerning, correcting, serving, and fallible followers of Christ. The implied author also shows that Women can be resistant to Jesus and hostile, deadly opponents to what God is doing. The implied author's discourses on women in Mark show that the determinative difference in every case has to do with how well they respond, or fail to respond, to what God is saying and doing in their lives.[1]

---

1. Mateus F. de Campos arrives at a similar conclusion for all characters in Mark where knowledge of Jesus is determined by their response to his revelation. See de Campos, *Markan Epistemology*, 745–66.

Bibliography

Abrams, M. H. *A Glossary of Literary Terms*. 10th ed. Boston: Cengage Learning, 2011.
Achtemeier, Paul J. *Mark*: Eugene, OR: Wipf & Stock, 2004.
Aernie, Jeffrey W. *Narrative Discipleship: Portraits of Women in the Gospel of Mark*. Eugene, OR: Pickwick, 2018.
Alter, Robert. *The Art of Biblical Narrative*. New York: Basic, 1981.
Aristotle. *Generation of Animals*. Translated by A. L. Peck. Loeb Classical Library 13. Cambridge, MA: Harvard University Press, 1942.
———. *Poetics*. Translated by S. H. Butcher. n.d.
Auerbach, Erich. *Mimesis: The Representation of Reality in Western Literature*. Translated by Willard R. Trask. 50th ann. ed. Princeton Classics. Princeton, NJ: Princeton University Press, 2013.
Bach, Alice. "Signs of the Flesh: Observations on Characterization in the Bible." In *Characterization in Biblical Literature*, edited by Elizabeth Struthers Malbon and Adele Berlin, 61–79. Semeia 6. Atlanta: Society of Biblical Literature, 1993.
Bal, Mieke. *Narratology: Introduction to the Theory of Narrative*. 2nd ed. Toronto: University of Toronto Press, 1997.
Balsdon, John Percy Vyvian Dacre. *Roman Women: Their History and Habits*. New York: Barnes & Noble, 1983.
Bassler, Jouette M. "The Parable of the Loaves." *Journal of Religion* 66.2 (1986) 157–72.
Bateman, Herbert W., IV. "Defining the Titles 'Christ' and 'Son of God' in Mark's Narrative Presentation of Jesus." *Journal of the Evangelical Theological Society* 50.3 (2007) 537–59.
Beernaert, P. Mourlon. "Jésus Controversé. Structure et Théologie de Marc 2, 1–3, 6," *Nouvelle Revue Théologique* 95.2 (1973) 129–49.
Bennema, Cornelis. "A Theory of Character in the Fourth Gospel with Reference to Ancient and Modern Literature." *Biblical Interpretation* 17.4 (2009) 375–421.
———. *A Theory of Character in New Testament Narrative*. Minneapolis, MN: Fortress, 2014.
Berlin, Adele. *Poetics and Interpretation of Biblical Narrative*. Winona Lake, IN: Eisenbrauns, 1994.
Blass, F., and A. Debrunner. *A Greek Grammar of the New Testament and Other Early Christian Literature*. Translated by Robert W. Funk. Chicago: University of Chicago Press, 1961.

Blomberg, Craig L. *Interpreting the Parables*. Downers Grove, IL: IVP Academic, 2009.
Bock, Darrell L. *Acts*. Baker Exegetical Commentary on the New Testament. Grand Rapids: Baker Academic, 2007.
———. *Luke 1:1—9:50*. Grand Rapids: Baker Academic, 1994.
Boomershine, Thomas E. "Mark 16:8 and the Apostolic Commission." *Journal of Biblical Literature* 100.2 (1981) 225–39.
Booth, Wayne C. "Resurrection of the Implied Author: Why Bother?" In *A Companion to Narrative Theory*, edited by James Phelan and Peter J. Rabinowitz, 75–88. Malden, MA: Blackwell, 2005.
———. *The Rhetoric of Fiction*. 2nd ed. Chicago: University of Chicago Press, 1983.
Bourdieu, Pierre. *The Algerians*. Translated by Alan C. M. Ross. Rev. ed. Boston: Beacon, 1962.
———. *The Logic of Practice*. Stanford: Stanford University Press, 1990.
———. *Masculine Domination*. Stanford: Stanford University Press, 2001.
———. *Outline of a Theory of Practice*. Cambridge: Cambridge University Press, 1977.
———. "Sentiment of Honour in Kabyle Society." In *Honour and Shame: The Values of Mediterranean Society*, edited by Jean G. Peristiany, 191–231, Chicago: University of Chicago Press, 1966.
Brown, Francis A., et al. *A Hebrew and English Lexicon of the Old Testament*. Oxford: Oxford University Press, 1959.
Brown, Raymond E. *The Death of the Messiah, From Gethsemane to the Grave*. 2 vols. New York: Doubleday, 1994.
———. "Gospel Miracles." In The *Bible in Current Catholic Thought*, edited by John L. McKenzie, 184–201. New York: Herder & Herder, 1962.
———. *Mary in the New Testament: A Collaborative Assessment by Protestant and Roman Catholic Scholars*. Edited by Karl P. Donfried et al. Philadelphia: Fortress, 1978.
Bruce, F. F. *New Testament History*. New York: Doubleday, 1980.
Burer, Michael H., et al., eds. *New English Translation [NET] Bible*. Full notes ed. Dallas: NET Bible, 2004.
Burnett, Fred W. "Characterization and Reader Construction of Characters in the Gospels." In *Characterization in Biblical Literature*, edited by Elizabeth Struthers Malbon and Adele Berlin, 3–28. Semeia 63. Atlanta: Society of Biblical Literature, 1993.
Carson, Anne. "Dirt and Desire: The Phenomenology of Female Pollution in Antiquity." In *Constructions of the Classical Body*, edited by James I. Porter, 77–100. Ann Arbor: University of Michigan Press, 2002.
Catchpole, David R. "The Fearful Silence of the Women at the Tomb: A Study in Markan Theology." *Journal of Theology for South Africa* 18 (1977) 3–10.
Chatman, Seymour. *Story and Discourse: Narrative Structure in Fiction and Film*. Ithaca, NY: Cornell University Press, 1980.
Chisholm, Robert B. *Handbook on the Prophets: Isaiah, Jeremiah, Lamentations, Ezekiel, Daniel, Minor Prophets*. Grand Rapids: Baker Academic, 2002.
Chrysologus, Peter. *Selected Sermons*. Washington, DC: Catholic University of America Press, 2005.
Cohick, Lynn H. *Women in the World of the Earliest Christians: Illuminating Ancient Ways of Life*. Grand Rapids: Baker Academic, 2009.
Connolly, Michele A. *Disorderly Women and the Order of God: An Australian Feminist Reading of the Gospel of Mark*. London: T&T Clark, 2018.

Corley, Kathleen E. *Private Women, Public Meals: Social Conflict in the Synoptic Tradition*. Peabody, MA: Hendrickson, 1993.

Cranfield, C. E. B. *The Gospel According to St Mark: An Introduction and Commentary*. 1959. Reprint, London: Cambridge University Press, 1974.

Culpepper, R. Alan. *Anatomy of the Fourth Gospel*. Philadelphia: Fortress, 1983.

———. "Mark 6:17–29 in Its Narrative Context: Kingdoms in Conflict." In *Mark as Story: Retrospect and Prospect*, edited by Kelly R. Iverson and Christopher W. Skinner, 145–63. Society of Biblical Literature 65. Atlanta: Society of Biblical Literature, 2011.

Dana, H. E., and Julius R. Mantey. *A Manual Grammar of the Greek New Testament*. New York: Macmillan, 1955.

Danker, Frederick W., et al. *Greek-English Lexicon of the New Testament and Other Early Christian Literature*. 3rd ed. Chicago: University of Chicago Press, 2000.

Danove, Paul L. "The Narrative Rhetoric of Mark's Characterization of Peter." In *Character Studies and the Gospel of Mark*, edited by Christopher W. Skinner and Matthew Ryan Hauge, 152–73. Library of New Testament Studies 483. New York: Bloomsbury, T&T Clark, 2014.

de Campos, Mateus F. "Markan Epistemology and the Problem of Incomprehension." *Journal of the Evangelical Theological Society* 64.4 (2021) 745–66.

de Villiers, Pieter G. R. "The Powerful Transformation of the Young Man in Mark 14:51–52 and 16:5." *Hervormde Teologiese Studies* 66.1 (2010) 1–7.

Deppe, Dean B. *The Theological Intentions of Mark's Literary Devices: Markan Intercalations, Frames, Allusionary Repetitions, Narrative Surprises, and Three Types of Mirroring*. Eugene, OR: Wipf & Stock, 2015.

Derrett, J. Duncan M. "Eating Up the Houses of Widows: Jesus' Comment on Lawyers?" *Novum Testamentum* 14.1 (1972) 1–9.

Dewey, Joanna. *Disciples of the Way: Mark on Discipleship*. Cincinnati: Women's Division, Board of Global Ministries, United Methodist Church, 1976.

———. "Mark as Aural Narrative: Structures as Clues to Understanding." *Sewanee Theological Review* 36.1 (1992) 45–56.

———. "Mark as Interwoven Tapestry: Forecasts and Echoes for a Listening Audience." *Catholic Biblical Quarterly* 53.2 (1991) 221–36.

———. *Markan Public Debate: Literary Technique, Concentric Structure, and Theology in Mark 2:1—3:6*. Dissertation Series. Atlanta: Scholars, 1980.

———. "Women in the Gospel of Mark." *Word & World* 26.1 (2006) 22–29.

DiCicco, Mario M. "What Can One Give in Exchange for One's Life? A Narrative-Critical Study of the Widow and Her Offering, Mark 12:41–44." *Currents in Theology and Mission* 25.6 (1998) 441–49.

Donaldson, Laura E. "Cyborgs, Ciphers, and Sexuality: Re-Theorizing Literary and Biblical Characters." In *Characterization in Biblical Literature*, edited by Elizabeth Struthers Malbon and Adele Berlin, 81–96. Semeia 63. Atlanta: Society of Biblical Literature, 1993.

Dowd, Sharyn. *Reading Mark: A Literary and Theological Commentary on the Second Gospel*. Reading the New Testament. Macon, GA: Smyth & Helwys, 2000.

Downing, F. Gerald. *Doing Things with Words in the First Christian Century*. London: T&T Clark International, 2004.

———. "In Quest of First-Century CE Galilee." *Catholic Biblical Quarterly* 66.1 (2004) 78–97.

———. "Markan Intercalation in Cultural Context." In *Doing Things with Words in the First Christian Century*, by F. Gerald Downing, 118–32. London: T&T Clark International, 2004.

———. "The Nature(s) of Christian Women and Men." *Theology* 108 (2005) 178–84.

Duff, Paul Brooks. "The March of the Divine Warrior and the Advent of the Greco-Roman King: Mark's Account of Jesus' Entry into Jerusalem." *Journal of Biblical Literature* 111.1 (1992) 55–71.

Edersheim, Alfred. *Life and Times of Jesus the Messiah—Enhanced Version*. 1.1 ed. Grand Rapids: Christian Classics Ethereal Library, 2009.

Edwards, Catharine. "The Suffering Body: Philosophy and Pain in Seneca's Letters." In *Constructions of the Classical Body*, edited by James I. Porter, 252–86. Ann Arbor: University of Michigan Press, 2002.

Edwards, James R. "Markan Sandwiches: The Significance of Interpolations in Markan Narratives." *Novum Testamamentum* 31.3 (1989) 193–216.

Erickson, Millard J. *Christian Theology*. 2nd ed. Grand Rapids: Baker Academic, 1998.

Evans, Christopher Francis. "I Will Go Before You into Galilee." *The Journal of Theological Studies* 5.1 (1954) 3–18.

Evans, Craig A. *Mark 8:27–16:20*. Edited by Bruce M. Metzger. Rev. ed. Word Biblical Commentary 34B. Grand Rapids: Zondervan Academic, 2015.

Farmer, William Reuben. *The Last Twelve Verses of Mark*. Monograph Series (Society for New Testament Studies) 25. Cambridge: Cambridge University Press, 1974.

Farrer, Austin. *St Matthew and St Mark*. Westminster: Dacre, 1954.

Fee, G. D., and W. R. Farmer. "Last Twelve Verses of Mark (Book Review)." *Journal of Biblical Literature* 94 (1975) 461–64.

Finley, Moses I. "Review of Henri Daniel-Rops's Daily Life in Palestine at the Time of Christ." *New Statesman*, November 1, 1963. 47–48.

Fokkelman, J. P. *Narrative Art and Poetry in the Books of Samuel: A Full Interpretation Based on Stylistic and Structural Analyses*. Vols. 1–2. Assen, Netherlands: Van Gorcum, 1981, 1986.

Forster, E. M. *Aspects of the Novel*. New York: Harvest, 1927.

Fowler, Robert M. *Let the Reader Understand: Reader-Response Criticism and the Gospel of Mark*. Minneapolis, MN: Fortress, 1991.

———. *Loaves and Fishes: The Function of the Feeding Stories in the Gospel of Mark*. Subsequent ed. Chico, CA: Society of Biblical Literature, 1981.

France, R. T. *The Gospel of Mark*. Grand Rapids: Eerdmans, 2002.

Gardner, A. Edward. "Imperfect and Faithful Followers: The Young Man at Gethsemane and the Young Man at the Tomb in the Gospel of Mark." *Encounter* 71.2 (2010) 33–43.

Geddert, Timothy J. "Beginning Again (Mark 16:1–8)." *Direction* 33.2 (2004) 150–57.

———. *Mark*. Believers Church Bible Commentary. Scottdale, PA: Herald, 2001.

———. *Watchwords: Mark 13 in Markan Eschatology*. London: Bloomsbury Academic, 2015.

Glahn, Sandra, ed. *Vindicating the Vixens: Revisiting Sexualized, Vilified, and Marginalized Women of the Bible*. Grand Rapids: Kregel Academic, 2017.

Glancy, Jennifer A. *Corporal Knowledge: Early Christian Bodies*. New York: Oxford University Press, 2010.

———. "Early Christianity, Slavery, and Women's Bodies." In *Beyond Slavery: Overcoming Its Religious and Sexual Legacies*, edited by Bernadette J. Brooten, 143–58. New York: Palgrave Macmillan, 2010.

———. "Jesus, the Syrophoenician Woman, and Other First Century Bodies." *Biblical Interpretation* 18.4–5 (2010) 342–63.

Glickman, S. Craig. *Knowing Christ: Life-Changing Glimpses of Our Lord*. Chicago: Moody, 1980.

———. "The Temptation Account in Matthew and Luke." PhD diss., University of Basel, 1983.

Goppelt, Leonhard. *Typos: The Typological Interpretation of the Old Testament in the New*. Translated by Donald H. Madvig. Grand Rapids: Eerdmans, 1982.

Grassi, Joseph A. *The Hidden Heroes of the Gospels: Female Counterparts of Jesus*. London: Marshall Morgan and Scott Lamp, 1989.

Grudem, Wayne. *Evangelical Feminism and Biblical Truth: An Analysis of More Than One Hundred Disputed Questions*. Reprint, Wheaton, IL: Crossway, 2012.

———. *Systematic Theology: An Introduction to Biblical Doctrine*. Grand Rapids: Zondervan, 1994.

Guelich, Robert A. *Mark 1—8:26*. Edited by David Allen Hubbard and Glenn W. Barker. Word Biblical Commentary 34A. Grand Rapids: Zondervan Academic, 2015.

Gundry, Robert Horton. *Mark: A Commentary on His Apology for the Cross*. Grand Rapids: Eerdmans, 2000.

Hallett, Judith P. "Women's Lives in the Ancient Mediterranean." In *Women & Christian Origins*, edited by Ross Shepard Kraemer and Mary Rose D'Angelo, 13–34. New York: Oxford University Press, 1999.

Hamm, Dennis. "Acts 3:1–10: The Healing of the Temple Beggar as Lucan Theology." *Biblica* 67.3 (1986) 305–19.

———. "Acts 3:12–26: Peter's Speech and the Healing of the Man Born Lame." *Perspectives in Religious Studies* 11.3 (1984) 199–217.

Harrington, Wilfrid. *New Testament Message: A Biblical-Theological Commentary*. New Testament Message 4. Dublin: Veritas, 1979.

Harrocks, Rebecca. "Jesus' Gentile Healings: The Absence of Bodily Contact and the Requirement of Faith." In *The Body in Biblical, Christian, and Jewish Texts*, edited by Joan E. Taylor, 83–101. Library of Second Temple Studies 85. New York: Bloomsbury T&T Clark, 2014.

Hesiod. *Theogony. Works and Days. Testimonia*. Edited by Glenn W. Most. Loeb Classical Library 1. Cambridge, MA: Harvard University Press, 2018.

Hippocrates. *Nature of Man, Regimen in Health, Humours, Aphorisms*. Translated by W. H. S. Jones. Loeb Classical Library 4. Cambridge, MA: Harvard University Press, 1931.

Hoehner, Harold W. *Herod Antipas: A Contemporary of Jesus Christ*. Grand Rapids: Zondervan, 1980.

Homer. *Iliad*. Edited by Jeffrey Henderson. Translated by A. T. Murray and William F. Wyatt. Vol. 2. Cambridge, MA: Harvard University Press, 1999.

———. *Odyssey*. Translated by A. T. Murray and George E. Dimock. Vol. 2. Loeb Classical Library 105. Cambridge, MA: Harvard University Press, 1919.

Iersel, Bas M. van. "Concentric Structures in Mark 1:14—3:35 (4:1) with Some Observations on Method." *Biblical Interpretation* 3.1 (1995) 75–98.

———. *Mark*. London; New York: Bloomsbury T&T Clark, 2005.

———. *Mark: A Reader-Response Commentary*. Journal for the Study of the New Testament 164. Sheffield: Sheffield Academic, 1998.

Jackson, Howard M. "Why the Youth Shed His Cloak and Fled Naked: The Meaning and Purpose of Mark 14:51–52." *Journal of Biblical Literature* 116.2 (1997) 273–89.

Jenkins, Allan K. "Young Man or Angel?" *The Expository Times* 94.8 (1983) 237–40.

Jodamus, Johnathan. "Paul, the 'Real' Man: Constructions and Representations of Masculinity in 1 Corinthians." *African Journal of Gender and Religion* 23.2 (2017) 68–94.

Johnson, Steven R. "The Identity and Significance of the *Neaniskos* in Mark." *Forum (Genova)* 8.1–2 (1992) 123–39.

Jongkind, Dirk, ed. *The Greek New Testament: Sample Selection The Gospel of Mark*. Tyndale House Cambridge. Wheaton, IL: Cambridge University Press; Crossway, 2017.

Josephus, Flavius. *Complete Works*. Edited by William Whiston. Grand Rapids: Kregel, 1960.

———. *Jewish Antiquities*. Translated by Ralph Marcus and Allen Wikgren. Vol. 7. Cambridge, MA: Harvard University Press, 1963.

———. *The Life. Against Apion*. Translated by H. St. J. Thackeray. Cambridge, MA: Harvard University Press, 1926.

Joynes, Christine E. "The Sound of Silence: Interpreting Mark 16:1–8 through the Centuries." *Interpretation: A Journal of Bible & Theology* 65.1 (2011) 18–29.

Juvenal. *Juvenal and Persius*. Edited by Susanna Morton Brand. Loeb Classical Library. Cambridge, MA: Harvard University Press, 2004.

Kelhoffer, James A. *Miracle and Mission: The Authentication of Missionaries and Their Message in the Longer Ending of Mark*. Wissenschaftliche Untersuchungen Zum Neuen Testament 2. Reihe 112. Tubingen, DE: Mohr (Siebeck), 2000.

Kermode, Frank. *The Genesis of Secrecy: On the Interpretation of Narrative*. Cambridge, MA: Harvard University Press, 1980.

Kerr, F. "The Enigmatic Gospel." *New Blackfriars* 93.1048 (2012) 629–30.

Kiley, Bernadette. "The Servant Girl in the Markan Passion Narrative: An Alternative Feminist Reading." *Lutheran Theological Journal* 41.1 (2007) 48–57.

Kingsbury, Jack Dean. *Conflict in Mark: Jesus, Authorities, Disciples*. Minneapolis, MN: Fortress, 1989.

———. "The Gospel of Mark in Current Research." *Religious Studies Review* 5.2 (1979) 101–7.

Knust, Jennifer Wright. *Abandoned to Lust: Sexual Slander and Ancient Christianity*. New York: Columbia University Press, 2005.

Koehler, Ludwig, et al. *The Hebrew and Aramaic Lexicon of the Old Testament*. Edited and translated by Mervyn E. J. Richardson. 4 vols. Leiden; Boston: Brill Academic, 1994–1999.

Kolatch, Alfred J. *Who's Who in the Talmud*. Rev. ed. New York: Jonathan David, 1981.

Kozar, Joseph Vlcek. "The Owl and the Pussycat: An Off-Kilter Reading of the Widow's Honorable Action at the Temple Treasury in Mark 12:41–44." *Proceedings* 28 (2008) 41–53.

Kraemer, Ross S. "Jewish Women and Christian Origins: Some Caveats." In *Women & Christian Origins*, edited by Ross Shepard Kraemer and Mary Rose D'Angelo, 35–49. New York: Oxford University Press, 1999.

———. "Jewish Women and Women's Judaism(s) at the Beginning of Christianity." In *Women & Christian Origins*, edited by Ross Shepard Kraemer and Mary Rose D'Angelo, 50–79. New York: Oxford University Press, 1999.
Kubiś, Adam. "The Poor Widow's Mites: A Contextual Reading of Mark 12:41–44." *The Biblical Annals* 3.2 (2013) 339–81.
Kuruvilla, Abraham. *Mark: A Theological Commentary for Preachers*. Eugene, OR: Cascade, 2012.
———. "The Naked Runaway and the Enrobed Reporter of Mark 14 and 16: What Is the Author Doing with What He Is Saying?" *Journal of the Evangelical Theological Society* 54.3 (2011) 527–45.
———. *Privilege the Text!: A Theological Hermeneutic for Preaching*. New ed. Chicago: Moody, 2013.
———. "'What Is the Author Doing with What He Is Saying?' Pragmatics and Preaching—An Appeal!" *Journal of the Evangelical Theological Society* 60.3 (2017) 557–80.
Kurz, William S. *Reading Luke-Acts: Dynamics of Biblical Narrative*. Louisville: Westminster John Knox, 1993.
Lachs, Samuel Tobias. *A Rabbinic Commentary on the New Testament: The Gospels of Matthew, Mark, and Luke*. Hoboken, NJ: KTAV, 1987.
Lane, William L. *The Gospel According to Mark: The English Text with Introduction, Exposition, and Notes*. Grand Rapids: Eerdmans, 1974.
———. "Gospel of Mark in Current Study." *Southwestern Journal of Theology* 21.1 (1978) 7–21.
Le Peau, Andrew T. *Mark Through Old Testament Eyes: A Background and Application Commentary*. New Testament Commentary Series: Through Old Testament Eyes. Grand Rapids: Kregel Academic, 2017.
Lee, Harper. *Go Set a Watchman: A Novel*. New York: Harper, 2015.
———. *To Kill a Mockingbird*. New York: Grand Central, 1988.
Levine, Baruch A. *Leviticus ויקרא: The Traditional Hebrew Text with the New JPS Translation Commentary*. JPS Torah Commentary. Philadelphia: Jewish Publication Society, 1989.
Lightfoot, R. H. *The Gospel Message of St Mark:* London: Oxford University Press, 1950.
Lincoln, Andrew T. "The Promise and the Failure: Mark 16:7, 8." *Journal of Biblical Literature* 108.2 (1989) 283–300.
Louw, Johannes P., et al., eds. *Greek-English Lexicon of the New Testament: Based on Semantic Domains*. Vol. 1. New York: United Bible Societies, 1988.
Lucian. *The Works of Lucian of Samosata*. Translated by H. W. Fowler and F. G. Oxford. 4 vols. Oxford: Clarendon, 1905.
Lyons-Pardue, Kara J. *Gospel Women and the Long Ending of Mark*. London: T&T Clark, 2020.
Magness, J. Lee. *Marking the End: Sense and Absence in the Gospel of Mark*. Eugene, OR: Wipf & Stock, 2002.
Malbon, Elizabeth Struthers. "Fallible Followers: Women and Men in the Gospel of Mark." *Semeia* 28 (1983) 29–48.
———. "The Jesus of Mark and the Sea of Galilee." *Journal of Biblical Literature* 103.3 (1984) 363–77.

———. "The Major Importance of the Minor Characters in Mark." In *The New Literary Criticism and the New Testament*, edited by Elizabeth Malbon and Edgar V. McKnight, 58–86. Sheffield: Sheffield Academic, 1994.

———. "The Poor Widow in Mark and Her Poor Rich Readers." *Catholic Biblical Quarterly* 53.4 (1991) 589–604.

Malbon, Elizabeth Struthers, and Adele Berlin, eds. *Characterization in Biblical Literature*. Semeia 63. Atlanta: Society of Biblical Literature, 1993.

Malick, David E. "The Contribution of Codex Bezae Cantabrigiensis to an Understanding of Women in the Book of Acts." *Journal of Greco-Roman Christianity and Judaism* 4 (2007) 158–83.

———. "An Examination of Jesus' View of Women through Three Intercalations in the Gospel of Mark." *Priscilla Papers* 27.3 (2013) 4–15.

Malina, Bruce J. *The New Testament World: Insights from Cultural Anthropology*. Louisville: Westminster John Knox, 2001.

———. "Social Sciences and Biblical Interpretation." *Interpretation: A Journal of Bible & Theology* 36 (1982) 229–42.

Mann, C. S. *Mark: A New Translation with Introduction and Commentary*. Anchor Bible 27. Garden City, NJ: Doubleday, 1986.

Margolin, Uri. "Character." In *Cambridge Companion to Narrative*, edited by David Herman, 66–69. Cambridge: Cambridge University Press, 2007.

Marsman, Hennie J. *Women in Ugarit and Israel: Their Social and Religious Position in the Context of the Ancient Near East*. Leiden; Boston: Brill, 2003.

Martin, Francis, ed. *Acts*. Vol. 5. Downers Grove, IL: IVP Academic, 2006.

May, David M. "Mark 3:20–35 from the Perspective of Shame/Honor." *Biblical Theological Bulletin* 17.3 (1987) 83–87.

McCraken, David. "Character in the Boundary: Bakhtin's Interindividuality in Biblical Narratives." In *Characterization in Biblical Literature*, edited by Elizabeth Struthers Malbon and Adele Berlin, 29–42. Semeia 63. Atlanta: Society of Biblical Literature, 1993.

Metzger, Bruce M., ed. *Oxford Annotated Apocrypha: The Apocrypha of the Old Testament: Revised Standard Version; Containing the Third and Fourth Books of the Maccabees and Psalm 151*. Expanded ed. New York: Oxford University Press, 1977.

———. *A Textual Commentary on the Greek New Testament*. 2nd ed. Stuttgart: Deutsche Bibelgesellschaft, 1994.

Metzger, Bruce M., and Bart D. Ehrman. *The Text of the New Testament: Its Transmission, Corruption, and Restoration*. 4th ed. New York: Oxford University Press, 2005.

Meyers, Carol L. *Discovering Eve: Ancient Israelite Women in Context*. New York: Oxford University Press, 1988.

Miller, Jeffery D. "A Defense of Gender-Accurate Bible Translation." In *Discovering Biblical Equality: Complementarity without Hierarchy*, edited by Ronald Price et al., 473–88. 3rd ed. Downers Grove, IL: IVP, 2021.

Miller, Susan. "Women Characters in Mark's Gospel." In *Character Studies and the Gospel of Mark*, edited by Christopher W. Skinner and Matthew Ryan Hauge, 174–93. Library of New Testament Studies 483. New York: Bloomsbury T&T Clark, 2014.

———. *Women in Mark's Gospel*. JSNT Supplement Series 259. London: T&T Clark International, 2004.

Moore, Stephen D. *Literary Criticism and the Gospels: The Theoretical Challenge*. New Haven, CT: Yale University Press, 1989.
Moss, Candida R. "The Man with the Flow of Power: Porous Bodies in Mark 5:25–34." *Journal of Biblical Literature* 129.3 (2010) 507–19.
Moulton, James Hope, and George Milligan. *Vocabulary of the Greek Testament*. Grand Rapids: Eerdmans, 1982.
Mpolo, A. Mpevo. "L'offrande de La Veuve Pauvre En Marc 12,41–44: Compliment Ou Déploration?" *Theoforum* 37.3 (2006) 259–86.
Munro, Winsome. "Women Disciples: Light from Secret Mark." *Journal of Feminist Studies in Religion* 8.1 (1992) 47–64.
———. "Women Disciples in Mark." *Catholic Biblical Quarterly* 44.2 (1982) 225–41.
Nash, Bryan A. "Point of View and the Women's Silence: A Reading of Mark 16:1–8." *Restoration Quarterly* 57.4 (2015) 225–32.
Neirynck, F. *Duality in Mark: Contributions to the Study of the Markan Redaction*. Rev. ed. Bibliotheca Ephemeridum Theologicarum Lovaniensium 31. Leuven: Leuven University, Uitgeverÿ Peeters, 1988.
Neusner, Jacob. *The Babylonian Talmud: A Translation and Commentary*. Peabody, MA: Hendrickson, 2011.
———. *The Mishnah: A New Translation*. Reprint, New Haven, CT: Yale University Press, 1991.
Neyrey, Jerome H., ed. *The Social World of Luke-Acts: Models for Interpretation*. Peabody, MA: Hendrickson, 1991.
Nineham, D. E. *Saint Mark*. Westminster: Penguin, 1973.
Nünning, Ansgar F. "Reconceptualizing Unreliable Narration: Synthesizing Cognitive and Rhetorical Approaches." In *A Companion to Narrative Theory*, edited by James Phelan and Peter J. Rabinowitz, 89–107. Malden, MA; Oxford: Blackwell, 2005.
O'Reilly, Leo. *Word and Sign in the Acts of the Apostles*. Roma: Gregorian & Biblical, 1987.
Osborne, Grant R. *The Hermeneutical Spiral: A Comprehensive Introduction to Biblical Interpretation*. Rev. and exp. ed. Downers Grove, IL: IVP Academic, 2007.
Oyen, Geert van. "Intercalation and Irony in the Gospel of Mark." In *Four Gospels, Festschrift Frans Neirynck*, edited by C. M. Tuckett, 949–74. Louvain, BE: Peeters, 1992.
Parsons, Mikeal C. "Christian Origins and Narrative Openings: The Sense of a Beginning in Acts 1–5." *Review & Expositor* 87.3 (1990) 403–22.
Parunak, H Van Dyke. "Oral Typesetting: Some Uses of Biblical Structure." *Biblica* 62.2 (1981) 153–68.
———. "Transitional Techniques in the Bible." *Journal of Biblical Literature* 102.4 (1983) 525–48.
Payne, Philip Barton. *Man and Woman, One in Christ: An Exegetical and Theological Study of Paul's Letters*. Grand Rapids: Zondervan, 2009.
Pentecost, J. Dwight, and John Danilson. *The Words and Works of Jesus Christ: A Study of the Life of Christ*. Grand Rapids: Zondervan, 2000.
Peristiany, J. G. *Honour and Shame—The Values of Mediterranean Society*. London: Weidenfeld & Nicholson, 1965.
Perkinson, James W. "A Canaanitic Word in the Logos of Christ; or the Difference the Syro-Phoenician Woman Makes to Jesus." *Semeia* 75 (1996) 61–85.

Pesch, Rudolf. *Das Markusevangelium, 2: Kommentar Zu Kap 8,27—16,20*. Fribourg, CH: Herder, 1980.

Petersen, Norman R. "Point of View in Mark's Narrative." *Semeia* 12 (1978) 97–121.

———. "When Is the End Not the End: Literary Reflections on the Ending of Mark's Narrative." *Interpretation* 34.2 (1980) 151–66.

Philo. *On the Contemplative Life*. Translated by F. H. Colson. Vol. 9. Cambridge, MA: Harvard University Press, 1941.

———. *On the Decalogue. On the Special Laws*. Translated by F. H. Colson. Vol. 3. Cambridge, MA: Harvard University Press, 1937.

———. *Questions on Genesis*. Translated by Ralph Marcus. Philo Suppl. 1. Cambridge, MA: Harvard University Press, 1953.

Plautus. *Amphitryon. The Comedy of Asses. The Pot of Gold. The Two Bacchises. The Captives*. Edited and translated by Wolfgang de Melo. Loeb Classical Library 60. Cambridge, MA: Harvard University Press, 2011.

Plutarch. *Lives: Theseus and Romulus; Lycurgus and Numa; Solon and Publicola*. Translated by Bernadotte Perrin. Vol. 1. Cambridge, MA: Harvard University Press, 1914.

Pomeroy, Sarah. *Goddesses, Whores, Wives, and Slaves: Women in Classical Antiquity*. New York: Schocken, 1995.

Porter, Stanley E. *Idioms of the Greek New Testament*. 2nd ed. Sheffield: Bloomsbury T&T Clark, 1992.

Prince, Gerald. "Introduction of the Study of the Narratee." In *Essentials of the Theory of Fiction*, edited by Michael J. Hoffman and Patrick D. Murphy, 213–33. Durham, NC: Duke University Press, 1996.

Rabinowitz, Peter J. "Truth in Fiction: A Reexamination of Audiences." *Critical Inquiry* (1977) 121–41.

Rambo, Shelly. "Trauma and Faith: Reading the Narrative of the Hemorrhaging Woman." *International Journal of Practical Theology* 13.2 (2009) 233–57.

Resseguie, James L. *Narrative Criticism of the New Testament: An Introduction*. Grand Rapids: Baker Academic, 2005.

Rhoads, David M., and Donald Michie. *Mark as Story: An Introduction to the Narrative of a Gospel*. Philadelphia: Fortress, 1982.

Rhoads, David M., et al. *Mark as Story: An Introduction to the Narrative of a Gospel*. 3rd ed. Minneapolis, MN: Fortress, 2012.

Rimmon-Kenan, Shlomith. *Narrative Fiction: Contemporary Poetics*. 2nd ed. Philadelphia: Routledge, 2003.

Robertson, A. T. *A Grammar of the Greek New Testament In The Light of Historical Research*. Nashville: Broadman, 1934.

Ross, Allen P. *A Commentary on the Psalms*. Vol. 1. Grand Rapids: Kregel Academic & Professional, 2011.

———. *Creation and Blessing: A Guide to the Study and Exposition of the Book of Genesis*. Grand Rapids: Baker Book House, 1988.

———. *Holiness to the Lord: A Guide to the Exposition of the Book of Leviticus*. Grand Rapids: Baker Academic, 2002.

Ryken, Leland. *Literature of the Bible*. Grand Rapids: Zondervan, 1980.

Safrai, Shmuel. "The Place of Women in First-Century Synagogues." *Priscilla Papers* 16.1 (2002) 9–12.

———. "The Role of Women in the Temple." *Jerusalem Perspective* 2.1 (1989) 5–6.

Sarna, Nahum M. *JPS Torah Commentary: Genesis*. Philadelphia: Jewish Publication Society, 2001.

Sawyer, Deborah F. *Women and Religion in the First Christian Centuries*. London; New York: Routledge, 1996.

Scholes, Robert, et al. *The Nature of Narrative: Revised and Expanded*. 40th ann. ed. Oxford; New York: Oxford University Press, 2006.

Schürer, Emil. *A History of the Jewish People in the Time of Jesus Christ*. 5 vols. Peabody, MA: Hendrickson, 1994.

———. *The History of the Jewish People in the Age of Jesus Christ*. Vol. 2. Edinburgh: T&T Clark, 1890.

Schüssler Fiorenza, Elisabeth. *In Memory of Her: A Feminist Theological Reconstruction of Christian Origins*. New York: Crossroad, 1983.

Selvidge, Marla J. "Mark 5:25–34 and Leviticus 15:19–20: A Reaction to Restrictive Purity Regulations." *Journal of Biblical Literature* 103.4 (1984) 619.

Seneca the Younger. *The Epistles of Seneca*. Translated by Richard M. Gummere. Vol. 1. Loeb Classical Library. Cambridge, MA: Harvard University Press, 1917.

Shepherd, Tom. *Markan Sandwich Stories: Narration, Definition, and Function*. Andrews University Seminary Doctoral Dissertation. Berrien Springs, MI: Andrews University Press, 1993.

———. "The Narrative Function of Markan Intercalation." *New Testament Studies* 41 (1995) 522–40.

Silva, Moisés. "The Place of Historical Reconstruction in New Testament Criticism." In *Hermeneutics, Authority, and Canon*, edited by D. A. Carson and John D. Woodbridge, 103–33. Grand Rapids: Zondervan, 1986.

Smith, Abraham. "Tyranny Exposed: Mark's Typological Characterization of Herod Antipas (Mark 6:14–29)." *Biblical Interpretation* 14.3 (2006) 259–93.

Smith, Geoffrey. "A Closer Look at the Widow's Offering: Mark 12:41–44." *Journal of the Evangelical Theological Society* 40.1 (1997) 27–36.

Sperber, Daniel. "Mark 12:42 and Its Metrological Background: A Study in Ancient Syriac Versions." *Novum Testammentum* 9.3 (1967) 178–90.

Stein, Robert H. *Mark*. Grand Rapids: Baker Academic, 2008.

Sternberg, Meir. *The Poetics of Biblical Narrative: Ideological Literature and the Drama of Reading*. Reprint, Bloomington: Indiana University Press, 1987.

Stewart, Eric C. "Masculinity in the New Testament and Early Christianity." *Biblical Theology Bulletin* 46.2 (2016) 91–102.

Stock, Augustine. "Hinge Transitions in Mark's Gospel." *Biblical Theology Bulletin* 15.1 (1985) 27–31.

———. *The Method and the Message of Mark*. Wilmington, DE: Michael Glazier, 1989.

———. "The Structure of Mark: A Five-Fold Concentric Framework." *Bible Today* (1985) 291–96.

Sugirtharajah, R. S. "The Widow's Mites Revalued." *Expository Times* 103.2 (1991) 42–43.

Talbert, Charles H. *Literary Patterns, Theological Themes, and the Genre of Luke-Acts*. Society of Biblical Literature Monograph Series 20. Missoula, MT: Society of Biblical Literature and Scholars, 1974.

———. *Reading Acts: A Literary and Theological Commentary*. Macon, GA: Smyth & Helwys, 2016.

Tannehill, Robert C. "Disciples in Mark: The Function of a Narrative Role." *Journal of Religion* 57.4 (1977) 386–405.

———. "The Functions of Peter's Mission Speeches in the Narrative of Acts." *New Testament Studies* 37.3 (1991) 400–414.

———. *The Gospel According to Luke*. Vol. 1 of *The Narrative Unity of Luke-Acts: A Literary Interpretation*. Philadelphia, PA: Fortress, 1986.

Thayer, Joseph Henry. *Greek-English Lexicon of the New Testament Being Grimm's Wilke's Clavis Novi Testamenti*. Grand Rapids: Zondervan, 1977.

Thiessen, Matthew. *Jesus and the Forces of Death: The Gospels' Portrayal of Ritual Impurity within First-Century Judaism*. Grand Rapids: Baker Academic, 2020.

Thompson, J. A. *The Book of Jeremiah*. New International Commentary on the Old Testament. Grand Rapids: Eerdmans, 1980.

Thompson, Marianne Meye. "'God's Voice You Have Never Heard, God's Form You Have Never Seen': The Characterization of God in the Gospel of John." In *Characterization in Biblical Literature*, edited by Elizabeth Struthers Malbon and Adele Berlin, 177–204. Semeia 63. Atlanta: Society of Biblical Literature, 1993.

Todorov, Tzvetan. "The Categories of Literary Narrative." Translated by Joseph Kestner. *Papers on Language & Literature* 50.3/4 (2014) 381–424.

Tolbert, Mary Ann. *Sowing the Gospel: Mark's World in Literary-Historical Perspective*. Minneapolis, MN: Fortress, 1989.

Tomashevsky, Boris Viktorovich. "Thematics." In *Russian Formalist Criticism: Four Essays*, edited by Lee T. Lemon, 61–95. Translated by Marion J. Reis. Lincoln: University of Nebraska Press, 1965.

Torgovnick, Marianna. *Closure in the Novel*. Princeton: Princeton University Press, 1981.

Uspensky, Boris. *A Poetics of Composition: The Structure of the Artistic Text and Typology of a Compositional Form*. Translated by Valentina Zavarin and Susan Wittig. 2nd ed. Berkley: University of California Press, 1973.

Van Eck, Ernest. *Galilee and Jerusalem in Mark's Story of Jesus: A Narratological and Social Scientific Reading*. Hervormde Teologiese Studies Supplementum 7. Pretoria, South Africa: University of Pretoria Press, 1995.

Villiers, Pieter G. R. de. "The Powerful Transformation of the Young Man in Mark 14:51–52 and 16:5." *Hervormode Teologiese Studies* 66.1 (2010) 1–7.

Voelz, James W. *Mark-Concordia Commentary*. Saint Louis, MO: Concordia, 2013.

Von Rad, Gerhard. *Genesis: A Commentary*. Rev. ed. Philadelphia: Westminster John Knox, 1972.

Vorster, Willem S. "Characterization of Peter in the Gospel of Mark." *Neotestamentica* 21.1 (1987) 57–76.

Wall, Robert W. *The Acts of the Apostles, Introduction to Epistolary Literature, the Letter to the Romans, the First Letter to the Corintheans*. Vol. 10 of *The New Interpreter's Bible*. Nashville: Abingdon, 2003.

Wallace, Daniel B. *Greek Grammar Beyond the Basics: An Exegetical Syntax of the New Testament with Scripture, Subject, and Greek Word Indexes*. Grand Rapids: Zondervan, 1997.

———. "Mark 16:8 as the Conclusion to the Second Gospel." In *Perspectives on the Ending of Mark: Four Views*, edited by David A. Black, 1–39. Nashville: B&H Academic, 2008.

Walters, Jonathan. "Invading the Roman Body: Manliness and Impenetrability in Roman Thought." In *Roman Sexualities*, edited by Judith P. Hallett and Marilyn B. Skinner, 29–43. Princeton: Princeton University Press, 1997.

Waltke, Bruce K., and Cathi J. Fredricks. *Genesis: A Commentary*. Grand Rapids: Zondervan, 2001.

Wenham, Gordon. *Genesis*. Vol. 2. Word Biblical Commentary. Dallas: Thomas Nelson, 1994.

Westfall, Cynthia Long. *Paul and Gender: Reclaiming the Apostle's Vision for Men and Women in Christ*. Grand Rapids: Baker Academic, 2016.

Wilhoit, Jim, and Leland Ryken. *Effective Bible Teaching*. Grand Rapids: Baker Academic, 1998.

Wilkinson, J. Harvie. *Cosmic Constitutional Theory: Why Americans Are Losing Their Inalienable Right to Self-Governance*. Oxford: Oxford University Press, 2012.

Williams, Joel F. "Does Mark's Gospel Have an Outline?" *Journal of the Evangelical Theological Society* 49.3 (2006) 505–25.

———. *Other Followers of Jesus: Minor Characters as Major Figures in Mark's Gospel*. Journal for the Study of the New Testament. Sheffield: JSOT, 1994.

Witherington, Ben, III. *Women and the Genesis of Christianity*. Cambridge; New York: Cambridge University Press, 1990.

———. *Women in the Earliest Churches*. Reprint, Cambridge; New York: Cambridge University Press, 1991.

———. *Women in the Ministry of Jesus: A Study of Jesus' Attitudes to Women and Their Roles as Reflected in His Earthly Life*. Cambridge; New York: Cambridge University Press, 1987.

Wolff, Hans Walter. *Hosea: A Commentary on the Book of the Prophet Hosea*. Edited by Paul D. Hanson. Translated by Gary Stansell. Hermeneia—A Critical and Historical Commentary on the Bible. Philadelphia: Fortress, 1973.

Wright, Addison G. "The Widow's Mites: Praise or Lament—a Matter of Context." *Catholic Biblical Quarterly* 44.2 (1982) 256–65.

Wright, George Al. "Markan Intercalations: A Study in the Plot of the Gospel." PhD diss., Southern Baptist Theological Seminary, 1985.

Yencich, Danny. "Sowing the Passion at Olivet: Mark 13–15 in a Narrative Frame." *Stone-Campbell Journal* 20.2 (2017) 189–200.

Zeitlin, Forma I. "Reflections on Erotic Desire in Archaic and Classical Greece." In *Constructions of the Classical Body*, edited by James I. Porter, 50–76. Ann Arbor: University of Michigan Press, 2002.

www.ingramcontent.com/pod-product-compliance
Lightning Source LLC
Chambersburg PA
CBHW061434300426
44114CB00014B/1680